The

Spiritual Liberation

of Women

Spiritualizing the World, vol 12

The

Spiritual

Liberation

of

Women

KIM MICHAELS

MORE TO LIFE PUBLISHING

www.morepublish.com

For foreign and translation rights,

contact: info@ morepublish.com

ISBN: 978-87-93297-76-0

Cover art by Sandra Singer

The information and insights in this book should not be considered as a form of therapy, advice, direction, diagnosis, and/or treatment of any kind. This information is not a substitute for medical, psychological, or other professional advice, counseling and care. All matters pertaining to your individual health should be supervised by a physician or appropriate health-care practitioner. No guarantee is made by the author or the publisher that the practices described in this book will yield successful results for anyone at any time. They are presented for informational purposes only, as the practice and proof rests with the individual.

For more information: *www.ascendedmasterlight.com and www.transcendencetoolbox.com*

Content

INTRODUCTION

This book belongs to the series *Spiritualizing the World*. The books in this series are given by the ascended masters as workbooks that provide the knowledge and practical tools we need in order to make a contribution to solving concrete world problems. This book contains the knowledge and the tools we need in order to start a new cycle of the liberation of women. These books do not contain foundational knowledge about ascended masters and their teachings. In order to make the most efficient use of this book, you need to have a general knowledge of the following topics:

- You need to know who the ascended masters are, how they give their teachings and how you can make the best use of them on a personal and planetary level. You can find extensive teachings on this in the books: *How You Can Help Change the World* and *The Power of Self*.

- You need to know how the earth functions as a cosmic schoolroom. You need to know your own role and the authority you have as a spiritual being in embodiment. You need to know the role of the ascended masters and how only we who are in embodiment can give them the authority to use their unlimited power to affect change on earth. You can find more on these topics in the first book in this series: *How You Can Help Change the World*.

- You need to know how to use the practical tools given by the ascended masters. You can find more on this topic in: *How You Can Help Change the World* and on the website: *www.transcendencetoolbox.com.*

- You need to know about the existence and methods of the dark forces who are ultimately responsible for creating problems on earth. You can find foundational teachings on this in: *Cosmology of Evil.*

How to use this book

There is no one way of using the teachings and tools in this book. However, if you want to make a significant contribution to solving world problems, it is suggested that you start by following this program:

- You read one of the chapters in the book completely in order to increase your understanding of the topic.

- You give the invocation associated with that chapter once a day for nine days while studying the same chapter again.

The reasoning behind this program is that the chapters in the book form a progression. As you give an invocation for one chapter, you are also clearing your own consciousness from certain energies and illusions. This makes it easier for you to absorb and apply the teachings from the next chapter.

You can of course also read the book all the way through and then select one or more invocation(s) that you give several times. It is always more powerful to give an invocation once a day for nine or 33 days.

Because some of the invocations in this book are quite long, they have been divided into two or more parts. It takes about 15-20 minutes to give each part. If you prefer, you can give all of the parts for one invocation in succession. In that case, you do not need to give the sealing after the first invocation or the preamble to the next. You give a preamble in the beginning, continue through the parts and give a sealing in the end.

1 | THERE IS NO FINAL TRUTH ABOUT WOMEN

I am the Ascended Master Mother Mary. It is my great joy to open this conference because it is truly a very significant step in what we have planned for moving this planet closer and closer to Saint Germain's Golden Age. We have decided to dedicate this coming decade of the 2020s to the issue of women: not only the liberation of women, but the raising of awareness of all aspects of women's situation on this planet.

Truly, it is time. It is in some ways long overdue, but in other ways it is just the right time to focus attention on women's situation and the many ways in which women have been suppressed and exploited, not by men but by other forces that we naturally will talk about. You will see in this coming decade that many, many people (who are not familiar with ascended masters, and do not need to be familiar with ascended masters) will pick up on the need to focus attention on women's situation, to debate various issues related to women's situation and to make drastic physical changes in society to improve women's situation.

The hidden force behind positive change

Now naturally, my beloved, we do not want to in any way imply that the ascended masters and the people who are aware of ascended masters are the only people on the planet who are working to improve the situation for women. We very much recognize that for a long time there have been many people in embodiment, both men and women, who have been taking steps to improve the situation of women. It is not so that we as ascended masters want to take credit. On the other hand, you must recognize as ascended master students that the ascended masters are behind and involved with any improvement, any progression in the upward movement that takes place on this planet.

It is because we are the spiritual custodians, the spiritual guardians, for this planet. We are the ones who are releasing specific energies, specific ideas, and as we have said before, we are broadcasting these energies, broadcasting these ideas into the collective consciousness, into the energy field of the planet, into the identity body, the mental body, the emotional body of the planet. This means that when these signals are sent from us, people can pick up on it. They can pick up on the ideas, they can feel the energies and therefore, they can suddenly begin to become aware and to take action, to debate various issues that they would not have been able to debate on their own.

Quite frankly, this planet has been so heavily influenced by the fallen beings, by the dark forces, and there is so much fear-based lower energy in the identity, mental and emotional bodies of the planet, that human beings would not be able to liberate themselves from this if it were not for the ascended masters. Again, this is not to detract from the fact that many people have been able to tune in to our energies and our ideas and have been willing to act upon them. We honor these people for doing so, even if they do not know about our existence, and as I said they do not have to know about our existence. We are not looking for ascended master students to go out there and say: "What you are doing is only because of the ascended masters." We are looking for you as ascended master students to know the dynamic on this planet, thereby you can also know realistically how important it is for you to make the calls, to reinforce the energies, to broadcast the energies and the ideas into the collective consciousness so that more and more people can pick up on them. You can then act, as we have said before, as the tip of the spear, the forerunners. You can act as those who can make the calls to cut free other people who are in positions in society to make the decisions, to take the actions, so that they will be able to act, which they otherwise would have not been able to do, had it not been for your calls.

Equality is primarily a psychological process

Naturally, it is not so that by the advent of this conference, this will start women's liberation. Obviously, the process of liberating women has been going on for well over a century in many of the so-called modern democracies. You also see that there are nations in the world that are lagging behind. When you step back from your own nation, your own situation, you see that when you look at the situation of women around the planet, and look at many different societies, you see that there are some vast, vast differences. You can see for example that there are a number of nations (what we call the modern democracies) that have made great improvements to women's situation. There is much greater awareness of the need to create equality between men and women.

Now, we cannot necessarily say that there is any society that has achieved equality between men and women because this is a rather long and complicated process. We *can* say that there are some nations that have taken action to create laws that promote the equality of men and women. Even those laws have not had the full impact that they could have, and the reason for this is that the liberation of women, the equality between men and women, is not a *legal* process. It is not even a *physical* process. It is a *psychological* process. It requires changes in the emotional body, the mental body and the identity body of a society and of individuals. Therefore, it is not so that a society could, tomorrow, enact a set of laws that would bring about total equality between men and women, or would liberate women from any oppression or limitation. It could not be done legally, because it is not an entirely legal or political process. As I said, it requires a shift.

Now, naturally, a country can enact laws that will bring that society towards the liberation of women, towards equality between men and women. It will take time before this filters through the collective consciousness and the individual consciousness of the people living in that society. Now, some countries have made great strides in the psychological process, but none has yet achieved what *can* be achieved, and what *will* be achieved in the golden age. Now, this is partly because it is not so that there is a specific goal that can be defined. You need to be careful as ascended master students that you do not fix your minds on a specific goal. You need to recognize here that what we are giving you through this messenger, through other messengers over the last century or so, is what we have called *progressive* revelation.

No absolute goal to achieve

There are too many ascended master students in the time of the last century or so who have focused too much attention on the word *revelation,* and too little attention on the word *progressive.* You see, my beloved, what is it that the fundamentalist Christians for example or the fundamentalist Muslims, or the fundamentalists of any color always say? They say: "We have the absolute truth. Our religious scripture is an absolute truth revealed directly by God." The Koran, the Bible, whatever scriptures you have, (even the materialist paradigm, the Communist Manifesto, whatever you have) there are people who believe: "Here is an absolute truth." Well, if something is an absolute truth, how could it ever be improved upon? How could it ever be changed? If something was an absolute truth, where would be the room for progressive revelation?

Of course, these fundamentalists will deny progressive revelation through the ascended masters or any other source. You as ascended master students need to step up and recognize here that regardless of what was said or implied through previous ascended master dispensations, it has never been our goal to bring forth an absolute or final revelation. If a revelation is *progressive,* how could it be *final?* How could it be absolute? Where would be the room for the progressive element?

Now, in our teachings on fanaticism, we said that the basic definition of fanaticism is that you hold a viewpoint that you think could not be improved upon. This is the essence of fanaticism. Whether you are a fundamentalist Christian, a Marxist, a Muslim or an ascended master student, if you say: "Here is a teaching given through this messenger, through this dispensation, that is an absolute truth, an absolute revelation," then you have stepped into the fanatical mindset and then you are denying progressive revelation. In your mind, you are denying us the ability to bring forth a higher revelation. Do you understand, my beloved, how important it is to keep this in your mind? As we have said before, the Golden Age of Saint Germain is not a final goal, a definite goal.

It is not so that Saint Germain has a plan, and when this and this and this has been implemented, the golden age will be manifest, and the golden age will then remain constant for the next 2,000 years. This is not Saint Germain's plan and Saint Germain's vision. As he has said himself, as others of us have said, the potential for what can be achieved in the next 2,000 years is very, very far beyond what you see manifest on the planet right now. It is so far beyond that there is hardly anybody in embodiment who could fathom, or even accept, the potential of what can be achieved. Because there is such a huge gap between current conditions and the potential for Saint Germain's Golden Age, there is no way to cross that gap in one leap, or even in one short evolution. It will take a very long process, and that process must of necessity have many different stages.

You see that what we aim to do right now, and what we aimed to do in the 1970s or the 1930s with our progressive revelation, has never been to give you some final revelation, not even a final revelation for the golden age. We aim to give a revelation that will take the planet from where it is now to the next level up. Then, when a critical mass of people have made that transition in consciousness, we aim to give a higher revelation that will take the planet to the next level. This process will continue through many different stages as the golden age progresses.

Now, I know very well, my beloved, that there are students of previous dispensations who have believed that they had some final revelation, or that they had the teaching that was meant to guide planet earth spiritually for the next 2,000 years of the Aquarian age. This is because these students were not able to grasp what I have just told you. They were not able to accept it because they were still, as we have said before, trapped in the Piscean mindset, and therefore they needed what you see so prevalent in the Piscean Age: the belief that we have the final truth. In order to step beyond the Piscean mindset, to pass the initiations of Pisces and to step into the Aquarian mindset, you need to let go of this dream of having a final truth, a final revelation. Who can do this? Well, some men can do it. *Some men* will understand, but many more *women* have the potential to do this.

The idea of a final truth is used to suppress women

Why is it important to do this? Well, my beloved, what is one of the primary means right now that is being used around the world to suppress women and keep women in a fixed station in society, in life, in their own minds, in the minds of men? Is it not the idea that there is some final truth? How many women around the world are being held in a fixed position because their society believes that Christianity has brought forth a final revelation, and that the Bible is the Word of God, and that it does not need to be expanded upon today. Therefore, they think that the few things that were said about women in the Bible are some absolute truth that should stand for all time. Such as, that women should remain silent in the churches, or that women are responsible for the fall of man and therefore should be kept out of decision-making positions in the church hierarchy because women are dangerous and could abort God's plan for saving the world, and they could send all people to hell.

These are beliefs that you may not see in writing. You may rarely hear them spoken in a public setting. I can assure you that millions upon millions of Christians hold these beliefs because they believe that the Bible is the word of God, an absolute truth, and could never be expanded upon. Look at Islamic countries and look at how many Muslims have the same belief about the Koran, and therefore believe that whatever was said about the Bible at the time of Mohammed, based on a male-dominated culture, that this is some absolute truth that should stand for all time. Look at the Hindu religion, look at India, look at China. Look how they have certain beliefs that they believe define women's situation in society, their station in society. There are even people who are materialists, who are atheists, who despise all religion but who still believe that evolution must have defined certain differences between men and women – not only physically, but even psychologically – so that women are inferior to men because evolution has made it so.

Naturally, one of the primary goals, one of the primary milestones on the road to the liberation of women, is to challenge the idea that there is any truth on earth that is absolute or final, and that could never be expanded upon. Will men do this, my beloved? Not in the near future, I can assure you. Perhaps there would be some future time when men would be open enough, when a critical mass of men would be open enough to challenge this belief. It would take a very, very long time, certainly beyond the lifetime of any of you who are in embodiment. If we are to make a significant leap forward, not only in the liberation of women, but in the liberation of men as well, then women need to step up and challenge this idea of the absolute, final truth.

Naturally, this idea is also keeping men in a fixed position because these absolute truths that you have, whether the Bible or the Koran or other scriptures, they also define fixed roles for men, and men are trapped in these roles, even if they do not recognize it consciously. This is one of the opportunities that women have. It is also one of the challenges in this decade of the 2020s. Will women be willing to step up and challenge this idea of an absolute truth and bring forth the awareness (bring it into the public debate) of how this very idea limits not only women but men and societies as well.

The most dangerous idea in the world

We have said before that the fall of the Soviet Union, the collapse of the Soviet Union, marked the end of the era of ideology. The era where societies were based on a specific ideology, be it religious, political or materialistic, and people believed that if only they could make their society live up to this absolute truth, then all problems would be solved and it would be an ideal world. It is time to bring out to public awareness that this is a false idea. It is a dangerous, non-constructive idea that has led to most of the conflicts you have seen in history, that has led to world wars and incredible atrocities and persecution. Why is this so, my beloved? Because, if one country or a group of countries believe they have the absolute idea and that their idea can bring forth the ideal society or the ideal state on earth, then they are automatically set in conflict with those who do not share their idea. They automatically have to somehow persuade or force other people to accept their idea, otherwise the ideal state on earth cannot be manifest.

The reality, my beloved, is that in the Aquarian age, in the Golden Age of Saint Germain, there will not be one ideology, one religion, one political philosophy that will dominate the earth. Nor will there be several rivaling ideologies that will fight each other for domination over the earth. As we move further and further into the golden age, the influence of these ideologies, these thought systems, will fall away gradually and more and more people will wake up and realize how trapped they were, how trapped societies were in these ideologies and thought systems. More and more people will be able and willing to see that we need to move away from this and we need to make a conscious, deliberate effort to move away from these ideas that are thought to be absolute.

Women should be kept out of decision-making

Now I know very well, my beloved (as I said earlier) that if you step back and look at women's situation all over the world, you might say that what I have said about ideologies and belief systems applies mainly to women in the modern democracies because that is where there is the openness to debate different things in society, that is where women have the opportunity to speak out. As you can see very clearly, a great part of the Islamic world, a great part of India, China, Asia, also have thought systems that are thought to be absolute, so even in those societies it is an important topic. It may not be the easiest one for women to start out with. It may not be the first one, but we will surely during this conference bring out other issues that need to be addressed, and that may be easier for women in these nations, in these areas, to deal with, but still, it is certainly applicable.

You look at South America that is still so dominated by the Catholic church and you can clearly see that women are trapped there because the Catholic church, the Catholic mindset, is based on the idea of an absolute truth. It is based on a very fixed idea of women being responsible for the fall, and therefore, my beloved, you can clearly see in the Catholic church how women are not allowed to hold decision-making positions. Do not fail to realize that, in any country that is dominated by the Catholic religion, there will be an underlying, often unspoken, consciousness that says that women should actually be kept out of *all* decision-making positions because if they are not to be trusted in the church, how can they be trusted in the government or in business? This is something you will see in any country that is dominated by the Catholic belief system. You will also see it in some Christian, Protestant, Lutheran societies where you have the same underlying attitude. You can go back to the time of Luther, you can go back to look at Luther himself and see that he was by no means open to the equality between the sexes.

Now, if you take a look at Africa, you can see again there is a certain dominance there by the Catholic religion in some nations, Protestant Christianity in other nations. In some nations you have Islam. What you see in Africa is that there is a set of beliefs that go back to the religions that were there before Muslims or Christians started having an influence on the African continent. You may call them tribal religions or whatever, but you will see that there are some beliefs that linger still and that are very dominant in many countries. You will see that even though Christianity and Christian ministers often believe that they are there to eradicate the superstitious beliefs of these older religions, they have in many cases not made very much impact on these beliefs. People have just incorporated them into their Christian or Muslim beliefs.

There are certain of these ideas that are very much limiting to women, holding women in certain fixed positions in society again often being suspicious of women, especially women who have power. You still have the belief that certain women are witches, which is of course something you find in various parts of the world but more so in Africa than in most other places. You have this belief that any woman who has power must be a witch, and this is something you see of course going back to the medieval ages in Europe. You see some of that same attitude in many African areas where you see a certain attitude towards women that has been carried on from these older religions, and that is based on certain "infallible" or never-questioned ideas. "This is just the way women are. This is just the way men are, and this is the way the relationship between men and women should be."

In many cases it can be difficult to point to a scripture or a specific belief that is clearly articulated but it is there in the collective consciousness, often so subtle that very few people think to even question it. This, of course is where there is a great need that those women who are more aware, who are more advanced in consciousness, will begin to identify these beliefs and question them. Write down what has never been written down. Speak what has rarely been spoken and identify and challenge these beliefs.

Medieval treatment of women

Now, my beloved, you may look at the planet and you could make up a map if you wanted to. I am not saying you *should,* but you *could* make up a map that shows where women have more rights, have more equality and where they have less rights and less equality, where they are less suppressed, more suppressed, more liberated, less liberated. You could therefore identify certain nations where you can see clearly that the situation of women today is far behind where it is in the more advanced modern democracies. You can see for example that there are nations in Africa, in the Middle East, in India, where women are treated in a way that is medieval. In other words, they are treated in the same way, or even sometimes in a worse way, than the way women were treated in medieval Europe.

You can very clearly see that these nations have a very long way to go. Now, if you look at these nations and if you could see what I see in the collective consciousness, you would also see that there are these huge collective entities, these beasts in the collective consciousness of these societies, and they are so powerful in these nations that they can overpower the minds of most women. They also of course overpower the minds of most men, but I am focusing here on women. If you look at certain nations, you can see for example that the collective consciousness is at a certain level, there is a certain beast that is very dominant and that is suppressing women. You can see that this beast is so strong that it is overpowering the minds of most women, the vast majority of women in some cases.

How ascended master students can help women

You who have been fortunate enough to grow up in a modern democracy, or in a country where women have more opportunity and more equality, should be very careful when you look at these nations. You must be very careful not to believe that all women who have embodied in these nations are overpowered by this collective consciousness. You should be very careful to think that women in these nations are somehow at a lower level of spiritual growth, at a lower level of evolution than you are yourselves. I can assure you that there are very mature souls who have chosen to embody in all nations around the world specifically to bring those societies forward. In every nation, regardless of how, should we say *backwards*, it might seem, there are very courageous souls who have embodied there, as women, some men of course too but I am focusing again on women. There are women embodied in those nations who are mature, advanced souls who chose to embody there so they could grow up in these situations, so they could be exposed to this collective programming, this collective brainwashing, as you might say, for it is a programming that goes far beyond the brain because it goes into the emotional, mental and identity bodies. These souls have chosen to embody there to be exposed to this, so they know what other women are going through, and so that they can then liberate themselves from it and thereby demonstrate that it can be done. They can also then gradually rise to positions where they can begin to challenge their societies with these new ideas.

First of all, you need to hold in your mind that this is so. There are women in all of these nations, some men as well, who are as mature spiritually as you are who have grown up in the more liberated countries. You also need to make the calls that those souls will be cut free to fulfill what is in their Divine plans. This is where you can have a major impact. When you look at these souls, you can see that there are some that are so mature from past lives that they will be able on their own to break through the collective resistance in their nation. There is also a larger group of souls who find it more difficult to break through and those are the ones especially that can be helped by your calls. This is where you can have a tremendous impact as ascended master students, of making the calls that these women will be cut free to wake up and fulfil the highest potential that they defined in their Divine plans, perhaps even go beyond what they dared to envision before they came into embodiment. This can be a major factor where you as ascended master students can have an impact.

You recognize I am sure that when we do a conference like this, we stand here from the ascended master perspective and we look at the planet. We are not planning in this conference to address every issue related to women. What we are doing is we are looking at the planet, the collective consciousness, then we are looking at our students. How many students do we have? What level of consciousness do you have? What is your willingness to devote your time and energy to this? We are in no way blaming anybody. We are in no way saying that you *should* be at a higher level or not. We are simply making a realistic assessment and then we are saying: "Now we have the opportunity to put on this conference, what is a realistic goal for what we can release without overwhelming or overburdening our students where they feel it is just too much for them to deal with?"

We are looking at a realistic assessment of how can the students of the ascended masters (as you are today and as you will be growing in the coming decades) how can you have the greatest possible impact on the liberation of women? What ideas, what tools can we give you that will have the greatest possible impact in the next one or two decades? Now, the teachings will not necessarily be applicable only in that time frame, because in other nations they can be applicable in future decades, but we are still making a realistic assessment, saying: "What can we bring to your attention now that can have the greatest possible impact on improving the situation that is there now?" In other words, we are not trying to bring forth some ultimate result that will be centuries into the golden age. We are trying to improve the situation that is there now, to bring us to the next phase where there can then be released higher ideas for the liberation of women, for the liberation of men, for the equality between the sexes.

This is our goal. This is a very practical-realist goal that when you give the calls and the invocations that will be based on this conference, when you study the teachings, when you, perhaps, find ways to share these teachings (as we have told you several times to share them in whatever context that is relevant for you personally), then you can indeed have a major impact. You can be those forerunners who will make this coming decade of the 2020s a real step forward in improving the situation of women on this planet. You know, some of you at least, that in America they have a way for measuring your eyesight. They give it a number and they say that normal vision is 20/20. It is simply the way they measure it. Therefore, you have this popular saying in America that "Hindsight is 20/20." In other words, it is always easy to look back, and you have perfect vision when you are looking back about what should have been done and how things should have been evolving. With this conference, we aim to give an impulse into the collective consciousness so that foresight will also be 20/20, because not only you as ascended master students, but the many people who are playing a role (and have it in their Divine plan to play a role) will have perfect vision to see what is a practical-realist goal for the liberation of women in this decade.

An evaluation of the potential of various nations

I have said that there are many mature souls who have chosen to embody in these less developed countries in order to bring forth the liberation of women there. Of course, there are also many souls, in fact, many more mature souls, who have chosen to embody in the modern democracies, in the more evolved countries, or even in those who are somewhat in between in order to bring those societies forward. In a sense, you could say that when you look at the nations in the world, there are some nations that are so far behind where the modern democracies are at that in the next decade it is not realistic that those nations can catch up to where the modern democracies are at today. I will not say which nations because I do not want to put any kind of pessimistic outlook into your minds, but realistically, there are some nations that will need several decades to catch up to the point of the liberation of women, equality among the sexes, where you see the modern democracies are at today.

There is a large group of nations that are somewhat behind where the modern democracies are at, or who are even among what we can call modern democracies, but not as advanced in terms of the liberation of women. These nations can indeed catch up in the next decade, so there is a tremendous potential for this large, middle group that they can come very, very close in the next decade to where the most advanced nations are at today in terms of equality among the sexes and the liberation of women.

Now, that being said of course I do not want you to fix in your minds that the more advanced nations will stand still in the next decade. Of course, they will not. There will be some of you for whom it is a goal to help your own nations catch up to where the more advanced nations are at today. There will be some of you who have chosen to embody in the more advanced nations because you want to bring those nations forward from where they are today. You want to bring a greater awareness of the liberation of women, a greater awareness of the need for equality among the sexes.

Equality among the sexes does not mean sameness

In this context, I want to briefly remark, even though we may say more about this, that when we are talking about the equality among the sexes, equality does not mean sameness. Naturally, we do, as ascended masters, (and Saint Germain very much wants in the golden age) that there is legal equality among the sexes, that the laws that apply to society apply equally to men and women. We want to see that women are given equal opportunity in the workplace, certainly equal pay for doing the same job, and that women are not confined to certain kinds of jobs where there is lesser pay. We do want to see that, from an outer legal, societal, practical framework, there is equality among the sexes.

Of course, there will always be, at least for the foreseeable future on planet earth, the physical differences and the different roles of mothers and giving birth to children, so equality does not necessarily mean sameness. It certainly means a shift where you see the equal value of men and women, and that women have an equal contribution to make to society. That is precisely why we need to overcome this idea that there is some absolute truth that was defined 2,000 years ago, or however many years ago, that because it is an absolute revelation from God should define the role of men and women, and the relationship between men and women.

Look at the technological development

My beloved, as ascended master students, you can do this but you can also make the calls that people will be able to do this. Simply step back and look at history. Go back and look at the time of Abraham and look at Jewish society. Look at Middle Eastern society as it was back then. Go back and look at the time of Jesus. Go back and look at the time of Mohammed. Look at how societies back then had the patriarchal mindset, were dominated by men and already had a certain attitude towards women. Now, look at those same societies from a technological viewpoint. Look at what has happened in the area of technology in the last 2,000 years, or even 3,000 or 4,000 years. Would you want to go back and live in a society as it was 2,000 years ago where you are out there with a pick and picking in the soil, trying to make something grow in the dry climate so that you can sustain yourself? Would you want to be making a living that way? If you do not want to turn the clock back technologically, why do you want your society to live as if the clock was turned back when it comes to the view of men and women and their roles? Is it not obvious that as technology has progressed, society needs to progress in the way it looks at men and women?

Abandoning the patriarchal mindset

Is it not equally obvious that in order for this to happen, a critical mass of people must begin to question and eventually abandon the idea that there could ever be a particular scripture that was an absolute infallible revelation that should stand for all time? Look at the Bible. Look at the Koran. Look at the Torah. Is it not obvious that the way language was used, the way ideas were formulated, the basic mindset, the basic paradigm, the way people looked at life back then, was colored by this patriarchal male-dominated mindset? Therefore, is it not obvious that even God the Almighty could not bring forth an ultimate revelation back then because the people trapped in this mindset would not have been able to accept it?

My beloved, God could not have told Abraham to give equality to his wife or wives. God could not have told Moses to promote equality among the sexes. God could not even have said this through Jesus, even though Jesus actually did not discriminate between men and women, regardless of what some of the scriptures do. Jesus, in his teachings and in his actions, did not discriminate between men and women. This is not accurately portrayed in the Christian scriptures because the people who wrote down the Christian scriptures were still so trapped in that male-dominated mindset.

There is a large group of people in the world today who are ready to step up and recognize this consciously. Many have already realized it in past lives. Many have realized it at the identity and mental levels, even at the emotional level, but it has not broken through to the physical. That is again where your calls can have a tremendous impact in making more and more people awaken from this mindset that we cannot question a scripture that was written down centuries or millennia ago because it was somehow given by God, and therefore it must be infallible. Of course God is infallible, but the people receiving a revelation are not infallible, never have been, never will be. Therefore, there never *has been,* there never *will be* any absolute revelation on this planet. When I say never, I mean as long as it is an unnatural planet. On a natural planet, you can discuss whether you even need revelation.

The calls you can make (that can have a tremendous impact) is for people to awaken from this and see this as obviously as you yourself see it. I trust that even some of you who may have been involved with previous ascended master organizations will be willing to take this dictation and step up so that you also see it. You see the reality of progressive revelation that we of the ascended masters have much more to give than what we can possibly give today. This is not a limitation of the messenger, of the students, but it is a limitation of the collective consciousness, and therefore this has been the same in all previous ages. There has never been an age on earth where perfect progressive revelation could be given. You see the teachings we have given. You are living in an unascended sphere that will progress until it ascends, but even after your sphere ascends, there is still progression towards higher levels of consciousness. How could there ever be something that was absolute? How could there ever be a statement expressed in words that could be absolute, that could not be expanded upon?

The myth of a scripture without errors

Now, be careful to recognize here that the fallen beings are very clever in manipulating people because they have mixed up the idea of revelation and Divine scripture with the idea of infallibility. They absolutely want people to believe that there can be no errors in the Bible, or the Koran, or in the Hindu scriptures or the Buddhist scriptures. They absolutely want people to believe this, but why do they want people to believe it? Because this shuts the door to progressive revelation.

The fallen beings have made so many people believe that if anything additional was said after the Christian scriptures were written down, then that would mean that the Christian scriptures were not infallible and there must be errors in them. There are people, as we have said, who have such a need for security that they need to believe they have an infallible belief system, and if they believe in this system and follow its rules, they are guaranteed to be saved after this lifetime. There are people who have not been willing to give up this belief. That is why they are so fanatical about adhering to fundamentalist Christianity, fundamentalist Islam, the Catholic church, the Hindu religion, the Buddhist religion, other religions. They will not consider any changes because they will be plunged into this unbearable fear.

My beloved, there are fewer and fewer people in the world who are trapped in this, and why is this so? Because the belief in these infallible belief systems has now been around for a very long time, which means that many, many people have, in their past lives, grown up in one of these infallible belief systems. They have believed in its claim that if they follow the system, they are guaranteed to be saved after this lifetime. Then, they pass from the screen of life. They go up to their life review, and they see that they have not qualified for their ascension because they have not raised their consciousness. You do not raise your consciousness to the ascended level by following an outer belief system.

Here, they have to go down in embodiment again, and when they have done this enough times (and quite frankly, some people have to do it many times) they come into embodiment being not quite so sure that there is an infallible belief system. Many, many people have gone through this process in past lives. They are at the point where all that is needed is that they break through at the conscious level and realize, and pull down to the conscious awareness, what they already know in their identity and mental bodies. They have to overcome that fear in the emotional body that blocks these insights from coming through to the physical mind.

This is where your calls can have an impact. You can really help millions of people come to that realization: We no longer need to believe that a scripture is infallible. We can be open to new ideas. We can be open to the possibility that we do not have to treat women in our society the way they were treated at the time of Mohammed, or the time of Jesus, or the time of Abraham or Moses, or the time of the Vedas or the Buddha. We do not have, in this modern society, to treat women the way they were treated thousands of years ago. This is a realization that is there in the collective consciousness. It has broken through in many societies, but there are many more where it is very close to breaking through. It is a realistic goal that it can break through in this next decade of the 2020s. It is a realistic goal.

Therefore, we ask you to keep this in your minds, to make the calls for it, and to accept it for yourselves that this is happening. Again, of course men are more prone to become victims of these absolutist belief systems and the epic mindset. Therefore, women are the ones who have the greatest potential to be the forerunners for this breakthrough where societies will begin to abandon this absolutist aspect of the epic mindset.

With this, I have given you what I wanted to give you. I thank you for your attention for this dictation, for your willingness to be part of this conference. We are grateful that so many people from around the world have chosen to be part of this conference, and we look forward to what we can release in the coming days. Therefore, I seal you in the love and the joy of the heart of the Divine Mother.

NOTE: This dictation was given May 30th, 2020.

2 | AWAKENING WOMEN TO QUESTION INFALLIBLE TRUTH (PART 1)

In the name of the I AM THAT I AM, Jesus Christ, I use the authority that I have as a being in embodiment on earth to call upon Mother Mary to reinforce my calls and use my chakras to project the statements in this invocation into the collective consciousness and awaken people to the awareness that will liberate both men and women from all psychological and spiritual thralldom to the fallen beings. Awaken people to the reality that we are spiritual beings and that we can co-create a new future by working with the ascended masters. I especially call for ...

[Make your own calls here.]

Part 1

1. Mother Mary, awaken women to the need to focus attention on women's situation, to debate various issues related to women's situation and to make drastic physical changes in society to improve women's situation.

O blessed Mary, Mother mine,
there is no greater love than thine,
as we are one in heart and mind,
my place in hierarchy I find.

O Mother Mary, generate,
the song that does accelerate,
the earth into a higher state,
all matter does now scintillate.

2. Mother Mary, awaken women to recognize that the ascended masters
are behind and involved with any improvement because you are the spiritual guardians for this planet.

I came to earth from heaven sent,
as I am in embodiment,
I use Divine authority,
commanding you to set earth free.

O Mother Mary, generate,
the song that does accelerate,
the earth into a higher state,
all matter does now scintillate.

3. Mother Mary, awaken women to the energies and ideas that you are
broadcasting into the collective consciousness and the energy field of the
planet.

I call now in God's sacred name,
for you to use your Mother Flame,
to burn all fear-based energy,
restoring sacred harmony.

O Mother Mary, generate,
the song that does accelerate,
the earth into a higher state,
all matter does now scintillate.

4. Mother Mary, awaken women to pick up on the ideas, to feel the energies and to take action to debate various issues that they are not able to debate on their own.

Your sacred name I hereby praise,
collective consciousness you raise,
no more of fear and doubt and shame,
consume it with your Mother Flame.

**O Mother Mary, generate,
the song that does accelerate,
the earth into a higher state,
all matter does now scintillate.**

5. Mother Mary, awaken women to the fact that this planet has been so heavily influenced by the fallen beings, and there is so much fear-based lower energy in the identity, mental and emotional bodies of the planet, that we human beings would not be able to liberate ourselves if it were not for the ascended masters.

All darkness from the earth you purge,
your light moves as a mighty surge,
no force of darkness can now stop,
the spiral that goes only up.

**O Mother Mary, generate,
the song that does accelerate,
the earth into a higher state,
all matter does now scintillate.**

6. Mother Mary, awaken women to see how important it is to make the calls, to reinforce the energies, to broadcast the energies and the ideas into the collective consciousness so that more and more people can pick up on them.

All elemental life you bless,
removing from them man-made stress,
the nature spirits are now free,
outpicturing Divine decree.

O Mother Mary, generate,
the song that does accelerate,
the earth into a higher state,
all matter does now scintillate.

7. Mother Mary, awaken those women who can act as the tip of the spear, the forerunners, who are in positions in society to make the decisions, to take the actions, so that they will be able to do what they came here to do.

I raise my voice and take my stand,
a stop to war I do command,
no more shall warring scar the earth,
a golden age is given birth.

O Mother Mary, generate,
the song that does accelerate,
the earth into a higher state,
all matter does now scintillate.

8. Mother Mary, awaken women to see that the liberation of women, the equality between men and women, is not a legal process. It is not even a *physical* process. It is a *psychological* process.

As Mother Earth is free at last,
disasters belong to the past,
your Mother Light is so intense,
that matter is now far less dense.

O Mother Mary, generate,
the song that does accelerate,
the earth into a higher state,
all matter does now scintillate.

9. Mother Mary, awaken women to see that equality requires changes in the emotional body, the mental body and the identity body of a society and of individuals.

In Mother Light the earth is pure,
the upward spiral will endure,

prosperity is now the norm,
God's vision manifest as form.

O Mother Mary, generate,
the song that does accelerate,
the earth into a higher state,
all matter does now scintillate.

Part 2

1. Mother Mary, awaken women to see that even if society enacted a set of laws that would bring about total equality between men and women, or would liberate women from any oppression or limitation, it could not be done legally because it is not an entirely legal or political process. It requires a shift in consciousness.

O blessed Mary, Mother mine,
there is no greater love than thine,
as we are one in heart and mind,
my place in hierarchy I find.

O Mother Mary, generate,
the song that does accelerate,
the earth into a higher state,
all matter does now scintillate.

2. Mother Mary, awaken women to see that it will take time before a change filters through the collective consciousness, and the individual conscious-ness of the people living in that society. It is a psychological process.

I came to earth from heaven sent,
as I am in embodiment,
I use Divine authority,
commanding you to set earth free.

O Mother Mary, generate,
the song that does accelerate,

the earth into a higher state,
all matter does now scintillate.

3. Mother Mary, awaken women to see that women need to let go of the belief that there is a final truth. Women need to let go of this dream of having a final truth, a final revelation because only women have the potential to do this.

I call now in God's sacred name,
for you to use your Mother Flame,
to burn all fear-based energy,
restoring sacred harmony.

O Mother Mary, generate,
the song that does accelerate,
the earth into a higher state,
all matter does now scintillate.

4. Mother Mary, awaken women to see that one of the primary means that is being used around the world to suppress women and keep women in a fixed station is the idea that there is some final truth.

Your sacred name I hereby praise,
collective consciousness you raise,
no more of fear and doubt and shame,
consume it with your Mother Flame.

O Mother Mary, generate,
the song that does accelerate,
the earth into a higher state,
all matter does now scintillate.

5. Mother Mary, awaken women to see that many women around the world are being held in a fixed position because their society believes that Christianity has brought forth a final revelation and that the Bible is the Word of God, and that it does not need to be expanded upon today.

All darkness from the earth you purge,
your light moves as a mighty surge,

no force of darkness can now stop,
the spiral that goes only up.

O Mother Mary, generate,
the song that does accelerate,
the earth into a higher state,
all matter does now scintillate.

6. Mother Mary, awaken women to see that many people believe that what was said about women in the Bible is an absolute truth that should stand for all time. Thus women should remain silent in the churches, women are responsible for the fall of man and should be kept out of decision-making positions because women are dangerous and could abort God's plan for saving the world.

All elemental life you bless,
removing from them man-made stress,
the nature spirits are now free,
outpicturing Divine decree.

O Mother Mary, generate,
the song that does accelerate,
the earth into a higher state,
all matter does now scintillate.

7. Mother Mary, awaken women to see that millions of Christians hold these beliefs because they believe that the Bible is the word of God. Many Muslims have the same belief about the Koran.

I raise my voice and take my stand,
a stop to war I do command,
no more shall warring scar the earth,
a golden age is given birth.

O Mother Mary, generate,
the song that does accelerate,
the earth into a higher state,
all matter does now scintillate.

8. Mother Mary, awaken women to see that in the Hindu religion, in India, in China they have certain beliefs that define women's situation in society, their station in society. Even some materialists believe that evolution defined differences between men and women so that women are inferior to men because evolution has made it so.

As Mother Earth is free at last,
disasters belong to the past,
your Mother Light is so intense,
that matter is now far less dense.

O Mother Mary, generate,
the song that does accelerate,
the earth into a higher state,
all matter does now scintillate.

9. Mother Mary, awaken women to see that one of the primary milestones on the road to the liberation of women is to challenge the idea that there is any truth on earth that is absolute or final. Men cannot do this, but women can step up and challenge this idea of the absolute, final truth.

In Mother Light the earth is pure,
the upward spiral will endure,
prosperity is now the norm,
God's vision manifest as form.

O Mother Mary, generate,
the song that does accelerate,
the earth into a higher state,
all matter does now scintillate.

Part 3

1. Mother Mary, awaken women to see that this idea is also keeping men in a fixed position because these absolute truths also define fixed roles for men, and men are trapped in these roles, even if they do not recognize it consciously.

O blessed Mary, Mother mine,
there is no greater love than thine,
as we are one in heart and mind,
my place in hierarchy I find.

O Mother Mary, generate,
the song that does accelerate,
the earth into a higher state,
all matter does now scintillate.

2. Mother Mary, awaken women to see that in this decade of the 2020s, women need to expose how the idea of an absolute truth limits not only women but men and societies as well.

I came to earth from heaven sent,
as I am in embodiment,
I use Divine authority,
commanding you to set earth free.

O Mother Mary, generate,
the song that does accelerate,
the earth into a higher state,
all matter does now scintillate.

3. Mother Mary, awaken women to see that the era of ideology is over. We can no longer allow ourselves to believe that if a society is based on a specific ideology, and lives up to an absolute truth, then all problems will be solved and it will be an ideal world.

I call now in God's sacred name,
for you to use your Mother Flame,
to burn all fear-based energy,
restoring sacred harmony.

O Mother Mary, generate,
the song that does accelerate,
the earth into a higher state,
all matter does now scintillate.

4. Mother Mary, awaken women to see that this is a false idea. It is a dangerous, non-constructive idea that has led to most of the conflicts we have seen in history, that has led to world wars and incredible atrocities and persecution.

Your sacred name I hereby praise,
collective consciousness you raise,
no more of fear and doubt and shame,
consume it with your Mother Flame.

O Mother Mary, generate,
the song that does accelerate,
the earth into a higher state,
all matter does now scintillate.

5. Mother Mary, awaken women to see that if one country or a group of countries believe they have the absolute idea and that their idea can bring forth the ideal society, then they are automatically set in conflict with those who do not share their idea.

All darkness from the earth you purge,
your light moves as a mighty surge,
no force of darkness can now stop,
the spiral that goes only up.

O Mother Mary, generate,
the song that does accelerate,
the earth into a higher state,
all matter does now scintillate.

6. Mother Mary, awaken women to see that in the coming age, there will not be one ideology, one religion, one political philosophy that will dominate the earth. Nor will there be several rivaling ideologies that will fight each other for domination over the earth.

All elemental life you bless,
removing from them man-made stress,
the nature spirits are now free,
outpicturing Divine decree.

O Mother Mary, generate,
the song that does accelerate,
the earth into a higher state,
all matter does now scintillate.

7. Mother Mary, awaken women to see that the influence of ideologies and thought systems will fall away as people wake up and realize how trapped they were, how trapped societies were in these ideologies and thought systems.

I raise my voice and take my stand,
a stop to war I do command,
no more shall warring scar the earth,
a golden age is given birth.

O Mother Mary, generate,
the song that does accelerate,
the earth into a higher state,
all matter does now scintillate.

8. Mother Mary, awaken women to make a conscious, deliberate effort to move away from these ideas that are thought to be absolute.

As Mother Earth is free at last,
disasters belong to the past,
your Mother Light is so intense,
that matter is now far less dense.

O Mother Mary, generate,
the song that does accelerate,
the earth into a higher state,
all matter does now scintillate.

9. Mother Mary, awaken women to see that the Catholic church, the Catholic mindset, is based on the idea of an absolute truth. It is based on a fixed idea of women being responsible for the fall, and therefore they should not be allowed to hold decision-making positions.

In Mother Light the earth is pure,
the upward spiral will endure,
prosperity is now the norm,
God's vision manifest as form.

O Mother Mary, generate,
the song that does accelerate,
the earth into a higher state,
all matter does now scintillate.

Part 4

1. Mother Mary, awaken women to see that in any country dominated by the Catholic religion, there will be an underlying, often unspoken, consciousness that says that women should be kept out of *all* decision-making positions because if they are not to be trusted in the church, how can they be trusted in the government or in business?

O blessed Mary, Mother mine,
there is no greater love than thine,
as we are one in heart and mind,
my place in hierarchy I find.

O Mother Mary, generate,
the song that does accelerate,
the earth into a higher state,
all matter does now scintillate.

2. Mother Mary, awaken women to see that this is also found in some Christian, Protestant, Lutheran societies where we have the same underlying attitude.

I came to earth from heaven sent,
as I am in embodiment,
I use Divine authority,
commanding you to set earth free.

O Mother Mary, generate,
the song that does accelerate,
the earth into a higher state,
all matter does now scintillate.

3. Mother Mary, awaken women to see that in Africa there is a set of beliefs that go back to the tribal religions and they are very limiting to women, being suspicious of women, especially women who have power.

I call now in God's sacred name,
for you to use your Mother Flame,
to burn all fear-based energy,
restoring sacred harmony.

O Mother Mary, generate,
the song that does accelerate,
the earth into a higher state,
all matter does now scintillate.

4. Mother Mary, awaken women to see that there is still an underlying belief that any woman who has power must be a witch, and thus society cannot let women come to power.

Your sacred name I hereby praise,
collective consciousness you raise,
no more of fear and doubt and shame,
consume it with your Mother Flame.

O Mother Mary, generate,
the song that does accelerate,
the earth into a higher state,
all matter does now scintillate.

5. Mother Mary, awaken women to see that in many African areas there is an attitude towards women that is based on "infallible" or never-questioned ideas: "This is just the way women are. This is just the way men are, and this is the way the relationship between men and women should be."

All darkness from the earth you purge,
your light moves as a mighty surge,
no force of darkness can now stop,
the spiral that goes only up.

O Mother Mary, generate,
the song that does accelerate,
the earth into a higher state,
all matter does now scintillate.

6. Mother Mary, awaken women to see that it can be difficult to point to a scripture or a specific belief that is clearly articulated but it is there in the collective consciousness, often so subtle that very few people think to question it.

All elemental life you bless,
removing from them man-made stress,
the nature spirits are now free,
outpicturing Divine decree.

O Mother Mary, generate,
the song that does accelerate,
the earth into a higher state,
all matter does now scintillate.

7. Mother Mary, awaken women to identify these beliefs and question them, speak what has rarely been spoken and identify and challenge these beliefs.

I raise my voice and take my stand,
a stop to war I do command,
no more shall warring scar the earth,
a golden age is given birth.

O Mother Mary, generate,
the song that does accelerate,
the earth into a higher state,
all matter does now scintillate.

8. Mother Mary, awaken women to see that there are very mature souls who have chosen to embody in all nations around the world specifically to bring those societies forward.

As Mother Earth is free at last,
disasters belong to the past,
your Mother Light is so intense,
that matter is now far less dense.

O Mother Mary, generate,
the song that does accelerate,
the earth into a higher state,
all matter does now scintillate.

9. Mother Mary, awaken women to see that in every nation, regardless of how backwards it might seem, there are very courageous souls who have embodied there as women so they could grow up in these situations.

In Mother Light the earth is pure,
the upward spiral will endure,
prosperity is now the norm,
God's vision manifest as form.

O Mother Mary, generate,
the song that does accelerate,
the earth into a higher state,
all matter does now scintillate.

Sealing

In the name of the I AM THAT I AM, I accept that Archangel Michael, Astrea and Shiva form an impenetrable shield around myself and all constructive people, sealing us from all fear-based energies in all four octaves. I accept that the Light of God is consuming and transforming all fear-based energies that make up the dark forces working against the liberation of women on earth!

3 | AWAKENING WOMEN TO QUESTION INFALLIBLE TRUTH (PART 2)

In the name of the I AM THAT I AM, Jesus Christ, I use the authority that I have as a being in embodiment on earth to call upon Mother Mary to reinforce my calls and use my chakras to project the statements in this invocation into the collective consciousness and awaken people to the awareness that will liberate both men and women from all psychological and spiritual thralldom to the fallen beings. Awaken people to the reality that we are spiritual beings and that we can co-create a new future by working with the ascended masters. I especially call for ...

[Make your own calls here.]

Part 1

1. Mother Mary, awaken women to overcome the collective programming of the emotional, mental and identity bodies so they liberate themselves from it and thereby demonstrate that it can be done.

O blessed Mary, Mother mine,
there is no greater love than thine,
as we are one in heart and mind,
my place in hierarchy I find.

O Mother Mary, generate,
the song that does accelerate,
the earth into a higher state,
all matter does now scintillate.

2. Mother Mary, awaken women so they can rise to positions where they can begin to challenge their societies with new ideas.

I came to earth from heaven sent,
as I am in embodiment,
I use Divine authority,
commanding you to set earth free.

O Mother Mary, generate,
the song that does accelerate,
the earth into a higher state,
all matter does now scintillate.

3. Mother Mary, awaken women in all nations to fulfill what is in their Divine plans. Help them break through the collective resistance in their nations.

I call now in God's sacred name,
for you to use your Mother Flame,
to burn all fear-based energy,
restoring sacred harmony.

O Mother Mary, generate,
the song that does accelerate,
the earth into a higher state,
all matter does now scintillate.

4. Mother Mary, awaken the most spiritually mature women to fulfil the highest potential that they defined in their Divine plans, even go beyond what they dared to envision before they came into embodiment.

> Your sacred name I hereby praise,
> collective consciousness you raise,
> no more of fear and doubt and shame,
> consume it with your Mother Flame.

> **O Mother Mary, generate,**
> **the song that does accelerate,**
> **the earth into a higher state,**
> **all matter does now scintillate.**

5. Mother Mary, awaken those people who can tune in and receive the higher ideas for the liberation of women, for the liberation of men, for the equality between the sexes.

> All darkness from the earth you purge,
> your light moves as a mighty surge,
> no force of darkness can now stop,
> the spiral that goes only up.

> **O Mother Mary, generate,**
> **the song that does accelerate,**
> **the earth into a higher state,**
> **all matter does now scintillate.**

6. Mother Mary, awaken women to find ways to share these teachings and be the forerunners who will make this coming decade of the 2020s a real step forward in improving the situation of women on this planet.

> All elemental life you bless,
> removing from them man-made stress,
> the nature spirits are now free,
> outpicturing Divine decree.

> **O Mother Mary, generate,**
> **the song that does accelerate,**

the earth into a higher state,
all matter does now scintillate.

7. Mother Mary, awaken women to have perfect vision to see what is a practical, realist goal for the liberation of women in this decade of the 2020s.

> I raise my voice and take my stand,
> a stop to war I do command,
> no more shall warring scar the earth,
> a golden age is given birth.

> **O Mother Mary, generate,**
> **the song that does accelerate,**
> **the earth into a higher state,**
> **all matter does now scintillate.**

8. Mother Mary, awaken the many mature souls who have chosen to embody in less developed countries in order to bring forth the liberation of women there.

> As Mother Earth is free at last,
> disasters belong to the past,
> your Mother Light is so intense,
> that matter is now far less dense.

> **O Mother Mary, generate,**
> **the song that does accelerate,**
> **the earth into a higher state,**
> **all matter does now scintillate.**

9. Mother Mary, awaken the mature souls who have chosen to embody in the more evolved countries, or even in those who are somewhat in between in order to bring those societies forward.

> In Mother Light the earth is pure,
> the upward spiral will endure,
> prosperity is now the norm,
> God's vision manifest as form.

O Mother Mary, generate,
the song that does accelerate,
the earth into a higher state,
all matter does now scintillate.

Part 2

1. Mother Mary, awaken women in those nations who are not as advanced in terms of the liberation of women so they can catch up in the next decade and come close to where the most advanced nations are at today in terms of equality among the sexes and the liberation of women.

O blessed Mary, Mother mine,
there is no greater love than thine,
as we are one in heart and mind,
my place in hierarchy I find.

O Mother Mary, generate,
the song that does accelerate,
the earth into a higher state,
all matter does now scintillate.

2. Mother Mary, awaken women who have chosen to embody in the more advanced nations to bring those nations forward from where they are today, to bring a greater awareness of the liberation of women, a greater awareness of the need for equality among the sexes.

I came to earth from heaven sent,
as I am in embodiment,
I use Divine authority,
commanding you to set earth free.

O Mother Mary, generate,
the song that does accelerate,
the earth into a higher state,
all matter does now scintillate.

3. Mother Mary, awaken women to see the way to create legal equality among the sexes so that the laws apply equally to men and women.

> I call now in God's sacred name,
> for you to use your Mother Flame,
> to burn all fear-based energy,
> restoring sacred harmony.

> **O Mother Mary, generate,**
> **the song that does accelerate,**
> **the earth into a higher state,**
> **all matter does now scintillate.**

4. Mother Mary, awaken women to see how to get equal opportunity in the workplace, equal pay for doing the same job, and that women are not confined to certain kinds of jobs where there is lesser pay.

> Your sacred name I hereby praise,
> collective consciousness you raise,
> no more of fear and doubt and shame,
> consume it with your Mother Flame.

> **O Mother Mary, generate,**
> **the song that does accelerate,**
> **the earth into a higher state,**
> **all matter does now scintillate.**

5. Mother Mary, awaken women to see that equality does not necessarily mean sameness. It means a shift where we see the equal value of men and women, and that women have an equal contribution to make to society.

> All darkness from the earth you purge,
> your light moves as a mighty surge,
> no force of darkness can now stop,
> the spiral that goes only up.

> **O Mother Mary, generate,**
> **the song that does accelerate,**

the earth into a higher state,
all matter does now scintillate.

6. Mother Mary, awaken women to see that this is why we need to over-come the idea that there is some truth from the past that is an absolute revelation from God that should define the role of men and women, and the relationship between men and women.

All elemental life you bless,
removing from them man-made stress,
the nature spirits are now free,
outpicturing Divine decree.

O Mother Mary, generate,
the song that does accelerate,
the earth into a higher state,
all matter does now scintillate.

7. Mother Mary, awaken women to see that in the past most societies had the patriarchal mindset. They were dominated by men and already had a certain attitude towards women.

I raise my voice and take my stand,
a stop to war I do command,
no more shall warring scar the earth,
a golden age is given birth.

O Mother Mary, generate,
the song that does accelerate,
the earth into a higher state,
all matter does now scintillate.

8. Mother Mary, awaken women to see that those same societies have made tremendous technological progress so why should they live as if the clock was turned back when it comes to the view of men and women and their roles?

As Mother Earth is free at last,
disasters belong to the past,

your Mother Light is so intense,
that matter is now far less dense.

O Mother Mary, generate,
the song that does accelerate,
the earth into a higher state,
all matter does now scintillate.

9. Mother Mary, awaken women to see that as technology has progressed, society needs to progress in the way it looks at men and women.

In Mother Light the earth is pure,
the upward spiral will endure,
prosperity is now the norm,
God's vision manifest as form.

O Mother Mary, generate,
the song that does accelerate,
the earth into a higher state,
all matter does now scintillate.

Part 3

1. Mother Mary, awaken women to question and eventually abandon the idea that there could ever be a particular scripture that was an absolute infallible revelation that should stand for all time.

O blessed Mary, Mother mine,
there is no greater love than thine,
as we are one in heart and mind,
my place in hierarchy I find.

O Mother Mary, generate,
the song that does accelerate,
the earth into a higher state,
all matter does now scintillate.

2. Mother Mary, awaken women to see that the Bible, the Koran, the Torah were brought fourth at a time when people looked at life through the patriarchal male-dominated mindset.

I came to earth from heaven sent,
as I am in embodiment,
I use Divine authority,
commanding you to set earth free.

O Mother Mary, generate,
the song that does accelerate,
the earth into a higher state,
all matter does now scintillate.

3. Mother Mary, awaken women to see that even God the Almighty could not bring forth an ultimate revelation back then because the people trapped in this mindset would not have been able to accept it.

I call now in God's sacred name,
for you to use your Mother Flame,
to burn all fear-based energy,
restoring sacred harmony.

O Mother Mary, generate,
the song that does accelerate,
the earth into a higher state,
all matter does now scintillate.

4. Mother Mary, awaken women to see that God could not have told Abraham or Moses to promote equality among the sexes.

Your sacred name I hereby praise,
collective consciousness you raise,
no more of fear and doubt and shame,
consume it with your Mother Flame.

O Mother Mary, generate,
the song that does accelerate,

the earth into a higher state,
all matter does now scintillate.

5. Mother Mary, awaken women to see that Jesus did not discriminate between men and women, but this is not accurately portrayed in the Christian scriptures because the people who wrote down the scriptures were still trapped in that male-dominated mindset.

All darkness from the earth you purge,
your light moves as a mighty surge,
no force of darkness can now stop,
the spiral that goes only up.

O Mother Mary, generate,
the song that does accelerate,
the earth into a higher state,
all matter does now scintillate.

6. Mother Mary, awaken the large group of people who are ready to step up and consciously let go of the mindset that we cannot question a scripture that was written down centuries or millennia ago because it was somehow given by God, and therefore it must be infallible.

All elemental life you bless,
removing from them man-made stress,
the nature spirits are now free,
outpicturing Divine decree.

O Mother Mary, generate,
the song that does accelerate,
the earth into a higher state,
all matter does now scintillate.

7. Mother Mary, awaken women to see that although God is infallible, the people receiving a revelation are not infallible. There never *has been,* there never *will be* any absolute revelation on this planet.

I raise my voice and take my stand,
a stop to war I do command,

no more shall warring scar the earth,
a golden age is given birth.

O Mother Mary, generate,
the song that does accelerate,
the earth into a higher state,
all matter does now scintillate.

8. Mother Mary, awaken women to see the reality of progressive revelation and that the ascended masters have much more to give than what can possibly be given today.

As Mother Earth is free at last,
disasters belong to the past,
your Mother Light is so intense,
that matter is now far less dense.

O Mother Mary, generate,
the song that does accelerate,
the earth into a higher state,
all matter does now scintillate.

9. Mother Mary, awaken women to see that because of the collective consciousness, there has never been an age on earth where perfect progressive revelation could be given.

In Mother Light the earth is pure,
the upward spiral will endure,
prosperity is now the norm,
God's vision manifest as form.

O Mother Mary, generate,
the song that does accelerate,
the earth into a higher state,
all matter does now scintillate.

Part 4

1. Mother Mary, awaken women to see that those who are manipulating mankind have mixed up the idea of revelation and Divine scripture with the idea of infallibility. They want people to believe that there can be no errors in the scriptures because this shuts the door to progressive revelation.

O blessed Mary, Mother mine,
there is no greater love than thine,
as we are one in heart and mind,
my place in hierarchy I find.

O Mother Mary, generate,
the song that does accelerate,
the earth into a higher state,
all matter does now scintillate.

2. Mother Mary, awaken women from the belief that if anything additional was said after the Christian scriptures were written down, then that would mean that the Christian scriptures were not infallible and there must be errors in them.

I came to earth from heaven sent,
as I am in embodiment,
I use Divine authority,
commanding you to set earth free.

O Mother Mary, generate,
the song that does accelerate,
the earth into a higher state,
all matter does now scintillate.

3. Mother Mary, awaken women from the need for security that makes them believe they have an infallible belief system, and if they believe in this system and follow its rules, they are guaranteed to be saved after this lifetime.

I call now in God's sacred name,
for you to use your Mother Flame,
to burn all fear-based energy,
restoring sacred harmony.

O Mother Mary, generate,
the song that does accelerate,
the earth into a higher state,
all matter does now scintillate.

4. Mother Mary, awaken women to see that people who are *not* willing to give up this belief become fanatics because of their unbearable fear.

Your sacred name I hereby praise,
collective consciousness you raise,
no more of fear and doubt and shame,
consume it with your Mother Flame.

O Mother Mary, generate,
the song that does accelerate,
the earth into a higher state,
all matter does now scintillate.

5. Mother Mary, awaken people who in past lives have grown up in one of these infallible belief systems and who have directly experienced that the promise of an external salvation is false.

All darkness from the earth you purge,
your light moves as a mighty surge,
no force of darkness can now stop,
the spiral that goes only up.

O Mother Mary, generate,
the song that does accelerate,
the earth into a higher state,
all matter does now scintillate.

6. Mother Mary, awaken people to break through at the conscious level and pull down to the conscious awareness what they already know in their

identity and mental bodies. Help them overcome the fear in the emotional
body that blocks these insights from coming through to the physical mind.

> All elemental life you bless,
> removing from them man-made stress,
> the nature spirits are now free,
> outpicturing Divine decree.

> **O Mother Mary, generate,**
> **the song that does accelerate,**
> **the earth into a higher state,**
> **all matter does now scintillate.**

7. Mother Mary, awaken people to the realization: We no longer need to
believe that a scripture is infallible. We can be open to new ideas. We can
be open to the possibility that we do not have to treat women in our society the way they were treated in the past.

> I raise my voice and take my stand,
> a stop to war I do command,
> no more shall warring scar the earth,
> a golden age is given birth.

> **O Mother Mary, generate,**
> **the song that does accelerate,**
> **the earth into a higher state,**
> **all matter does now scintillate.**

8. Mother Mary, awaken women to see that we do not have, in this modern
society, to treat women the way they were treated thousands of years ago.
I call for this realization to break through in this next decade of the 2020s.

> As Mother Earth is free at last,
> disasters belong to the past,
> your Mother Light is so intense,
> that matter is now far less dense.

> **O Mother Mary, generate,**
> **the song that does accelerate,**

**the earth into a higher state,
all matter does now scintillate.**

9. Mother Mary, awaken women to see that men are more prone to become victims of these absolutist belief systems and the epic mindset. Therefore, women are the ones who have the greatest potential to be the forerunners for this breakthrough where societies will begin to abandon this absolutist aspect of the epic mindset.

In Mother Light the earth is pure,
the upward spiral will endure,
prosperity is now the norm,
God's vision manifest as form.

**O Mother Mary, generate,
the song that does accelerate,
the earth into a higher state,
all matter does now scintillate.**

Sealing

In the name of the I AM THAT I AM, I accept that Archangel Michael, Astrea and Shiva form an impenetrable shield around myself and all constructive people, sealing us from all fear-based energies in all four octaves. I accept that the Light of God is consuming and transforming all fear-based energies that make up the dark forces working against the liberation of women on earth!

4 | THE UNKNOWN FORCES BEHIND THE SUPPRESSION OF WOMEN

I am the Ascended Master Portia. I take this opportunity to give *you* the opportunity to step up higher in your willingness to receive progressive revelation. If we step back, far back, far back into space and look at earth, what do we see? What do we see about this planet that stands out from a cosmic perspective? The one thing that stands out is that for a very long time, humankind has been trapped in a particular mindset. This is the mindset of being very focused on yourself and thinking, feeling, sensing or never questioning that there is something beyond your current level of consciousness. It is the inability, or for the fallen beings the unwillingness, to admit that there is a higher state of consciousness than what you have right now—and therefore, a higher perspective on everything.

What does this, we might call it, *narcissistic* state of consciousness cause people to do? A very simple thing. It causes them to project, based on their current state of consciousness, beyond themselves and their immediate environment. In other words, human beings (manipulated by the fallen beings, I admit, but nevertheless) have been trapped in thinking that you can look at current conditions on earth, and based on current conditions on earth you can project what reality is like beyond earth. You can project how the universe functions. You can project what the spiritual realm or heaven is like. You can even project what God is like, based on what you observe currently on earth.

Humanity is stuck in a closed loop

You think that what you observe currently on earth has some reality to it or has some connection to reality. Therefore, it can tell you something about the entire cosmos, even God, and this something should then be universally, absolutely, eternally true because you cannot even conceive that your consciousness could be wrong, could be limited, could be colored, could be subjective, could be completely out of touch with reality. When you look at earth from this cosmic perspective that I am seeking to give to you – not only in the words but in the vibration, in the light that I am releasing – what you see on earth is that people on earth are trapped in a closed loop. They are in a very limited state of consciousness, but they fail to acknowledge that they are in a limited state of consciousness, and therefore, they think they are able to recognize absolute truth. They think that based on what they see, based on what they have in their minds, they can project the absolute truth about God, or the entire cosmos, or the laws of nature, or the political necessity, or historical necessity or whatever you have.

I Portia, who hold the office of the Goddess of Opportunity, I hereby shatter that matrix! I *shatter, shatter, shatter, shatter, shatter, shatter, shatter, shatter, shatter* that matrix in the identity, mental and emotional realms! I shatter it so that there is a new opportunity for those who are willing to see beyond it, and to suddenly, as happened to Paul on the road to Damascus, have the scales fall from their eyes. They see how limited, how nonsensical, how out of touch with reality that this mindset really is. I grant you that two thousand years ago, or three thousand years ago or a thousand years ago, it was difficult for people to do this because they thought that the earth was all there was. Many thought that the earth was the center of the universe and their universe was just a small bubble around the earth, and there was the sky, and beyond the sky was God and the angels.

Today, my beloved, who can fail to realize that the universe is vast, is perhaps infinite? Who can fail to have heard that there are billions of galaxies with millions or billions of stars, with even untold billions of planets? The universe is so vast that there has not been time for light, which travels so fast, to reach earth from the furthest reaches of the cosmos. There has not been time since the universe began. You all know this! Hardly anyone on earth has not heard about this and knows the size of the universe you live in. Therefore, you should be able to mentally step back and realize that you live on one little planet that literally is like a speck of dust on an infinite beach. One grain of sand on an infinite beach, *that* is what your planet is like.

Do you seriously believe – and I speak into the collective consciousness because I know you, our students, do not believe this, but nevertheless, it needs to be spoken – do you seriously believe that this little grain of sand and how things are on this little grain of sand can tell you anything at all about the totality of the cosmos or what is beyond the cosmos, namely the Creator itself? How can you possibly maintain the illusion that you can sit here on earth and look at this planet and look how limited it is, and you can think this can tell you something about the cosmos, about God or about the spiritual realm? How can you think this?

How can a primitive planet tell you about the cosmos?

Now, go the other way, instead of looking beyond the earth and stepping back, now step right into the earth. Go around this planet and look at the conditions. We are focusing on women. Look at these women who are being lured or kidnapped in their teenage years in some little village in Eastern Europe, in Asia, in Africa, wherever it may be. They are being lured by the promise of a better life or they are just outright being kidnapped. They are being held captive. They are being brutally beaten and raped by their captors. Then, they are perhaps even getting hooked on drugs. They are told that they have to work as prostitutes to pay back the debt they have incurred for being kidnapped. How do you have to pay somebody to kidnap you and hold you against your will?

Look at the conditions in India for example where a girl from early childhood is made to believe that she is worthless because she is a girl. What is her only option? To hope that some man will have pity upon her and marry her so she can be his slave physically and sexually for the rest of her life, still feeling worthless the entire time. Do you think this is *natural?* Do you think this is the highest condition found anywhere in the universe? Do you think then that this planet is a high planet? When you look at how women are being treated around the planet, do you think this is a high planet? Do you think that a primitive planet like this can tell you anything about the rest of the cosmos and of God? This is a nonsensical state of consciousness. It is completely out of touch with reality. It is so nonsensical that there are beings who will not even look at the earth. They will not put their attention on earth because they do not want to reinforce anything they see.

The masters must step down their light

We who are ascended masters who are working with earth, we have, in a sense, in order to work with earth, had to step down our consciousness and our light to where we can still work with earth without reinforcing the conditions that we see on this planet. Now, when I say reinforce, I do not necessarily mean that this strengthens them. It means that if I, given the consciousness that I have, were to look at female prostitution, human trafficking, with the fullness of my awareness, the light flowing over the bridge of my attention would be so strong that it would inflate these conditions so that they would be acted out in more and more extreme ways. Therefore, this would have very destructive consequences, not only for the people who are perpetrating these actions against women, but even for the women, for the societies, for the institutions that are allowing money laundering and all of these things. In other words, it would have such an accelerating effect that things would simply begin to fall apart, blow apart, be inflated to the point where society could not ignore it. It would be such a dramatic change that it could have very destructive consequences.

If I were to do this, you might say: "Well, wouldn't it be better to just get it over with, to have these things fall apart so that we can move on and have better conditions for women on this planet?" This is because again, there is a misconception about the planet. You think, even ascended master students can sometimes think this, that there is a certain condition that we of the ascended masters want to see manifest, that Saint Germain has this perfect matrix for the golden age, like many students in previous ascended master organizations believed, with wonderful cities with golden buildings and gold in the streets and all of this stuff.

What have we told you time and time again? We are working within the constraints of free will. What is the cause for why you have the current conditions on earth? Because you, humanity, collectively have chosen to enter a certain level of consciousness. The conditions you see, including the mistreatment of women, are simply out-picturings in the physical of that state of consciousness. You have used your free will to enter that state of consciousness. Our goal is not simply to remove a certain condition from the earth, but to gradually raise the collective and individual consciousness to where at least a critical mass of people, hopefully a majority of people, can choose to rise above that state of consciousness so that these manifestations can be removed from the earth.

The collective consciousness is in a bubble

You see, my beloved, when you step back from earth again and look at it from a cosmic perspective, you see that planet earth is one of these planets (we have called it unnatural planets) where free will has been allowed to outplay itself to a very extreme degree. That is why the planet has been enveloped in this fog, this cloud. That is why the collective consciousness is in this bubble where people cannot see. They cannot see beyond their own consciousness and they project onto the universe and God what they *can* see. Because they think that what they can see has some universal, absolute validity and reality that can really say something about these greater things.

My beloved, what a misunderstanding, what a complete illusion! Again, I Portia say, *shatter, shatter, shatter* that illusion in the identity realm! *Shatter, shatter, shatter* that illusion in the mental realm! *Shatter, shatter, shatter* that illusion in the emotional realm! And this time I also say *shatter, shatter, shatter* that illusion in the physical realm, for it is time that people begin to wake up, that a critical mass of people begin to wake up and realize that human beings are in such a limited state of consciousness that we cannot recognize any higher reality or higher truth.

There is no absolute truth anywhere on earth

Therefore, everything that we see on earth is a reflection of our state of consciousness. Did you hear me? There is so much discussion on earth about what is true, what is real. Who has the final truth? Is it the Christian religion, the Hindu religion, Islam? Is it materialism? Is it Communism? Is it this, is it that? Who has the final truth, or rather which one of the thought systems on earth is the ultimate one, is the real one? This has been going on for a very, very long time where there has been this assumption that there must be some truth on earth. There must be something on earth that is true in an ultimate sense, that is infallible, that is given from a higher source.

It is a complete illusion! There is no absolute truth anywhere on earth, because the collective consciousness is too limited. It is not a matter of determining which one of the existing truths is the absolute truth. It is not a matter of bringing forth an absolute truth, a new teaching that is the absolute truth. It is a matter of recognizing that the key to improving conditions on earth is to raise consciousness and that this goes through several stages. There is a very, very long way to go before the collective consciousness is at a level where a real higher truth can be brought forth.

Now, you are saying: "But what are you then doing giving us this dictation? Are you not saying that you are giving us an absolute truth by saying there is no absolute truth?" This, my beloved, is exactly how the fallen consciousness reasons about everything. Saying there is no absolute truth is not claiming that my statement is an absolute truth. Can you not then turn this around and say: "But if you are saying that there is no absolute truth, then your statement must be an absolute truth. And therefore, you are contradicting yourself." You see my beloved, this is the fallen consciousness that reasons in a closed loop by using what we have called the linear mind. This mindset has no reality to it.

When I say there is no absolute truth on earth, I am not saying there is no absolute truth. I am saying that given the current level of the collective consciousness, it would not be possible for people to recognize an absolute truth. It would not be possible even for the ascended masters or for God himself to bring forth an absolute truth on earth. Those who are wise will recognize this, and recognize that what you can recognize right now, what you can grasp, what you can understand will be limited by your current state of consciousness. Even if you were at the 144th level of consciousness and close to ascending, what you can grasp on this dense planet is still limited by your level of consciousness. There is so much more to grasp, to experience, to see when you ascend. The difference between the consciousness of an ascended master and an unascended person is *huge,* is a quantum leap, is a qualitative difference. There is no comparison. There is no way that we could even give you an impression of what it is like to be in our state of consciousness because until you experience it, it will not be real for you.

You understand that there is a risk involved with giving you a teaching expressed in words, as we have hinted at before. The risk is that you can form a mental image in your mind of what truth is like or what the ascended state is like and then you project that with your mind. Now, you may think, as many people think, that they can form an image of God here on earth. Then, they are projecting that image onto God. When they project the image, it has some impact on God or reality. This is of course a complete illusion.

It is foolishness to think we can understand reality

Projecting an image, an idol, does have an impact, but the impact is primarily on your own state of consciousness. As soon as you formulate an image in your mind that you think represents some absolute truth, and you project this out (whether you project it on God or reality or the universe or other people) what do you do? You close your mind to a higher understanding, a higher experience—and you think that you can understand truth. The illusion that has been hanging over this planet for a very long time (and which has been reinforced in many of the modern nations that have become so intellectual and linear) is that you can *understand* reality.

There are things you can *understand.* You can understand things in your own environment, but what you can understand in your environment is determined by your level of consciousness. That which is beyond earth, your immediate environment, you cannot understand fully. You can grasp it, you can *experience* it, but you cannot *understand* it. Understanding with the mind implies a fundamental duality between the knower and the known, between the subject that is trying to know and the object it is trying to know about. There is a fundamental subject-object duality that always exists in the mental mind. You cannot go beyond it with the four lower bodies.

You cannot go beyond it with the identity level either because even at the identity level you see yourself as a subject, as an individual, as a being, as a human person. You are seeing a world outside of you that you are relating to. You are therefore observing, understanding, at a distance. This cannot ever give you an *experience* of truth. What have we said? There is a core of your being, which we have called pure awareness or the Conscious You. It is what mystics have been talking about throughout the ages, using different words and different names. The reality is you have the ability to step outside of your current state of mind, your current perception filter, your four lower bodies. Again, whatever you want to call it, you can step outside of it and experience a reality that is beyond it. This is how you can grasp, *experience* truth.

You are experiencing it because the subject-object duality is suspended, is transcended. Therefore, at least for a brief moment, you experience oneness between the knower and the known. This is how you can, not really *know,* but *experience* a reality. Once you have had that experience, you come back to a "normal" state of consciousness. If you now try to describe your experience by using the words and concepts that are in your normal state of consciousness, then you have already removed yourself from the experience, and any description you give will be less than the experience.

Now, my beloved, why is this a topic that we are bringing up in a conference on the liberation of women? Well, because as Mother Mary said, you cannot liberate women without challenging the idea that there is some absolute scripture from the past or some necessity of nature that defines what a woman is and what a man is. I am simply taking this one step further and saying there is no way to really challenge the oppression of women without realizing that you cannot know reality through the mind, but only by stepping outside the mind. Quite frankly, anyone who looks at spiritual, New Age, mystical, even traditional religions will see that women are much more active in such organizations. Women are much more open to these ideas, women are more likely to carry these ideas forward and to begin to talk about them, to practice them, to have these experiences, and thereby, being the open door for transforming this view.

A logical explanation for the abuse of women

Where did this view come from? Well again, let us take a look at earth. Let me take the example again of young women who are kidnapped and forced into prostitution. Now, ask yourself this. What causes men – for it is in most cases men who are behind this, even though women may in some cases participate – what causes men to kidnap a young woman, or in some cases a young boy even, and force them into prostitution just so that they can make some money? Is it really just to make money? Could these men not find another way to make money if they really wanted to? Why are men allowing themselves to become the instruments for these inhuman acts? Is it just because they are desperate to make money? No, my beloved. It is because they are not thinking. They are not conscious. They are not *aware.*

What does it mean that they are not aware? Well, their minds are taken over by something. This is an idea that many, many women (who have never heard of ascended masters, and who do not need to hear of ascended masters) are ready to grasp. When you look at men who are abusing women—and some women will know this personally because they are being abused by their husbands or partners, whether it is sexually or by being beaten up or verbally abused. If you look at these men and look them in the eye when they are doing this, you can see it is not a human being who is doing this. At least, not a human being who is aware, who has sensitivity, who has compassion for life. Therefore, you must say, especially if you see that a man can behave differently in other situations, you must say something has taken over that person's mind when he is doing this.

What then is that something? This is where women can become open to the idea that there are these, what we have called collective entities, collective beasts, that are energy beings that are created by all of the energy and attention that people have fed into this over a long period of time. Alcohol has been used for a very long time on this planet and when someone is drunk, you can see the person is not there. What is there? The alcohol entity that has taken over the person's mind.

Once you realize this, you realize that there are indeed certain unseen forces that can take over people's minds. Of course, they can take over the minds of women as well as men, but the reality is that men are more taken over by these energetic beings than women, in general. There are more men that are trapped in these very destructive entities, alcohol, violence, forcing people into prostitution, rape, all of these things that are very, very destructive. Therefore, if we are to free society from this, women are the ones who have the biggest opportunity to do this, to become aware that these beings exist, to start to talk about it, to say there is something here that we need to understand. We need to explore this scientifically. We need to explore it through psychology. We need to explore it even through alternative methods, even alternative ideas and spiritual ideas until we understand this phenomenon.

What is it that takes over the minds of our men when they are abusing us? What is it? What is it that takes over the minds of our sisters who have been abused, who are limited, who do not think they deserve anything better in life, who think they can only have a certain life where they are dependent on this man who is abusing them? What is it that makes a woman think that because she has been manipulated or forced into this situation, she has to endure this for the rest of her life, possibly for 60, 70 years? Is that not also something that is taking over the minds of these women so that they cannot even imagine a way out, an alternative?

Narcissistic men and other beings abusing women

When you realize this as women (that there is something that can take over people's minds), then you can take this, after this idea has been absorbed and accepted, you can take it one step further and you can go back to what I said. Why do we have the idea that it is possible for us human beings on earth to know truth and that certain ideas that we can grasp with the mind are real, have some reality or truth to them? Where does this entire concept come from? Then, you can perhaps begin to realize that it comes from certain narcissistic men in embodiment who are seeking to manipulate others for their own purposes, often to gain power. Again, you have the perennial examples of a person like Hitler, who was using these ideas of the Aryan race and the superhuman to manipulate the German people, but there are certainly many others around the world. You can then begin to ask yourself why the Catholic church has been suppressing women for now 17 centuries of its existence, and it shows no real change of attitude? Why is this?

You may say: "Well, there are certain men in embodiment who are promoting this kind of suppression of women," but can you explain it only by looking at men in embodiment? Or do you need to step a little further back and say perhaps even Hitler or some popes had their minds taken over by something? Then, you can make the distinction that when a man's mind is taken over by the alcohol entity and he is drinking himself into this agitated state of mind where he starts beating up his wife, this alcohol entity is not really a thinker. It has no real thought. It has no sophisticated reasoning power. It just wants men to drink and there may be a violence entity that wants them to be violent, but beyond that there is no real thinking and reasoning process.

When you see that behind the suppression of women, going back through time, there is a set of very sophisticated ideas that are based on a quite sophisticated reasoning process, then you can step up and say: "But where do these ideas come from? Which mind is able to think up ideas like this? Was Hitler really that smart? He showed no real signs of being intelligent, being a genius of any kind. Where did he get his ideas from?" Then, at least some women will be stepping up to the ideas we have given you, that there are certain narcissistic beings (that we have called *fallen* beings) who are not necessarily in embodiment, but who are existing in a higher realm, the identity and mental realms, and who are from there seeking to manipulate human beings.

These are the beings who have come up with all of these ideas that you see throughout history that have been defined or proclaimed as the absolute truth. What you can then begin to realize is that the fallen beings—why are they doing this? Why are they creating an image of God and projecting, or seeking to project onto reality that this is the real God? Why do they think they can know God at a distance? Well, because what happened when the fallen beings fell was that they created an even stronger subject-object duality than what most of you have, whether you are human beings on earth or avatars that came from a natural planet.

The process of falling is reinforcing or creating a subject-object duality that is much stronger than what you experience as an avatar or as an inhabitant on earth. That is why the fallen beings cannot actually have these mystical experiences that I talked about. They cannot step outside of their minds and experience the reality of God because they have closed their minds so firmly. It is not that the fallen beings have lost the opportunity to do this, but they have closed their minds so firmly that there is such a gravitational pull inside their own minds that the Conscious You cannot free itself from that pull and experience neutral or pure awareness. Therefore, they cannot experience the Creator. A fallen being cannot experience God's Being and can therefore not know or experience the reality of God, so it must relate to God through an image.

Of course, the fallen beings are firmly convinced that their image of God is reality. There are some fallen beings that have a little more reasoning and may doubt this, but they then see that the image they have created of God is such a fantastic tool for manipulating human beings that they are not really willing to question it. This of course keeps them trapped as well in the closed loop of their own minds, which is really one simple definition of the fallen consciousness: the mind has become a closed loop from which there is no way out. This is the tool they have been using now for so long to manipulate men. Of course, men are manipulated by this and women are manipulated by it.

The decision to make men the superior sex

You see, the fallen beings did something at a very early stage that can be used against their control on this planet. There was a point where certain fallen beings, including the Dark Master that we have talked to you about, made the decision that they would make men the superior sex on earth and women the inferior sex. Now, my beloved, be careful here. They might as well have made the other decision and made women the superior sex and men the inferior sex. This is the case on a few other unnatural planets. On earth, they chose to make men the superior sex. What does that mean? Well, it means, my beloved, that from a certain perspective there is an advantage to being a man on earth.

You look at many societies where women are basically the servants or even the slaves of men. They do all the work and they raise the children. In some cases, they even have to provide the physical living, while the men study the Torah, or drink or do whatever. Even though it is not a real advantage, you can say that there are some men that experience that even though they have a very uncomfortable life, it is at least less uncomfortable than the life of women. This means what? This means that men are far less likely to start questioning this. Men are not the ones who can free planet earth from this mindset.

The women are the ones who are on the receiving end of this mindset that men are superior. They are the ones who are being held back. They are the ones who are being pushed down and limited. Therefore, they have a stronger drive to free themselves from this manipulation. There is a greater opportunity that women can be the forerunners for freeing the planet from this oppression, and this is something that the fallen beings do not know what to do with. Some fallen beings have speculated: "Did we make a mistake by making women the inferior sex? Should we have made men the inferior sex?" Some of them, when they think about it, even realize that it did not matter. Whatever they had chosen, there would have been the same dynamic: The sex that was suppressed has a stronger drive to free itself from the suppression, and therefore they are more likely to open their minds to seeing through the manipulation and the schemes of the fallen beings, seeing the lies they are based on.

This is inevitable because this is the reality of life on an unnatural planet. Once you go into duality, there are two opposite polarities. In order for you to have power, to have advantages, to be superior, you must elevate the one polarity and push down the other. This is the mechanics of duality. As they say on earth: "You are damned if you do and damned if you don't." Or rather, whatever you do has a cost. Whatever you do has advantages and disadvantages. For a time you can enjoy the advantages, but because of the nature of duality, the nature of the density of planet earth, there will come a point where the disadvantages to what you have done will come back to haunt you. When they do, there is really nothing you can do about it.

The cosmic wheels will liberate women

My beloved, listen to what I am saying here. The fallen beings have made certain choices. They have generated certain ideas that have suppressed women and elevated men. There has been a long period of time where neither men nor women have questioned this, but because of the changing cycles, this time is coming to an end. This cycle is coming to an end. This has something to do with the fact that we of the ascended masters are releasing light. It has something to do with the fact that people in embodiment have called for these changes. It has something to do with, as Mother Mary said, that when you have been in embodiment as a woman, who was enslaved by men for a certain number of times, you come into embodiment with this inner knowing that this is not right, and it needs to change and you have the drive to change it. All of these things are coming together, and we are now at a point where the cosmic wheels, so to speak, are turning and bringing forth a liberation of women.

Of course, this is subject to free will. The fallen beings will do everything they can to prevent women from waking up. They cannot stop women from making the decision to start to awaken themselves and look at new ideas and free themselves from this oppression. When women make the decision that they want change, then the fallen beings will not be able to stop it. They can try to postpone it by keeping women ignorant, keeping them passive, keeping them not having the knowledge or the determination to free themselves. Once women begin to awaken themselves and make the higher, more aware decisions that they want change in society and in their lives, the fallen beings will not be able to stop it. There is nothing they can do to stop the movement of the liberation of women.

Sure, they can delay it, as they have done even in the modern democracies. They can delay it even more in some Islamic countries, African nations, what have you, but they cannot *stop* it. You have the concept of a point of no return. Well, the point of no return has been reached, and that is why we are releasing these teachings: to reinforce that, so that more and more women can wake up, so that more women can make the calls and wake up even more women, so that the snowball keeps rolling and rolling, getting bigger and bigger, encompassing more and more women who become part of this unified movement that simply comes to this realization: "We will no longer tolerate the suppression of women on this planet of ours, because we claim planet earth as *our* planet."

When this happens, when this gains momentum, the fallen beings will have nothing they can do to counteract it. They cannot stop it. They cannot divert it. They must simply watch as they lose the dominance they have over this planet and over these male-dominated societies who will not remain male-dominated, but will indeed become more and more balanced. You will not see on earth the emergence of matriarchal societies that are dominated by women. The extreme feminists' dream that suddenly women would have the same power as men have had for so long, will not come to pass. Because as the suppression of women has been driven by the fallen beings, then the extreme feminist movement and their attempt to elevate women to have the same power as men, is also driven by the fallen beings, although a very small minority of them who are opposing the other fallen beings.

The fallen beings are unavoidably divided

For as always, the fallen beings are divided amongst themselves, as they must be when they go into duality. There cannot be a fully unified movement of fallen beings, except if you go to the level of those who are simply using different factions of fallen beings to create conflict and chaos on earth. Even that is not unified because there will always be one being who seeks to gain superiority and there will always be at least one who wants that superiority, possibly even a group of beings who want to take over. Therefore, there will be a rivalry that from time to time will result in open conflict. United we stand, divided we fall. And when we have already fallen, we can only be divided. We can never stand united.

These are the concepts that I wanted to give you for now. We have of course much more to say. What I want to end with is this idea, again. This address is meant to give everyone, including ascended master students, the opportunity to open your minds to progressive revelation. We have said it before. We of the ascended masters can give teachings for a certain level of consciousness, but there is always an element of the teachings that will help people transcend that level of consciousness. Those who use a given teaching to transcend the level of consciousness that is the target of the teaching, they can move on, they can recognize progressive revelation in the next form, in the next messenger. Those who will not use the teaching to transcend that level of consciousness cannot recognize the new teaching.

Those who move on need to recognize that when we have said something through one organization, when we start a new dispensation to bring forth a new level of progressive revelation, we cannot be limited by what was said earlier. What was said earlier was said for a specific level of consciousness. It was not an ultimate reality. It does not mean it was wrong, it was false, it had errors, but it means it is not the highest perspective that can be given. This means that all previous dispensations were given for a certain level of consciousness and they therefore contain certain ideas about men and women, about the soul – male souls, female souls, twin flames, this or that – that were limited to what could be given to that level of consciousness.

Today, we have moved to a higher level. It is not an absolute level, but it is a higher level for the Aquarian age, and therefore we aim to give a higher teaching about men and women, about twin flames, about souls. This is what other masters will expound upon as we move on with this conference.

I therefore thank you for giving me this opportunity to release this teaching, to use your chakras and auras wherever you are around this planet, to radiate this powerful impulse into the collective consciousness. Therefore I say: "May you use the opportunity to transcend yourself."

NOTE: This dictation was given May 30, 2020.

5 | INVOKING AWARENESS OF UNSEEN FORCES (PART 1)

In the name of the I AM THAT I AM, Jesus Christ, I use the authority that I have as a being in embodiment on earth to call upon Portia to reinforce my calls and use my chakras to project the statements in this invocation into the collective consciousness and awaken people to the awareness that will liberate both men and women from all psychological and spiritual thralldom to the fallen beings. Awaken people to the reality that we are spiritual beings and that we can co-create a new future by working with the ascended masters. I especially call for ...

[Make your own calls here.]

Part 1

1. Beloved Portia, awaken women to see that humankind is trapped in the mindset of being very focused on ourselves and thinking, feeling, sensing that there is nothing beyond our current level of consciousness.

O Portia, in your own retreat,
with Mother's Love you do me greet.

As all my tests I now complete,
old patterns I no more repeat.

O Portia, opportunity,
I am beyond duality.
I focus now internally,
with you I grow eternally.

2. Beloved Portia, awaken women to see that we are trapped by an inability to admit that there is a higher state of consciousness than what we have right now—and therefore, a higher perspective on everything.

O Portia, Justice is your name,
upholding Cosmic Honor Flame,
No longer will I play the game,
of seeking to remain the same.

O Portia, opportunity,
I am beyond duality.
I focus now internally,
with you I grow eternally.

3. Beloved Portia, awaken women to see that this *narcissistic* state of consciousness causes us to project, based on our current state of consciousness, beyond ourselves and our immediate environment.

O Portia, in the cosmic flow,
one with you, I ever grow.
I am the chalice here below,
of cosmic justice you bestow.

O Portia, opportunity,
I am beyond duality.
I focus now internally,
with you I grow eternally.

4. Beloved Portia, awaken women to see that human beings are trapped in thinking that we can look at current conditions on earth, and based on

current conditions we can project what reality is like beyond earth, how the universe functions, what the spiritual realm is like.

O Portia, cosmic balance bring,
eternal hope, my heart does sing.
Protected by your Mother's wing,
I feel at one with everything.

O Portia, opportunity,
I am beyond duality.
I focus now internally,
with you I grow eternally.

5. Beloved Portia, awaken women to see that we think that what we observe on earth has some reality to it. Therefore, it can tell us something about the entire cosmos, and this is universally, absolutely, eternally true.

O Portia, bring the Mother Light,
to set all free from darkest night.
Your Love Flame shines forever bright,
with Saint Germain now hold me tight.

O Portia, opportunity,
I am beyond duality.
I focus now internally,
with you I grow eternally.

6. Beloved Portia, awaken women to see that our consciousness could be wrong, could be limited, could be colored, could be subjective, could be completely out of touch with reality.

O Portia, in your mastery,
I feel transforming chemistry.
In your light of reality,
I find the golden alchemy.

O Portia, opportunity,
I am beyond duality.

I focus now internally,
with you I grow eternally.

7. Beloved Portia, awaken women to see that people on earth are trapped in a closed loop. They are in a very limited state of consciousness, but they fail to acknowledge that they are in a limited state of consciousness, and therefore, they think they are able to recognize absolute truth.

O Portia, in the cosmic stream,
I am awake from human dream.
Removing now the ego's beam,
I earn my place on cosmic team.

O Portia, opportunity,
I am beyond duality.
I focus now internally,
with you I grow eternally.

8. Beloved Portia, awaken women to see that people think that based on what they see, based on what they have in their minds, they can project the absolute truth about God, or the entire cosmos, or the laws of nature, or the political necessity, or historical necessity.

O Portia, you come from afar,
you are a cosmic avatar.
So infinite your repertoire,
you are for earth a guiding star.

O Portia, opportunity,
I am beyond duality.
I focus now internally,
with you I grow eternally.

9. Beloved Portia, I call for you to shatter that matrix! *Shatter, shatter, shatter, shatter, shatter, shatter, shatter, shatter, shatter* that matrix in the identity, mental and emotional realms!

O Portia, I am confident,
I am a cosmic instrument.

I came to earth from heaven sent,
to help bring forward her ascent.

O Portia, opportunity,
I am beyond duality.
I focus now internally,
with you I grow eternally.

Part 2

1. Beloved Portia, shatter the matrix so there is a new opportunity for people to see beyond it, and to suddenly have the scales fall from their eyes, seeing how limited, how nonsensical, how out of touch with reality this mindset really is.

O Portia, in your own retreat,
with Mother's Love you do me greet.
As all my tests I now complete,
old patterns I no more repeat.

O Portia, opportunity,
I am beyond duality.
I focus now internally,
with you I grow eternally.

2. Beloved Portia, help women realize that we live on one little planet that is like one grain of sand on an infinite beach. This little grain of sand and how things are on here *cannot* tell us anything about the totality of the cosmos or what is beyond the cosmos, namely the Creator itself.

O Portia, Justice is your name,
upholding Cosmic Honor Flame,
No longer will I play the game,
of seeking to remain the same.

O Portia, opportunity,
I am beyond duality.

**I focus now internally,
with you I grow eternally.**

3. Beloved Portia, awaken women from the illusion that we can sit here on earth and look at this planet and look how limited it is, and we can think this can tell us something about the cosmos or about God or about the spiritual realm.

O Portia, in the cosmic flow,
one with you, I ever grow.
I am the chalice here below,
of cosmic justice you bestow.

**O Portia, opportunity,
I am beyond duality.
I focus now internally,
with you I grow eternally.**

4. Beloved Portia, awaken women to see that when we look at how women are mistreated around the planet, we cannot allow ourselves to think this is natural, this is the highest condition found anywhere in the universe.

O Portia, cosmic balance bring,
eternal hope, my heart does sing.
Protected by your Mother's wing,
I feel at one with everything.

**O Portia, opportunity,
I am beyond duality.
I focus now internally,
with you I grow eternally.**

5. Beloved Portia, awaken women to see that this planet is *not* a high planet. When we look at how women are being treated around the planet, we cannot think this is a high planet. Therefore, a primitive planet like this *cannot* tell us anything about the rest of the cosmos.

O Portia, bring the Mother Light,
to set all free from darkest night.

Your Love Flame shines forever bright,
with Saint Germain now hold me tight.

O Portia, opportunity,
I am beyond duality.
I focus now internally,
with you I grow eternally.

6. Beloved Portia, awaken women to see that this is a nonsensical state of consciousness. It is completely out of touch with reality.

O Portia, in your mastery,
I feel transforming chemistry.
In your light of reality,
I find the golden alchemy.

O Portia, opportunity,
I am beyond duality.
I focus now internally,
with you I grow eternally.

7. Beloved Portia, awaken women to see that the cause for why we have the current conditions on earth is that we have collectively chosen to enter a certain level of consciousness.

O Portia, in the cosmic stream,
I am awake from human dream.
Removing now the ego's beam,
I earn my place on cosmic team.

O Portia, opportunity,
I am beyond duality.
I focus now internally,
with you I grow eternally.

8. Beloved Portia, awaken women to see that current conditions, including the mistreatment of women, are simply out-picturings in the physical of that state of consciousness.

O Portia, you come from afar,
you are a cosmic avatar.
So infinite your repertoire,
you are for earth a guiding star.

O Portia, opportunity,
I am beyond duality.
I focus now internally,
with you I grow eternally.

9. Beloved Portia, awaken women to see that we need to raise the collective and individual consciousness to where at least a critical mass of people can choose to rise above that state of consciousness so that these manifestations can be removed from the earth.

O Portia, I am confident,
I am a cosmic instrument.
I came to earth from heaven sent,
to help bring forward her ascent.

O Portia, opportunity,
I am beyond duality.
I focus now internally,
with you I grow eternally.

Part 3

1. Beloved Portia, awaken women to see that on earth free will has been allowed to outplay itself to a very extreme degree. That is why the planet has been enveloped in this fog, and the collective consciousness is in this bubble where people cannot see.

O Portia, in your own retreat,
with Mother's Love you do me greet.
As all my tests I now complete,
old patterns I no more repeat.

**O Portia, opportunity,
I am beyond duality.
I focus now internally,
with you I grow eternally.**

2. Beloved Portia, awaken women to see that we cannot see beyond our own consciousness and we think that what we can see has some universal, absolute validity and reality. This is a misunderstanding, a complete illusion!

O Portia, Justice is your name,
upholding Cosmic Honor Flame,
No longer will I play the game,
of seeking to remain the same.

**O Portia, opportunity,
I am beyond duality.
I focus now internally,
with you I grow eternally.**

3. Beloved Portia, *shatter, shatter, shatter* that illusion in the identity realm! *Shatter, shatter, shatter* that illusion in the mental realm! *Shatter, shatter, shatter* that illusion in the emotional realm! *Shatter, shatter, shatter* that illusion in the physical realm.

O Portia, in the cosmic flow,
one with you, I ever grow.
I am the chalice here below,
of cosmic justice you bestow.

**O Portia, opportunity,
I am beyond duality.
I focus now internally,
with you I grow eternally.**

4. Beloved Portia, awaken women to see that we human beings are in such a limited state of consciousness that we cannot recognize any higher reality or higher truth.

O Portia, cosmic balance bring,
eternal hope, my heart does sing.
Protected by your Mother's wing,
I feel at one with everything.

O Portia, opportunity,
I am beyond duality.
I focus now internally,
with you I grow eternally.

5. Beloved Portia, awaken women to see the futility of the discussion about what is true, what is real. It is based on this assumption that there must be some truth on earth. There must be something on earth that is true in an ultimate sense, that is infallible, that is given from a higher source.

O Portia, bring the Mother Light,
to set all free from darkest night.
Your Love Flame shines forever bright,
with Saint Germain now hold me tight.

O Portia, opportunity,
I am beyond duality.
I focus now internally,
with you I grow eternally.

6. Beloved Portia, awaken women to see that this is a complete illusion! There is no absolute truth anywhere on earth, because the collective consciousness is too limited.

O Portia, in your mastery,
I feel transforming chemistry.
In your light of reality,
I find the golden alchemy.

O Portia, opportunity,
I am beyond duality.
I focus now internally,
with you I grow eternally.

7. Beloved Portia, awaken women to see that it is not a matter of determining which one of the existing truths is the absolute truth. It is not a matter of bringing forth a new teaching that is the absolute truth.

> O Portia, in the cosmic stream,
> I am awake from human dream.
> Removing now the ego's beam,
> I earn my place on cosmic team.

> **O Portia, opportunity,**
> **I am beyond duality.**
> **I focus now internally,**
> **with you I grow eternally.**

8. Beloved Portia, awaken women to see that it is a matter of recognizing that the key to improving conditions on earth is to raise consciousness and that this goes through several stages. There is a very long way to go before the collective consciousness is at a level where a real higher truth can be brought forth.

> O Portia, you come from afar,
> you are a cosmic avatar.
> So infinite your repertoire,
> you are for earth a guiding star.

> **O Portia, opportunity,**
> **I am beyond duality.**
> **I focus now internally,**
> **with you I grow eternally.**

9. Beloved Portia, awaken women to see that given the current level of the collective consciousness, it would not be possible for people to recognize an absolute truth. It would not be possible to bring forth an absolute truth on earth.

> O Portia, I am confident,
> I am a cosmic instrument.
> I came to earth from heaven sent,
> to help bring forward her ascent.

O Portia, opportunity,
I am beyond duality.
I focus now internally,
with you I grow eternally.

Part 4

1. Beloved Portia, awaken women to see that what we can recognize right now, what we can grasp, what we can understand will be limited by our current state of consciousness.

O Portia, in your own retreat,
with Mother's Love you do me greet.
As all my tests I now complete,
old patterns I no more repeat.

O Portia, opportunity,
I am beyond duality.
I focus now internally,
with you I grow eternally.

2. Beloved Portia, awaken women to see that many people think they can form an image of God and when they project the image, it has some impact on God or reality. This is a complete illusion.

O Portia, Justice is your name,
upholding Cosmic Honor Flame,
No longer will I play the game,
of seeking to remain the same.

O Portia, opportunity,
I am beyond duality.
I focus now internally,
with you I grow eternally.

3. Beloved Portia, awaken women to see that projecting an image, an idol, does have an impact, but the impact is primarily on our own state of consciousness.

O Portia, in the cosmic flow,
one with you, I ever grow.
I am the chalice here below,
of cosmic justice you bestow.

O Portia, opportunity,
I am beyond duality.
I focus now internally,
with you I grow eternally.

4. Beloved Portia, awaken women to see that as soon as we formulate an image in our minds that we think represents some absolute truth, and we project this out, we close our minds to a higher understanding, a higher experience.

O Portia, cosmic balance bring,
eternal hope, my heart does sing.
Protected by your Mother's wing,
I feel at one with everything.

O Portia, opportunity,
I am beyond duality.
I focus now internally,
with you I grow eternally.

5. Beloved Portia, awaken women to see that the illusion that has been hanging over this planet for a very long time, and which has been reinforced in many of the modern nations that have become very intellectual and linear, is that we can *understand* reality.

O Portia, bring the Mother Light,
to set all free from darkest night.
Your Love Flame shines forever bright,
with Saint Germain now hold me tight.

**O Portia, opportunity,
I am beyond duality.
I focus now internally,
with you I grow eternally.**

6. Beloved Portia, awaken women to see that there are things we can *understand*. We can understand things in our own environment, but it is determined by our level of consciousness.

O Portia, in your mastery,
I feel transforming chemistry.
In your light of reality,
I find the golden alchemy.

**O Portia, opportunity,
I am beyond duality.
I focus now internally,
with you I grow eternally.**

7. Beloved Portia, awaken women to see that what is beyond earth, our immediate environment, we cannot understand fully. We can grasp it, we can *experience* it, but we cannot *understand* it.

O Portia, in the cosmic stream,
I am awake from human dream.
Removing now the ego's beam,
I earn my place on cosmic team.

**O Portia, opportunity,
I am beyond duality.
I focus now internally,
with you I grow eternally.**

8. Beloved Portia, awaken women to see that understanding with the mind implies a fundamental duality between the knower and the known, between the subject that is trying to know and the object it is trying to know about.

O Portia, you come from afar,
you are a cosmic avatar.

So infinite your repertoire,
you are for earth a guiding star.

O Portia, opportunity,
I am beyond duality.
I focus now internally,
with you I grow eternally.

9. Beloved Portia, awaken women to see that there is a fundamental sub-ject-object duality that always exists in the mental mind. We cannot go beyond it with the four lower bodies.

O Portia, I am confident,
I am a cosmic instrument.
I came to earth from heaven sent,
to help bring forward her ascent.

O Portia, opportunity,
I am beyond duality.
I focus now internally,
with you I grow eternally.

Sealing

In the name of the I AM THAT I AM, I accept that Archangel Michael, Astrea and Shiva form an impenetrable shield around myself and all con-structive people, sealing us from all fear-based energies in all four octaves. I accept that the Light of God is consuming and transforming all fear-based energies that make up the dark forces working against the liberation of women on earth!

6 | INVOKING AWARENESS OF UNSEEN FORCES (PART 2)

In the name of the I AM THAT I AM, Jesus Christ, I use the authority that I have as a being in embodiment on earth to call upon Portia to reinforce my calls and use my chakras to project the statements in this invocation into the collective consciousness and awaken people to the awareness that will liberate both men and women from all psychological and spiritual thralldom to the fallen beings. Awaken people to the reality that we are spiritual beings and that we can co-create a new future by working with the ascended masters. I especially call for ...

[Make your own calls here.]

Part 1

1. Beloved Portia, awaken women to see that when we see ourselves as subjects, we are observing, understanding, at a distance. This cannot ever give us an *experience* of truth.

O Portia, in your own retreat,
with Mother's Love you do me greet.

As all my tests I now complete,
old patterns I no more repeat.

O Portia, opportunity,
I am beyond duality.
I focus now internally,
with you I grow eternally.

2. Beloved Portia, awaken women to see that there is a core of our beings, and it gives us the ability to step outside of our current state of mind, our current perception filter, our four lower bodies. We can experience a reality that is beyond it and this is how we can grasp, *experience* truth.

O Portia, Justice is your name,
upholding Cosmic Honor Flame,
No longer will I play the game,
of seeking to remain the same.

O Portia, opportunity,
I am beyond duality.
I focus now internally,
with you I grow eternally.

3. Beloved Portia, awaken women to see that we are experiencing truth because the subject-object duality is suspended, is transcended. We experience oneness between the knower and the known. This is how we can *experience* a reality.

O Portia, in the cosmic flow,
one with you, I ever grow.
I am the chalice here below,
of cosmic justice you bestow.

O Portia, opportunity,
I am beyond duality.
I focus now internally,
with you I grow eternally.

4. Beloved Portia, awaken women to see that we cannot describe our experience by using the words and concepts that are in our normal state of consciousness. We will remove ourselves from the experience, and any description will be less than the experience.

> O Portia, cosmic balance bring,
> eternal hope, my heart does sing.
> Protected by your Mother's wing,
> I feel at one with everything.

> **O Portia, opportunity,**
> **I am beyond duality.**
> **I focus now internally,**
> **with you I grow eternally.**

5. Beloved Portia, awaken women to see that we cannot liberate women without challenging the idea that there is some absolute scripture from the past or some necessity of nature that defines what a woman is and what a man is.

> O Portia, bring the Mother Light,
> to set all free from darkest night.
> Your Love Flame shines forever bright,
> with Saint Germain now hold me tight.

> **O Portia, opportunity,**
> **I am beyond duality.**
> **I focus now internally,**
> **with you I grow eternally.**

6. Beloved Portia, awaken women to see that there is no way to challenge the oppression of women without realizing that we cannot know reality through the mind, but only by stepping outside the mind.

> O Portia, in your mastery,
> I feel transforming chemistry.
> In your light of reality,
> I find the golden alchemy.

O Portia, opportunity,
I am beyond duality.
I focus now internally,
with you I grow eternally.

7. Beloved Portia, awaken women to see that women are much more open to these ideas than men, and women are more likely to carry these ideas forward and be the open door for transforming this view.

O Portia, in the cosmic stream,
I am awake from human dream.
Removing now the ego's beam,
I earn my place on cosmic team.

O Portia, opportunity,
I am beyond duality.
I focus now internally,
with you I grow eternally.

8. Beloved Portia, awaken women to see that when men allow themselves to become the instruments for inhumane acts against women, it is because they are not thinking. They are not conscious. They are not *aware*.

O Portia, you come from afar,
you are a cosmic avatar.
So infinite your repertoire,
you are for earth a guiding star.

O Portia, opportunity,
I am beyond duality.
I focus now internally,
with you I grow eternally.

9. Beloved Portia, awaken women to see that their minds are taken over by something. When men are abusing women, it is not a human being who is doing this, at least not a human being who is aware, who has sensitivity, who has compassion for life.

O Portia, I am confident,
I am a cosmic instrument.
I came to earth from heaven sent,
to help bring forward her ascent.

O Portia, opportunity,
I am beyond duality.
I focus now internally,
with you I grow eternally.

Part 2

1. Beloved Portia, awaken women to see that there are collective entities, collective beasts, that are energy beings that are created by all of the energy and attention that people have fed into this over a long period of time.

O Portia, in your own retreat,
with Mother's Love you do me greet.
As all my tests I now complete,
old patterns I no more repeat.

O Portia, opportunity,
I am beyond duality.
I focus now internally,
with you I grow eternally.

2. Beloved Portia, awaken women to see that alcohol has been used for a very long time on this planet and when someone is drunk, the person is not there. What is there is the alcohol entity that has taken over the person's mind.

O Portia, Justice is your name,
upholding Cosmic Honor Flame,
No longer will I play the game,
of seeking to remain the same.

O Portia, opportunity,
I am beyond duality.
I focus now internally,
with you I grow eternally.

3. Beloved Portia, awaken women to see that there are unseen forces that can take over people's minds, and men are more likely to be taken over by these energetic beings than women.

O Portia, in the cosmic flow,
one with you, I ever grow.
I am the chalice here below,
of cosmic justice you bestow.

O Portia, opportunity,
I am beyond duality.
I focus now internally,
with you I grow eternally.

4. Beloved Portia, awaken women to see that if we are to free society from this, women are the ones who have the biggest opportunity to do this, to become aware that these beings exist.

O Portia, cosmic balance bring,
eternal hope, my heart does sing.
Protected by your Mother's wing,
I feel at one with everything.

O Portia, opportunity,
I am beyond duality.
I focus now internally,
with you I grow eternally.

5. Beloved Portia, awaken women to see that we need to explore this scientifically, through psychology and alternative ideas. We need to understand what takes over the minds of our men when they are abusing us.

O Portia, bring the Mother Light,
to set all free from darkest night.

Your Love Flame shines forever bright,
with Saint Germain now hold me tight.

O Portia, opportunity,
I am beyond duality.
I focus now internally,
with you I grow eternally.

6. Beloved Portia, awaken women to see that we need to understand what takes over the minds of our sisters who have been abused, who are limited, who do not think they deserve anything better in life, who think they can only have a certain life where they are dependent on this man who is abusing them.

O Portia, in your mastery,
I feel transforming chemistry.
In your light of reality,
I find the golden alchemy.

O Portia, opportunity,
I am beyond duality.
I focus now internally,
with you I grow eternally.

7. Beloved Portia, awaken women to see that we need to understand what makes a woman think that because she has been manipulated or forced into this situation, she has to endure this for the rest of her life and cannot imagine a way out.

O Portia, in the cosmic stream,
I am awake from human dream.
Removing now the ego's beam,
I earn my place on cosmic team.

O Portia, opportunity,
I am beyond duality.
I focus now internally,
with you I grow eternally.

8. Beloved Portia, awaken women to see that there are certain narcissistic men in embodiment who are seeking to manipulate others for their own purposes, often to gain power.

O Portia, you come from afar,
you are a cosmic avatar.
So infinite your repertoire,
you are for earth a guiding star.

**O Portia, opportunity,
I am beyond duality.
I focus now internally,
with you I grow eternally.**

9. Beloved Portia, awaken women to ask why the Catholic church has been suppressing women for 17 centuries, and it shows no real change of attitude.

O Portia, I am confident,
I am a cosmic instrument.
I came to earth from heaven sent,
to help bring forward her ascent.

**O Portia, opportunity,
I am beyond duality.
I focus now internally,
with you I grow eternally.**

Part 3

1. Beloved Portia, awaken women to see that there are certain men in embodiment who are promoting this kind of suppression of women, but we cannot explain it only by looking at men in embodiment.

O Portia, in your own retreat,
with Mother's Love you do me greet.

As all my tests I now complete,
old patterns I no more repeat.

O Portia, opportunity,
I am beyond duality.
I focus now internally,
with you I grow eternally.

2. Beloved Portia, awaken women to see that when a man is drinking and starts beating up his wife, this alcohol entity is not really a thinker. It has no real thought. It has no sophisticated reasoning power. It just wants men to drink or be violent.

O Portia, Justice is your name,
upholding Cosmic Honor Flame,
No longer will I play the game,
of seeking to remain the same.

O Portia, opportunity,
I am beyond duality.
I focus now internally,
with you I grow eternally.

3. Beloved Portia, awaken women to see that behind the suppression of women, there is a set of very sophisticated ideas that are based on an elaborate reasoning process. We must ask which kind of mind is able to think up ideas like this?

O Portia, in the cosmic flow,
one with you, I ever grow.
I am the chalice here below,
of cosmic justice you bestow.

O Portia, opportunity,
I am beyond duality.
I focus now internally,
with you I grow eternally.

4. Beloved Portia, awaken women to see that there are certain narcissistic beings who are not necessarily in embodiment, but who are existing in a higher realm, the identity and mental realms, and who are from there seeking to manipulate human beings.

O Portia, cosmic balance bring,
eternal hope, my heart does sing.
Protected by your Mother's wing,
I feel at one with everything.

**O Portia, opportunity,
I am beyond duality.
I focus now internally,
with you I grow eternally.**

5. Beloved Portia, awaken women to see that these are the beings who have come up with all of these ideas that are defined or proclaimed as the absolute truth.

O Portia, bring the Mother Light,
to set all free from darkest night.
Your Love Flame shines forever bright,
with Saint Germain now hold me tight.

**O Portia, opportunity,
I am beyond duality.
I focus now internally,
with you I grow eternally.**

6. Beloved Portia, awaken women to see that these narcissistic beings have an even stronger subject-object duality than what most people have.

O Portia, in your mastery,
I feel transforming chemistry.
In your light of reality,
I find the golden alchemy.

**O Portia, opportunity,
I am beyond duality.**

I focus now internally,
with you I grow eternally.

7. Beloved Portia, awaken women to see that such beings have created an image of God that is a powerful tool for manipulating human beings.

O Portia, in the cosmic stream,
I am awake from human dream.
Removing now the ego's beam,
I earn my place on cosmic team.

O Portia, opportunity,
I am beyond duality.
I focus now internally,
with you I grow eternally.

8. Beloved Portia, awaken women to see that these beings are trapped in the closed loop of their own minds, and they cannot see its unreality.

O Portia, you come from afar,
you are a cosmic avatar.
So infinite your repertoire,
you are for earth a guiding star.

O Portia, opportunity,
I am beyond duality.
I focus now internally,
with you I grow eternally.

9. Beloved Portia, awaken women to see that these narcissistic beings made the decision that they would make men the superior sex on earth and women the inferior sex. This means that from a certain perspective there is an advantage to being a man on earth.

O Portia, I am confident,
I am a cosmic instrument.
I came to earth from heaven sent,
to help bring forward her ascent.

O Portia, opportunity,
I am beyond duality.
I focus now internally,
with you I grow eternally.

Part 4

1. Beloved Portia, awaken women to see that in many societies women are the servants or even the slaves of men. They do all the work and they raise the children.

O Portia, in your own retreat,
with Mother's Love you do me greet.
As all my tests I now complete,
old patterns I no more repeat.

O Portia, opportunity,
I am beyond duality.
I focus now internally,
with you I grow eternally.

2. Beloved Portia, awaken women to see that men are far less likely to start questioning this. Men are not the ones who can free planet earth from this mindset.

O Portia, Justice is your name,
upholding Cosmic Honor Flame,
No longer will I play the game,
of seeking to remain the same.

O Portia, opportunity,
I am beyond duality.
I focus now internally,
with you I grow eternally.

3. Beloved Portia, awaken women to see that women are the ones who are on the receiving end of the mindset that men are superior. We are the ones

who are being held back. We are the ones who are being pushed down and limited.

> O Portia, in the cosmic flow,
> one with you, I ever grow.
> I am the chalice here below,
> of cosmic justice you bestow.

> **O Portia, opportunity,**
> **I am beyond duality.**
> **I focus now internally,**
> **with you I grow eternally.**

4. Beloved Portia, awaken women to see that women have a stronger drive to free ourselves from this manipulation. There is a greater opportunity that women can be the forerunners for freeing the planet from this oppression, and this is something that the narcissistic beings do not know what to do with.

> O Portia, cosmic balance bring,
> eternal hope, my heart does sing.
> Protected by your Mother's wing,
> I feel at one with everything.

> **O Portia, opportunity,**
> **I am beyond duality.**
> **I focus now internally,**
> **with you I grow eternally.**

5. Beloved Portia, awaken women to see that the sex that is suppressed has a stronger drive to free itself from the suppression, and therefore they are more likely to open their minds to seeing through the manipulation and the schemes of the narcissistic beings, seeing the lies they are based on.

> O Portia, bring the Mother Light,
> to set all free from darkest night.
> Your Love Flame shines forever bright,
> with Saint Germain now hold me tight.

O Portia, opportunity,
I am beyond duality.
I focus now internally,
with you I grow eternally.

6. Beloved Portia, awaken women to see that the narcissistic beings have made certain choices. They have generated certain ideas that have suppressed women and elevated men.

O Portia, in your mastery,
I feel transforming chemistry.
In your light of reality,
I find the golden alchemy.

O Portia, opportunity,
I am beyond duality.
I focus now internally,
with you I grow eternally.

7. Beloved Portia, awaken women to see that there has been a long period of time where neither men nor women have questioned this, but because of the changing cycles, this time is coming to an end. This cycle is coming to an end.

O Portia, in the cosmic stream,
I am awake from human dream.
Removing now the ego's beam,
I earn my place on cosmic team.

O Portia, opportunity,
I am beyond duality.
I focus now internally,
with you I grow eternally.

8. Beloved Portia, awaken women to see that we are now at a point where the cosmic wheels are turning and bringing forth a liberation of women.

O Portia, you come from afar,
you are a cosmic avatar.

So infinite your repertoire,
you are for earth a guiding star.

O Portia, opportunity,
I am beyond duality.
I focus now internally,
with you I grow eternally.

9. Beloved Portia, awaken women to see that although the narcissistic beings will do everything they can to prevent women from waking up, they cannot stop us from making the decision to awaken ourselves and look at new ideas and free ourselves from this oppression.

O Portia, I am confident,
I am a cosmic instrument.
I came to earth from heaven sent,
to help bring forward her ascent.

O Portia, opportunity,
I am beyond duality.
I focus now internally,
with you I grow eternally.

Part 5

1. Beloved Portia, awaken women to see that when women make the decision that they want change, then the narcissistic beings will not be able to stop it. They can try to postpone it by keeping women ignorant, keeping them passive, keeping them not having the knowledge or the determination to free themselves.

O Portia, in your own retreat,
with Mother's Love you do me greet.
As all my tests I now complete,
old patterns I no more repeat.

O Portia, opportunity,
I am beyond duality.
I focus now internally,
with you I grow eternally.

2. Beloved Portia, awaken women to see that once women begin to awaken themselves and make the higher, more aware decisions that they want change in society and in their lives, the narcissistic beings will not be able to stop it.

O Portia, Justice is your name,
upholding Cosmic Honor Flame,
No longer will I play the game,
of seeking to remain the same.

O Portia, opportunity,
I am beyond duality.
I focus now internally,
with you I grow eternally.

3. Beloved Portia, awaken women to see that there is nothing the narcissistic beings can do to stop the movement of the liberation of women. The point of no return has been reached.

O Portia, in the cosmic flow,
one with you, I ever grow.
I am the chalice here below,
of cosmic justice you bestow.

O Portia, opportunity,
I am beyond duality.
I focus now internally,
with you I grow eternally.

4. Beloved Portia, awaken women to make the calls and wake up even more women, so that the snowball keeps rolling, getting bigger, encompassing more women who become part of this unified movement.

O Portia, cosmic balance bring,
eternal hope, my heart does sing.
Protected by your Mother's wing,
I feel at one with everything.

O Portia, opportunity,
I am beyond duality.
I focus now internally,
with you I grow eternally.

5. Beloved Portia, awaken women to the realization: "We will no longer tolerate the suppression of women on this planet of ours, because we claim planet earth as *our* planet."

O Portia, bring the Mother Light,
to set all free from darkest night.
Your Love Flame shines forever bright,
with Saint Germain now hold me tight.

O Portia, opportunity,
I am beyond duality.
I focus now internally,
with you I grow eternally.

6. Beloved Portia, awaken women to see that when this gains momentum, the narcissistic beings will have nothing they can do to counteract it. They cannot stop it. They cannot divert it. They must simply watch as they lose the dominance they have over this planet.

O Portia, in your mastery,
I feel transforming chemistry.
In your light of reality,
I find the golden alchemy.

O Portia, opportunity,
I am beyond duality.
I focus now internally,
with you I grow eternally.

7. Beloved Portia, awaken women to overthrow these male-dominated societies who will not remain male-dominated, but will indeed become more and more balanced.

O Portia, in the cosmic stream,
I am awake from human dream.
Removing now the ego's beam,
I earn my place on cosmic team.

**O Portia, opportunity,
I am beyond duality.
I focus now internally,
with you I grow eternally.**

8. Beloved Portia, awaken women to see beyond the extreme feminists' dream that suddenly women would have the same power as men have had for so long.

O Portia, you come from afar,
you are a cosmic avatar.
So infinite your repertoire,
you are for earth a guiding star.

**O Portia, opportunity,
I am beyond duality.
I focus now internally,
with you I grow eternally.**

9. Beloved Portia, awaken women to see that as the suppression of women has been driven by the narcissistic beings, then the extreme feminist movement and their attempt to elevate women to have the same power as men, is also driven by such beings.

O Portia, I am confident,
I am a cosmic instrument.
I came to earth from heaven sent,
to help bring forward her ascent.

O Portia, opportunity,
I am beyond duality.
I focus now internally,
with you I grow eternally.

Sealing

In the name of the I AM THAT I AM, I accept that Archangel Michael, Astrea and Shiva form an impenetrable shield around myself and all constructive people, sealing us from all fear-based energies in all four octaves. I accept that the Light of God is consuming and transforming all fear-based energies that make up the dark forces working against the liberation of women on earth!

7 | YOU WERE NOT CREATED AS A MAN OR A WOMAN

I am the Ascended Master Omega, or if you will, the Cosmic Being Omega, as I am not strictly an ascended master, having not ascended from earth. What I aim to give you here, is a perspective that goes beyond and will challenge most of the religions that you currently see on earth, that you have seen throughout history on earth, at least since the fallen beings were allowed to embody here but even before.

This messenger was many years ago given an experience of being transported in his finer bodies, or rather in his Conscious You as we say today, to the Central Sun to experience the presence of Alpha and myself. He has described the experience and some of you will know it. The important point of this is that the office that Alpha and I hold, is the cosmic gateway (so to speak) between the Creator and its creation.

It is only through this office that you can have an experience of the Creator and the Creator's Being. It is also only through this office and the lineage of ascended masters, going all the way to the masters working with earth, that you could take a message from the Creator. Of course, the Creator can do whatever it desires to do, but very rarely would give a message through an unascended messenger because there is such a confusion on earth, such contradictions, so many theories and religions about God and the ultimate God.

All images of God block your experience of God

The important point that I want to get across here is that when you experience the Creator's Being, you experience directly something that is beyond all form. You live in a world of form, everything in this world has form. It may not be a visible form, a form you can hear, touch, smell, it may be a thought, a feeling, but they are also forms. Even a subtle sense of identity has a form, any image you might have of God also has form but the real Creator is beyond form.

Now, you may say: "Does that mean that the Creator has no characteristics, no individuality, no personality, is there nothing that could describe the Creator?" Well, the answer to that question is "yes and no." Of course, your Creator, *our* Creator, the Creator of this world of form has what you could call an individuality. It is not an individuality that could be compared to, described by, any form that you see in this world of form. It is not an individuality that could be described by any words, even words that the Creator could give you. There are no words, there are no forms, there are no images that could capture the Creator's Being. That is why we, for lack of a better word, say that the Creator has no form, is beyond form, has transcended form, is transcendent of form, that you need to transcend your attachment to form and go into the full purity and neutralness of the Conscious You in order to experience the Creator's Being.

You need to recognize here that while the Creator is the originator of the world of form in which you live, the Creator itself is beyond its creation. There is not even a similarity between the Creator and its creation. There is, as Portia said, nothing that you can grasp, or see, or experience on earth that you can use to reason backwards and say, this tells me something about the Creator.

If you try to do this, you go into the mind, the linear mind, that is a subject, which is attempting to picture, understand an object. If you go into this mind and attempt to comprehend God, you cannot comprehend God, you can only understand an idol, an image of God, and it can never be God, it can only be an idol. Therefore, it is not in alignment with reality but if you think it is in alignment with reality, it becomes a false image, a false god, a false idol. For that matter, all idols are false but nevertheless you get my meaning.

The Creator is not a male god

The reality that I wish to bring out here is this: Regardless of the images, the idols that have been created on earth, the Creator is not male, the Creator is not a male God. The concept of male and female is completely meaningless when it comes to the real God that is beyond form. How could there be a distinction of male and female in something that is beyond form, when male and female exist only in the world of form. For that matter, they exist only on the kind of planets that you are used to and that you see here on earth.

If you take the *My Lives* book and look at the description given there, you can see that on a natural planet there is not a need for physical child-birth. Therefore, there is not a need for two sexes as you have here on earth where you have physical bodies with sexual organs that can impregnate the one body, and therefore bring forth a physical child that grows inside that body until it is born and becomes independent of the body. This process is not there on a natural planet. You can talk about male and female, masculine and feminine on a natural planet but not in the way you talk about it on earth.

My point is that what you see as male and female on earth is a very primitive concept only existing on dense-matter planets. Therefore, it is completely meaningless to want to apply this to the Creator. Now then, why do you even have this concept? Does it have no reality to it? Well, again the answer to that question is "yes and no." The way most people look at the concept of male and female on earth has no reality to it. There is a deeper reality, a higher reality that I will expound upon.

The Creator is beyond form. The Creator starts out with an intent to create, a will to create, a world that has form. As we have described before, before the Creator has created anything, there is only a void, a void meaning there is no form, at least as you define form in this world of form. What does the Creator have to do to create form? Well, the void can be described with the word *undifferentiated,* there is no differentiation in the void. Therefore, you cannot define what you see in your world of form where you have one form that is set apart from another form and therefore in a sense both forms are defined in relation to each other, or they are defined in relation to the void that has no form. There is either no form, or there is *this* form, which is different from *that* form. This is in a sense, the beginning of creating a world of form. You have to define something that is set apart from the void, then you have to create something else that is distinct from the other form.

Now, it may be tempting to think that you create one first and then the other but you actually do not, you create two, you create them as pairs. You create the two forms at the same time and that is the beginning of differentiation. There is the differentiation that there is a form that is different from the void, but at the level of form there are at least two forms that are set apart from each other. This is how the Creator differentiates. Once you have created these two basic elements, then from there you can create more. The two basic elements that your Creator decided to use to create its world of form, was an expanding and a contracting force. Now, I know some of you will be curious and say: "Was that the only choice, were those the only options, are there other worlds of form that are different?" The answer to that is "yes" but it would be very difficult for you to fathom this because you are created in this particular world of form and you tend to look at everything based on the differentiation that created your world of form. Do not stress your minds by even comprehending this, focus on mastering the world of form you are in. Then, when you attain the Creator consciousness, you can comprehend these other options.

How a sphere is created

The Creator chose an expanding and a contracting force. This was not at a level at all where it can be said to have anything to do with male and female, masculine and feminine as you see it on earth. It had absolutely nothing to do with it. There was simply a differentiation into an outgoing force that would continue to go out and expand indefinitely. Then the contracting force that could balance the outgoing force so that a certain form could be maintained in that state, in a certain state over what you would call time but time of course is a relative concept. In the very beginning, your concept of time did not really apply, but I am using a word with which you are familiar.

In other words, a form could be created and maintained because the contracting force balanced the expanding force. The original differentiation into these two forces went through several complex steps, until the Creator had defined what we have called the first sphere that was set apart from the void. In this sphere was defined a certain relationship between the expanding and the contracting force. This relationship, this ratio we might call it, determined the density of that first sphere, thereby setting the pattern or the boundaries for what kind of forms could be created.

Now, this led to the creation of the first two self-aware beings. These were not the Alpha and Omega that you know, because I and Alpha are in the Central Sun of this unascended sphere. We have attained these offices, we were not created originally in the first sphere to hold this office. There were originally two beings that you may also call Alpha and Omega if you wish, or the beginning or the ending, and they were the first self-aware beings generated out of the Creator's Being. They, when they had become self-aware, were given the task of actually defining the balance between the expanding and the contracting force. The Creator had set a certain ratio or certain boundary, but within that there was room for a specific definition of this balancing force and that was determined by these first two beings.

They then took on the responsibility for defining what could be done by the self-aware beings that were created after this, after themselves, what they could do with free will. They had free will but only within the parameters defined for their sphere. This is not really a limitation of free will because in a world of form—well, forms have to be defined. Therefore, you cannot say that this limits your free will. A decision has to be made that defines certain parameters, then beings exercise their free will within those parameters until they ascend and become permanent beings. Then, they can define parameters themselves.

You see here that this is the basis for a sphere and the pattern has been repeated until we come to your sphere. This is where Alpha and Omega, myself and Alpha come in. We were appointed to this office to serve as Alpha and Omega, the beginning and the ending. It is because we had attained this in a previous sphere and we were then appointed to define the parameters for this sphere. In other words, we would define the beginning and the ending. The beginning was the starting point for this sphere. The ending was the highest potential it can reach and at that point it is ready to ascend. What happens in between those two points is determined by the free-will choices of the beings in that sphere.

The messenger has described that when he was experiencing the Central Sun, there were two thrones, Alpha and I were sitting on the two thrones. Between those two was a white cube of translucent white material that emitted white light. This has been called the Cosmic Cube, the Cube of Christ and other names. It is because it is this cube that actually defines not only the beginning and the ending of a sphere, but the specific (we might call it) ratio or geometry that allows beings in a given sphere to transcend themselves. I know this is abstract to wrap your minds around, I am deliberately making it abstract because if you think you can grasp this with the linear, intellectual, outer mind, then as Portia said, you are mistaken. You may be able to use these words, if you are willing to go beyond the outer mind, to thereby have an experience that shows this to you, an experience that is beyond words. On the other hand, if you fixate your mind on the words, then that will prevent you from having the experience. *That* is the challenge we face as ascended masters communicating from a higher level of consciousness.

The Christ ratio determines self-transcendence

The Cosmic Cube or the Cube of Christ, is the balancing factor between the outgoing, the expanding and the contracting force. Your sphere is created in the same way as the first sphere, in the sense that there is an outgoing and a contracting force, and a form can only be upheld by the two being balanced. What determines the balance between the outgoing and the contracting force in your sphere, is precisely the white cube or what we call the Christ mind. This is what balances the two forces. Only then can you create something that has enduring value. Now, what does this mean? We have before said that only by balancing the two forces can you create something that can be maintained over time.

This is true enough, but not the highest understanding. The deeper reality is that the Christ, the definition of the Christ ratio for your particular sphere, determines the increments by which you can transcend yourself. In other words, you will know if you have studied a little bit of quantum physics, that there was a time where scientists believed that energy was a continuous phenomenon, that an energy wave, such as light, was a continuous phenomenon. Then it was discovered that this was not correct, that light is actually a discrete phenomenon, in the sense that light is radiated in discrete packages, called "quanta." That is why you have the concept of the quantum leap because the light cannot have any value. It can only have this value, the next value up, the next value up, the next value up—and there is a specific interval between these values.

You will know, as we have given the example before of Zeno's paradox, that you can divide the distance between two points into smaller increments indefinitely. You can take the difference between the number one and the number two, and you can divide it indefinitely into smaller and smaller numbers, as you can keep going towards bigger and bigger numbers. This is in a sense, an infinite loop. It is not really an infinite linear scale because there can be no such thing as an infinite linear scale, there can only be an infinite loop. Nevertheless, the point is that creation is not infinitely divisible, there are discrete intervals. There is a discrete jump where you can jump from one level to the next, thereby you transcend yourself or you can go down to the next level. There is no in between, you are either at this level or you are at that level, or you are at the lower level, there is no continuous movement.

This is why you have on planet earth, 144 different levels of consciousness and this is why you go from one to the other. That is why you cannot go below it because then you cannot stay on earth. You cannot go above it because then you ascend from earth. This is determined, this interval, this quantum leap, the cosmic quantum leap is determined by the values coded into the Cosmic Cube between the thrones of Alpha and myself. We have determined this within the parameters set by previous spheres, we have determined what it would be for our sphere.

Alpha and myself are differentiated, we are differentiated so that we are two different beings. You have to be very careful and really comprehend, really *experience* the reality of our teachings on non-duality because we are not dualistic beings, we are not in opposition to each other. There is no way that Alpha and I could destroy something, we are only creative beings. Why is that? Because we actually would never go against the upward movement of the entire world of form, we are committed to the growth of this sphere. We are therefore, continually having this figure-eight flow between us that is actually upholding the balance, the Christ balance, of the entire sphere. Truly, this balance that we uphold and that we have defined, sets the matrix for everything that happens in terms of raising your sphere up towards higher and higher levels. In the totality of your sphere there are many more than 144 levels. On dense-matter planets like earth, there are only 144 levels defined.

What you see, is that Christ can then be seen as this ratio, this specific geometric ratio between the expanding and the contracting forces. It can be seen as a value, although you cannot put a number on it on earth. It is beyond the numbers that you have. I know that there are various theories and teachings out there that want to associate a certain number with the Christ mind. It is not the ultimate understanding because the Christ mind cannot be confined to this. However, the mind of anti-christ *can* be confined to certain numbers that go against the upward movement, that go against self-transcendence.

Seeking to define Christ in order to get power

You understand that the Christ mind is self-transcendence. As we have said with progressive revelation, it never stands still. It could never be defined in an absolute term that could never change. You may, as some people have experienced, grasp the Christ at a certain point. Jesus has even explained in one of his profound dictations, how the Christ is like a horse that runs into town and whirls up the dust as it runs, and some people are covered in dust. When it comes back, other people who did not see the horse, sense the dust and sense there is something special about that person. Some people may even run along with the horse or may even jump on top of it for a while and then they jump off. Now they come out and now they say: "What I experienced was the Christ and this is how the Christ is." The moment you define Christ, you have lost Christ, for Christ has already transcended itself. If you want to keep pace with Christ, you must continually transcend yourself and not believe that you have the final experience, the final understanding, the final theory, the final doctrine. Once you try to fixate Christ, you have lost Christ and gone into anti-christ.

Why do certain beings, such as the fallen beings, attempt to fixate Christ? Well, because Christ is the ultimate power in an unascended sphere and they want to use that power for their own purposes. Of course, it cannot be done because Christ is the Oneness of all life and constantly transcending itself, as the sphere is transcending itself. The moment you try to fixate Christ so you can use it to gain power for yourself, where you are refusing to transcend yourself but you want to maintain that power, then it is not Christ you are having; it is anti-christ. It can be no other way. Christ is the ultimate power, as even the song you were playing of the Hallelujah chorus, the King of Kings and Lord of Lords because Christ is above anything on earth. Which of course most people cannot fathom and certainly the fallen beings cannot fathom. Therefore, they cannot fathom Christ, they can only construct a false image of Christ and that is anti-christ.

The origin of masculine and feminine

What do you see then that the fallen beings have done? Well, they have taken the concept of the expanding and contracting forces, they have perverted them by comparing them to the masculine and feminine that you see on earth. Now, what have I said? There is a huge difference between what you can see on earth and the Creator, what you can see on earth in an unascended sphere. Even what you can see on earth and the natural planets in your sphere, there is a huge gap. Therefore, to take the ideas of these cosmic forces and associate them with something as dense and as primitive as male and female bodies on a dense-matter planet like earth, has no reality to it whatsoever. It is a complete attempt to manipulate people. What the fallen beings have done is that they have looked at their limited understanding of creation, they have sensed that there is an expanding force, there is a contracting force. They have then attempted to create a fixed image of these forces and their interaction. This is what cannot be done.

If you were to attempt to create a fixed image of Alpha and myself, the moment you had created the image in your mind that operates in time, we would have transcended ourselves and no longer live up to the image, the same with the Christ. What the fallen beings have done is, they have taken these two forces and they have pulled them into their dualistic view and they have said: "One is male, one is female, the male is superior and the female is inferior." In other words, they have pulled the cosmic forces that are beyond your sphere into their own limited view, their perception filter, their state of consciousness, their dualistic view, where one dualistic polarity has to be defined in opposition to the other dualistic polarity.

In other words, instead of being two forces that are (should we say) complementary, they are now opposites, they pull in opposite directions. Of course, you will say with the outer, linear, logical, rational, analytical mind, you will say: "But surely the outgoing force is going in the opposite direction than the contracting force." Yes, from a linear perspective, but the world of form is not linear, it is spherical. What would happen if you keep going out in the same direction and keep going for long enough, as even Einstein intuited? You come back to your starting point from the other direction. The problem is, this would take you so long that no form could be maintained on a planet like earth. There has to be something that balances that outgoing, in order to maintain a form. But can you really say that *that* is opposite? Nay, it is just balancing so that there is a form that can be maintained. There is no contradiction, there is no opposition, there is no form breaking down another.

When you are not in duality, you can use the expanding and contracting forces to create something, you can create many different forms so they are not in opposition to each other, they do not break down each other, they do not destroy each other. Once you go into duality, well you are still creating the same way, but now the two forces have become opposites, they work against each other.

Now, it is as if there is a resistance, there is an opposition to anything you want to create and to maintaining it over time or transcending it. First, there is an opposition to maintaining something over time so you can experience it for some time, but there is also opposition if you want to transcend it because you become trapped in your own creation. The fallen beings have taken these two cosmic forces, pulled them into a dualistic worldview and now they are opposites, they appear to be opposites. Therefore, the masculine must have certain qualities that are in opposition to the feminine, and once you have defined these two as opposites, what can you then do? You can add the hallmark, so to speak, of the fallen beings, you create a value judgment, you define a value judgment that says the expanding force, the masculine element is superior and the female is inferior. You transfer that to how it is on earth and therefore you say, men are superior to women and therefore women should submit themselves to male dominance.

This is how they have created the opposition between the sexes. Do you see what I said earlier, that the Creator cannot in any way be construed to be masculine or feminine? The Creator is not a dualistic being, cannot be looked at through the dualistic mindset because then you create a false god. That is indeed what the fallen beings have done on this planet. They have created many false gods. As we have said (and which I know will be difficult to accept for many, many religious people, even many spiritual people) the Old Testament god Jehovah is a false god created by the fallen beings. Any god that is seen as masculine or feminine, as you define masculine and feminine on earth, is a false god. For that manner, any god who has form as you define form on earth is a false god.

The dilemma

Now, of course you could say there are ascended masters, and the dilemma that we have faced is that in order to even enable you to relate to us, we must portray ourselves in a form that you can relate to, that you can deal with in your minds. That is why in previous dispensations there has been a certain image created of certain masters. The reality is that you cannot create an image of an ascended master because an ascended master is constantly transcending itself. We have the example of El Morya who was known through several previous dispensations and came to a point where he realized that so many students had become trapped in a particular image of him that it was no longer actually helping their growth. He decided to take the unprecedented step of changing his name to Master MORE. This is what ascended masters sometimes have to do to shake people out of worshiping an idol. It is not that El Morya/Master MORE was affected by the image projected by the students, but the students were affected by it because they had now created an idol of El Morya/Master MORE that they were worshiping. They had lost the real master because he had moved on and transcended himself, but they were holding on to the idol so they could not move on with him.

In a sense, you could say here that we have given you images that we are masculine and feminine masters. It is not that there is no reality to it as such, because Alpha and myself, we hold a certain polarity. Alpha holds the polarity of the expanding force, I hold the polarity of the contracting force. There is a certain reality there of a differentiation, but it is not the way you look at male and female on earth. It has been necessary for us to give you these images so that you can relate to us. We have also said that you need to look beyond the images because as you reach a certain level of consciousness, you go beyond male and female. For that matter, in order to ascend from earth, you need to go beyond the images of male and female that is in the collective consciousness on earth.

You do not ascend as a man or a woman, you ascend as a neutral being. It is not necessarily that you become what they call an androgynous being, although that terminology can be used. We would rather have you think of this so that you become neutral in terms of gender identity and gender roles. This does not mean you have to go to the extreme that you see in some people in Japan where they try in their appearance and their behavior to act almost androgynous, so it is difficult to tell whether it is a man or a woman. You do not need to now seek to change or go beyond, or suppress the sexuality of your body. In your mind, you become more and more neutral. You reach a certain level of consciousness where you are clearly in a male or a female body, but you as a being are not identifying yourself as a man or a woman but as a spiritual being. That is incidentally, why this messenger can be a messenger for a conference on the liberation of women because he is not seeing himself as a man or a woman but as a spiritual being.

All gender images were created on earth and are unreal

With this, I simply want to give you some ideas to ponder. First of all, you can look at this idea that there are male and female masters and you can transcend those traditional gender images and gender roles. A female master like Mother Mary can be very stern and very direct, which is a quality many ascended master students have associated with the male masters, but a male master can also be soft, loving and kind. You would do well to start to soften up your view of ascended masters so you do not identify us as male or female based on what you see on earth.

The next step would then be to start softening up the way you look at yourselves. As I said, as you go towards the 144th level of consciousness, you become less and less concerned about masculine and feminine, male and female. Naturally, you are still in a male or female body but there comes a point where you say: "So what. Why should that limit me in my spiritual growth or my expression of who I am on earth? I will be who I will be, express what I will express, regardless of whether I am in a male or female body."

Now, as Portia was preparing you to understand, this is where we also need you to start looking beyond the teachings given in previous dispensations. It was said that you were created as a masculine or feminine soul, but this was a teaching that could be given at the time based on the mindset, the Piscean mindset, and the collective consciousness. We have given you the teachings on the Conscious You. What have we said about the Conscious You? It is a formless being. It is pure awareness. It has no form. The Conscious You is not male or female. Your soul may have a male dominance or a female dominance, but that was not because you were created that way by God or by your I AM Presence. It was because the Conscious

You, as you started exercising your free will in the density of planet earth, you created a certain identity in your identity body, certain matrices in your mental body, certain feelings in your emotional body, certain patterns of feelings. Over many lifetimes, this has created a set of selves. There are some of those selves that were created while you were in a female body, there were some that were created while you were in a male body.

Now, all of you have been in female bodies in many embodiments and in male bodies in many embodiments. These selves, that we can say are masculine and feminine selves, may have been reinforced over a very long period of time, over many, many embodiments. What happens to you is that when you come down in your present lifetime, you are coming down in a male or a female body. For most people, what happens is, if you come into a male body, as you are in the womb and you are integrating with the body, the male selves are activated and the female selves are suppressed. If you come into a female body, obviously the opposite happens. Now, there are some people where this does not quite happen, they are sort of in an in-between state where some male selves are active and some female selves are active. That is why they can come in and they are either confused about their sexual orientation, or they are convinced that they have a different sexual orientation than their physical body, they are in the wrong body as many people feel. This is also something that has happened over many lifetimes.

Now, there are some old teachings (that go back a long time) that say that homosexual people are at a higher level of spiritual development. Well, again the answer to that is: it is both true and untrue. It is not necessarily the case for everybody. You cannot say that everybody who is a homosexual has a high spiritual attainment. In fact the vast majority of homosexuals have no higher attainment than the average person. They have in some recent lifetimes, either switched between male and female, or they have some very severe traumas for both male and female embodiments and they are (so to speak), their auras are so scattered that they do not have a clear male or female orientation. They are switching between different selves not really knowing where they belong and they cannot establish a coherent identity.

However, there are some homosexual people who have been in both male and female embodiments for so long that they have started softening up their gender identity. They are not so identified with the sex of the physical body. This is the case for some, which is a teaching that goes beyond what we have given before. It will no doubt be a comfort to many and it will no doubt be used by some who are not actually at a higher level of attainment, but let me not confuse you here. This teaching does not mean that homosexuality is an ideal. It does not mean that in order to raise your level of consciousness and ascend, you have to go through a homosexual phase. The vast majority of people do not do this. There are some that do but the vast majority do not need to do this because they actually come to a point where it is no problem for them to switch into the selves that are aligned with the sex of their body.

Transcending the basic conflict on earth

Where does all this lead to? Well, it leads to the fact that you need to begin to contemplate here some very important concepts that relate to the liberation of women. Number One. God is neither male nor female, the Creator is beyond any kind of gender difference that you could possibly define on earth. The idea that God is a masculine God is false, completely false, created by the fallen beings, deliberately put upon this planet in order to manipulate and create conflict between men and women. What more basic conflict can you create on a planet like earth, than having a conflict between men and women?

The second idea. In the spiritual realm there is a differentiation between masculine and feminine but it is completely beyond the gender roles defined on earth. It is not dualistic and there is no value judgment. There are two cosmic forces that are equally necessary for creation. There is the Christ, which balances the two forces. The Christ is beyond gender, the Christ is not male, is not female, it cannot be characterized by gender. It is neutral, if you want to use any word, which of course is limited.

The third level is that in your being, you are neither male nor female, you are the Conscious You, you are gender neutral, you are pure awareness, you are beyond these gender roles. That means what? It means that whatever gender roles are defined here on earth, you can free yourself from any and all of them. This goes equally for men and for women. As Portia said, in this cycle it is easier for women to free themselves from these gender roles and more necessary, since women have been suppressed. Nevertheless, men are also very strictly limited by their gender roles, even though they may have certain perks but they are still limited. You can free yourselves from it.

The concept of twin flames

What else can you learn? Well, let us look at the concept of twin flames, which was that you are created in a polarity with another soul that had the opposite polarity to yours, that you were only complete when you were together. Again, there is a certain reality to the concept but it was limited to what could be given at the time. You were not created in a polarity. You were created as the Conscious You, which is not incomplete in itself because it has no structure. How could there be incompleteness? How could there be an imbalance? How could you be male or female?

You were not created in a polarity, you are a unique independent being. You can ascend as that independent being without ever meeting any other being. Why do we have the concept of twin flames? Because after people fell into duality, they were assigned (not all people on earth but many of the more spiritual people and those who were starting to climb the ladder of consciousness), they were assigned another being, another soul if you will, so that those two together could balance each other. This was not something created in the spiritual realm, it was created as a reaction to falling into duality.

Does that mean that twin flames are the perfect love who are made for each other? Hollywood nonsense, my beloved! It means you are made for each other, in the sense that there are certain beings who have the exact qualities that can bring out what they have not seen in themselves. They can force it out, force the conflict, force them to look at themselves if they want to grow. There also comes a point where you reach a certain level of consciousness where you do not need a twin flame because you have built this willingness to look at yourself, you do not need a person who is the opposite or has opposite qualities. You can still enjoy being in a relationship because you can complement each other, it is not something that is forced upon you.

If you look back at the concept of twin flames, you will see that there was a certain subtle element of force that was brought into this. There was a certain sense that if you thought this other person was your twin flame, then you *should* be together with that person and you should be able to have a perfect and harmonious relationship. This put enormous strain on those couples who either were told by a previous messenger or who believed by themselves that they were twin flames. In many cases, the relationships failed because of unrealistic expectations. Any close relationship where two people feel drawn to each other is because they have something to learn from each other, but they only learn it by transcending, by being willing to look at themselves and see: "What is the other person bringing out in me?" If they suppress this because they suppress all conflict and think they should have the happily-ever-after relationship, then they will not grow and eventually the relationship will break up so that they can grow separately.

Then, what about ascended masters—are we not twin flames, Alpha and myself, Portia and Saint Germain? Well, according to the concept that was given in previous dispensations, yes. You see again, Saint Germain and Portia, when they were originally created were not created as twin flames. After they ascended they formed a polarity so that they can hold an office—because most spiritual offices in the ascended realm have a masculine and feminine polarity that holds the expanding and contracting forces and balances them with the Christ. You can assign, or be assigned, or be attracted to another ascended master in this polarity, which in the old days were called twin flames but which we do not really use anymore, because we want you to look beyond the concept and realize there is much more to it.

There is always more to experience

Basically if you have followed me through this very long discourse, which of course is born from the fact that I am beyond time and space, even though you are not, you will realize one thing: There is always more to it. There is no final revelation as Portia said. There is always more to it. Why is this so, my beloved? Well, first of all because, as we have said, until you experience the greatest being, it is just a concept that you are trying to understand at a distance. We are always seeking to urge you to transcend your present level of consciousness and experience something higher because that is the Christ principle, the Christ movement.

The moment you think you have a concept of God, of ascended masters, of yourself, of earth, of the cosmos, your growth stops. Because now you are sitting there and you are essentially saying: "Don't bother me, God, don't bother me ascended masters. Now I finally figured it out, now I see exactly how creation works. I have it all worked out in my linear, analytical mind. I have this perfect image of exactly how the world works and this makes me feel so secure. My ego is just so secure because now I know how the world works. I know I am going to be saved and I can feel really superior to all these other people who don't know how the world works. I want to continue to experience that feeling longer, so don't bother me, don't disturb me and tell me there is more to it. Because I've got it all figured out based on the Summit Lighthouse teachings, the I AM teachings, the Christian fundamentalist teachings, the Hindu teachings, the Muslim teachings, the Buddhic teachings, whatever you have."

Of course, my beloved I bow to your free will. I respect your free will. If you want to have that experience, you can have it for as long as you want but then my address is not for you. My address is for those who have had enough of having the same experience, who want to reconnect to the Christ and the upward self-transcending movement that is the purpose of creating a world of form.

With this my beloved, I seal you in the figure-eight flow of Alpha and Omega and I say to you, ponder the white cube, the Cosmic Cube, the Christ cube. Envision yourself sitting on it, feeling the flow between Alpha and myself. Then you will know your beginning and you might be able to glimpse your ending, at least your ending on earth, through your ascension. With this, I thank you for enduring this long release, which has been an important milestone for the raising of the collective consciousness on earth. It is finished.

NOTE: This dictation was given May 30, 2020.

8 | INVOKING FREEDOM FROM ALL PREDEFINED ROLES (PART 1)

In the name of the I AM THAT I AM, Jesus Christ, I use the authority that I have as a being in embodiment on earth to call upon Omega to reinforce my calls and use my chakras to project the statements in this invocation into the collective consciousness and awaken people to the awareness that will liberate both men and women from all psychological and spiritual thralldom to the fallen beings. Awaken people to the reality that we are spiritual beings and that we can co-create a new future by working with the ascended masters. I especially call for ...

[Make your own calls here.]

Part 1

1. Omega, awaken women to see that the Creator's Being is beyond all form, but we live in a world of form and everything in this world has form.

Omega, I now meditate,
upon your throne in cosmic gate.

I'm born out of the figure-eight,
that Alpha and you co-create.

O Song of Life, you vitalize,
all hearts you truly synchronize.
O Sacred Sound, you alchemize,
turn earth into a paradise.

2. Omega, awaken women to see that thoughts and feelings are also forms. Even a subtle sense of identity has a form, any image we might have of God also has form but the real Creator is beyond form.

Omega, in your sacred space,
my cosmic parents I embrace.
I see that it is such a grace,
that I take part in cosmic race.

O Song of Life, you vitalize,
all hearts you truly synchronize.
O Sacred Sound, you alchemize,
turn earth into a paradise.

3. Omega, awaken women to see that there are no words, there are no forms, there are no images that could capture the Creator's Being. The Creator has no form, is beyond form, has transcended form, is transcendent of form.

Omega in the Central Sun,
you show me life is cosmic fun.
And thus a victory is won,
my homeward journey has begun.

O Song of Life, you vitalize,
all hearts you truly synchronize.
O Sacred Sound, you alchemize,
turn earth into a paradise.

4. Omega, awaken women to see that we need to transcend our attachment to form and go into the full purity and neutralness of the Conscious You, in order to experience the Creator's Being.

Omega, femininity
is doorway to infinity.
With you I have affinity,
to know my own divinity.

**O Song of Life, you vitalize,
all hearts you truly synchronize.
O Sacred Sound, you alchemize,
turn earth into a paradise.**

5. Omega, awaken women to see that while the Creator is the originator of the world of form, the Creator itself is beyond its creation. Nothing we can grasp or experience on earth can be used to reason backwards and say this tells me something about the Creator.

Omega, in your cosmic flow,
my plan divine I clearly know.
My heart is now a lamp aglow,
as love on all I do bestow.

**O Song of Life, you vitalize,
all hearts you truly synchronize.
O Sacred Sound, you alchemize,
turn earth into a paradise.**

6. Omega, awaken women to see that if we try to do this, we go into the linear mind that is a subject, which is attempting to understand an object.

Omega, cosmic Mother Flame,
this is the light from which I came.
As I take part in cosmic game,
Christ victory I do proclaim.

**O Song of Life, you vitalize,
all hearts you truly synchronize.**

**O Sacred Sound, you alchemize,
turn earth into a paradise.**

7. Omega, awaken women to see that if we go into this mind and attempt to comprehend God, we cannot comprehend God, we can only understand an idol, an image of God and it can never be God, it can only be an idol.

Omega, I now comprehend,
why I did to earth descend.
And thus I fully do intend,
to help this planet to ascend.

**O Song of Life, you vitalize,
all hearts you truly synchronize.
O Sacred Sound, you alchemize,
turn earth into a paradise.**

8. Omega, awaken women to see that an image is not in alignment with reality but if we think it *is* in alignment with reality, it becomes a false image, a false god, an idol.

Omega, I do now aspire,
to join the ranks of cosmic choir.
My heart burns with a Christic fire,
that is this planet's sanctifier.

**O Song of Life, you vitalize,
all hearts you truly synchronize.
O Sacred Sound, you alchemize,
turn earth into a paradise.**

9. Omega, awaken women to see that regardless of the images, the idols that have been created on earth, the Creator is not male, the Creator is not a male God.

Omega, my heart is ablaze,
my life is in an upward phase.

Come teach me now the secret phrase,
so that I can this planet raise.

**O Song of Life, you vitalize,
all hearts you truly synchronize.
O Sacred Sound, you alchemize,
turn earth into a paradise.**

Part 2

1. Omega, awaken women to see that the concept of male and female is completely meaningless when it comes to the real God that is beyond form. How could there be a distinction of male and female in something that is beyond form, when male and female exist only in the world of form.

Omega, I now meditate,
upon your throne in cosmic gate.
I'm born out of the figure-eight,
that Alpha and you co-create.

**O Song of Life, you vitalize,
all hearts you truly synchronize.
O Sacred Sound, you alchemize,
turn earth into a paradise.**

2. Omega, awaken women to see that male and female on earth is a very primitive concept only existing on dense-matter planets. It is completely meaningless to want to apply this to the Creator.

Omega, in your sacred space,
my cosmic parents I embrace.
I see that it is such a grace,
that I take part in cosmic race.

**O Song of Life, you vitalize,
all hearts you truly synchronize.**

**O Sacred Sound, you alchemize,
turn earth into a paradise.**

3. Omega, awaken women to see that in order to create a world of form, the Creator must define differentiation so that one form is set apart from another form and both forms are defined in relation to each other, or they are defined in relation to the void that has no form.

Omega in the Central Sun,
you show me life is cosmic fun.
And thus a victory is won,
my homeward journey has begun.

**O Song of Life, you vitalize,
all hearts you truly synchronize.
O Sacred Sound, you alchemize,
turn earth into a paradise.**

4. Omega, awaken women to see that one must create two forms at the same time and that is the beginning of differentiation. There is the differentiation that there is a form that is different from the void, but at the level of form there are at least two forms that are set apart from each other.

Omega, femininity
is doorway to infinity.
With you I have affinity,
to know my own divinity.

**O Song of Life, you vitalize,
all hearts you truly synchronize.
O Sacred Sound, you alchemize,
turn earth into a paradise.**

5. Omega, awaken women to see that the two basic elements that our Creator decided to use to create its world of form, was an expanding and a contracting force.

Omega, in your cosmic flow,
my plan divine I clearly know.

My heart is now a lamp aglow,
as love on all I do bestow.

**O Song of Life, you vitalize,
all hearts you truly synchronize.
O Sacred Sound, you alchemize,
turn earth into a paradise.**

6. Omega, awaken women to see that the Creator chose an expanding and a contracting force. This had nothing to do with male and female as we see it on earth.

Omega, cosmic Mother Flame,
this is the light from which I came.
As I take part in cosmic game,
Christ victory I do proclaim.

**O Song of Life, you vitalize,
all hearts you truly synchronize.
O Sacred Sound, you alchemize,
turn earth into a paradise.**

7. Omega, awaken women to see that this was a differentiation into an outgoing force, that would continue to go out and expand indefinitely, and the contracting force that could balance the outgoing force so that a certain form could be maintained.

Omega, I now comprehend,
why I did to earth descend.
And thus I fully do intend,
to help this planet to ascend.

**O Song of Life, you vitalize,
all hearts you truly synchronize.
O Sacred Sound, you alchemize,
turn earth into a paradise.**

8. Omega, awaken women to see that a form could be created and maintained because the contracting force balanced the expanding force, and

the Creator defined a certain relationship between the expanding and the contracting force.

> Omega, I do now aspire,
> to join the ranks of cosmic choir.
> My heart burns with a Christic fire,
> that is this planet's sanctifier.

> **O Song of Life, you vitalize,**
> **all hearts you truly synchronize.**
> **O Sacred Sound, you alchemize,**
> **turn earth into a paradise.**

9. Omega, awaken women to see that this relationship, this ratio, determined the density of matter, thereby setting the pattern or the boundaries for what kind of forms could be created.

> Omega, my heart is ablaze,
> my life is in an upward phase.
> Come teach me now the secret phrase,
> so that I can this planet raise.

> **O Song of Life, you vitalize,**
> **all hearts you truly synchronize.**
> **O Sacred Sound, you alchemize,**
> **turn earth into a paradise.**

Part 3

1. Omega, awaken women to see that there is a balancing factor between the expanding and the contracting force. There is an outgoing and a contracting force, and a form can only be upheld by the two being balanced.

> Omega, I now meditate,
> upon your throne in cosmic gate.
> I'm born out of the figure-eight,
> that Alpha and you co-create.

**O Song of Life, you vitalize,
all hearts you truly synchronize.
O Sacred Sound, you alchemize,
turn earth into a paradise.**

2. Omega, awaken women to see that the definition of the Christ ratio for our particular sphere determines the increments by which we can transcend ourselves.

Omega, in your sacred space,
my cosmic parents I embrace.
I see that it is such a grace,
that I take part in cosmic race.

**O Song of Life, you vitalize,
all hearts you truly synchronize.
O Sacred Sound, you alchemize,
turn earth into a paradise.**

3. Omega, awaken women to see that Christ is this ratio, this specific geometric ratio between the expanding and the contracting forces. The Christ mind is self-transcendence.

Omega in the Central Sun,
you show me life is cosmic fun.
And thus a victory is won,
my homeward journey has begun.

**O Song of Life, you vitalize,
all hearts you truly synchronize.
O Sacred Sound, you alchemize,
turn earth into a paradise.**

4. Omega, awaken women to see that the moment we define Christ, we have lost Christ, for Christ has already transcended itself. If we want to keep pace with Christ, we must continually transcend ourselves and not believe that we have the final experience, the final understanding, the final theory, the final doctrine.

Omega, femininity
is doorway to infinity.
With you I have affinity,
to know my own divinity.

**O Song of Life, you vitalize,
all hearts you truly synchronize.
O Sacred Sound, you alchemize,
turn earth into a paradise.**

5. Omega, awaken women to see that once we try to fixate Christ, we have lost Christ and gone into anti-christ. Certain beings attempt to fixate Christ because Christ is the ultimate power in an unascended sphere and they want to use that power for their own purposes.

Omega, in your cosmic flow,
my plan divine I clearly know.
My heart is now a lamp aglow,
as love on all I do bestow.

**O Song of Life, you vitalize,
all hearts you truly synchronize.
O Sacred Sound, you alchemize,
turn earth into a paradise.**

6. Omega, awaken women to see that this cannot be done because Christ is the Oneness of all life and constantly transcending itself. The moment we try to fixate Christ so we can use it to gain power, then it is not Christ we are having; it is anti-christ.

Omega, cosmic Mother Flame,
this is the light from which I came.
As I take part in cosmic game,
Christ victory I do proclaim.

**O Song of Life, you vitalize,
all hearts you truly synchronize.
O Sacred Sound, you alchemize,
turn earth into a paradise.**

7. Omega, awaken women to see that Christ is the ultimate power because Christ is above anything on earth.

> Omega, I now comprehend,
> why I did to earth descend.
> And thus I fully do intend,
> to help this planet to ascend.

> **O Song of Life, you vitalize,**
> **all hearts you truly synchronize.**
> **O Sacred Sound, you alchemize,**
> **turn earth into a paradise.**

8. Omega, awaken women to see that the narcissistic beings, the fallen beings, cannot fathom Christ, they can only construct a false image of Christ and that is anti-christ.

> Omega, I do now aspire,
> to join the ranks of cosmic choir.
> My heart burns with a Christic fire,
> that is this planet's sanctifier.

> **O Song of Life, you vitalize,**
> **all hearts you truly synchronize.**
> **O Sacred Sound, you alchemize,**
> **turn earth into a paradise.**

9. Omega, awaken women to see that the fallen beings have taken the concept of the expanding and contracting forces, they have perverted them by comparing them to the masculine and feminine we see on earth.

> Omega, my heart is ablaze,
> my life is in an upward phase.
> Come teach me now the secret phrase,
> so that I can this planet raise.

> **O Song of Life, you vitalize,**
> **all hearts you truly synchronize.**

**O Sacred Sound, you alchemize,
turn earth into a paradise.**

Part 4

1. Omega, awaken women to see that to take the ideas of these cosmic forces and associate them with something as dense and as primitive as male and female bodies on a dense-matter planet like earth, has no reality to it whatsoever.

Omega, I now meditate,
upon your throne in cosmic gate.
I'm born out of the figure-eight,
that Alpha and you co-create.

**O Song of Life, you vitalize,
all hearts you truly synchronize.
O Sacred Sound, you alchemize,
turn earth into a paradise.**

2. Omega, awaken women to see that this is an attempt to manipulate people. The fallen beings have looked at their limited understanding of creation, they have sensed that there is an expanding force, there is a contracting force. They have then attempted to create a fixed image of these forces and their interaction. This is what cannot be done.

Omega, in your sacred space,
my cosmic parents I embrace.
I see that it is such a grace,
that I take part in cosmic race.

**O Song of Life, you vitalize,
all hearts you truly synchronize.
O Sacred Sound, you alchemize,
turn earth into a paradise.**

3. Omega, awaken women to see that the fallen beings have taken these two forces and they have pulled them into their dualistic view and they have said: "One is male, one is female, the male is superior and the female is inferior."

> Omega in the Central Sun,
> you show me life is cosmic fun.
> And thus a victory is won,
> my homeward journey has begun.

> **O Song of Life, you vitalize,**
> **all hearts you truly synchronize.**
> **O Sacred Sound, you alchemize,**
> **turn earth into a paradise.**

4. Omega, awaken women to see that the fallen beings have pulled the cosmic forces that are beyond our sphere into their own limited view, their perception filter, their state of consciousness, their dualistic view, where one dualistic polarity has to be defined in opposition to the other dualistic polarity.

> Omega, femininity
> is doorway to infinity.
> With you I have affinity,
> to know my own divinity.

> **O Song of Life, you vitalize,**
> **all hearts you truly synchronize.**
> **O Sacred Sound, you alchemize,**
> **turn earth into a paradise.**

5. Omega, awaken women to see that instead of being two forces that are complementary, they are now opposites, they pull in opposite directions.

> Omega, in your cosmic flow,
> my plan divine I clearly know.
> My heart is now a lamp aglow,
> as love on all I do bestow.

**O Song of Life, you vitalize,
all hearts you truly synchronize.
O Sacred Sound, you alchemize,
turn earth into a paradise.**

6. Omega, awaken women to see that there has to be something that balances the outgoing force in order to maintain a form. But it is not opposite; it is just balancing so that form can be maintained. There is no contradiction, there is no opposition, there is no form breaking down another.

Omega, cosmic Mother Flame,
this is the light from which I came.
As I take part in cosmic game,
Christ victory I do proclaim.

**O Song of Life, you vitalize,
all hearts you truly synchronize.
O Sacred Sound, you alchemize,
turn earth into a paradise.**

7. Omega, awaken women to see that when we are not in duality, we can use the expanding and contracting forces to create something, we can create many different forms so they are not in opposition to each other, they do not break down each other, they do not destroy each other.

Omega, I now comprehend,
why I did to earth descend.
And thus I fully do intend,
to help this planet to ascend.

**O Song of Life, you vitalize,
all hearts you truly synchronize.
O Sacred Sound, you alchemize,
turn earth into a paradise.**

8. Omega, awaken women to see that once we go into duality, we are still creating the same way, but now the two forces have become opposites, they work against each other.

Omega, I do now aspire,
to join the ranks of cosmic choir.
My heart burns with a Christic fire,
that is this planet's sanctifier.

**O Song of Life, you vitalize,
all hearts you truly synchronize.
O Sacred Sound, you alchemize,
turn earth into a paradise.**

9. Omega, awaken women to see that in duality there is a resistance, there is an opposition to anything we want to create and to maintaining it over time or transcending it.

Omega, my heart is ablaze,
my life is in an upward phase.
Come teach me now the secret phrase,
so that I can this planet raise.

**O Song of Life, you vitalize,
all hearts you truly synchronize.
O Sacred Sound, you alchemize,
turn earth into a paradise.**

Sealing

In the name of the I AM THAT I AM, I accept that Archangel Michael, Astrea and Shiva form an impenetrable shield around myself and all constructive people, sealing us from all fear-based energies in all four octaves. I accept that the Light of God is consuming and transforming all fear-based energies that make up the dark forces working against the liberation of women on earth!

9 | INVOKING FREEDOM FROM ALL PREDEFINED ROLES (PART 2)

In the name of the I AM THAT I AM, Jesus Christ, I use the authority that I have as a being in embodiment on earth to call upon Omega to reinforce my calls and use my chakras to project the statements in this invocation into the collective consciousness and awaken people to the awareness that will liberate both men and women from all psychological and spiritual thralldom to the fallen beings. Awaken people to the reality that we are spiritual beings and that we can co-create a new future by working with the ascended masters. I especially call for …

[Make your own calls here.]

Part 1

1. Omega, awaken women to see that there is an opposition to maintaining something over time, so we can experience it for some time, but there is also opposition if we want to transcend it because we become trapped in our own creation.

Omega, I now meditate,
upon your throne in cosmic gate.
I'm born out of the figure-eight,
that Alpha and you co-create.

O Song of Life, you vitalize,
all hearts you truly synchronize.
O Sacred Sound, you alchemize,
turn earth into a paradise.

2. Omega, awaken women to see that the fallen beings have taken these two cosmic forces, pulled them into a dualistic worldview and now they appear to be opposites. Therefore, the masculine must have certain qualities that are in opposition to the feminine.

Omega, in your sacred space,
my cosmic parents I embrace.
I see that it is such a grace,
that I take part in cosmic race.

O Song of Life, you vitalize,
all hearts you truly synchronize.
O Sacred Sound, you alchemize,
turn earth into a paradise.

3. Omega, awaken women to see that once the fallen beings had defined these two as opposites, they defined a value judgment that says the expanding force, the masculine element, is superior and the female is inferior.

Omega in the Central Sun,
you show me life is cosmic fun.
And thus a victory is won,
my homeward journey has begun.

O Song of Life, you vitalize,
all hearts you truly synchronize.
O Sacred Sound, you alchemize,
turn earth into a paradise.

4. Omega, awaken women to see that the fallen beings transferred that and said men are superior to women and therefore women should submit themselves to male dominance.

> Omega, femininity
> is doorway to infinity.
> With you I have affinity,
> to know my own divinity.

> **O Song of Life, you vitalize,**
> **all hearts you truly synchronize.**
> **O Sacred Sound, you alchemize,**
> **turn earth into a paradise.**

5. Omega, awaken women to see that this is how the fallen beings have created the opposition between the sexes.

> Omega, in your cosmic flow,
> my plan divine I clearly know.
> My heart is now a lamp aglow,
> as love on all I do bestow.

> **O Song of Life, you vitalize,**
> **all hearts you truly synchronize.**
> **O Sacred Sound, you alchemize,**
> **turn earth into a paradise.**

6. Omega, awaken women to see that the fallen beings have created many false gods, and even the Old Testament god, Jehovah, is a false god created by the fallen beings. Any god that is seen as masculine or feminine is a false god. Any god who has form is a false god.

> Omega, cosmic Mother Flame,
> this is the light from which I came.
> As I take part in cosmic game,
> Christ victory I do proclaim.

> **O Song of Life, you vitalize,**
> **all hearts you truly synchronize.**

**O Sacred Sound, you alchemize,
turn earth into a paradise.**

7. Omega, awaken women to see that we do not ascend as a man or a woman, we ascend as a neutral being, we become neutral in terms of gender identity and gender roles.

Omega, I now comprehend,
why I did to earth descend.
And thus I fully do intend,
to help this planet to ascend.

**O Song of Life, you vitalize,
all hearts you truly synchronize.
O Sacred Sound, you alchemize,
turn earth into a paradise.**

8. Omega, awaken women to see that we do not need to change, go beyond or suppress the sexuality of the body. In our minds, we become more and more neutral.

Omega, I do now aspire,
to join the ranks of cosmic choir.
My heart burns with a Christic fire,
that is this planet's sanctifier.

**O Song of Life, you vitalize,
all hearts you truly synchronize.
O Sacred Sound, you alchemize,
turn earth into a paradise.**

9. Omega, awaken women to see that we reach a certain level of consciousness where we are in a male or a female body, but we are not identifying ourselves as men or women but as spiritual beings.

Omega, my heart is ablaze,
my life is in an upward phase.
Come teach me now the secret phrase,
so that I can this planet raise.

O Song of Life, you vitalize,
all hearts you truly synchronize.
O Sacred Sound, you alchemize,
turn earth into a paradise.

Part 2

1. Omega, awaken women to see that as we rise to higher levels of consciousness, we become less and less concerned about masculine and feminine, male and female.

Omega, I now meditate,
upon your throne in cosmic gate.
I'm born out of the figure-eight,
that Alpha and you co-create.

O Song of Life, you vitalize,
all hearts you truly synchronize.
O Sacred Sound, you alchemize,
turn earth into a paradise.

2. Omega, awaken women to see that we are still in a male or female body but there comes a point where we say: "So what. Why should that limit me in my spiritual growth or my expression of who I am on earth? I will be who I will be, express what I will express, regardless of whether I am in a male or female body."

Omega, in your sacred space,
my cosmic parents I embrace.
I see that it is such a grace,
that I take part in cosmic race.

O Song of Life, you vitalize,
all hearts you truly synchronize.
O Sacred Sound, you alchemize,
turn earth into a paradise.

3. Omega, awaken women to see that the core of our beings is the Conscious You, which is a formless being. It is pure awareness. It has no form. The Conscious You is not male or female.

> Omega in the Central Sun,
> you show me life is cosmic fun.
> And thus a victory is won,
> my homeward journey has begun.

> **O Song of Life, you vitalize,**
> **all hearts you truly synchronize.**
> **O Sacred Sound, you alchemize,**
> **turn earth into a paradise.**

4. Omega, awaken women to see that the soul may have a male dominance or a female dominance, but that is not because it was created that way.

> Omega, femininity
> is doorway to infinity.
> With you I have affinity,
> to know my own divinity.

> **O Song of Life, you vitalize,**
> **all hearts you truly synchronize.**
> **O Sacred Sound, you alchemize,**
> **turn earth into a paradise.**

5. Omega, awaken women to see that as we started exercising free will in the density of planet earth, we created a certain identity, certain matrices in the mental body and certain patterns of feelings.

> Omega, in your cosmic flow,
> my plan divine I clearly know.
> My heart is now a lamp aglow,
> as love on all I do bestow.

> **O Song of Life, you vitalize,**
> **all hearts you truly synchronize.**

**O Sacred Sound, you alchemize,
turn earth into a paradise.**

6. Omega, awaken women to see that over many lifetimes, this has created a set of selves. Some of those selves were created while we were in a female body, some were created while we were in a male body.

Omega, cosmic Mother Flame,
this is the light from which I came.
As I take part in cosmic game,
Christ victory I do proclaim.

**O Song of Life, you vitalize,
all hearts you truly synchronize.
O Sacred Sound, you alchemize,
turn earth into a paradise.**

7. Omega, awaken women to see that all of us have been in female bodies in many embodiments and in male bodies in many embodiments. These masculine and feminine selves may have been reinforced over a very long period of time.

Omega, I now comprehend,
why I did to earth descend.
And thus I fully do intend,
to help this planet to ascend.

**O Song of Life, you vitalize,
all hearts you truly synchronize.
O Sacred Sound, you alchemize,
turn earth into a paradise.**

8. Omega, awaken women to see that when we come down in our present lifetime, we are coming down in a male or a female body. If we come into a male body, the male selves are activated and the female selves are suppressed.

Omega, I do now aspire,
to join the ranks of cosmic choir.

My heart burns with a Christic fire,
that is this planet's sanctifier.

O Song of Life, you vitalize,
all hearts you truly synchronize.
O Sacred Sound, you alchemize,
turn earth into a paradise.

9. Omega, awaken women to see that for some people, some male selves are active and some female selves are active. That is why they are either confused about their sexual orientation, or they are convinced that they have a different sexual orientation than their physical body, they are in the wrong body.

Omega, my heart is ablaze,
my life is in an upward phase.
Come teach me now the secret phrase,
so that I can this planet raise.

O Song of Life, you vitalize,
all hearts you truly synchronize.
O Sacred Sound, you alchemize,
turn earth into a paradise.

Part 3

1. Omega, awaken women to see that ideally we come to a point where it is no problem for us to switch into the selves that are aligned with the sex of the body.

Omega, I now meditate,
upon your throne in cosmic gate.
I'm born out of the figure-eight,
that Alpha and you co-create.

O Song of Life, you vitalize,
all hearts you truly synchronize.

O Sacred Sound, you alchemize,
turn earth into a paradise.

2. Omega, awaken women to see that God is neither male nor female, the Creator is beyond any kind of gender difference that we could possibly define on earth.

Omega, in your sacred space,
my cosmic parents I embrace.
I see that it is such a grace,
that I take part in cosmic race.

O Song of Life, you vitalize,
all hearts you truly synchronize.
O Sacred Sound, you alchemize,
turn earth into a paradise.

3. Omega, awaken women to see that the idea that God is a masculine God is completely false, created by the fallen beings, deliberately put upon this planet in order to manipulate and create conflict between men and women. What more basic conflict can one create than having a conflict between men and women?

Omega in the Central Sun,
you show me life is cosmic fun.
And thus a victory is won,
my homeward journey has begun.

O Song of Life, you vitalize,
all hearts you truly synchronize.
O Sacred Sound, you alchemize,
turn earth into a paradise.

4. Omega, awaken women to see that in the spiritual realm there is a differentiation between masculine and feminine but it is completely beyond the gender roles defined on earth. It is not dualistic and there is no value judgment.

Omega, femininity
is doorway to infinity.
With you I have affinity,
to know my own divinity.

O Song of Life, you vitalize,
all hearts you truly synchronize.
O Sacred Sound, you alchemize,
turn earth into a paradise.

5. Omega, awaken women to see that there are two cosmic forces that are equally necessary for creation. There is the Christ which balances the two forces. The Christ is beyond gender, the Christ is not male, is not female, it cannot be characterized by gender. It is neutral.

Omega, in your cosmic flow,
my plan divine I clearly know.
My heart is now a lamp aglow,
as love on all I do bestow.

O Song of Life, you vitalize,
all hearts you truly synchronize.
O Sacred Sound, you alchemize,
turn earth into a paradise.

6. Omega, awaken women to see that our beings are neither male nor female, we are the Conscious You, we are gender neutral, we are pure awareness, we are beyond these gender roles.

Omega, cosmic Mother Flame,
this is the light from which I came.
As I take part in cosmic game,
Christ victory I do proclaim.

O Song of Life, you vitalize,
all hearts you truly synchronize.
O Sacred Sound, you alchemize,
turn earth into a paradise.

7. Omega, awaken women to see that whatever gender roles are defined here on earth, we can free ourselves from any and all of them. This goes equally for men and for women.

Omega, I now comprehend,
why I did to earth descend.
And thus I fully do intend,
to help this planet to ascend.

O Song of Life, you vitalize,
all hearts you truly synchronize.
O Sacred Sound, you alchemize,
turn earth into a paradise.

8. Omega, awaken women to see that in this cycle it is easier for women to free themselves from these gender roles and more necessary, since women have been suppressed.

Omega, I do now aspire,
to join the ranks of cosmic choir.
My heart burns with a Christic fire,
that is this planet's sanctifier.

O Song of Life, you vitalize,
all hearts you truly synchronize.
O Sacred Sound, you alchemize,
turn earth into a paradise.

9. Omega, awaken women to see that men are also strictly limited by their gender roles, even though they may have certain advantages but they are still limited.

Omega, my heart is ablaze,
my life is in an upward phase.
Come teach me now the secret phrase,
so that I can this planet raise.

O Song of Life, you vitalize,
all hearts you truly synchronize.

**O Sacred Sound, you alchemize,
turn earth into a paradise.**

Part 4

1. Omega, awaken women to see that we were not created in a polarity, we were created as the Conscious You, which is not incomplete in itself because it has no structure. How could there be incompleteness? How could there be an imbalance? How could we be male or female?

> Omega, I now meditate,
> upon your throne in cosmic gate.
> I'm born out of the figure-eight,
> that Alpha and you co-create.

> **O Song of Life, you vitalize,
> all hearts you truly synchronize.
> O Sacred Sound, you alchemize,
> turn earth into a paradise.**

2. Omega, awaken women to see that we were not created in a polarity, we are unique independent beings. We can ascend as independent beings without ever meeting any other being.

> Omega, in your sacred space,
> my cosmic parents I embrace.
> I see that it is such a grace,
> that I take part in cosmic race.

> **O Song of Life, you vitalize,
> all hearts you truly synchronize.
> O Sacred Sound, you alchemize,
> turn earth into a paradise.**

3. Omega, awaken women to see that after people fell into duality, they were assigned another being so that those two together could balance each

other. This was not something created in the spiritual realm, it was created
as a reaction to falling into duality.

> Omega in the Central Sun,
> you show me life is cosmic fun.
> And thus a victory is won,
> my homeward journey has begun.

> **O Song of Life, you vitalize,**
> **all hearts you truly synchronize.**
> **O Sacred Sound, you alchemize,**
> **turn earth into a paradise.**

4. Omega, awaken women to see that twin flames are beings who have the
exact qualities that can bring out what we have not seen in ourselves. They
can force it out, force the conflict, force us to look at ourselves if we want
to grow.

> Omega, femininity
> is doorway to infinity.
> With you I have affinity,
> to know my own divinity.

> **O Song of Life, you vitalize,**
> **all hearts you truly synchronize.**
> **O Sacred Sound, you alchemize,**
> **turn earth into a paradise.**

5. Omega, awaken women to see that we can reach a level of consciousness where we do not need a twin flame because we have built the willingness to look at ourselves, we do not need a person who is the opposite or
has opposite qualities.

> Omega, in your cosmic flow,
> my plan divine I clearly know.
> My heart is now a lamp aglow,
> as love on all I do bestow.

**O Song of Life, you vitalize,
all hearts you truly synchronize.
O Sacred Sound, you alchemize,
turn earth into a paradise.**

6. Omega, awaken women to see that there is always more to grasp and experience by going beyond understanding at a distance. We need to transcend our present level of consciousness and experience something higher because that is the Christ principle, the Christ movement.

Omega, cosmic Mother Flame,
this is the light from which I came.
As I take part in cosmic game,
Christ victory I do proclaim.

**O Song of Life, you vitalize,
all hearts you truly synchronize.
O Sacred Sound, you alchemize,
turn earth into a paradise.**

7. Omega, awaken women to see that the moment we think we have a concept of God, of ourselves, of earth, our growth stops. We are no longer willing to look beyond the concept defined by an outer teaching, we do not want to be disturbed by a higher awareness.

Omega, I now comprehend,
why I did to earth descend.
And thus I fully do intend,
to help this planet to ascend.

**O Song of Life, you vitalize,
all hearts you truly synchronize.
O Sacred Sound, you alchemize,
turn earth into a paradise.**

8. Omega, awaken women to see that this very idea is what has been used to suppress women because a religious scripture or scientific doctrine is said to have defined the role of women and it must stand for all time.

Omega, I do now aspire,
to join the ranks of cosmic choir.
My heart burns with a Christic fire,
that is this planet's sanctifier.

O Song of Life, you vitalize,
all hearts you truly synchronize.
O Sacred Sound, you alchemize,
turn earth into a paradise.

9. Omega, awaken women to see that there are no predefined roles for women on this planet. We have the right to break free from all limitations put upon women and completely redefine what it means to be a spiritual being expressing itself through a female body on earth.

Omega, my heart is ablaze,
my life is in an upward phase.
Come teach me now the secret phrase,
so that I can this planet raise.

O Song of Life, you vitalize,
all hearts you truly synchronize.
O Sacred Sound, you alchemize,
turn earth into a paradise.

Sealing

In the name of the I AM THAT I AM, I accept that Archangel Michael, Astrea and Shiva form an impenetrable shield around myself and all constructive people, sealing us from all fear-based energies in all four octaves. I accept that the Light of God is consuming and transforming all fear-based energies that make up the dark forces working against the liberation of women on earth!

10 | NO WOMAN IS FREE UNTIL ALL WOMEN ARE FREE

I am the Ascended Master Saint Germain, and I wish to continue what has been said by other masters and build upon this by giving you some thoughts about how the fallen beings have managed to take away the freedom of both men and women. Now, as we have explained, the fallen beings took the basic creative forces, the expanding and the contracting forces, and turned them into dualistic polarities. They perverted them because once you have turned something into a dualistic polarity, you can pervert it beyond what it originally was.

Let us look at the expanding force first. How have the fallen beings perverted it? Well, the expanding force wants to expand. Now, as we have said, there is no point in expansion because the purpose of using the expanding force is to create some form that is sustainable for a time. If there was only expansion and nothing balancing expansion, no form would be created, no form could be upheld. You may have some form created for a fleeting moment, but then it will be gone or transformed into another form the next moment. What the fallen beings have done is they have taken this drive to create, this drive to expand, and they have perverted it by saying that there should be no rules and no restrictions to what you can do with your free will. If you really have free will, you should be able to do anything you want. Therefore, there should be no rules, no restrictions, no consequences and no repercussions for anything that the fallen beings do.

Rebellion against the mechanics of the universe

We have explained to you that there was a point where certain beings in an unascended sphere had refused to transcend their state of consciousness so that they were not ready to ascend when the rest of the sphere was ready to ascend. These beings (who had not yet fallen) had set themselves up on certain planets as having a very high degree of power. When they were confronted by the ascended masters with the need to transcend their mindset and ascend with the rest of their sphere, they rebelled against this. They refused to let go of this mindset because they thought that if they really had free will, they should be allowed to do anything they wanted for as long as they wanted, and there should be no ascended master who could come in and upset the apple cart and disturb their sense that they had all power on their particular planet. When they were confronted by the ascended masters and they realized that they did not have all power, and that free will does not mean you can do anything you want for as long as you want, and that there are consequences for what you do, then they rebelled against this. They refused to transcend themselves and therefore they fell into the next sphere that was created.

We have said before that the fact that your choices have consequences is not a restriction of your free will. As we have explained, you live in a world of form that was created with a certain matrix, a certain Christ matrix, a certain density of matter and energy. You start out as a co-creator who is creating within that matrix. Once you ascend, you can keep rising until you can define your own matrix. You start out as a co-creator, and as a co-creator you have free will, but you do not have what you might call an unrestricted free will. Because you are co-creating within the parameters defined by those who are above you, those who are ascended beings and who are one with the whole and therefore will not set parameters that will damage some beings and elevate others to a privileged position. We have also said that if you did not see a consequence of your choices, how would you know you have made a choice?

The purpose of being a co-creator is not to create a particular creation and stay with that indefinitely. The purpose of being a co-creator is to create something and when you experience what you have created, you have the opportunity to transcend the consciousness from which you created it so you can move forward. *That* is the purpose of life and that is what the vast majority of beings in an unascended sphere are engaged in. Now, the fallen beings refused to transcend the consciousness through which they had created these privileged positions for themselves, for on an entire planet with billions of lifestreams, a handful of fallen beings had set themselves up as the leaders who had absolute power and absolute privilege. Basically, the other billions of beings on that planet were just slaves, working for the benefit of the elite, very similar to what you see on earth in the current situation, and what you have seen in the past.

The denial of responsibility and the power elite

This is one of the perversions of the expanding force of the Father when it is pulled down to the level of a dualistic polarity. It makes people think that there should be no restrictions, that they should be allowed to do anything they want, and there should be no consequences. You will see this in the world, how there are people who believe this. You will see how this has even given rise to some belief systems. For example, you will see that in the Christian religion, especially with the formation of the Catholic church but even before, there was a denial of reincarnation, a refusal to incorporate reincarnation in the official Christian doctrines and this is basically a denial of consequences. People are denying that they can have consequences that can, for choices they have made in this lifetime, come back to them in a future lifetime, or that certain things that happened to them in this lifetime are the result of choices they made in a previous lifetime. In other words, one perversion of the expanding force is that people deny responsibility. They refuse consequences and therefore they think that whatever happens in this lifetime was not the result of choices they made in a past life, it was just a result of conditions beyond their control and they deny that anything they do in this lifetime could have repercussions in a future lifetime.

Now, you also have scientific materialists or communists who also deny reincarnation for much the same reason. Many, or at least some, of the primary philosophers behind materialism also refuse to take responsibility beyond this particular lifetime. Now, of course you can look at the planet and you can see that there are certain men that are affected by this mindset and they often form a certain power elite. They are men who believe they have a special authority, a special ability, especially the ability to be leaders, to rule over others and therefore they tend to, in any society, set themselves up as the elite who has power. This can be in the government where they will, if the opportunity is there, set themselves up as dictators. It can also be in a democratic society where they attempt to be elected leaders, but then attempt to take on more powers and in a sense, undermine democracy. This is what you see in some nations. You see it for example in Poland with the current government. You see it in Russia with Putin and you have seen other examples of it, including Churchill in England during the war and of course Hitler. You can debate whether he was democratically elected or not, but at least there was an election that brought him to power.

This is one way, but it is not only in government that these people will set themselves up. You can find it in the business community where they attempt to become owners of these large businesses where they set themselves up as the monopoly capitalists to attempt to gain a monopoly. They can attempt to become CEOs of businesses who, then again, act basically as if they were the dictator of that business and they have all power. You also see an intellectual elite, it can be philosophers, it can be people in educational institutions, especially in the universities, who set themselves up in a position where nobody can really object, nobody can protest against them. They are the ones who define what is true or not true. You see this in terms of certain people who are promoting a materialist agenda, and who are basically holding the educational institutions of the world, especially in the modern democracies, in an iron grip of materialism and will not allow any kind of research or theories that question the materialist paradigm or the materialist gospel, as we might say.

You find this of course in all areas of society, but especially in the areas I have mentioned. Of course you have the religious area where they will also attempt to set themselves up, not necessarily as the ones defining a new religion, even though that happens as well, but even as the leaders of an ancient religion such as the Pope who has, seemingly, all power in the Catholic religion, and a small group of clerics in Islam who also have tremendous power there.

The force that pressures all men to accept certain roles

Of course, when you look at the situation, you can see that not all men are in this mindset of wanting to have power or wanting to have privilege, at least not in terms of gaining a position in these particular institutions. You do see that there is a tendency in the collective consciousness, there is a sort of pressure on all men and it is of course created by a collective beast that was originally defined by the fallen beings but has been reinforced by many men over these many, many thousands of years of male-dominated or patriarchal societies. It is basically that the fallen beings have created this dynamic where they themselves have set themselves up as a privileged power elite. They are forcing the majority of men in the society into specific roles that support their privilege and their power. It may be that they are forced to be soldiers, they are forced to live a certain lifestyle, such as the peasants in feudal societies or as the workers in industry, where they do all the labor that makes all the money but the capitalists reap all the benefits.

The fallen beings, through the power elite, have forced the majority of men into a situation where they feel a certain dis-empowerment, they do not feel they are masters of their own destiny. They have limited choices in life. They might have had dreams when they were young but they could not fulfill them. They had to settle for something less to get money to live their lives and therefore they feel frustrated.

The pressure to be sexually active

Now, what has happened for many men is of course that they have also been the victims of another pressure that is created by, or put upon them by, this collective beast and it is the pressure of sexuality, male sexuality, where men feel this pressure to be sexually active, to find a woman where they can have sex and be sexually active. This, along with another power elite, the religious power elite, has pressured men into thereby marrying women. It has caused many men to go into a relationship, into a marriage at a fairly early age.

They have then, especially in the past, for example in Catholic societies, denied contraception. They have made their wives pregnant at a fairly early age and suddenly this man who may have had dreams about what he would do in his life is now tied down to a woman and children and there has to be bread on the table and the woman is taking care of the children, so who has to go out and make the money by getting whatever job seems available at the time? Well, the man has to do this so he feels disempowered. What does he blame for this state? Well, most men are not aware enough to blame the fallen beings and the power elite so they end up blaming their wives. It is because they are married that they have to settle for this second-rate job and cannot fulfill their dreams.

What do they do? Well, they fall prey to this pressure from the collective consciousness that is a perversion of the male expanding force, that they can at least have some compensation for their sense of being powerless if they have power over their wives and children, if they are the man in the house, if they are the one who determines everything and makes the decisions. This is of course what causes men to accept this male-dominated family structure and it is what causes other men to take their frustration to a level where they become abusive towards their wives and children whether physically or emotionally or in other ways.

You see this entire dynamic that the fallen beings have set up that traps men into this role where they feel disempowered and it is all because they have to do the work that enables the power elite to stay in their privileged positions where they have power and they have a comfortable lifestyle and more wealth than they could ever need. The men are trapped and as a result of that, they abuse their power towards their women and if the women submit to this, then they are also trapped. Now, obviously you, whether you are men or women, if you are concerned about bringing society forward towards the golden age, you can make the calls for this, for the binding and consuming of these beasts, for the binding of the mindset, the fallen beings and so on.

Perversion of the contracting force

Let us now move on to look at how the fallen beings have perverted the contracting force. One perversion of the expanding force is that you seek to gain power, a perversion of the contracting force is that you become passive. You become docile, you become unwilling to make decisions and take initiative and you become focused on having a comfortable daily life. You shut down any ambition, any dreams, you are just focused on your personal daily situation and you just want to be somewhat comfortable. We have talked at length about how all people have this tendency in their psychology that you need a certain sense of security in order to feel that you have your life under some sort of control, and once you have that sense of security, you are reluctant to give it up. What have the fallen beings created? They have created societies that are dominated by the men that have defined a role for women where women are the ones who should focus on being wives and mothers, raising their children, making the family function, staying at home, thereby being financially dependent on their men. This of course causes many women to actually accept that this is their lot in life, this is all they can do. It is a perversion of the contracting force that you are satisfied with current conditions. You feel secure, maybe even comfortable, if current conditions are not too bad. Then you tend to stay in those conditions for a long time because you do not want to risk the uncertainty of breaking out of the fold. You see so many women who are staying in a marriage or a relationship that really has no growth, has no transcendence, but it has a certain level of security and comfortability because after all, the husband is bringing home enough money and he is not so bad, he is not abusive and so on.

You see also women who are in more abusive relationships and you often see that the very women who managed to break free, they do it because the abuse becomes so severe that they can no longer handle it. This of course is a very unfortunate situation for women to be in, which I have great compassion for. All of us have great compassion for it and we do not wish this upon anyone. The only way to break free of this situation and to really change it at the level of society is that women begin to see this as a perversion of the contracting force and they free themselves from the desire for security and reconnect to the desire that all people have, whether they are in a male or female body, the desire to grow, the desire to transcend, the desire in essence to experience more than they are experiencing right now.

The never-ending desire to own

Here comes the next level of perversion perpetrated by the fallen beings. Another perversion of the expanding force of the Father, or the expanding force in general, is that it wants to move on, it wants to experience something different. It wants to experience more of what it wants to have, whether it is power, whether it is money, whether it is possessions, whether it is sex, whether it is this or that. There is a tendency in the expanding force to want more, and when it is perverted into a dualistic polarity, this means you want to have more of something, not because you want to experience it, but because you want to *own* it. You want to keep it. You want to accumulate it because it is never enough. You can never have enough of something when you are in this mindset. You can look at the obvious example: money. There may be some point where a man has started his own business and it has started to go well, and suddenly he is making more money and he has an experience of making more money. It is an experience he needs to have. It is even a constructive experience in the sense that it can help him move forward and transcend his level of consciousness. He feels: "I am really making money" and he has an experience from making money. If he continues to make more and more money, as some of the richest people in the world have done, there comes a point where you no longer get any enjoyment out of making the money. Now, you are trapped by this collective beast that has overtaken your mind and you cannot stop, you cannot say: "It's enough." You want more and more money. Now, it is not about the experience of *making* the money, it is in a sense about the experience of *having* the money. Even so, can you ever have the experience of having enough money? Well, you *can*, because some men have come to that point and they have said: "This is enough." Some men cannot, and especially the fallen beings of course cannot. They want to own more and more money, more and more possessions or they want to have more and more power.

The perversion of the expanding force is that you can never have enough and the perversion of the contracting force is that you are not allowed to have more, that you are not worthy to have more, that there is a certain station in life and this is your lot. You see in many women that they have become trapped in that mindset. If you go to some of the less developed countries, for example India or Africa, you will see women who have grown up from early childhood being, so to speak, programmed to accept that they have very limited options in life.

This is even worse in a country like India where women are brought up, girls are brought up, to think they are essentially worthless, they are worthless as human beings, they are even worthless in their own family. Even their own parents or brothers do not think they are worth anything. Society does not think they are worth anything. Probably God, the Hindu gods, do not think they are really worth anything and so on. They grow up with this mindset that they may see that other people have something, but they accept: "It's not for me. I'm not worthy to have it. I can't have it. I'm not allowed to have it. I'm not good enough. I'm not smart enough. I'm not capable enough to have it." This is the perversion of the contracting force.

Finding balance by finding a higher purpose

What is it that can break this stalemate? What can break it? We have talked about the potential that women can balance men. Well, what has happened already to a large degree is that many women in the more developed nations have started to break free of this mindset. Many, many women have refused to accept the traditional gender roles defined by their society and culture. They have for example said: "Why can't I, as a woman, have an education? Why can't I, as a woman, have a good job, have a career? Why can't I have a nice house, a nice car? Why can't I have affluence? Why can't I be self-sufficient economically so I do not need to depend on my husband and so I can leave him if he is abusive or if the relationship isn't growing?" Many, many women have already started breaking through this.

You have to be very, very careful that you do not, then, after breaking through this perversion of the contracting force become trapped in a perversion of the expanding force, feeling that you want more and more. Even women can go into not feeling they have enough. It may not be the same things that many men want. Many women do not want power. They do not necessarily want money for the sake of having money, but they want money for the sake of being able to do something or buy something, have a bigger, nicer house, go on vacation, this or that. There can come a point where women get caught up. They free themselves from the perversion of the contracting force of thinking they cannot have this, but now they get caught up in the perversion of the masculine force wanting more and more and it is never enough.

Now, many women in the more developed nations, especially, have started to find some balance. There was a certain period of this very materialistic focus in societies where many women were focused on getting these outer things. Many women have now started to find balance and of course some men have also started to find balance. The biggest potential here is that women can find that balance where they have a balance of the contracting force so that they do not want more than what makes them comfortable. How can this happen? Well, it can only happen if these women, as many women are beginning to do, find some higher purpose for their lives than what has been defined by their culture, especially in the western consumer cultures. Women need to discover a purpose and it can be in the beginning, psychological healing. It can be self-development, self-improvement, what Abraham Maslow called the self-actualization needs that are at the top of the pyramid of needs. Many women have started to pursue various ways of developing themselves, actualizing themselves. It can be through mindfulness, through yoga, through various therapy or discussion groups, many, many things that are not necessarily a high spiritual teaching or esoteric spiritual teaching but are more universal forms of spiritual teachings. Many more are of course ready to discover a higher teaching and realize that there is a purpose to life, which is not just to develop yourself to get better than you are right now, but that there is actually a goal. There is a higher state of consciousness that human beings can attain than what you see around you in your societies that have been dominated by Christianity, which took out the spiritual path, and by materialism, which never had the spiritual path.

Women can help men find purpose

If women can see this, they could begin to balance men so that men can be pulled out, or can pull themselves out, of this mindset of: "It's never enough. I need to have more and more." Women can then inspire men to first come to the realization: "But how much money do we really need? Isn't it enough that we have a nice house, a functioning car and that we can go on vacation? Now that we have all of these things, isn't it time to look at other things, look at what is really important to us in life, how we experience life, how we experience ourselves?" Then, men can also become open to this path of self-improvement, mindfulness, improving yourself and even for some, raising your consciousness to a distinctly higher level.

This is a realistic potential in the coming decade that many, many women in the more developed nations will make this transition. Of course, as we have said, there are also advanced souls in many not so developed nations that can also make this transition and realize there is a spiritual path. You can raise your consciousness and by doing so you can have a greater impact on improving conditions even in the less developed nations. This of course requires that balance, and the balance can come partly again because some souls have incarnated so many times in particular situations that they have started to find a balance. They have gone to various extremes in past lifetimes and they have become more aware of the need to find balance. It can also really come because you who are the ascended master students make the calls for people to be cut free to see this, to discover some higher purpose, some spiritual purpose, that life is not just about living, life is not just about accumulating material possessions or raising your children or having a career or having money or achieving these outer materialistic goals.

The shift we are looking for, the shift that I especially am looking for, at this stage of the golden age is the shift that I was hoping would have occurred a long time ago. I have said before that my purpose for sponsoring the development of all this technology that you see in the more developed nations is precisely to give people free time so that they do not spend all their time and energy just making a living and surviving physically. Instead, they have time, attention, energy and money left over to pursue other things in life, other than empty entertainment or the eternal quest for more and more that is never enough. *That* was my hope and there is a realistic potential that a critical mass of people will make that switch in the coming decade. Primarily, it will be women, but as the women make the shift, gradually they will start to pull the men in as well. Of course, some men have already made it. Many more *can* make it.

Still it is primarily women who are at the point where they can make this shift and realize that: "Once we have attained a certain level of material comfortability, we don't need more material goods, we need something else. We need some content in our lives, some purpose that is a higher purpose, a more spiritual purpose, a purpose that reaches beyond ourselves where we first of all develop ourselves, but even then, expand our awareness to what can we do for others. How can we use our level of comfortability, of material wealth, of awareness, of knowledge to help others?" This is a shift that also can begin to occur. Of course, it has already started to occur, but there can be an acceleration in this coming decade where primarily women in the more developed democracies begin to realize that they have been fortunate to grow up in very privileged societies where they have had far, far better conditions than the vast majority of women around the planet.

Women helping women

Now, one of the aspects of being a woman on earth is of course motherhood. Motherhood is in its essence, when it is balanced, it is the act or the mindset of doing something beyond yourself, of doing something for others. That is what you do for your children, even for your husband in the family. Many women are already in the mindset of doing for others. There are now many, many women who have gotten to a point where the children are grown, they are becoming self-sufficient so there is a real potential that they can take that momentum they have on nurturing others and transfer that to people who are less fortunate than themselves. It can be people in their own societies of course, but it can be people in the less developed parts of the world, especially the women there.

There is a real potential, there is a real need, for a new kind of women's movement that promotes solidarity between women, that promotes the idea that it is necessary for women in the more developed countries, women who have greater privileges than those in the less developed countries, to reach out to their sisters in these other countries and seek to help them in various ways. I will not here define these ways because there are many. Some women are already engaged in this, but many more can come up, and the ideas will surely be released. I do not want to put any limitation on this. You can of course help people directly or you can help them by promoting change in their societies, even by using the governments of the more developed democracies to reach out to the governments in the less developed nations and offer them various assistances or even put pressure on them where it is necessary to apply pressure.

When you take this mother-nurturing momentum that many women have and you expand it to go beyond your own children, to look at either children in those less developed nations or the women there, you can see that, as a woman in a privileged modern democracy, is it really acceptable to you that millions of girls at a very young age are exposed to female genital mutilation, female circumcision? Is that really acceptable to women in the democratic world? Is it acceptable to women in the democratic world that girls in India are considered worthless, may be sold as slaves by their families or forced into marriages? Is it really acceptable to women in the modern democratic world that so many Islamic women are forced to live a very isolated life where they have to cover themselves up to their faces, where they cannot go out, they cannot get a driver's license. They do not have the basic freedoms that the women in the democratic nations have grown up to take for granted. Is that really acceptable to you?

This of course ties in with who I am and the Flame of Freedom that I hold for earth. I am the primary spiritual representative for the Flame of Freedom for earth. You, women in the modern democracies, you have grown up in free societies. You have had a very large degree of freedom in those societies where even from girlhood you could choose to get an education if you wanted. You had a realistic possibility of getting that education and doing something with it. You have grown up with an incredible freedom. You did not have to marry whom your parents told you to marry. You did not even have to marry. You could get a job and become self-sufficient. You did not have to wear a particular kind of dress. You did not have to cover your body. Nobody mutilated your genitals so you could not have sexual pleasure.

Can you not awaken from the tendency to take this freedom for granted and look at how many women around the planet do not have these basic freedoms? Can you, then, not make the switch in your mind and say: "It is not acceptable to me that the majority of women on this planet do not have the freedoms that I have grown up with, and it is not enough for me to focus on my own life, enjoying these freedoms, knowing that so many other women are not free. I *must,* I *will,* because I desire to, and it is in my Divine plan to, use my freedom to give freedom to other women, to make sure that other nations, other societies recognize the equality, the equal value of women, the equal rights of women, and the equal freedom and opportunity of women."

No woman is truly free until every woman is free

This truly is the highest possible use of the freedoms that you have grown up with in these modern nations that are in a sense very, very privileged. The question is: Will you allow the men in these privileged nations to continue to be trapped in this mindset that "it's never enough" and they are still only focused on themselves gaining more and more of this and that, but never being satisfied because it is never enough. Or will you be the driving force that awakens these privileged societies to say: "But we already have so much that we have enough to help others and the purpose of getting what we have is not to get more and more on a merry-go-round that never leads anywhere. The purpose of getting what we have is so we are free to help others and we can use our freedom to give greater freedom to those who are still limited, still oppressed, still unfree."

I hold the Flame of Freedom for the earth. Too many people, men and women alike in those nations that consider themselves to be free, have not grasped, have not locked in to, have not felt in their hearts my Flame of Freedom. If they had felt it, it would not be acceptable to them that so many people around the world are unfree. They would have used their freedom to expand the freedom of others. Therefore, I say into the collective consciousness: "Wake up and experience the Flame of Freedom!

It is already there in your heart. Allow it to burn through the resistance in your identity, mental and emotional bodies, even in your physical cells so you can feel that Flame of Freedom and begin to express it in giving freedom to others, securing freedom for others."

We need a Women's Liberation Movement where the women who are already liberated and have a high degree of freedom do not stop there, but make a real effort to secure the same freedom for their sisters in other nations, in other parts of the world that are not yet free. They are not *yet* free. *Will* they be free? Well, only if you decide that their freedom is important to you, important enough that you will use your freedom to do something for them. This is not to say that all people need to do something physically.

Many of you who are spiritual people can have a greater impact by doing the spiritual work and making the calls but there are many women out there (and again, I speak into the collective consciousness) who have it in your Divine plans to do something physically for other women around the globe. This is why you came into embodiment in these privileged societies where you had the freedom as women, so you could come to that point where you had enough of the outer things that you now were free, you had your freedom of attention and even the physical, economic freedom to do something for others.

Therefore, it is time, starting in this year 2020 going through the next decade, it is time to awaken, it is time to start or rekindle these women's movements that promote solidarity between women around the world and who will have the motto: "No woman is truly free until *every* woman is free."

That, my beloved, was my release, that was my gift, my contribution and I thank you for being the broadcast stations who have broadcast this into the collective consciousness. With this, I seal you in the Flame of Freedom, the joyful aspect of the Flame of Freedom.

NOTE: This dictation was given May 30, 2020.

11 | INVOKING THE FREEDOM OF WOMEN EVERYWHERE (PART 1)

In the name of the I AM THAT I AM, Jesus Christ, I use the authority that I have as a being in embodiment on earth to call upon Saint Germain to reinforce my calls and use my chakras to project the statements in this invocation into the collective consciousness and awaken people to the awareness that will liberate both men and women from all psychological and spiritual thralldom to the fallen beings. Awaken people to the reality that we are spiritual beings and that we can co-create a new future by working with the ascended masters. I especially call for …

[Make your own calls here.]

Part 1

1. Saint Germain, I call forth your judgment upon the fallen beings who have managed to take away the freedom of both men and women.

O Saint Germain, you do inspire,
my vision raised forever higher,

with you I form a figure-eight,
your Golden Age I co-create.

O Saint Germain, what love you bring,
it truly makes all matter sing,
your violet flame does all restore,
with you we are becoming more.

2. Saint Germain, I call forth your judgment upon the fallen beings who took the basic creative forces, the expanding and the contracting forces, and turned them into dualistic polarities, perverting them beyond what they originally were.

O Saint Germain, what Freedom Flame,
released when we recite your name,
acceleration is your gift,
our planet it will surely lift.

O Saint Germain, what love you bring,
it truly makes all matter sing,
your violet flame does all restore,
with you we are becoming more.

3. Saint Germain, I call forth your judgment upon the fallen beings who have taken the drive to create, the drive to expand, and have perverted it by saying that there should be no rules and no restrictions to what you can do with your free will.

O Saint Germain, in love we claim,
our right to bring your violet flame,
from you Above, to us below,
it is an all-transforming flow.

O Saint Germain, what love you bring,
it truly makes all matter sing,
your violet flame does all restore,
with you we are becoming more.

4. Saint Germain, I call forth your judgment upon the fallen beings who have said that if you really have free will, you should be able to do anything you want. There should be no rules, no restrictions, no consequences and no repercussions for anything that the fallen beings do.

O Saint Germain, I love you so,
my aura filled with violet glow,
my chakras filled with violet fire,
I am your cosmic amplifier.

O Saint Germain, what love you bring,
it truly makes all matter sing,
your violet flame does all restore,
with you we are becoming more.

5. Saint Germain, I call forth your judgment upon the fallen beings who refused to transcend their state of consciousness and ascend because they did not want to let go of their power.

O Saint Germain, I am now free,
your violet flame is therapy,
transform all hang-ups in my mind,
as inner peace I surely find.

O Saint Germain, what love you bring,
it truly makes all matter sing,
your violet flame does all restore,
with you we are becoming more.

6. Saint Germain, I call forth your judgment upon the fallen beings who rebelled and refused to let go of their mindset that if they really had free will, they should be allowed to do anything they wanted for as long as they wanted.

O Saint Germain, my body pure,
your violet flame for all is cure,
consume the cause of all disease,
and therefore I am all at ease.

**O Saint Germain, what love you bring,
it truly makes all matter sing,
your violet flame does all restore,
with you we are becoming more.**

7. Saint Germain, I call forth your judgment upon the fallen beings who rebelled against the ascended masters who disturbed their sense that they had all power on their particular planet.

O Saint Germain, I'm karma-free,
the past no longer burdens me,
a brand new opportunity,
I am in Christic unity.

**O Saint Germain, what love you bring,
it truly makes all matter sing,
your violet flame does all restore,
with you we are becoming more.**

8. Saint Germain, I call forth your judgment upon the fallen beings who rebelled against being confronted by the ascended masters and shown that they did not have all power and that there are consequences for what you do.

O Saint Germain, we are now one,
I am for you a violet sun,
as we transform this planet earth,
your Golden Age is given birth.

**O Saint Germain, what love you bring,
it truly makes all matter sing,
your violet flame does all restore,
with you we are becoming more.**

9. Saint Germain, I call forth your judgment upon the fallen beings who refused to transcend themselves and therefore fell into the next sphere that was created.

O Saint Germain, the earth is free,
from burden of duality,
in oneness we bring what is best,
your Golden Age is manifest.

O Saint Germain, what love you bring,
it truly makes all matter sing,
your violet flame does all restore,
with you we are becoming more.

Part 2

1. Saint Germain, I call forth your judgment upon the fallen beings who refused to transcend the consciousness through which they had created these privileged positions for themselves.

O Saint Germain, you do inspire,
my vision raised forever higher,
with you I form a figure-eight,
your Golden Age I co-create.

O Saint Germain, what love you bring,
it truly makes all matter sing,
your violet flame does all restore,
with you we are becoming more.

2. Saint Germain, I call forth your judgment upon the fallen beings who had set themselves up as the leaders who had absolute power and privilege so that billions of beings were just slaves working for the benefit of the elite.

O Saint Germain, what Freedom Flame,
released when we recite your name,
acceleration is your gift,
our planet it will surely lift.

O Saint Germain, what love you bring,
it truly makes all matter sing,
your violet flame does all restore,
with you we are becoming more.

3. Saint Germain, I call forth your judgment upon the fallen beings who have pulled the expanding force of the Father down to the level of a dualistic polarity and think there should be no restrictions, that they should be allowed to do anything they want, and there should be no consequences.

O Saint Germain, in love we claim,
our right to bring your violet flame,
from you Above, to us below,
it is an all-transforming flow.

O Saint Germain, what love you bring,
it truly makes all matter sing,
your violet flame does all restore,
with you we are becoming more.

4. Saint Germain, I call forth your judgment upon the fallen beings who used the Catholic church to deny reincarnation, who refused to incorporate reincarnation in the official Christian doctrines, because of their denial of consequences.

O Saint Germain, I love you so,
my aura filled with violet glow,
my chakras filled with violet fire,
I am your cosmic amplifier.

O Saint Germain, what love you bring,
it truly makes all matter sing,
your violet flame does all restore,
with you we are becoming more.

5. Saint Germain, I call forth your judgment upon the fallen beings who deny that choices they have made in this lifetime, can come back to them in a future lifetime, or who deny that certain things that happened to them in this lifetime are the result of choices they made in a previous lifetime.

O Saint Germain, I am now free,
your violet flame is therapy,
transform all hang-ups in my mind,
as inner peace I surely find.

O Saint Germain, what love you bring,
it truly makes all matter sing,
your violet flame does all restore,
with you we are becoming more.

6. Saint Germain, I call forth your judgment upon the fallen beings who have perverted the expanding force and used it to deny responsibility, so they think that whatever happens in this lifetime was not the result of choices they made in a past life, it was just a result of conditions beyond their control.

O Saint Germain, my body pure,
your violet flame for all is cure,
consume the cause of all disease,
and therefore I am all at ease.

O Saint Germain, what love you bring,
it truly makes all matter sing,
your violet flame does all restore,
with you we are becoming more.

7. Saint Germain, I call forth your judgment upon the fallen beings behind the scientific materialists or communists who deny reincarnation for much the same reason.

O Saint Germain, I'm karma-free,
the past no longer burdens me,
a brand new opportunity,
I am in Christic unity.

O Saint Germain, what love you bring,
it truly makes all matter sing,
your violet flame does all restore,
with you we are becoming more.

8. Saint Germain, I call forth your judgment upon the fallen beings behind the primary philosophers of materialism who refuse to take responsibility beyond this particular lifetime.

O Saint Germain, we are now one,
I am for you a violet sun,
as we transform this planet earth,
your Golden Age is given birth.

O Saint Germain, what love you bring,
it truly makes all matter sing,
your violet flame does all restore,
with you we are becoming more.

9. Saint Germain, I call forth your judgment upon the fallen beings who form a power elite because they believe they have a special authority, a special ability, especially the ability to be leaders, to rule over others.

O Saint Germain, the earth is free,
from burden of duality,
in oneness we bring what is best,
your Golden Age is manifest.

O Saint Germain, what love you bring,
it truly makes all matter sing,
your violet flame does all restore,
with you we are becoming more.

Part 3

1. Saint Germain, I call forth your judgment upon the fallen beings in any society who tend to set themselves up as the elite who has power.

O Saint Germain, you do inspire,
my vision raised forever higher,
with you I form a figure-eight,
your Golden Age I co-create.

**O Saint Germain, what love you bring,
it truly makes all matter sing,
your violet flame does all restore,
with you we are becoming more.**

2. Saint Germain, I call forth your judgment upon the fallen beings who set themselves up as dictators and those in democratic societies who attempt to take on more powers and undermine democracy.

O Saint Germain, what Freedom Flame,
released when we recite your name,
acceleration is your gift,
our planet it will surely lift.

**O Saint Germain, what love you bring,
it truly makes all matter sing,
your violet flame does all restore,
with you we are becoming more.**

3. Saint Germain, I call forth your judgment upon the fallen beings in the business community who attempt to become owners of large businesses where they set themselves up as the monopoly capitalists who attempt to gain a monopoly.

O Saint Germain, in love we claim,
our right to bring your violet flame,
from you Above, to us below,
it is an all-transforming flow.

**O Saint Germain, what love you bring,
it truly makes all matter sing,
your violet flame does all restore,
with you we are becoming more.**

4. Saint Germain, I call forth your judgment upon the fallen beings who become CEOs of businesses and act as if they were the dictator of that business and they have all power.

O Saint Germain, I love you so,
my aura filled with violet glow,
my chakras filled with violet fire,
I am your cosmic amplifier.

O Saint Germain, what love you bring,
it truly makes all matter sing,
your violet flame does all restore,
with you we are becoming more.

5. Saint Germain, I call forth your judgment upon the fallen beings who form an intellectual elite, such as philosophers, people in educational institutions, especially in the universities, who set themselves up in a position where nobody can object, nobody can protest against them.

O Saint Germain, I am now free,
your violet flame is therapy,
transform all hang-ups in my mind,
as inner peace I surely find.

O Saint Germain, what love you bring,
it truly makes all matter sing,
your violet flame does all restore,
with you we are becoming more.

6. Saint Germain, I call forth your judgment upon the fallen beings who define what is true or not true and are promoting a materialist agenda that is holding the educational institutions of the world, especially in the modern democracies, in an iron grip of materialism.

O Saint Germain, my body pure,
your violet flame for all is cure,
consume the cause of all disease,
and therefore I am all at ease.

O Saint Germain, what love you bring,
it truly makes all matter sing,
your violet flame does all restore,
with you we are becoming more.

7. Saint Germain, I call forth your judgment upon the fallen beings who will not allow any kind of research or theories that question the materialist paradigm or the materialist gospel.

O Saint Germain, I'm karma-free,
the past no longer burdens me,
a brand new opportunity,
I am in Christic unity.

O Saint Germain, what love you bring,
it truly makes all matter sing,
your violet flame does all restore,
with you we are becoming more.

8. Saint Germain, I call forth your judgment upon the fallen beings who set themselves up as the leaders of ancient religions such as the Pope who has all power in the Catholic religion, and a small group of clerics in Islam who also have tremendous power.

O Saint Germain, we are now one,
I am for you a violet sun,
as we transform this planet earth,
your Golden Age is given birth.

O Saint Germain, what love you bring,
it truly makes all matter sing,
your violet flame does all restore,
with you we are becoming more.

9. Saint Germain, I call forth your judgment upon the fallen beings who defined the collective beast behind male-dominated or patriarchal societies.

O Saint Germain, the earth is free,
from burden of duality,
in oneness we bring what is best,
your Golden Age is manifest.

O Saint Germain, what love you bring,
it truly makes all matter sing,

**your violet flame does all restore,
with you we are becoming more.**

Part 4

1. Saint Germain, I call forth your judgment upon the fallen beings who have created this dynamic where they have set themselves up as a privileged power elite and they are forcing the majority of men in the society into specific roles that support their privileges and power.

O Saint Germain, you do inspire,
my vision raised forever higher,
with you I form a figure-eight,
your Golden Age I co-create.

**O Saint Germain, what love you bring,
it truly makes all matter sing,
your violet flame does all restore,
with you we are becoming more.**

2. Saint Germain, I call forth your judgment upon the fallen beings who are forcing men to be soldiers, to live a certain lifestyle, such as the peasants in feudal societies or as the workers in industry, where they do all the labor that makes all the money but the capitalists reap all the benefits.

O Saint Germain, what Freedom Flame,
released when we recite your name,
acceleration is your gift,
our planet it will surely lift.

**O Saint Germain, what love you bring,
it truly makes all matter sing,
your violet flame does all restore,
with you we are becoming more.**

3. Saint Germain, I call forth your judgment upon the fallen beings who have forced the majority of men into a situation where they feel a certain dis-empowerment, they do not feel they are masters of their own destiny.

O Saint Germain, in love we claim,
our right to bring your violet flame,
from you Above, to us below,
it is an all-transforming flow.

O Saint Germain, what love you bring,
it truly makes all matter sing,
your violet flame does all restore,
with you we are becoming more.

4. Saint Germain, I call forth your judgment upon the fallen beings who have forced men to feel they have limited choices in life. They might have had dreams when they were young but they could not fulfill them. They had to settle for something less to get money to live their lives and therefore they feel frustrated.

O Saint Germain, I love you so,
my aura filled with violet glow,
my chakras filled with violet fire,
I am your cosmic amplifier.

O Saint Germain, what love you bring,
it truly makes all matter sing,
your violet flame does all restore,
with you we are becoming more.

5. Saint Germain, I call forth your judgment upon the fallen beings who have created the collective beast and the pressure of male sexuality, where men feel this pressure to be sexually active, to find a woman where they can have sex.

O Saint Germain, I am now free,
your violet flame is therapy,
transform all hang-ups in my mind,
as inner peace I surely find.

**O Saint Germain, what love you bring,
it truly makes all matter sing,
your violet flame does all restore,
with you we are becoming more.**

6. Saint Germain, I call forth your judgment upon the fallen beings behind the religious power elite that has pressured men into marrying women, has caused many men to go into a marriage at an early age.

O Saint Germain, my body pure,
your violet flame for all is cure,
consume the cause of all disease,
and therefore I am all at ease.

**O Saint Germain, what love you bring,
it truly makes all matter sing,
your violet flame does all restore,
with you we are becoming more.**

7. Saint Germain, I call forth your judgment upon the fallen beings behind the denial of contraception, such as in the Catholic church.

O Saint Germain, I'm karma-free,
the past no longer burdens me,
a brand new opportunity,
I am in Christic unity.

**O Saint Germain, what love you bring,
it truly makes all matter sing,
your violet flame does all restore,
with you we are becoming more.**

8. Saint Germain, I call forth your judgment upon the fallen beings who have manipulated men into making their wives pregnant at a fairly early age and suddenly this man who had dreams about what he would do in his life is tied down to a woman and children.

O Saint Germain, we are now one,
I am for you a violet sun,

as we transform this planet earth,
your Golden Age is given birth.

O Saint Germain, what love you bring,
it truly makes all matter sing,
your violet flame does all restore,
with you we are becoming more.

9. Saint Germain, I call forth your judgment upon the fallen beings who have pressured men into getting whatever job seems available so they feel disempowered.

O Saint Germain, the earth is free,
from burden of duality,
in oneness we bring what is best,
your Golden Age is manifest.

O Saint Germain, what love you bring,
it truly makes all matter sing,
your violet flame does all restore,
with you we are becoming more.

Sealing

In the name of the I AM THAT I AM, I accept that Archangel Michael, Astrea and Shiva form an impenetrable shield around myself and all constructive people, sealing us from all fear-based energies in all four octaves. I accept that the Light of God is consuming and transforming all fear-based energies that make up the dark forces working against the liberation of women on earth!

12 | INVOKING THE FREEDOM OF WOMEN EVERYWHERE (PART 2)

In the name of the I AM THAT I AM, Jesus Christ, I use the authority that I have as a being in embodiment on earth to call upon Saint Germain to reinforce my calls and use my chakras to project the statements in this invocation into the collective consciousness and awaken people to the awareness that will liberate both men and women from all psychological and spiritual thralldom to the fallen beings. Awaken people to the reality that we are spiritual beings and that we can co-create a new future by working with the ascended masters. I especially call for …

[Make your own calls here.]

Part 1

1. Saint Germain, I call forth your judgment upon the fallen beings who have manipulated men into blaming their wives, thinking it is because they are married that they have to settle for this second-rate job and cannot fulfill their dreams.

O Saint Germain, you do inspire,
my vision raised forever higher,
with you I form a figure-eight,
your Golden Age I co-create.

O Saint Germain, what love you bring,
it truly makes all matter sing,
your violet flame does all restore,
with you we are becoming more.

2. Saint Germain, I call forth your judgment upon the fallen beings who have created this pressure from the collective consciousness that is a perversion of the male expanding force, saying men can have some compensation for their sense of being powerless if they have power over their wives and children, if they are the man in the house.

O Saint Germain, what Freedom Flame,
released when we recite your name,
acceleration is your gift,
our planet it will surely lift.

O Saint Germain, what love you bring,
it truly makes all matter sing,
your violet flame does all restore,
with you we are becoming more.

3. Saint Germain, I call forth your judgment upon the fallen beings who have caused men to accept this male-dominated family structure, causing some men to become abusive towards their wives and children whether physically, emotionally or in other ways.

O Saint Germain, in love we claim,
our right to bring your violet flame,
from you Above, to us below,
it is an all-transforming flow.

O Saint Germain, what love you bring,
it truly makes all matter sing,

**your violet flame does all restore,
with you we are becoming more.**

4. Saint Germain, I call forth your judgment upon the fallen beings who have set up a dynamic that traps men into this role, where they feel disempowered, and it is all because they have to do the work that enables the power elite to stay in their privileged positions, where they have power and they have a comfortable lifestyle and more wealth than they could ever need.

O Saint Germain, I love you so,
my aura filled with violet glow,
my chakras filled with violet fire,
I am your cosmic amplifier.

**O Saint Germain, what love you bring,
it truly makes all matter sing,
your violet flame does all restore,
with you we are becoming more.**

5. Saint Germain, I call forth your judgment upon the fallen beings causing men to feel trapped so they abuse their power towards their women and if the women submit to this, then they are also trapped.

O Saint Germain, I am now free,
your violet flame is therapy,
transform all hang-ups in my mind,
as inner peace I surely find.

**O Saint Germain, what love you bring,
it truly makes all matter sing,
your violet flame does all restore,
with you we are becoming more.**

6. Saint Germain, I call forth your judgment upon and the binding and consuming of these beasts. I call for the consuming of the mindset and the binding of the fallen beings behind it.

O Saint Germain, my body pure,
your violet flame for all is cure,
consume the cause of all disease,
and therefore I am all at ease.

O Saint Germain, what love you bring,
it truly makes all matter sing,
your violet flame does all restore,
with you we are becoming more.

7. Saint Germain, I call forth your judgment upon the fallen beings who have perverted the contracting force by making people become passive, become docile, become unwilling to make decisions and take initiative, being focused on having a comfortable daily life.

O Saint Germain, I'm karma-free,
the past no longer burdens me,
a brand new opportunity,
I am in Christic unity.

O Saint Germain, what love you bring,
it truly makes all matter sing,
your violet flame does all restore,
with you we are becoming more.

8. Saint Germain, I call forth your judgment upon the fallen beings causing people to shut down any ambition, any dreams, being focused on their personal daily situation and wanting to be somewhat comfortable.

O Saint Germain, we are now one,
I am for you a violet sun,
as we transform this planet earth,
your Golden Age is given birth.

O Saint Germain, what love you bring,
it truly makes all matter sing,
your violet flame does all restore,
with you we are becoming more.

9. Saint Germain, I call forth your judgment upon the fallen beings who have created societies that are dominated by the men that have defined a role for women, where women are the ones who should focus on being wives and mothers, raising their children, making the family function, staying at home, thereby being financially dependent on their men.

O Saint Germain, the earth is free,
from burden of duality,
in oneness we bring what is best,
your Golden Age is manifest.

**O Saint Germain, what love you bring,
it truly makes all matter sing,
your violet flame does all restore,
with you we are becoming more.**

Part 2

1. Saint Germain, I call forth your judgment upon the fallen beings who have caused many women to accept that this is their lot in life, this is all they can do.

O Saint Germain, you do inspire,
my vision raised forever higher,
with you I form a figure-eight,
your Golden Age I co-create.

**O Saint Germain, what love you bring,
it truly makes all matter sing,
your violet flame does all restore,
with you we are becoming more.**

2. Saint Germain, I call forth your judgment upon the fallen beings who have used a perversion of the contracting force to make women feel satisfied with current conditions, feeling secure, maybe even comfortable if current conditions are not too bad.

O Saint Germain, what Freedom Flame,
released when we recite your name,
acceleration is your gift,
our planet it will surely lift.

**O Saint Germain, what love you bring,
it truly makes all matter sing,
your violet flame does all restore,
with you we are becoming more.**

3. Saint Germain, I call forth your judgment upon the fallen beings making women stay in those conditions for a long time because they do not want to risk the uncertainty of breaking out of the fold.

O Saint Germain, in love we claim,
our right to bring your violet flame,
from you Above, to us below,
it is an all-transforming flow.

**O Saint Germain, what love you bring,
it truly makes all matter sing,
your violet flame does all restore,
with you we are becoming more.**

4. Saint Germain, I call forth your judgment upon the fallen beings who are manipulating women into staying in a marriage that has no growth, has no transcendence, but it has a certain level of security and comfortability because after all, the husband is bringing home enough money and he is not abusive.

O Saint Germain, I love you so,
my aura filled with violet glow,
my chakras filled with violet fire,
I am your cosmic amplifier.

**O Saint Germain, what love you bring,
it truly makes all matter sing,
your violet flame does all restore,
with you we are becoming more.**

5. Saint Germain, I call forth your judgment upon the fallen beings manipulating women so they only break free of abusive relationships when the abuse becomes so severe that they can no longer handle it.

O Saint Germain, I am now free,
your violet flame is therapy,
transform all hang-ups in my mind,
as inner peace I surely find.

O Saint Germain, what love you bring,
it truly makes all matter sing,
your violet flame does all restore,
with you we are becoming more.

6. Saint Germain, I call forth your judgment upon the fallen beings who are trying to prevent a change at the level of society so that women begin to see this as a perversion of the contracting force and they free themselves from the desire for security and reconnect to the desire to grow.

O Saint Germain, my body pure,
your violet flame for all is cure,
consume the cause of all disease,
and therefore I am all at ease.

O Saint Germain, what love you bring,
it truly makes all matter sing,
your violet flame does all restore,
with you we are becoming more.

7. Saint Germain, I call forth your judgment upon the fallen beings who have used the tendency in the expanding force to want more, and who have perverted this into a dualistic polarity, causing people to want to own something.

O Saint Germain, I'm karma-free,
the past no longer burdens me,
a brand new opportunity,
I am in Christic unity.

O Saint Germain, what love you bring,
it truly makes all matter sing,
your violet flame does all restore,
with you we are becoming more.

8. Saint Germain, I call forth your judgment upon the fallen beings who have created this mindset where people want to own, want to keep it and where they can never have enough.

O Saint Germain, we are now one,
I am for you a violet sun,
as we transform this planet earth,
your Golden Age is given birth.

O Saint Germain, what love you bring,
it truly makes all matter sing,
your violet flame does all restore,
with you we are becoming more.

9. Saint Germain, I call forth your judgment upon the fallen beings behind the mindset that men can never have enough money but want more and more money, because it is not about the experience of *making* the money, it is about the experience of *having* the money.

O Saint Germain, the earth is free,
from burden of duality,
in oneness we bring what is best,
your Golden Age is manifest.

O Saint Germain, what love you bring,
it truly makes all matter sing,
your violet flame does all restore,
with you we are becoming more.

Part 3

1. Saint Germain, I call forth your judgment upon the fallen beings who want to own more and more money, more and more possessions or they want to have more and more power.

O Saint Germain, you do inspire,
my vision raised forever higher,
with you I form a figure-eight,
your Golden Age I co-create.

**O Saint Germain, what love you bring,
it truly makes all matter sing,
your violet flame does all restore,
with you we are becoming more.**

2. Saint Germain, I call forth your judgment upon the fallen beings who have perverted the expanding force by saying you can never have enough, and who have perverted the contracting force by saying you are not allowed to have more, that you are not worthy to have more, that there is a certain station in life and this is your lot.

O Saint Germain, what Freedom Flame,
released when we recite your name,
acceleration is your gift,
our planet it will surely lift.

**O Saint Germain, what love you bring,
it truly makes all matter sing,
your violet flame does all restore,
with you we are becoming more.**

3. Saint Germain, I call forth your judgment upon the fallen beings who have manipulated many women to become trapped in this mindset, being from early childhood programmed to accept that they have very limited options in life.

O Saint Germain, in love we claim,
our right to bring your violet flame,
from you Above, to us below,
it is an all-transforming flow.

O Saint Germain, what love you bring,
it truly makes all matter sing,
your violet flame does all restore,
with you we are becoming more.

4. Saint Germain, I call forth your judgment upon the fallen beings behind the mindset in India where girls are brought up to think they are worthless as human beings, they are even worthless in their own family.

O Saint Germain, I love you so,
my aura filled with violet glow,
my chakras filled with violet fire,
I am your cosmic amplifier.

O Saint Germain, what love you bring,
it truly makes all matter sing,
your violet flame does all restore,
with you we are becoming more.

5. Saint Germain, I call forth your judgment upon the fallen beings who are behind the mindset that causes girls to feel their own parents or brothers do not think they are worth anything. Society does not think they are worth anything. Even the gods do not think they are worth anything.

O Saint Germain, I am now free,
your violet flame is therapy,
transform all hang-ups in my mind,
as inner peace I surely find.

O Saint Germain, what love you bring,
it truly makes all matter sing,
your violet flame does all restore,
with you we are becoming more.

6. Saint Germain, I call forth your judgment upon the fallen beings who have caused women to accept: "It's not for me. I'm not worthy to have it. I can't have it. I'm not allowed to have it. I'm not good enough. I'm not smart enough. I'm not capable enough to have it."

O Saint Germain, my body pure,
your violet flame for all is cure,
consume the cause of all disease,
and therefore I am all at ease.

O Saint Germain, what love you bring,
it truly makes all matter sing,
your violet flame does all restore,
with you we are becoming more.

7. Saint Germain, I call forth your judgment upon the fallen beings seeking to prevent women in the more developed nations from breaking free of this mindset.

O Saint Germain, I'm karma-free,
the past no longer burdens me,
a brand new opportunity,
I am in Christic unity.

O Saint Germain, what love you bring,
it truly makes all matter sing,
your violet flame does all restore,
with you we are becoming more.

8. Saint Germain, I call forth your judgment upon the fallen beings who are seeking to make women stay in the traditional gender roles defined by their society and culture, feeling that a woman cannot have an education, cannot have a good job or a career.

O Saint Germain, we are now one,
I am for you a violet sun,
as we transform this planet earth,
your Golden Age is given birth.

**O Saint Germain, what love you bring,
it truly makes all matter sing,
your violet flame does all restore,
with you we are becoming more.**

9. Saint Germain, I call forth your judgment upon the fallen beings who are seeking to make women stay in the traditional gender roles defined by their society and culture, feeling that a woman cannot have a nice house, a nice car, cannot have affluence.

O Saint Germain, the earth is free,
from burden of duality,
in oneness we bring what is best,
your Golden Age is manifest.

**O Saint Germain, what love you bring,
it truly makes all matter sing,
your violet flame does all restore,
with you we are becoming more.**

Part 4

1. Saint Germain, I call forth your judgment upon the fallen beings who are seeking to make women stay in the traditional gender roles defined by their society and culture, feeling that women cannot be self-sufficient economically, but must depend on their husbands and cannot leave them if they are abusive.

O Saint Germain, you do inspire,
my vision raised forever higher,
with you I form a figure-eight,
your Golden Age I co-create.

**O Saint Germain, what love you bring,
it truly makes all matter sing,
your violet flame does all restore,
with you we are becoming more.**

2. Saint Germain, I call forth your judgment upon the fallen beings who are seeking to get women who break free of limitations to become trapped in another perversion of the expanding force, feeling that they want more and more.

> O Saint Germain, what Freedom Flame,
> released when we recite your name,
> acceleration is your gift,
> our planet it will surely lift.

> **O Saint Germain, what love you bring,**
> **it truly makes all matter sing,**
> **your violet flame does all restore,**
> **with you we are becoming more.**

3. Saint Germain, I call forth your judgment upon the fallen beings who are seeking to make women who free themselves from limitations get caught up in the perversion of the masculine force, wanting more and more and it is never enough.

> O Saint Germain, in love we claim,
> our right to bring your violet flame,
> from you Above, to us below,
> it is an all-transforming flow.

> **O Saint Germain, what love you bring,**
> **it truly makes all matter sing,**
> **your violet flame does all restore,**
> **with you we are becoming more.**

4. Saint Germain, I call forth your judgment upon the fallen beings who are seeking to prevent women from finding a balance of the contracting force so that they do not want more than what makes them comfortable.

> O Saint Germain, I love you so,
> my aura filled with violet glow,
> my chakras filled with violet fire,
> I am your cosmic amplifier.

**O Saint Germain, what love you bring,
it truly makes all matter sing,
your violet flame does all restore,
with you we are becoming more.**

5. Saint Germain, I call forth your judgment upon the fallen beings who are seeking to prevent women from finding some higher purpose for their lives than what has been defined by their culture, especially in the western consumer cultures.

O Saint Germain, I am now free,
your violet flame is therapy,
transform all hang-ups in my mind,
as inner peace I surely find.

**O Saint Germain, what love you bring,
it truly makes all matter sing,
your violet flame does all restore,
with you we are becoming more.**

6. Saint Germain, I call forth your judgment upon the fallen beings who seek to prevent women from finding a purpose in psychological healing, self-development, self-improvement, the self-actualization needs that are at the top of the pyramid of needs.

O Saint Germain, my body pure,
your violet flame for all is cure,
consume the cause of all disease,
and therefore I am all at ease.

**O Saint Germain, what love you bring,
it truly makes all matter sing,
your violet flame does all restore,
with you we are becoming more.**

7. Saint Germain, I call forth your judgment upon the fallen beings who are seeking to prevent women from finding ways of developing themselves, actualizing themselves, be it through mindfulness, yoga, various forms of therapy or discussion groups.

O Saint Germain, I'm karma-free,
the past no longer burdens me,
a brand new opportunity,
I am in Christic unity.

O Saint Germain, what love you bring,
it truly makes all matter sing,
your violet flame does all restore,
with you we are becoming more.

8. Saint Germain, I call forth your judgment upon the fallen beings who are seeking to prevent women from finding universal forms of spiritual teachings, realizing that there is a purpose to life, which is not just to develop yourself to get better than you are right now, but that there is actually a goal.

O Saint Germain, we are now one,
I am for you a violet sun,
as we transform this planet earth,
your Golden Age is given birth.

O Saint Germain, what love you bring,
it truly makes all matter sing,
your violet flame does all restore,
with you we are becoming more.

9. Saint Germain, I call forth your judgment upon the fallen beings who are seeking to prevent women from realizing that there is a higher state of consciousness than what they see around them in the societies that have been dominated by Christianity, which took out the spiritual path, and by materialism, which never had the spiritual path.

O Saint Germain, the earth is free,
from burden of duality,
in oneness we bring what is best,
your Golden Age is manifest.

O Saint Germain, what love you bring,
it truly makes all matter sing,

**your violet flame does all restore,
with you we are becoming more.**

Sealing

In the name of the I AM THAT I AM, I accept that Archangel Michael, Astrea and Shiva form an impenetrable shield around myself and all constructive people, sealing us from all fear-based energies in all four octaves. I accept that the Light of God is consuming and transforming all fear-based energies that make up the dark forces working against the liberation of women on earth!

13 | INVOKING THE FREEDOM OF WOMEN EVERYWHERE (PART 3)

In the name of the I AM THAT I AM, Jesus Christ, I use the authority that I have as a being in embodiment on earth to call upon Saint Germain to reinforce my calls and use my chakras to project the statements in this invocation into the collective consciousness and awaken people to the awareness that will liberate both men and women from all psychological and spiritual thralldom to the fallen beings. Awaken people to the reality that we are spiritual beings and that we can co-create a new future by working with the ascended masters. I especially call for …

[Make your own calls here.]

Part 1

1. Saint Germain, I call forth your judgment upon the fallen beings who are seeking to prevent women from balancing men so that men can be pulled out, or can pull themselves out, of this mindset of: "It's never enough. I need to have more and more."

O Saint Germain, you do inspire,
my vision raised forever higher,
with you I form a figure-eight,
your Golden Age I co-create.

O Saint Germain, what love you bring,
it truly makes all matter sing,
your violet flame does all restore,
with you we are becoming more.

2. Saint Germain, I call forth your judgment upon the fallen beings who are seeking to prevent women from inspiring men to come to the realization: "But how much money do we really need? Isn't it time to look at other things, look at what is really important to us in life, how we experience life, how we experience ourselves?"

O Saint Germain, what Freedom Flame,
released when we recite your name,
acceleration is your gift,
our planet it will surely lift.

O Saint Germain, what love you bring,
it truly makes all matter sing,
your violet flame does all restore,
with you we are becoming more.

3. Saint Germain, I call forth your judgment upon the fallen beings who are seeking to prevent women from inspiring men to become open to this path of self-improvement, mindfulness, improving yourself and even raising your consciousness to a distinctly higher level.

O Saint Germain, in love we claim,
our right to bring your violet flame,
from you Above, to us below,
it is an all-transforming flow.

O Saint Germain, what love you bring,
it truly makes all matter sing,

**your violet flame does all restore,
with you we are becoming more.**

4. Saint Germain, I call forth your judgment upon the fallen beings who are seeking to prevent women from making this transition and realizing we can raise our consciousness and thereby have a greater impact on improving conditions in our nations.

O Saint Germain, I love you so,
my aura filled with violet glow,
my chakras filled with violet fire,
I am your cosmic amplifier.

**O Saint Germain, what love you bring,
it truly makes all matter sing,
your violet flame does all restore,
with you we are becoming more.**

5. Saint Germain, cut people free to discover some higher purpose, some spiritual purpose, that life is not just about living, life is not just about accumulating material possessions or raising children or having a career or having money or achieving these outer materialistic goals.

O Saint Germain, I am now free,
your violet flame is therapy,
transform all hang-ups in my mind,
as inner peace I surely find.

**O Saint Germain, what love you bring,
it truly makes all matter sing,
your violet flame does all restore,
with you we are becoming more.**

6. Saint Germain, I call forth your judgment upon the fallen beings who are seeking to prevent women from waking up and using their free time to pursue other things in life, other than empty entertainment or the eternal quest for more and more that is never enough.

O Saint Germain, my body pure,
your violet flame for all is cure,
consume the cause of all disease,
and therefore I am all at ease.

**O Saint Germain, what love you bring,
it truly makes all matter sing,
your violet flame does all restore,
with you we are becoming more.**

7. Saint Germain, I call forth your judgment upon the fallen beings who are seeking to prevent women from making this switch in this decade of the 2020s so they will pull the men up as well.

O Saint Germain, I'm karma-free,
the past no longer burdens me,
a brand new opportunity,
I am in Christic unity.

**O Saint Germain, what love you bring,
it truly makes all matter sing,
your violet flame does all restore,
with you we are becoming more.**

8. Saint Germain, I call forth your judgment upon the fallen beings who are seeking to prevent women from realizing: "Once we have attained a certain level of material comfortability, we don't need more material goods, we need something else."

O Saint Germain, we are now one,
I am for you a violet sun,
as we transform this planet earth,
your Golden Age is given birth.

**O Saint Germain, what love you bring,
it truly makes all matter sing,
your violet flame does all restore,
with you we are becoming more.**

9. Saint Germain, I call forth your judgment upon the fallen beings who are seeking to prevent women from realizing: "We need some content in our lives, some purpose that is a higher purpose, a more spiritual purpose, a purpose that reaches beyond ourselves, where we develop ourselves and then expand our awareness to what can we do for others. How can we use our level of comfortability, of material wealth, of awareness, of knowledge to help others?"

O Saint Germain, the earth is free,
from burden of duality,
in oneness we bring what is best,
your Golden Age is manifest.

O Saint Germain, what love you bring,
it truly makes all matter sing,
your violet flame does all restore,
with you we are becoming more.

Part 2

1. Saint Germain, I call forth your judgment upon the fallen beings who are seeking to prevent women in the more developed democracies from realizing that they have had far better conditions than the vast majority of women around the planet, and they can use this to help other women.

O Saint Germain, you do inspire,
my vision raised forever higher,
with you I form a figure-eight,
your Golden Age I co-create.

O Saint Germain, what love you bring,
it truly makes all matter sing,
your violet flame does all restore,
with you we are becoming more.

2. Saint Germain, I call forth your judgment upon the fallen beings who are seeking to prevent women from realizing that the essence of motherhood

is the mindset of doing something beyond yourself, of doing something
for others.

> O Saint Germain, what Freedom Flame,
> released when we recite your name,
> acceleration is your gift,
> our planet it will surely lift.

> **O Saint Germain, what love you bring,**
> **it truly makes all matter sing,**
> **your violet flame does all restore,**
> **with you we are becoming more.**

3. Saint Germain, I call forth your judgment upon the fallen beings who
are seeking to prevent women from taking the momentum they have on
nurturing others and transferring it to people who are less fortunate than
themselves, either in their own societies or in the less developed parts of
the world.

> O Saint Germain, in love we claim,
> our right to bring your violet flame,
> from you Above, to us below,
> it is an all-transforming flow.

> **O Saint Germain, what love you bring,**
> **it truly makes all matter sing,**
> **your violet flame does all restore,**
> **with you we are becoming more.**

4. Saint Germain, I call forth your judgment upon the fallen beings who
are seeking to prevent women from creating a new kind of women's movement that promotes solidarity between women, that promotes the idea
that it is necessary for women in the more developed countries, women
who have greater privileges than those in the less developed countries, to
reach out to their sisters in these countries and seek to help them.

> O Saint Germain, I love you so,
> my aura filled with violet glow,

my chakras filled with violet fire,
I am your cosmic amplifier.

O Saint Germain, what love you bring,
it truly makes all matter sing,
your violet flame does all restore,
with you we are becoming more.

5. Saint Germain, I call forth your judgment upon the fallen beings who are seeking to prevent women from receiving the ideas from you of how they can find ways to help other women.

O Saint Germain, I am now free,
your violet flame is therapy,
transform all hang-ups in my mind,
as inner peace I surely find.

O Saint Germain, what love you bring,
it truly makes all matter sing,
your violet flame does all restore,
with you we are becoming more.

6. Saint Germain, I call forth your judgment upon the fallen beings who are seeking to prevent women from seeing how they can use the governments of the more developed democracies to reach out to the governments in the less developed nations and offer them assistance in how to help their own people.

O Saint Germain, my body pure,
your violet flame for all is cure,
consume the cause of all disease,
and therefore I am all at ease.

O Saint Germain, what love you bring,
it truly makes all matter sing,
your violet flame does all restore,
with you we are becoming more.

7. Saint Germain, I call forth your judgment upon the fallen beings who are seeking to prevent women from seeing how they can use the governments of the more developed democracies to put pressure on governments in less developed nations to improve the situation for women.

O Saint Germain, I'm karma-free,
the past no longer burdens me,
a brand new opportunity,
I am in Christic unity.

O Saint Germain, what love you bring,
it truly makes all matter sing,
your violet flame does all restore,
with you we are becoming more.

8. Saint Germain, I call forth your judgment upon the fallen beings who are seeking to prevent women from taking their mother-nurturing momentum and expanding it to go beyond their own children, to look at women and children in the less developed nations.

O Saint Germain, we are now one,
I am for you a violet sun,
as we transform this planet earth,
your Golden Age is given birth.

O Saint Germain, what love you bring,
it truly makes all matter sing,
your violet flame does all restore,
with you we are becoming more.

9. Saint Germain, I call forth your judgment upon the fallen beings who are seeking to prevent women from realizing that it is not acceptable to them that millions of girls at a very young age are exposed to female genital mutilation, female circumcision.

O Saint Germain, the earth is free,
from burden of duality,
in oneness we bring what is best,
your Golden Age is manifest.

**O Saint Germain, what love you bring,
it truly makes all matter sing,
your violet flame does all restore,
with you we are becoming more.**

Part 3

1. Saint Germain, I call forth your judgment upon the fallen beings who are seeking to prevent women from realizing that it is not acceptable to them that girls in India are considered worthless, may be sold as slaves by their families or forced into marriages.

O Saint Germain, you do inspire,
my vision raised forever higher,
with you I form a figure-eight,
your Golden Age I co-create.

**O Saint Germain, what love you bring,
it truly makes all matter sing,
your violet flame does all restore,
with you we are becoming more.**

2. Saint Germain, I call forth your judgment upon the fallen beings who are seeking to prevent women from realizing that it is not acceptable to them that so many Islamic women are forced to live a very isolated life where they have to cover themselves, where they cannot go out, they cannot get a driver's license.

O Saint Germain, what Freedom Flame,
released when we recite your name,
acceleration is your gift,
our planet it will surely lift.

**O Saint Germain, what love you bring,
it truly makes all matter sing,
your violet flame does all restore,
with you we are becoming more.**

3. Saint Germain, I call forth your judgment upon the fallen beings who are seeking to prevent women from realizing that it is not acceptable to them that so many women in other nations do not have the basic freedoms that they have grown up to take for granted.

> O Saint Germain, in love we claim,
> our right to bring your violet flame,
> from you Above, to us below,
> it is an all-transforming flow.

> **O Saint Germain, what love you bring,**
> **it truly makes all matter sing,**
> **your violet flame does all restore,**
> **with you we are becoming more.**

4. Saint Germain, awaken women in the modern democracies to see that they have grown up with an incredible freedom compared to so many women in other parts of the world.

> O Saint Germain, I love you so,
> my aura filled with violet glow,
> my chakras filled with violet fire,
> I am your cosmic amplifier.

> **O Saint Germain, what love you bring,**
> **it truly makes all matter sing,**
> **your violet flame does all restore,**
> **with you we are becoming more.**

5. Saint Germain, awaken women from the tendency to take this freedom for granted, and help them look at how many women around the planet do not have basic freedoms.

> O Saint Germain, I am now free,
> your violet flame is therapy,
> transform all hang-ups in my mind,
> as inner peace I surely find.

**O Saint Germain, what love you bring,
it truly makes all matter sing,
your violet flame does all restore,
with you we are becoming more.**

6. Saint Germain, awaken women to make the switch in their minds and say: "It is not acceptable to me that the majority of women on this planet do not have the freedoms that I have grown up with, and it is not enough for me to focus on my own life, enjoying these freedoms, knowing that so many other women are not free.

O Saint Germain, my body pure,
your violet flame for all is cure,
consume the cause of all disease,
and therefore I am all at ease.

**O Saint Germain, what love you bring,
it truly makes all matter sing,
your violet flame does all restore,
with you we are becoming more.**

7. Saint Germain, awaken women to make the switch in their minds and say: "I *must*, I *will*, because I desire to, and it is in my Divine plan to use my freedom to give freedom to other women, to make sure that other societies recognize the equal value of women, the equal rights of women, and the equal freedom and opportunity of women."

O Saint Germain, I'm karma-free,
the past no longer burdens me,
a brand new opportunity,
I am in Christic unity.

**O Saint Germain, what love you bring,
it truly makes all matter sing,
your violet flame does all restore,
with you we are becoming more.**

8. Saint Germain, awaken women to see that helping others is the highest possible use of the freedoms that we have grown up with in these modern nations that are very privileged.

O Saint Germain, we are now one,
I am for you a violet sun,
as we transform this planet earth,
your Golden Age is given birth.

**O Saint Germain, what love you bring,
it truly makes all matter sing,
your violet flame does all restore,
with you we are becoming more.**

9. Saint Germain, awaken women to say: "We will not allow the men in these privileged nations to continue to be trapped in this mindset that it's never enough and being only focused on themselves, gaining more and more of this and that, but never being satisfied because it is never enough.

O Saint Germain, the earth is free,
from burden of duality,
in oneness we bring what is best,
your Golden Age is manifest.

**O Saint Germain, what love you bring,
it truly makes all matter sing,
your violet flame does all restore,
with you we are becoming more.**

Part 4

1. Saint Germain, awaken women to say: "But we already have so much that we have enough to help others, and the purpose of getting what we have is not to get more and more on a merry-go-round that never leads anywhere. The purpose is so we are free to help others and we can use our freedom to give greater freedom to those who are still limited, still oppressed, still unfree."

O Saint Germain, you do inspire,
my vision raised forever higher,
with you I form a figure-eight,
your Golden Age I co-create.

O Saint Germain, what love you bring,
it truly makes all matter sing,
your violet flame does all restore,
with you we are becoming more.

2. Saint Germain, awaken women to grasp, to lock in to, to feel in their hearts your Flame of Freedom, so it is no longer acceptable to them that so many people around the world are unfree.

O Saint Germain, what Freedom Flame,
released when we recite your name,
acceleration is your gift,
our planet it will surely lift.

O Saint Germain, what love you bring,
it truly makes all matter sing,
your violet flame does all restore,
with you we are becoming more.

3. Saint Germain, awaken women to use their freedom to expand the freedom of others.

O Saint Germain, in love we claim,
our right to bring your violet flame,
from you Above, to us below,
it is an all-transforming flow.

O Saint Germain, what love you bring,
it truly makes all matter sing,
your violet flame does all restore,
with you we are becoming more.

4. Saint Germain, in oneness with you, I say into the collective consciousness: "Wake up and experience the Flame of Freedom! It is already there

in your heart. Allow it to burn through the resistance in your identity, mental and emotional bodies, even in your physical cells so you can feel that Flame of Freedom and begin to express it in giving freedom to others, securing freedom for others."

O Saint Germain, I love you so,
my aura filled with violet glow,
my chakras filled with violet fire,
I am your cosmic amplifier.

O Saint Germain, what love you bring,
it truly makes all matter sing,
your violet flame does all restore,
with you we are becoming more.

5. Saint Germain, awaken women to see that we need a Women's Liberation Movement, where the women who are already liberated and have a high degree of freedom do not stop there, but make a real effort to secure the same freedom for their sisters in other nations, in other parts of the world that are not yet free.

O Saint Germain, I am now free,
your violet flame is therapy,
transform all hang-ups in my mind,
as inner peace I surely find.

O Saint Germain, what love you bring,
it truly makes all matter sing,
your violet flame does all restore,
with you we are becoming more.

6. Saint Germain, awaken women to see that these women are not *yet* free, and they will be free only if we decide that their freedom is important to us, important enough that we will use our freedom to do something for them.

O Saint Germain, my body pure,
your violet flame for all is cure,
consume the cause of all disease,
and therefore I am all at ease.

O Saint Germain, what love you bring,
it truly makes all matter sing,
your violet flame does all restore,
with you we are becoming more.

7. Saint Germain, awaken women who have it in their Divine plans to do something physically for other women around the globe. Help them see that this is why they came into embodiment in these privileged societies where they had freedom as women.

O Saint Germain, I'm karma-free,
the past no longer burdens me,
a brand new opportunity,
I am in Christic unity.

O Saint Germain, what love you bring,
it truly makes all matter sing,
your violet flame does all restore,
with you we are becoming more.

8. Saint Germain, awaken women to see that they are at the point where they have enough of the outer things, they have freedom of attention and even the physical economic freedom to do something for others.

O Saint Germain, we are now one,
I am for you a violet sun,
as we transform this planet earth,
your Golden Age is given birth.

O Saint Germain, what love you bring,
it truly makes all matter sing,
your violet flame does all restore,
with you we are becoming more.

9. Saint Germain, awaken women to see that it is time to start or rekindle these women's movements that promote solidarity between women around the world and who will have the motto: "No woman is truly free until *every* woman is free."

O Saint Germain, the earth is free,
from burden of duality,
in oneness we bring what is best,
your Golden Age is manifest.

**O Saint Germain, what love you bring,
it truly makes all matter sing,
your violet flame does all restore,
with you we are becoming more.**

Sealing

In the name of the I AM THAT I AM, I accept that Archangel Michael, Astrea and Shiva form an impenetrable shield around myself and all constructive people, sealing us from all fear-based energies in all four octaves. I accept that the Light of God is consuming and transforming all fear-based energies that make up the dark forces working against the liberation of women on earth!

14 | WOMEN ARE NOT TO BLAME FOR THE FALL OF MAN

I am the Ascended Master Archangel Michael and I come to offer my assistance to all women on this planet who desire to be liberated and who are willing to do something to become liberated. Therefore, they are willing to break the spell that has been cast upon women by the fallen beings, by men, by the collective consciousness, by societies, by institutions, by religions, political parties, whatever you have.

You may think of me as a male master, but at the level of an archangel the normal concepts of male and female that you have on earth do not apply. I am completely beyond all of this. I am a universal being and if it may help you to think of me as having certain qualities, then fine. For many people, it actually does not help you to think of me as having male qualities. It would be more constructive to see me as a universal being. I am beyond anything on earth, which is precisely why I can serve to bind the fallen beings on earth who are otherwise masters of drawing people into some relative dualistic reaction. I am beyond all relativity, all duality and that is why the fallen beings cannot draw me into any kind of reaction to them, which is precisely why I can serve to bind them anytime there is a call for it from earth.

Naturally, I am not in embodiment. Therefore, I cannot just go in and do whatever I desire to do on planet earth, even though I could very,

very quickly, in fact in the blink of an eye, remove all fallen beings from earth. This is the power I have as an archangel of the First Ray. There is no power on earth that can stand against it precisely because any power on earth is dualistic and my power is not dualistic. Therefore, my power is the power of the entire universe because I am one with the greater whole, with the oneness of the universe, with the one Creator. That oneness can of course not be moved by any force that is divided. There is nothing that is divided that could possibly move oneness.

Divisions can move within oneness in an unascended sphere because that is allowed for the outplaying of free will. Divisions can move within oneness, but cannot move oneness. They can move within oneness when a sphere is set apart as an unascended sphere where free will is allowed to outplay itself, in the sense that beings can use their free will to ignore that they are part of the whole and start acting as separate beings. This is precisely what the fallen beings have done. This is what they have perpetrated on earth so that you have created this most basic illusion on earth, which is that men and women are separate beings.

Men and women are not separate beings

You have this very, very fundamental division that men and women are different. Out of this fundamental division springs all of the persecution, suppression of women. I know very well that when you are in embodiment on a planet like earth, it is difficult to look beyond the fact that your physical bodies are different. It is difficult to look beyond that, but you need to recognize that the fallen beings have taken the differences of the physical body and projected those differences upon you, as souls, as spiritual beings. They have projected that there is a difference between men and women. Of course, they have used religions to project, as we have explained, the idea that men are created differently by God, or even what you see in Genesis where God first created Adam and then, almost as an afterthought, he created Eve. Oh, yeah, Adam feels alone. We need to give him someone who can be there with him, and by the way, be his servant and fulfill his needs. So, we create woman as well.

What did we explain to you? All of creation is based on two forces: the expanding, the contracting. You cannot create anything without both of them. When you are not in duality, they are not separated. There is not one that comes first and one that comes later. The expanding force did not come before the contracting, they were created at the same time. They are created in a polarity. It is not a dualistic polarity. It is a creative polarity, but nevertheless, they are created at the same time.

You could not physically create man first and then create woman. It cannot be done. It is simply a product of the lower state of consciousness that people had at the time when Genesis was given to the people in the Middle East. This of course raises the question again: Who gave Genesis to the Jews or the forefathers of what you call the Jews today? Well, it was not the Almighty God who created the heaven and the earth. It was not the Creator itself. It was the fallen beings who gave Genesis and who gave certain statements in Genesis precisely to, right there at the very beginning, set men and women apart in a fundamental way that allowed them to then elevate men as the primary creation and women to a secondary, servant role.

Then, of course comes what is also built into Genesis and the story of the Garden of Eden where it was Eve who was tempted to eat that forbidden fruit. Well, my beloved, this is again a deliberate, malicious, aggressive lie of the fallen beings in order to create this fundamental, irreconcilable divide between men and women. Truly, there is no reality to it whatsoever. We have before said that there can be a certain symbolic value. We have in previous dispensations said for example that you can set up various polarities where you can say that the I AM Presence is the masculine aspect of your being and the soul is the feminine, and it was the soul that was tempted to go into duality, which is the forbidden fruit. It is not forbidden because it is an aspect of free will, but again this is how the fallen beings decided to portray it because it fits in with their overall agenda. It creates tremendous confusion.

Resistance from the male-dominated religions

How many Christians, Jews, Muslims have read the story of Genesis and been confused? Why did God put the fruit in the garden if he did not want them to eat it? Why put a fruit there and then say it is forbidden? Why did he say that if you eat of the fruit, you will surely die, but the serpent said: "You will not *surely* die" and they ate the fruit and they did not die? So who was right? Was God wrong and the serpent was right? Well, of course that is exactly what the fallen beings want you to believe—that they know better than God. That is what they have made many people believe. They have made many people act upon this even if they do not consciously believe it. They think the ideas that the fallen beings have put out on earth are more true than the ideas that come from the spiritual realm, from the ascended masters. You will see, when you look at planet earth today, how there is an incredible resistance to the ideas we are giving you at this conference and of course many of the other teachings we have given you over the years. There is an incredible resistance to this.

You take the three monotheistic religions who are all based on the Torah or the Old Testament, who all in some form recognize or acknowledge the story of Genesis as the creation story, and you will see that they are all discriminating against and putting down women. They are doing it precisely because they are still upholding this very old account of creation, even though the consciousness has moved on so far from what it was when Genesis was released. There are of course, as with everything else in the world, various estimates of when Genesis was released, but I can tell you that it actually goes far back beyond recorded history. You see that even if you take the normal time frame, and say that a few thousand years ago there was this tribe in the Middle East who received this teaching, look at how much society has moved on in those few thousand years. Look at the incredible changes that have happened in people's knowledge, in technology, in the development of society, the emergence of democracies and all of this. What sense does it make that there are so many billions of people on earth who are holding on to this ancient account and think that this must have been released by this superior God, and therefore it must be an infallible revelation that should stand for all time? It makes no sense whatsoever. Of course, many people, men and women alike, have started to realize this, which is why they are leaving these monotheistic religions behind. They realize that they have virtually nothing of value to say about the situation they face in a modern world, in a modern society.

My beloved, cycles change. Everything on earth evolves in cycles. This is something that you can even observe. You do not even need to look at the precession of the equinoxes, but you can just look at earth. There are seasons, but beyond the seasons of the year, there are cycles, there are cycles in society, there are cycles in the collective consciousness where people have been under a certain illusion, and after a time they begin to free themselves from it, and all of a sudden there is progress. There are new inventions, new ideas that are released.

Resisting or flowing with the cycles

Would it not be possible for people to come to this recognition that if we truly want what is best for the people in our society, we need to flow with the cycles? How are we going to flow with the cycles if we hold on to ideas that were released in a previous cycle? How can we flow with the cycles of time, the *inevitable* cycles of time, if we are holding on to an idea about men and women that is thousands of years old? It was released in a previous cycle where the collective consciousness was lower, the planet was very different, the energy of the planet was different, society was so different? How can we flow with the cycles, the inevitable, unchangeable, unconquerable, unstoppable cycles that move this planet in ways that no force on this planet, including the fallen beings, can resist? You know very well that there is the cycles of the different ages based on the precession of the equinoxes. Well, the equinoxes are star constellations that are far, far, far beyond earth. If you think about this logically, you realize that the earth cannot affect these remote star constellations. The earth has no way, there is no force on earth, whether it be the force of gravity or anything else, that can affect these remote stars. Therefore, there is no force on earth that can withstand or stop these cycles. The cycles are happening. Of course, given that people have free will, you can attempt to resist the cycles. You will have limited success, but you can have *some* success, as you clearly see that certain religions have been able to hold back changes in society for hundreds, if not thousands, of years.

You see that even though religions may hold back changes in some areas of human activity and society, they cannot completely hold back change. You see for example how the Christian religion, the Muslim religion, have held back certain changes, such as in the relationship between men and women, but they have not been able to hold back technological changes. The technology is still changing how people look at and believe in these religions and their doctrines and their ancient scriptures. You will see that even though for example Muslim societies are attempting to hold back certain changes in their societies, they cannot really hold back the technology.

It is one of these things that you can see also in the last years of the Soviet Union where the leaders of the Soviet Union were facing this dilemma: Would they deny their scientists to have computer technology in order to maintain control over their scientists? If they denied their scientist access to computers, and access to communicating with other scientists outside the Soviet Union, then they would inevitably fall behind the technological development of the rest of the world. It is exactly the same that the Muslim nations are facing. If they refuse their citizens to have access to communications technologies, such as the internet, then they will fall behind technologically, economically. Eventually this will then cause the population to rise up and say: "Why should we accept that we are living in poverty because we have these restrictive religious doctrines and laws that are preventing the progress of society?" You see, there is a limit to how far they can hold back, how much they can hold back, change.

Archangel Michael defends growth, not faith

Now, my role has been traditionally seen as the defender of faith. This is largely a misunderstanding. I am not really here to defend your faith, for faith is by most religious people, certainly Muslims and Christians, seen as something static. You have faith in the scriptures, the infallibility of the scriptures, you have faith in the promise of the Christian religion that you will be saved after this lifetime, even if you do not raise your consciousness. My role is not to defend anything static. My role is actually to defend your growth, those who are willing to grow, those who are willing to transcend themselves.

Therefore, my offer for this topic of the liberation of women is that I will offer to sponsor the development of an invocation that you can then give, women and men alike, where I will primarily bind the forces, the dark forces, the demons, entities, the collective entities that have been created that are holding back the liberation of women and serving to hold on to this suppression of women that is based on these very old ideas. I offer my considerable momentum to shatter these forces, to shatter the hold they have on the psychology of both men and women, the psychology of entire societies, the collective consciousness, this hypnotic state, this cloud that people are under.

Now, if you go to the Middle Ages, you will see (if you could really get into the minds of people back then) that they were hypnotized by Catholic doctrines and the Catholic claim to infallibility. They were literally hypnotized, their minds were clouded over by these collective entities that prevented people from seeing it. After the first scientists started to challenge the infallibility of papal doctrine, very very gradually some people started to break free. One person here, one person there, a few people there. What happens is that, like described by Paul on the road to Damascus, the scales fall from their eyes and suddenly they see how limited their previous view was. Of course, many people in the modern democracies have had this experience, not necessarily in this life but certainly in past lives, of waking up from the hypnotic state of medieval Christianity, whether Protestant or Catholic. Right now, you look at the Islamic world and you see that many, many people, their minds are completely clouded over by this hypnotic state created by fundamentalist Islam, by the beast behind it, by the false god behind it, this false god of Allah that they have created. This is a man-made god, just as the false god of Jehovah is a man-made god, originally created by the fallen beings, but reinforced by the millions of people who have worshiped this god.

You see that it is possible to make the calls for the shattering of this hypnotic state and I will then do what I can do according to the law, which is a complex equation. I cannot, even if you make the call, go in and use my full force to shatter these forces because there is always the outplaying of free will. You understand the equation here. When you make the call for a certain force to be bound or shattered I can do it to the extent that I give some people the opportunity to set themselves free, to awaken themselves from the hypnotic state. There is always the element of free will. They have to *choose* to make use of that opportunity. I can do what gives them an opportunity to free themselves from this weight, this cloud that they are under, but they have to choose to embrace it, to change their attitude, to change their outlook. If they do not do that, they actually go back into the cloud. They can be free of the cloud for a moment. Sometimes people get scared of this freedom, and they choose to go right back into the familiar, and in that case I can do no more for these people. They must be allowed to live out in the School of Hard Knocks whatever they need to experience until they either change, go out of embodiment, or whatever the case may be.

You see here that your calls can have an impact, but it is always subject to the free will of the people. Therefore, you cannot expect that you can make these calls and suddenly people and women everywhere will wake up and these forces will be completely removed, and the earth will change in the blink of an eye. Free will is a very complex equation, but I can assure you that by you making the calls, it will be much easier for people to choose to move on so that I can actually defend their growth as a progressive process, not something static that makes them think they should hold on to ideas that anybody who is not hypnotized can see are completely outdated and irrelevant to the situation of modern people.

This is my offer and surely I will work with the messenger to develop this invocation for the book. Therefore, you can use it as you see fit as part of the other invocations that will be made, and this will give you a very powerful tool for liberating women. Not only that the women will be liberated, but also the men will be liberated from their mental prison of thinking they have to have a certain male role that they have to fulfill for their entire lives. This actually, when they are honest with themselves (which they cannot do as long as they are hypnotized), but when they are honest, they can see how it limits them as well. Thus with this, I seal you in the power of the First Ray that I embody for this planet.

NOTE: This dictation was given May 31, 2020.

15 | INVOKING FREEDOM FROM FALSE GODS

In the name of the I AM THAT I AM, Jesus Christ, I use the authority that I have as a being in embodiment on earth to call upon Archangel Michael to reinforce my calls and use my chakras to project the statements in this invocation into the collective consciousness and awaken people to the awareness that will liberate both men and women from all psychological and spiritual thralldom to the fallen beings. Awaken people to the reality that we are spiritual beings and that we can co-create a new future by working with the ascended masters. I especially call for …

[Make your own calls here.]

Part 1

1. Archangel Michael, bind the fallen beings who have cast a spell upon women by using men, the collective consciousness, societies, institutions, religions and political parties.

> Archangel Michael, light so blue,
> my heart has room for only you.

My mind is one, no longer two,
your love for me is ever true.

Archangel Michael, you are here,
consuming now all doubt and fear.
Your Presence is forever near,
you are to me so very dear.

2. Archangel Michael, bind the fallen beings who are masters of drawing people into some relative dualistic reaction.

Archangel Michael, I will be,
all one with your reality.
No fear can hold me as I see,
this world no power has o'er me.

Archangel Michael, you are here,
consuming now all doubt and fear.
Your Presence is forever near,
you are to me so very dear.

3. Archangel Michael, bind the fallen beings who have used their free will to ignore that they are part of the whole and started acting as separate beings, thereby creating this most basic illusion on earth, which is that men and women are separate beings.

Archangel Michael, hold me tight,
shatter now the darkest night.
Clear my chakras with your light,
restore to me my inner sight.

Archangel Michael, you are here,
consuming now all doubt and fear.
Your Presence is forever near,
you are to me so very dear.

4. Archangel Michael, bind the fallen beings behind the fundamental division that men and women are different, which gives rise to all of the persecution and suppression of women.

Archangel Michael, now I stand,
with you the light I do command.
My heart I ever will expand,
till highest truth I understand.

Archangel Michael, you are here,
consuming now all doubt and fear.
Your Presence is forever near,
you are to me so very dear.

5. Archangel Michael, bind the fallen beings who have taken the differences of the physical body and projected those differences upon us, as souls, as spiritual beings. They have projected that there is a difference between men and women.

Archangel Michael, in my heart,
from me you never will depart.
Of hierarchy I am a part,
I now accept a fresh new start.

Archangel Michael, you are here,
consuming now all doubt and fear.
Your Presence is forever near,
you are to me so very dear.

6. Archangel Michael, bind the fallen beings who have used religions to project the idea that men are created differently by God, or even that God first created Adam and then, almost as an afterthought, created Eve.

Archangel Michael, sword of blue,
all darkness you are cutting through.
My Christhood I do now pursue,
discernment shows me what is true.

Archangel Michael, you are here,
consuming now all doubt and fear.
Your Presence is forever near,
you are to me so very dear.

7. Archangel Michael, bind the fallen beings who gave Genesis to the Jews and who gave certain statements in Genesis precisely to set men and women apart in a fundamental way that allowed them to then elevate men as the primary creation and women to a secondary, servant role.

Archangel Michael, in your wings,
I now let go of lesser things.
God's homing call in my heart rings,
my heart with yours forever sings.

**Archangel Michael, you are here,
consuming now all doubt and fear.
Your Presence is forever near,
you are to me so very dear.**

8. Archangel Michael, bind the fallen beings who built into Genesis and the story of the Garden of Eden that it was Eve who was tempted to eat the forbidden fruit.

Archangel Michael, take me home,
in higher spheres I want to roam.
I am reborn from cosmic foam,
my life is now a sacred poem.

**Archangel Michael, you are here,
consuming now all doubt and fear.
Your Presence is forever near,
you are to me so very dear.**

9. Archangel Michael, bind the fallen beings who created this deliberate, malicious, aggressive lie in order to create this fundamental, irreconcilable divide between men and women.

Archangel Michael, light you are,
shining like the bluest star.
You are a cosmic avatar,
with you I will go very far.

**Archangel Michael, you are here,
consuming now all doubt and fear.
Your Presence is forever near,
you are to me so very dear.**

Part 2

1. Archangel Michael, bind the fallen beings who created the lie of the forbidden fruit, which fits in with their overall agenda and creates tremendous confusion.

Archangel Michael, light so blue,
my heart has room for only you.
My mind is one, no longer two,
your love for me is ever true.

**Archangel Michael, you are here,
consuming now all doubt and fear.
Your Presence is forever near,
you are to me so very dear.**

2. Archangel Michael, bind the fallen beings behind the story that makes it seem like God lied to Adam and Eve but the serpent was right that they would not die by eating the fruit.

Archangel Michael, I will be,
all one with your reality.
No fear can hold me as I see,
this world no power has o'er me.

**Archangel Michael, you are here,
consuming now all doubt and fear.
Your Presence is forever near,
you are to me so very dear.**

3. Archangel Michael, bind the fallen beings who want people to believe that they know better than God, that the ideas which the fallen beings have

put out on earth are more true than the ideas that come from the spiritual realm, from the ascended masters.

Archangel Michael, hold me tight,
shatter now the darkest night.
Clear my chakras with your light,
restore to me my inner sight.

**Archangel Michael, you are here,
consuming now all doubt and fear.
Your Presence is forever near,
you are to me so very dear.**

4. Archangel Michael, bind the fallen beings who are behind the resistance to ascended master ideas and teachings.

Archangel Michael, now I stand,
with you the light I do command.
My heart I ever will expand,
till highest truth I understand.

**Archangel Michael, you are here,
consuming now all doubt and fear.
Your Presence is forever near,
you are to me so very dear.**

5. Archangel Michael, bind the fallen beings behind the three monotheistic religions who are all based on the Old Testament and who are all discriminating against and putting down women.

Archangel Michael, in my heart,
from me you never will depart.
Of hierarchy I am a part,
I now accept a fresh new start.

**Archangel Michael, you are here,
consuming now all doubt and fear.
Your Presence is forever near,
you are to me so very dear.**

6. Archangel Michael, bind the fallen beings who are causing people to uphold this very old account of creation, even though the consciousness has moved on so far from what it was when Genesis was released.

> Archangel Michael, sword of blue,
> all darkness you are cutting through.
> My Christhood I do now pursue,
> discernment shows me what is true.

> **Archangel Michael, you are here,**
> **consuming now all doubt and fear.**
> **Your Presence is forever near,**
> **you are to me so very dear.**

7. Archangel Michael, bind the fallen beings who have manipulated billions of people into holding on to this ancient account and think that this must have been released by this superior God, and therefore it must be an infallible revelation that should stand for all time.

> Archangel Michael, in your wings,
> I now let go of lesser things.
> God's homing call in my heart rings,
> my heart with yours forever sings.

> **Archangel Michael, you are here,**
> **consuming now all doubt and fear.**
> **Your Presence is forever near,**
> **you are to me so very dear.**

8. Archangel Michael, bind the fallen beings who are preventing people from recognizing that if we truly want what is best for the people in our society, we need to flow with the cycles we can observe on earth.

> Archangel Michael, take me home,
> in higher spheres I want to roam.
> I am reborn from cosmic foam,
> my life is now a sacred poem.

Archangel Michael, you are here,
consuming now all doubt and fear.
Your Presence is forever near,
you are to me so very dear.

9. Archangel Michael, bind the fallen beings who are manipulating people into this blindness where they cannot see that in order to flow with the inevitable cycles of time, we must let go of the idea about men and women that is thousands of years old, and was released in a previous cycle where the collective consciousness was lower, the planet was very different.

Archangel Michael, light you are,
shining like the bluest star.
You are a cosmic avatar,
with you I will go very far.

Archangel Michael, you are here,
consuming now all doubt and fear.
Your Presence is forever near,
you are to me so very dear.

Part 3

1. Archangel Michael, bind the fallen beings who have manipulated people into resisting the cosmic cycles through religions that have been able to hold back changes in society for hundreds or thousands of years.

Archangel Michael, light so blue,
my heart has room for only you.
My mind is one, no longer two,
your love for me is ever true.

Archangel Michael, you are here,
consuming now all doubt and fear.
Your Presence is forever near,
you are to me so very dear.

2. Archangel Michael, bind the fallen beings who have used the Christian and Muslim religions to hold back changes in the relationship between men and women.

Archangel Michael, I will be,
all one with your reality.
No fear can hold me as I see,
this world no power has o'er me.

Archangel Michael, you are here,
consuming now all doubt and fear.
Your Presence is forever near,
you are to me so very dear.

3. Archangel Michael, bind the fallen beings who have manipulated Muslims and Christians into seeing faith as something static.

Archangel Michael, hold me tight,
shatter now the darkest night.
Clear my chakras with your light,
restore to me my inner sight.

Archangel Michael, you are here,
consuming now all doubt and fear.
Your Presence is forever near,
you are to me so very dear.

4. Archangel Michael, bind the fallen beings who have manipulated people into having faith in the scriptures, the infallibility of the scriptures, having faith in the promise of the Christian religion that they will be saved after this lifetime, even if they do not raise their consciousness.

Archangel Michael, now I stand,
with you the light I do command.
My heart I ever will expand,
till highest truth I understand.

Archangel Michael, you are here,
consuming now all doubt and fear.

Your Presence is forever near,
you are to me so very dear.

5. Archangel Michael, bind the dark forces, the demons and the collective entities that are holding back the liberation of women and causing people to hold on to the suppression of women based on these very old ideas.

Archangel Michael, in my heart,
from me you never will depart.
Of hierarchy I am a part,
I now accept a fresh new start.

Archangel Michael, you are here,
consuming now all doubt and fear.
Your Presence is forever near,
you are to me so very dear.

6. Archangel Michael, shatter these forces, shatter the hold they have on the psychology of both men and women, the psychology of entire societies, the collective consciousness. Shatter this hypnotic state, this cloud that people are under.

Archangel Michael, sword of blue,
all darkness you are cutting through.
My Christhood I do now pursue,
discernment shows me what is true.

Archangel Michael, you are here,
consuming now all doubt and fear.
Your Presence is forever near,
you are to me so very dear.

7. Archangel Michael, bind the fallen beings who have caused people to be hypnotized by Catholic doctrines and the Catholic claim to infallibility.

Archangel Michael, in your wings,
I now let go of lesser things.
God's homing call in my heart rings,
my heart with yours forever sings.

**Archangel Michael, you are here,
consuming now all doubt and fear.
Your Presence is forever near,
you are to me so very dear.**

8. Archangel Michael, bind the collective entities that have hypnotized peoples' minds, causing them to be clouded over so they cannot see that these doctrines are not infallible.

Archangel Michael, take me home,
in higher spheres I want to roam.
I am reborn from cosmic foam,
my life is now a sacred poem.

**Archangel Michael, you are here,
consuming now all doubt and fear.
Your Presence is forever near,
you are to me so very dear.**

9. Archangel Michael, cut people free from this spell of infallibility so the scales can fall from their eyes and they suddenly see how limited their previous view was.

Archangel Michael, light you are,
shining like the bluest star.
You are a cosmic avatar,
with you I will go very far.

**Archangel Michael, you are here,
consuming now all doubt and fear.
Your Presence is forever near,
you are to me so very dear.**

Part 4

1. Archangel Michael, cut people free from the hypnotic state of Christianity, whether Protestant or Catholic.

Archangel Michael, light so blue,
my heart has room for only you.
My mind is one, no longer two,
your love for me is ever true.

**Archangel Michael, you are here,
consuming now all doubt and fear.
Your Presence is forever near,
you are to me so very dear.**

2. Archangel Michael, cut free people in the Islamic world, cut free the people whose minds are clouded over by this hypnotic state created by fundamentalist Islam.

Archangel Michael, I will be,
all one with your reality.
No fear can hold me as I see,
this world no power has o'er me.

**Archangel Michael, you are here,
consuming now all doubt and fear.
Your Presence is forever near,
you are to me so very dear.**

3. Archangel Michael, bind the beast behind fundamentalist Islam, bind the false god behind it, this false god of Allah that they have created.

Archangel Michael, hold me tight,
shatter now the darkest night.
Clear my chakras with your light,
restore to me my inner sight.

**Archangel Michael, you are here,
consuming now all doubt and fear.
Your Presence is forever near,
you are to me so very dear.**

4. Archangel Michael, bind the fallen beings who originally created this man-made gods of Allah that has been reinforced by the millions of people who have worshiped this god.

> Archangel Michael, now I stand,
> with you the light I do command.
> My heart I ever will expand,
> till highest truth I understand.

> **Archangel Michael, you are here,**
> **consuming now all doubt and fear.**
> **Your Presence is forever near,**
> **you are to me so very dear.**

5. Archangel Michael, bind the fallen beings who originally created this man-made god of Jehovah, that has been reinforced by the millions of people who have worshiped this god.

> Archangel Michael, in my heart,
> from me you never will depart.
> Of hierarchy I am a part,
> I now accept a fresh new start.

> **Archangel Michael, you are here,**
> **consuming now all doubt and fear.**
> **Your Presence is forever near,**
> **you are to me so very dear.**

6. Archangel Michael, bind the false god Jehovah and shatter this hypnotic state in order to give people the opportunity to set themselves free, to awaken themselves from the hypnotic state.

> Archangel Michael, sword of blue,
> all darkness you are cutting through.
> My Christhood I do now pursue,
> discernment shows me what is true.

> **Archangel Michael, you are here,**
> **consuming now all doubt and fear.**

**Your Presence is forever near,
you are to me so very dear.**

7. Archangel Michael, cut people free so they have the opportunity to free themselves from this weight, this cloud that they are under, so they can change their attitude and outlook.

Archangel Michael, in your wings,
I now let go of lesser things.
God's homing call in my heart rings,
my heart with yours forever sings.

**Archangel Michael, you are here,
consuming now all doubt and fear.
Your Presence is forever near,
you are to me so very dear.**

8. Archangel Michael, cut people free to move on so that you can defend their growth as a progressive process, not something static that makes them think they should hold on to ideas that anybody who is not hypnotized can see are completely outdated and irrelevant to the situation of modern people.

Archangel Michael, take me home,
in higher spheres I want to roam.
I am reborn from cosmic foam,
my life is now a sacred poem.

**Archangel Michael, you are here,
consuming now all doubt and fear.
Your Presence is forever near,
you are to me so very dear.**

9. Archangel Michael, cut free both women and men from their mental prison of thinking they have to have a certain role that they have to fulfill for their entire lives and that there is no alternative.

Archangel Michael, light you are,
shining like the bluest star.

You are a cosmic avatar,
with you I will go very far.

**Archangel Michael, you are here,
consuming now all doubt and fear.
Your Presence is forever near,
you are to me so very dear.**

Part 5

1. Archangel Michael, bind and consume the collective entities, the beasts in the collective consciousness of Africa, the Middle East and India that overpower the minds of most men and women, causing them to submit to their roles.

Archangel Michael, light so blue,
my heart has room for only you.
My mind is one, no longer two,
your love for me is ever true.

**Archangel Michael, you are here,
consuming now all doubt and fear.
Your Presence is forever near,
you are to me so very dear.**

2. Archangel Michael, bind and consume all beasts behind the suppression of women, the beasts that overpower the minds of the vast majority of women in some nations.

Archangel Michael, I will be,
all one with your reality.
No fear can hold me as I see,
this world no power has o'er me.

**Archangel Michael, you are here,
consuming now all doubt and fear.**

**Your Presence is forever near,
you are to me so very dear.**

3. Archangel Michael, bind and consume the fallen beings and collective entities behind female prostitution, human trafficking and the institutions that are allowing money laundering from these activities.

Archangel Michael, hold me tight,
shatter now the darkest night.
Clear my chakras with your light,
restore to me my inner sight.

**Archangel Michael, you are here,
consuming now all doubt and fear.
Your Presence is forever near,
you are to me so very dear.**

4. Archangel Michael, bind and consume the collective entities that keep men trapped in the abuse of alcohol, violence, forcing people into prostitution, rape and other destructive activities.

Archangel Michael, now I stand,
with you the light I do command.
My heart I ever will expand,
till highest truth I understand.

**Archangel Michael, you are here,
consuming now all doubt and fear.
Your Presence is forever near,
you are to me so very dear.**

5. Archangel Michael, bind and consume the fallen beings and collective entities that are seeking to prevent societies from realizing that these dark beings exist and how they overpower people's minds.

Archangel Michael, in my heart,
from me you never will depart.
Of hierarchy I am a part,
I now accept a fresh new start.

**Archangel Michael, you are here,
consuming now all doubt and fear.
Your Presence is forever near,
you are to me so very dear.**

6. Archangel Michael, bind and consume the fallen beings and collective entities that are seeking to prevent societies from realizing that we need to understand collective entities scientifically and through psychology.

Archangel Michael, sword of blue,
all darkness you are cutting through.
My Christhood I do now pursue,
discernment shows me what is true.

**Archangel Michael, you are here,
consuming now all doubt and fear.
Your Presence is forever near,
you are to me so very dear.**

7. Archangel Michael, I call for you to bind and remove from earth the fallen beings, including the Dark Master, who made the decision that they would make men the superior sex on earth and women the inferior sex.

Archangel Michael, in your wings,
I now let go of lesser things.
God's homing call in my heart rings,
my heart with yours forever sings.

**Archangel Michael, you are here,
consuming now all doubt and fear.
Your Presence is forever near,
you are to me so very dear.**

8. Archangel Michael, shatter the veil of ignorance that the fallen beings have created in order to hide their own existence, their agenda and their complete insensitivity to human beings.

Archangel Michael, take me home,
in higher spheres I want to roam.

I am reborn from cosmic foam,
my life is now a sacred poem.

Archangel Michael, you are here,
consuming now all doubt and fear.
Your Presence is forever near,
you are to me so very dear.

9. Archangel Michael, shatter the veil of ignorance so that all institutions that unwittingly support the agenda of the fallen beings will be exposed. Cut free all people who have the potential to free societies from the manipulation of the fallen beings.

Archangel Michael, light you are,
shining like the bluest star.
You are a cosmic avatar,
with you I will go very far.

Archangel Michael, you are here,
consuming now all doubt and fear.
Your Presence is forever near,
you are to me so very dear.

Sealing

In the name of the I AM THAT I AM, I accept that Archangel Michael, Astrea and Shiva form an impenetrable shield around myself and all constructive people, sealing us from all fear-based energies in all four octaves. I accept that the Light of God is consuming and transforming all fear-based energies that make up the dark forces working against the liberation of women on earth!

16 | CHRISTIANITY WAS NOT MEANT TO SUPPRESS WOMEN

I am the Ascended Master Jesus Christ. I have several things on my agenda for this release. First of all, I want to make as strong and direct of a contribution as I can possibly make to changing the abhorrent fact that the religion that claims to represent me on earth has been one of the strongest forces in recent history for the suppression of women. Let me make it very, very clear that it was never – *ever* – my intention to create a religious or spiritual movement that would suppress women.

I was, when I walked the earth 2,000 years ago, quite aware that any spiritual teaching that can be given on a dark planet like earth must be given in context, and the context is of course the collective consciousness. I was also aware that I had deliberately chosen to descend to the Middle East. Now, as I have said before, I did not take embodiment in the Middle East because it was a high spiritual region. It was not that there is anything particularly spiritual about the Middle East or the energies there. It is not, as many Christians call it, a *holy* land. I descended to the Middle East because it was, and unfortunately *is,* one of the darkest areas on earth. It has one of the lowest levels of energy, one of the lowest states of the collective consciousness. This was the case back then and it is still the case today.

Jesus' teachings were given in context

I came there for various reasons, partly because I came to bring the judgment of certain fallen beings, for which they needed to kill my physical body in order to receive that judgment. Therefore, I needed to embody where they were in embodiment. Also, I came to bring the judgment of the people and the consciousness in the Middle East and give them an opportunity to come up higher. Another reason was that if I could somehow manage to change the most dense people on earth, then there was a good chance of changing others as well.

You see here that the first illusion that needs to be shattered about Christianity is that I came to the Middle East because it was a *holy* place. The Middle East was back then in a very low state of the collective consciousness. What needs to be understood by recognizing this is that this set some limitations for the teachings that I could give at the time. I needed to give those teachings in context and therefore, I could not give a teaching at the time that would directly and openly challenge a male-dominated society because the people in the Middle East were not ready for this.

What I could do and what I did was that I demonstrated, through my actions and through the community that sprang up around me, that I treated women and men equally. I treated women and men with an equal potential to grow spiritually. I know that this can be difficult to ascertain from the scriptures, even from the New Testament where you for example see that I had only male disciples according to the scriptures. This is according to the *scriptures,* not according to *reality.* I had, first of all, more than 12 disciples and many of them were women. There was a just about equal proportion between men and women among those that I would call my direct disciples, meaning people who interacted with me.

Now, there are many misunderstandings that have crept in because of this unfortunate fact that the scriptures have written down a distorted view of my mission and my actions. One of the most insidious distortions is of course that there must be some difference between men and women, since Christ only had male disciples. Yeah, there were certain women that were obviously always around and maybe they were even the first to realize that Jesus had been resurrected and left the grave, but still, they are not really that important. What was important was the male disciples and of course primarily among them, Peter, who is said to have been the first pope (even though I do not recall ever using the terminology of a pope and anointing him as the Pope). Then Paul, who wrote down his various epistles. You see that this distortion begins right at the Christian scriptures. They did not give an accurate portrayal of my actual actions and my relationship with women, the way I treated women and they do not portray that I actually had female disciples.

What you see here is that from the very beginning, when the scriptures were written down and later when those particular scriptures were selected to be part of the official canon, a distortion was created. This was created because as soon as I had left embodiment, the equal relationship that I had attempted to create between men and women was very quickly abandoned or lost. There were certain groups that maintained this for some time after my departure, but some of them did not even retain it from the very start. For example, this applies to any movement led by Peter, who could not overcome his male chauvinist mindset (to be honest) and certain other groups as well. There was such a strong, patriarchal, male-dominant mentality in the Middle East that had been there for so long, that many of the early followers of Christ could not overcome it. They soon started to create various groups and sects that went right back to relegating women to a secondary role.

You are not inherently male or female

This was of course because the Old Testament had created, as Archangel Michael explained, this fundamental divide between men and women, making women responsible for the fall of man. You realize of course that you can create various polarities, as Archangel Michael said, between masculine and feminine. You can say the I AM Presence is the masculine aspect of your being, the soul or the Conscious You is the feminine polarity and therefore it was the Conscious You or the soul, whatever you choose to call it, that fell, that ate the forbidden fruit and went into duality. This happened whether you were in a male or female body. You can also look at it in a slightly different aspect where you can actually say that, as we have explained, when you were exposed to various traumatic situations (for example in the first embodiment where you encountered the fallen beings), you created certain selves and those selves may have, depending on whether you were in a male or female body at the time, a certain male or female orientation. You realize, I hope, that this was based again on context. You need to go back and say: Perhaps a very, very long time ago,

I was embodied in my first embodiment and I received my cosmic birth trauma and at that time I was in a female body and therefore, I created certain separate selves that have a female coloring, a female overlay. This may be the case, but you need to recognize that these selves were created based on the culture in which you first embodied and how women's roles were defined at that time. I can assure you that even if you take the time-frame we give in the *My Lives* book, that some avatars came to earth 2 million years ago, the fallen beings had already then distorted the view of women and created these dualistic roles for men and women.

What I am saying here is this. The female role is not something that you can look at as a universal thing. We have said before that God did not create men and women with a fundamental difference. Evolution has not brought forth men and women with a fundamental difference except of course at the physical body and the level of hormones and the functions of the physical body in terms of childbirth. There is on a spiritual level, no fundamental difference between men and women. You need to recognize here that even if you have certain selves that were created a long time ago, they are not based on some spiritual, universal definition that this is the way women are. They are based on the cultural context that was influenced by the fallen beings and their attempt to make men the dominant sex and women the inferior sex, in order to create that fundamental division and that fundamental conflict on earth.

The Christ mind sees no difference between men and women

What you need to recognize here is this. What is Christ? What did I, when I took embodiment as Jesus 2,000 years ago, come to represent to earth? I came to represent Christ and to demonstrate how a person with Christ consciousness brings a different perspective on everything. That is why, as I said, I treated men and women equally. This was shocking to many Jews at the time who were used to this fundamental difference in the way men and women were treated, even in a religious context, but in all other contexts. I treated men and women equally because to the Christ, to the Christ mind, men and women are not only of equal value, but of equal spiritual potential. In fact, you could say that to the Christ mind, there is no difference between men and women. The Christ mind looks at a person, and looks beyond the sex of the physical body, and looks at the being of that person.

The Christ mind sees that the core of this being is the Conscious You, which is neutral, gender neutral. Then, there is the I AM Presence, which is also gender neutral. Of course, the Conscious You may be trapped in and identified with a certain number of selves. These are not gender neutral, but this is not who the person really is so the Christ sees beyond this and looks at: How can the Christ help liberate that particular person from the separate selves that are limiting the Conscious You from expressing itself, from being an open door for the I AM Presence? How can the Christ liberate you from whatever is limiting you? There may be some selves that are of a male orientation, some of a female orientation or coloring but it does not really matter to the Christ.

The Christ does not set up any kind of value judgment. In a sense, you could say that the Christ does not treat women differently from men or men differently from women. It may of course express itself differently, whether it is addressing a female separate self or a male separate self, but nevertheless the goal is always to liberate the person from whatever it is trapped in.

Having said this, I hope I have made it clear that it was never my intention to create a religion that discriminated against and suppressed women—so why did this happen? Well, it happened in part because, as I said, many people did not even fathom that I treated men and women equally and they quickly lost it when I was not there. Many of the people who started writing down scriptures or creating different sects and groups had not encountered me personally. They just assumed again, they *projected* upon me that I was doing what they were doing. Therefore, I was looking at women the way they were looking at women, I was treating women the way they were treating women.

The Catholic church and Roman treatment of women

Then, of course comes this momentous change in the Christian movement, which is the formation of the Catholic church. There, you again need to look at context and you need to look at the status of women in Roman society. You can clearly see that they were in an inferior position. Not necessarily as bad as in some societies at the time but clearly, they were in an inferior position. Was there a female Roman emperor? Not that I recall and women were, in general, put in certain positions where they were prevented from being part of the decision-making process in society. They were in many other ways, limited. This was then transferred to the Christian religion because if you look at this again in context, you can see very clearly that the Roman, the *Roman* Catholic church, was created by the *Roman* Emperor Constantine as a political instrument for uniting his empire. You might say it was created in a desperate attempt to maintain control, his failing control of his empire. Therefore, it was not Constantine's intent to challenge these set institutions of Roman society, such as the relationship between men and women. He had no intention of challenging that. He had the intention of creating a new religion that was not so different that Romans could not accept it but that nevertheless, he hoped, could bring some unification of the empire under his control. He thought that if he could control the religion, it could help him control the empire. Of course, you can see historically that Constantine had great control over the early Roman Catholic church, including the doctrines of Nicaea that elevated me beyond the status of being a human being and therefore, beyond being an example to follow.

This then also meant that any remnant of awareness that I treated men and women equally could be set aside, because the Roman Catholic church was not meant to do what I did but to do what they said that I did. The Catholic church from its inception was not based on the true teachings of Christ. It was not based on any attunement with the universal Christ mind or with the Ascended Master Jesus Christ. It was an entirely man-made institution that did, as other masters have explained, create a man-made image and project that onto Christ. They created a man-made image of what Jesus Christ was like, what his message was like and they projected that upon—not me, but people's view of me. They reinforced it and built upon it for the next more than a thousand years and they are still trying to reinforce it today. You see of course how up through the centuries, this led to various conflicts, the Crusades, the Inquisition. When it comes to women, you see that for over a thousand years the Catholic church was an instrument for maintaining the suppression of women, maintaining the status quo where women had a clearly secondary position in society.

The witch hunts destroyed women's influence upon society

Then comes that period of the witch-hunts and what was the cause of this? Well, it was because of the fact that many, many women were starting to question status quo, not only in the Christian religion but in society as a whole. Many women were starting to question their role and why they should be in a secondary position in society. This was a movement that was seen as dangerous, not only by the Catholic church, but also by the secular leaders, the kings and the emperors of the Middle Ages. This then resulted in the witch-hunt processes where any woman who had any kind of knowledge beyond the norm, the accepted norm, was labeled as a witch and therefore persecuted—burned at the stake.

We might say that the witch-hunt processes were a deliberate and aggressive intent to stamp out the first feminist movement in Europe and again, Christianity played a key role, even though you cannot necessarily say that it was only the church that was behind this. There were also the secular leaders, and there was a certain taking advantage of popular superstitions in terms of witchcraft and dark forces that were believed in back then. This was what allowed this to even happen and people did not revolt against it.

Even beyond the witch-hunts, you see that up into the modern age, Christian movements, even Lutheran, Protestant movements, were against giving women the right to vote. You see how there was a great resistance to allowing women to gain any position in the Protestant Christian churches and there is even resistance today. There are male ministers in Protestant, Lutheran churches who are against the anointing of women as priests or bishops, who will not shake their hand and who will not interact with them. You see that even today, in the modern age, Christianity is an instrument for the suppression of women.

Why is it important for you to be aware of this? Well, for several reasons. First of all, you can make the calls for this. You can make the calls for the binding of the dark forces, the fallen beings and the collective entities that are behind this. There are some very strong collective entities that have been created by the Christian religion, both the Catholic church and the Protestant religions, that make men feel that they are superior, should be superior, and that women should be inferior. There are even those who make women accept this position so that many women who still see themselves as Christians, even many women in the modern democracies who still see themselves as Christians, have come to accept that women should have a secondary position. You can call for the binding of this so that people can be given an opportunity, as Archangel Michael said, to make the choice to let go of this mindset. Whether they will do so or not will then be up to them, but at least they have the opportunity that they do not have now where they are hypnotized by this mindset.

Can Christianity survive in the modern world?

Beyond this, there is a question that I would like to pose and I pose it primarily to women because you actually see that in many of the more developed nations, women are more active in Christian churches. They may not be ministers or bishops, but they are often doing much of the practical work in terms of keeping the church functioning, keeping services going and all of these things. Given that women are the primary driving force that keeps these churches going, women need to ask themselves a simple question and the question is this: "Can Christianity survive in a modern, developed nation? Does Christianity still have a place in these modern democracies that we live in? Does Christianity have any relevance in the very complex modern societies that we have now?" Then, women, at least *some,* can be cut free to see that the answer to that question depends on how you look at Christianity.

Is Christianity a static religion that must continue to work within the boundaries defined 17 centuries ago, or 20 centuries ago, when the first scriptures were written down? You will notice that the four gospels were written down by men. This is the question that those women who are engaged in Christian churches in the modern democracies need to ask themselves. Then, they need to recognize something very profound – which many women may not be able to recognize – they need to recognize that Christ represents change.

You can start with a recognition that obviously society has changed tremendously between when I walked the earth, when the Catholic church was formed, and today. Therefore, from even a common sense, rational perspective, it makes no sense to hold on to these doctrines and rituals, this view of men and women that was created back then, when the cultural context was entirely different. It is not beyond many, many people, both men and women, but primarily women, to realize that Christianity did emerge in a particular cultural context. Now that the cultural context has changed as dramatically as it has, it is necessary to make certain changes to the Christian church if it is to remain relevant.

You can also take the common sense perspective that if a religion is to be relevant to people, it must do something for them that helps them improve their daily lives. There are always two aspects of a religion. One is of course the entire concept of salvation, which I will set aside for now, but the other is the concept of how a religion impacts people's daily lives. Obviously, the challenges people face in their daily lives today in the modern world are very different from what it was when the Catholic church was formed, or when the Lutheran churches were formed centuries ago. Therefore, it is simply necessary to make changes so that you can help people address the problems and concerns they have today. If people do not find anything in the Christian religion that is relevant to their daily situation, how can they feel that the Christian religion is relevant and how can the church then survive?

Christ defines a geometric matrix for change

These are common sense perspectives, but beyond this, you who are ascended master students can realize and make the calls for the fact that Christ as a principle represents not only change, but self-transcendence. Omega expounded upon the fact that in the beginning, the expanding and contracting forces are created as a polarity, but what allows the creation of forms that can be maintained, is a balance between the two. The Christ, the universal Christ mind, is the very factor that helps maintain that balance. However, balance is not something static because the purpose of the entire universe, as she explained, is of course to grow, to facilitate the growth of consciousness of the self-aware beings who inhabit that world of form. As she explained, Christ defines a certain ratio, a certain interval, a certain geometry, for how change happens in a given sphere.

In your sphere there was, when it was created, defined a certain Christ factor. It is not really a number, it is a more complex geometrical shape, but it is what defines the density of matter. It also defines the levels of consciousness that self-aware beings can have whether it is on earth or natural planets. It defines these levels of consciousness and thereby defines the quantum jump that electrons or protons can go through as they jump from one energy level to another. Also, the quantum jump that you make in consciousness when you jump from one level of consciousness to the next. This then sets a certain progressive spiral, we might say, for how this unascended sphere evolves from its starting point towards its ascension point.

It is quite possible, and many beings have done this, that you can start out as a newly created being and you are in tune with this spiral of Christ, this upward spiral of Christ. You experience the level of consciousness at which you were created for a time and then after a time, you intuitively sense that now it is time to jump to the next level. You effortlessly let go of the sense of self you have at your primary level. You, in a sense, let that self die and you allow yourself to be reborn because after you make that quantum leap to the next level, you are reborn into a new sense of identity. You started with an identity in Christ, you are reborn into a new identity in Christ. This is a process I described when I said that: "He who seeks to save his life shall lose it, but he who is willing to lose his life for my sake, shall find eternal life."

You are created at a certain level of consciousness with a certain sense of identity and self, but you let that self die. You are willing to let that self die and go into this interval, this quantum interval, without knowing what will happen next. You trust that you will be reborn into a higher sense of self, and that is indeed what you are when you are willing to let the old die and experience that brief interval where you are free from any self and then reborn into another. This is Christ. This is the essence of Christ. It is what you might call a no-man's land, a no-woman's land, a no-self land. This cosmic interval where you have let the old die, but you have not yet entered the new. You are in between and then you experience Christ.

This does not necessarily mean that you can only experience Christ when you jump from one level of consciousness to the next but it does mean that you can only experience Christ when you are willing to let one particular separate self die. Perhaps I should even step back a little bit here, because what I gave you before was the ideal scenario, but what I am talking about now about letting separate selves die is of course after you have gone into duality and created separate selves.

Letting separate selves die to follow Christ

Let us look at that process. I said that it is possible for a lifestream to start out at a certain level where it was created, and to gradually follow the Christ spiral upwards from there. This means that such a being can follow the upward spiral defined for its unascended sphere without ever going into duality. It is using its free will all the time. It is just not choosing to use that free will to go into duality. Of course, it is a part of an unascended sphere to give lifestreams the opportunity to use their free will to go into duality, but when you go into duality, you are removing yourself from the upward Christ spiral. You cannot stay on that spiral and go into duality. You lose the attunement with that spiral. The fallen beings have reasoned that following the Christ spiral is a limitation of their free will because there are certain choices they cannot make and it is true. If you want to stay with the Christ spiral, you cannot make the choice to go into duality.

The question is whether that is really a limitation of your free will. You are the one who is making the choice. You can go into duality if you like, but as we have explained, if you make a choice and there is no consequence, how have you made the choice? There must be a difference. In other words, you cannot have your cake and eat it too. You cannot choose to go into duality and stay on the Christ spiral. Now, you can always come back to the Christ spiral, but you cannot be *on* the Christ spiral and *off* the Christ spiral at the same time. That is not a limitation of free will, but a function of a world of form where one form is set apart from another. You can draw a circle and you can draw a square, but you cannot draw a circle and a square at the same time because forms are distinct. That is how you create a world of form.

What happens is that some beings choose to go into duality in order to experience what this is like. As we have said many, many times, despite the overlay that has been created by the fallen beings of guilt and shame and all of this, there is no blame from the part of God for those who have made that choice. It is simply a natural part of the progression of a sphere that some lifestreams will make the choice to go into duality. The question is simply this: "Have you had enough of duality and do you want to come back to a higher state?" Then, the Christ is there for you.

Now, you will see that there is a statement in the Bible that has confused many Christians, which says: "Jesus Christ, the same yesterday, today and forever." Now, first of all, this is a statement that was made from a limited understanding and a failure to understand what I have just explained to you. There is some reality to it in the sense that Jesus Christ is not the same every day, all the time, but that the Christ principle is the same in the sense that it is always there as an alternative to duality. However far you have gone into duality, the Christ is always there to take you out of duality if you want. In order to take you out of duality, you must be willing to let a certain self die and to continue to do this until you have let all of the dualistic selves, all of the separate selves, die. Then, you can rejoin the Christ spiral defined for your sphere. What you see here is that the reality is that when you step into duality, when you make that first decision to step into duality, *that* is when you are limiting your free will. The choice to step into duality can be said to be the last free choice you make while you are into duality.

How duality limits free will

Why is this so? Well, because in duality, there are always two opposing polarities, there is always a tension, a conflict, between them. How do you go into duality? Well, you actually go into duality by creating a self that is based on one particular dualistic polarity. That particular dualistic polarity will be opposed by the opposite dualistic polarity and that means that you will be pushed, you will be in a state where there is a push and pull from these two different polarities, and that means that you are not now making a free choice. You are in one particular polarity, which is opposed by another dualistic polarity and you are forced to react to that opposition.

How will you deal with that opposition to the sense of self that you now have? When you are not in duality, nothing opposes your sense of self but when you go into duality, there will always be something that opposes your sense of self. As long as you are identified with a dualistic self, you will think, feel and experience that you cannot avoid reacting to that opposition. You *must* react. How do you react? By creating another self, but that new self is also dualistic. It also has an opposition, which you must react to and how do you react to that? By creating a third self and the third self has an opposition and you create a fourth self and this goes on indefinitely, building selves upon selves upon selves, until you come to that point where you decide: "I can't do this anymore. There must be a different way. What is the way out? God, show me a way out." *That,* then, is when the Christ can appear to you in some form that offers you a way out.

You see that the basic dualistic polarity that you can go into on a planet like earth is that in order to take embodiment on earth, you must be in a male or female body in any one embodiment. In order to go into and take embodiment in a male body or a female body, you must create a self based on that body and that self will of course be based on the cultural context in which you take embodiment. It will have an opposition and you must react to that by creating new selves, and so on and so forth, ad infinitum.

Now, I know that this may sound very discouraging, because there could be an infinite number of selves that you have created. Well actually, there cannot be an infinite number because time is not infinite, but there can be a very large number. Nevertheless, this is why Christ is there. This is the function of Christ. No matter what kind of separate dualistic selves you have created, Christ offers you the perspective, the realization, the experience, that you are not this particular self and therefore, you can let the self die and you will not die when the self dies. That is why I said:

He who is willing to lose his life, lose the life of that one self, in order to follow me, shall find the eternal life of going upwards, towards the point where you can again join the Christ spiral, which is eternal life, is eternal self-transcendence, or at least until the end of the cycle where your sphere ascends. Then, of course there is life beyond that in the ascended realm. This is the essence of Christ. It is self-transcendence.

A new form of Christianity driven by women

Now of course, because of what has happened to the Christian religion, Christ is not a universal term. Other mystical traditions have used different words for the same principle, but the reality here is that the most universal word that we can give you is "Christ," when you understand that Christ is that principle of self-transcendence. That is the essence of Christ. You can see this as ascended master students. You can begin to embody it in a more conscious way than you have done before.

You can make the calls that other people will begin to realize this because I tell you this: If the Christian religion is going to survive in the modern democracies, it must transcend itself. It must transcend this historical baggage of the Catholic church, the Jewish religion, the Old Testament and all of this baggage that the religion is still dragging along with it. You may look at an institution like the Catholic church and you may say: "But it has survived for 17 centuries and it is still there and it still has 1.3 billion members around the world." Its membership is dwindling in the modern democracies and what is happening in the modern democracies is simply a forewarning of what will happen on a worldwide scale.

The Catholic religion will not survive in the Golden Age of Saint Germain in its present form. The question is whether the Catholic tradition can transform itself, and that is, as I have said before, an open question. It is also possible that a new form of Christianity will emerge, or even several new forms of Christianity that can be focused on different things. If this is to happen, it will be driven primarily by women. It will also involve men, but it will be driven primarily by women who will be able and willing, many of them because you make the calls for them to become free to tune in to the mind of the ascended master Jesus Christ.

They may not even recognize me in a sense as an ascended master, but they may still be able to tune in and receive certain ideas that will allow them to suddenly have the scales fall from their eyes and they see it is necessary to go in a new direction. It is necessary to create a new Christian church that is more focused on people, serving people, helping people meet the challenges they face in the modern age. What are the challenges you meet in the modern age? In the modern democracies, you have people who have grown up and physical survival – their material needs – have never really been a challenge for them. They have been taken care of to the point where it did not eat up their attention.

What is the next logical step? It is to follow Maslow's pyramid of needs and go into the self-actualization needs. Well, would it be possible, even without knowing about ascended master teachings, to create a Christian church that was based on using the teachings and example of Christ to help people fulfill their needs for self-actualization? Well, of course that would be possible if there are people who are willing to tune in to my mind and receive these ideas. This is not contingent upon people recognizing an ascended master teaching. It is a matter of them tuning in to my mind and receiving these ideas. It is possible that this could happen. Some attempts have already been made by people who have more attunement and you can of course make the calls that this will spread. Quite frankly, I must tell you that I am non-attached to whether or not this happens. I am non-attached to whether or not a new form of Christianity emerges, or whether the Christian religion simply fades away, because then other forms of spiritual movements will emerge that are more suited to fulfilling people's needs in this age we are going into.

What I *will* say is that for a new form of Christianity to emerge, it will be necessary to simply take the Old Testament out of Christian scriptures. It will also be necessary to incorporate at least some of what are today popularly called the Gnostic Gospels, in order to get a more diversified scriptural background. Naturally, you could create a new form of Christianity based on the teachings I have given through this messenger alone but that is not as likely to happen. It is not so likely that people will be able to get rid of all the scriptures, but it should be possible for people to see that we need to simply let go of the Old Testament and incorporate some of the apocryphal scriptures, not necessarily all of them, because quite frankly some of them do not come from the Christ mind.

The Old Testament cannot give equality to women

Why is it necessary to let go of the Old Testament? Well, because as long as you believe that this is the word of God and was given through some infallible revelation, you will not be able to overcome this baggage that defines women as inferior to men and as the cause of the downfall of the entire human race. A new form of Christianity must leave this entire mindset behind, or it will have no chance whatsoever of surviving in the modern age. You must let go of this Old Testament baggage and there is no way to do it except by letting go of the Old Testament. There is very little that is relevant to modern people in the Old Testament, which is largely a history of the Jewish people and not relevant to those who are not Jewish. Let the Jews keep the Torah, let the Muslims keep the Old Testament books if they want, but move on into a new form of Christianity that is not just a new testament but a new attunement with the universal Christ mind that promotes growth, that promotes self-transcendence, not a static form of Christianity.

This of course is a big challenge because the fallen beings do not want this kind of a movement that is based on self-transcendence. They want to maintain the kind of Christianity you have had since the formation of the Catholic church, namely a kind of Christianity that denies your ability to self-transcend. What do they say? "Only the pope is to become Christ. Only the pope has direct contact with Christ. Only the ministers, the priests, are the mediators between God and men."

What did I actually come to give as the primary message I came with 2,000 years ago? There is no human being or human institution that is the mediator between Spirit and man. Only the Christ is the mediator, and the Christ is a universal mind that is beyond any division that you could possibly create on earth. Christ is always there for all people and where do you find Christ? Well, Christ resides in the kingdom of God and where is the kingdom of God located? It is located within you because the kingdom of God is your ability to become aware that you have a limited self, your ability to decide that you are willing to let that self die in order to follow Christ, in order to come up higher in consciousness and be reborn into a higher sense of self that is closer to the sense of self with which you were created. It was created out of the Christ mind and therefore, was attuned to the Christ spiral, the upward spiral of self-transcendence that drives the entire world of form. This is eternal life, this Christ spiral.

You cannot instantly switch and have eternal life. You can go through a period where you gradually, one by one, let these separate dualistic selves die and are reborn. *Then,* you can come to that point where you let the last self die and now you are rejoined with the Christ spiral and then you have eternal life, not in the physical body, but in your spiritual being, in your spiritual identity that you gradually reconnect to as you shed the snakeskin of these outer selves.

Thus, I seal you in that Christ flame of joy that I came to bring to this planet, and as I have said before, how many associate joy with Jesus Christ in Christianity? *That* shows you how much Christianity has been perverted, because what is Christ joy? It is the joy of allowing a limited self to die and being reborn in a more expanded sense of self. *That* gives you the highest form of joy that you can experience on a dark planet like earth. So, be sealed in that Christ flame of infinite joy.

NOTE: This dictation was given May 31, 2020.

17 | INVOKING A NEW FORM OF CHRISTIANITY (PART 1)

In the name of the I AM THAT I AM, Jesus Christ, I use the authority that I have as a being in embodiment on earth to call upon Jesus to reinforce my calls and use my chakras to project the statements in this invocation into the collective consciousness and awaken people to the awareness that will liberate both men and women from all psychological and spiritual thralldom to the fallen beings. Awaken people to the reality that we are spiritual beings and that we can co-create a new future by working with the ascended masters. I especially call for …

[Make your own calls here.]

Part 1

1. Beloved Jesus, awaken women to see that it was never your intention to create a religious or spiritual movement that would suppress women.

> O Jesus, blessed brother mine,
> I walk the path that you outline,
> a great example to us all,
> I follow now your inner call.

**O Jesus, let the Fire of Joy,
consume the devil's subtle ploy,
transfigured is our planet earth,
the golden age is given birth.**

2. Beloved Jesus, awaken women to see that any spiritual teaching that can be given on a dark planet like earth must be given in context, and the context is the collective consciousness.

O Jesus, open inner sight,
the ego wants to prove it's right,
but this I will no longer do,
I want to be all one with you.

**O Jesus, let the Fire of Joy,
consume the devil's subtle ploy,
transfigured is our planet earth,
the golden age is given birth.**

3. Beloved Jesus, awaken women to see that you took embodiment in the Middle East because it was one of the darkest areas on earth. It had one of the lowest levels of energy, one of the lowest states of the collective consciousness, and this is still the case today.

O Jesus, I now clearly see,
the Key of Knowledge given me,
my Christ self I hereby embrace,
as you fill up my inner space.

**O Jesus, let the Fire of Joy,
consume the devil's subtle ploy,
transfigured is our planet earth,
the golden age is given birth.**

4. Beloved Jesus, shatter the illusion that you came to the Middle East because it was a *holy* place.

O Jesus, show me serpent's lie,
expose the beam in my own eye,

as Christ discernment you me give,
in oneness I forever live.

**O Jesus, let the Fire of Joy,
consume the devil's subtle ploy,
transfigured is our planet earth,
the golden age is given birth.**

5. Beloved Jesus, awaken women to see that the collective consciousness set some limitations for the teachings that you could give at the time. You could not give a teaching at the time that would directly and openly challenge a male-dominated society because the people in the Middle East were not ready for this.

O Jesus, I am truly meek,
and thus I turn the other cheek,
when the accuser attacks me,
I go within and merge with thee.

**O Jesus, let the Fire of Joy,
consume the devil's subtle ploy,
transfigured is our planet earth,
the golden age is given birth.**

6. Beloved Jesus, awaken women to see that you demonstrated, through your actions and through the community that sprang up around you, that you treated women and men with an equal potential to grow spiritually.

O Jesus, ego I let die,
surrender ev'ry earthly tie,
the dead can bury what is dead,
I choose to walk with you instead.

**O Jesus, let the Fire of Joy,
consume the devil's subtle ploy,
transfigured is our planet earth,
the golden age is given birth.**

7. Beloved Jesus, awaken women to see that you did not have only male disciples. There was an equal proportion between men and women among those that were your direct disciples.

O Jesus, help me rise above,
the devil's test through higher love,
show me separate self unreal,
my formless self you do reveal.

**O Jesus, let the Fire of Joy,
consume the devil's subtle ploy,
transfigured is our planet earth,
the golden age is given birth.**

8. Beloved Jesus, shatter the illusion that there must be some difference between men and women, since Christ only had male disciples.

O Jesus, what is that to me,
I just let go and follow thee,
with this I do pass ev'ry test,
to find with you eternal rest.

**O Jesus, let the Fire of Joy,
consume the devil's subtle ploy,
transfigured is our planet earth,
the golden age is given birth.**

9. Beloved Jesus, awaken women to see that the Christian scriptures do not give an accurate portrayal of your actions and your relationship with women, the way you treated women and they do not portray that you had female disciples.

O Jesus, fiery master mine,
my heart now melting into thine,
I love with heart and mind and soul,
the God who is my highest goal.

**O Jesus, let the Fire of Joy,
consume the devil's subtle ploy,**

**transfigured is our planet earth,
the golden age is given birth.**

Part 2

1. Beloved Jesus, awaken women to see that from the very beginning, when the scriptures were written down and later when those particular scriptures were selected to be part of the official canon, a distortion was created.

O Jesus, blessed brother mine,
I walk the path that you outline,
a great example to us all,
I follow now your inner call.

**O Jesus, let the Fire of Joy,
consume the devil's subtle ploy,
transfigured is our planet earth,
the golden age is given birth.**

2. Beloved Jesus, awaken women to see that as soon as you had left embodiment, the equal relationship that you had attempted to create between men and women was abandoned or lost.

O Jesus, open inner sight,
the ego wants to prove it's right,
but this I will no longer do,
I want to be all one with you.

**O Jesus, let the Fire of Joy,
consume the devil's subtle ploy,
transfigured is our planet earth,
the golden age is given birth.**

3. Beloved Jesus, awaken women to see that the movement led by Peter could not overcome his male chauvinist mindset.

O Jesus, I now clearly see,
the Key of Knowledge given me,
my Christ self I hereby embrace,
as you fill up my inner space.

**O Jesus, let the Fire of Joy,
consume the devil's subtle ploy,
transfigured is our planet earth,
the golden age is given birth.**

4. Beloved Jesus, awaken women to see that there was such a strong, patriarchal, male-dominant mentality in the Middle East that many of the early
followers of Christ could not overcome it, and they created various groups
and sects that relegated women to a secondary role.

O Jesus, show me serpent's lie,
expose the beam in my own eye,
as Christ discernment you me give,
in oneness I forever live.

**O Jesus, let the Fire of Joy,
consume the devil's subtle ploy,
transfigured is our planet earth,
the golden age is given birth.**

5. Beloved Jesus, awaken women to see that the female role is not a universal thing. God did not create men and women with a fundamental
difference. Evolution has not brought forth men and women with a fundamental difference except of course in the physical body.

O Jesus, I am truly meek,
and thus I turn the other cheek,
when the accuser attacks me,
I go within and merge with thee.

**O Jesus, let the Fire of Joy,
consume the devil's subtle ploy,
transfigured is our planet earth,
the golden age is given birth.**

6. Beloved Jesus, awaken women to see that there is, on a spiritual level, no fundamental difference between men and women.

> O Jesus, ego I let die,
> surrender ev'ry earthly tie,
> the dead can bury what is dead,
> I choose to walk with you instead.

> **O Jesus, let the Fire of Joy,**
> **consume the devil's subtle ploy,**
> **transfigured is our planet earth,**
> **the golden age is given birth.**

7. Beloved Jesus, awaken women to see that we have certain selves that were created a long time ago, but they are not based on some spiritual, universal definition that this is the way men and women are.

> O Jesus, help me rise above,
> the devil's test through higher love,
> show me separate self unreal,
> my formless self you do reveal.

> **O Jesus, let the Fire of Joy,**
> **consume the devil's subtle ploy,**
> **transfigured is our planet earth,**
> **the golden age is given birth.**

8. Beloved Jesus, awaken women to see that all separate selves are based on the cultural context that was influenced by the fallen beings and their attempt to make men the dominant sex and women the inferior sex, in order to create that fundamental division and that fundamental conflict on earth.

> O Jesus, what is that to me,
> I just let go and follow thee,
> with this I do pass ev'ry test,
> to find with you eternal rest.

O Jesus, let the Fire of Joy,
consume the devil's subtle ploy,
transfigured is our planet earth,
the golden age is given birth.

9. Beloved Jesus, awaken women to see that you came to represent Christ and to demonstrate how a person with Christ consciousness brings a different perspective on everything.

O Jesus, fiery master mine,
my heart now melting into thine,
I love with heart and mind and soul,
the God who is my highest goal.

O Jesus, let the Fire of Joy,
consume the devil's subtle ploy,
transfigured is our planet earth,
the golden age is given birth.

Part 3

1. Beloved Jesus, awaken women to see that you treated men and women equally because to the Christ, to the Christ mind, men and women are not only of equal value, but of equal spiritual potential.

O Jesus, blessed brother mine,
I walk the path that you outline,
a great example to us all,
I follow now your inner call.

O Jesus, let the Fire of Joy,
consume the devil's subtle ploy,
transfigured is our planet earth,
the golden age is given birth.

2. Beloved Jesus, awaken women to see that to the Christ mind, there is no difference between men and women. The Christ mind looks at a person,

and looks beyond the sex of the physical body, and looks at the being of
that person.

> O Jesus, open inner sight,
> the ego wants to prove it's right,
> but this I will no longer do,
> I want to be all one with you.

> **O Jesus, let the Fire of Joy,**
> **consume the devil's subtle ploy,**
> **transfigured is our planet earth,**
> **the golden age is given birth.**

3. Beloved Jesus, awaken women to see that the Christ mind sees that the
core of this being is the Conscious You, which is neutral, gender neutral.
Then, there is the I AM Presence, which is also gender neutral.

> O Jesus, I now clearly see,
> the Key of Knowledge given me,
> my Christ self I hereby embrace,
> as you fill up my inner space.

> **O Jesus, let the Fire of Joy,**
> **consume the devil's subtle ploy,**
> **transfigured is our planet earth,**
> **the golden age is given birth.**

4. Beloved Jesus, awaken women to see that the Conscious You may be
trapped in and identified with a certain number of selves. These are not
gender neutral, but this is not who the person really is, so the Christ sees
beyond this and looks at how it can help liberate that particular person
from the separate selves.

> O Jesus, show me serpent's lie,
> expose the beam in my own eye,
> as Christ discernment you me give,
> in oneness I forever live.

O Jesus, let the Fire of Joy,
consume the devil's subtle ploy,
transfigured is our planet earth,
the golden age is given birth.

5. Beloved Jesus, awaken women to see that the Christ looks at how it can help liberate you from whatever is limiting you. There may be some selves that are of a male orientation, some of a female orientation but it does not matter to the Christ.

O Jesus, I am truly meek,
and thus I turn the other cheek,
when the accuser attacks me,
I go within and merge with thee.

O Jesus, let the Fire of Joy,
consume the devil's subtle ploy,
transfigured is our planet earth,
the golden age is given birth.

6. Beloved Jesus, awaken women to see that the Christ does not set up any kind of value judgment. The Christ does not treat women differently from men or men differently from women. The goal is always to liberate the person from whatever it is trapped in.

O Jesus, ego I let die,
surrender ev'ry earthly tie,
the dead can bury what is dead,
I choose to walk with you instead.

O Jesus, let the Fire of Joy,
consume the devil's subtle ploy,
transfigured is our planet earth,
the golden age is given birth.

7. Beloved Jesus, awaken women to see that Christianity became a male-dominated religion because those who started writing down scriptures or creating different sects and groups *projected* upon you that you were looking

at women the way they were looking at women, you were treating women
the way they were treating women.

O Jesus, help me rise above,
the devil's test through higher love,
show me separate self unreal,
my formless self you do reveal.

O Jesus, let the Fire of Joy,
consume the devil's subtle ploy,
transfigured is our planet earth,
the golden age is given birth.

8. Beloved Jesus, awaken women to see that the formation of the Catholic
church was influenced by the fact that in Roman society women were in
an inferior position.

O Jesus, what is that to me,
I just let go and follow thee,
with this I do pass ev'ry test,
to find with you eternal rest.

O Jesus, let the Fire of Joy,
consume the devil's subtle ploy,
transfigured is our planet earth,
the golden age is given birth.

9. Beloved Jesus, awaken women to see that in Roman society women
were put in certain positions where they were prevented from being part
of the decision-making process.

O Jesus, fiery master mine,
my heart now melting into thine,
I love with heart and mind and soul,
the God who is my highest goal.

O Jesus, let the Fire of Joy,
consume the devil's subtle ploy,

**transfigured is our planet earth,
the golden age is given birth.**

Part 4

1. Beloved Jesus, awaken women to see that the *Roman* Catholic church, was created by the *Roman* Emperor Constantine as a political instrument for uniting his empire.

> O Jesus, blessed brother mine,
> I walk the path that you outline,
> a great example to us all,
> I follow now your inner call.

> **O Jesus, let the Fire of Joy,
> consume the devil's subtle ploy,
> transfigured is our planet earth,
> the golden age is given birth.**

2. Beloved Jesus, awaken women to see that it was not Constantine's intent to challenge these set institutions of Roman society, such as the relationship between men and women.

> O Jesus, open inner sight,
> the ego wants to prove it's right,
> but this I will no longer do,
> I want to be all one with you.

> **O Jesus, let the Fire of Joy,
> consume the devil's subtle ploy,
> transfigured is our planet earth,
> the golden age is given birth.**

3. Beloved Jesus, awaken women to see that Constantine had great control over the early Roman Catholic church, including the doctrines of Nicaea that elevated you beyond the status of being a human being and therefore, beyond being an example to follow.

O Jesus, I now clearly see,
the Key of Knowledge given me,
my Christ self I hereby embrace,
as you fill up my inner space.

O Jesus, let the Fire of Joy,
consume the devil's subtle ploy,
transfigured is our planet earth,
the golden age is given birth.

4. Beloved Jesus, awaken women to see that any remnant of awareness that you treated men and women equally could be set aside, because the Roman Catholic church was not meant to do what you did but to do *what they said* that you did.

O Jesus, show me serpent's lie,
expose the beam in my own eye,
as Christ discernment you me give,
in oneness I forever live.

O Jesus, let the Fire of Joy,
consume the devil's subtle ploy,
transfigured is our planet earth,
the golden age is given birth.

5. Beloved Jesus, awaken women to see that the Catholic church from its inception was not based on the true teachings of Christ. It was not based on any attunement with the universal Christ mind or with the Ascended Master Jesus Christ.

O Jesus, I am truly meek,
and thus I turn the other cheek,
when the accuser attacks me,
I go within and merge with thee.

O Jesus, let the Fire of Joy,
consume the devil's subtle ploy,
transfigured is our planet earth,
the golden age is given birth.

6. Beloved Jesus, awaken women to see that the Catholic church was an entirely man-made institution that created a man-made image and projected it onto Christ.

O Jesus, ego I let die,
surrender ev'ry earthly tie,
the dead can bury what is dead,
I choose to walk with you instead.

**O Jesus, let the Fire of Joy,
consume the devil's subtle ploy,
transfigured is our planet earth,
the golden age is given birth.**

7. Beloved Jesus, awaken women to see that the church fathers created a man-made image of what Jesus Christ was like, what your message was like and they projected that upon not you, but people's view of you.

O Jesus, help me rise above,
the devil's test through higher love,
show me separate self unreal,
my formless self you do reveal.

**O Jesus, let the Fire of Joy,
consume the devil's subtle ploy,
transfigured is our planet earth,
the golden age is given birth.**

8. Beloved Jesus, awaken women to see that this image has been reinforced and built upon for more than a thousand years and they are still trying to reinforce it today.

O Jesus, what is that to me,
I just let go and follow thee,
with this I do pass ev'ry test,
to find with you eternal rest.

**O Jesus, let the Fire of Joy,
consume the devil's subtle ploy,**

**transfigured is our planet earth,
the golden age is given birth.**

9. Beloved Jesus, awaken women to see that for over a thousand years the Catholic church was an instrument for maintaining the suppression of women, maintaining the status quo where women had a secondary position in society.

O Jesus, fiery master mine,
my heart now melting into thine,
I love with heart and mind and soul,
the God who is my highest goal.

**O Jesus, let the Fire of Joy,
consume the devil's subtle ploy,
transfigured is our planet earth,
the golden age is given birth.**

Sealing

In the name of the I AM THAT I AM, I accept that Archangel Michael, Astrea and Shiva form an impenetrable shield around myself and all constructive people, sealing us from all fear-based energies in all four octaves. I accept that the Light of God is consuming and transforming all fear-based energies that make up the dark forces working against the liberation of women on earth!

18 | INVOKING A NEW FORM OF CHRISTIANITY (PART 2)

In the name of the I AM THAT I AM, Jesus Christ, I use the authority that I have as a being in embodiment on earth to call upon Jesus to reinforce my calls and use my chakras to project the statements in this invocation into the collective consciousness and awaken people to the awareness that will liberate both men and women from all psychological and spiritual thralldom to the fallen beings. Awaken people to the reality that we are spiritual beings and that we can co-create a new future by working with the ascended masters. I especially call for …

[Make your own calls here.]

Part 1

1. Beloved Jesus, awaken women to see that when many women were starting to question status quo, not only in the Christian religion but in society as a whole, the Catholic church started the witch hunts.

O Jesus, blessed brother mine,
I walk the path that you outline,

a great example to us all,
I follow now your inner call.

**O Jesus, let the Fire of Joy,
consume the devil's subtle ploy,
transfigured is our planet earth,
the golden age is given birth.**

2. Beloved Jesus, awaken women to see that when women were starting to question their role and why they should be in a secondary position in society, this was a movement that was seen as dangerous, not only by the Catholic church, but also by the secular leaders, the kings and the emperors of the Middle Ages.

O Jesus, open inner sight,
the ego wants to prove it's right,
but this I will no longer do,
I want to be all one with you.

**O Jesus, let the Fire of Joy,
consume the devil's subtle ploy,
transfigured is our planet earth,
the golden age is given birth.**

3. Beloved Jesus, awaken women to see that this resulted in the witch-hunt processes, where any woman who had any kind of knowledge beyond the accepted norm, was labeled as a witch and therefore persecuted or burned at the stake.

O Jesus, I now clearly see,
the Key of Knowledge given me,
my Christ self I hereby embrace,
as you fill up my inner space.

**O Jesus, let the Fire of Joy,
consume the devil's subtle ploy,
transfigured is our planet earth,
the golden age is given birth.**

4. Beloved Jesus, awaken women to see that the witch-hunt processes were a deliberate and aggressive intent to stamp out the first feminist movement in Europe and Christianity played a key role.

> O Jesus, show me serpent's lie,
> expose the beam in my own eye,
> as Christ discernment you me give,
> in oneness I forever live.

> **O Jesus, let the Fire of Joy,**
> **consume the devil's subtle ploy,**
> **transfigured is our planet earth,**
> **the golden age is given birth.**

5. Beloved Jesus, awaken women to see that up into the modern age, Christian movements, even Lutheran, Protestant movements, were against giving women the right to vote.

> O Jesus, I am truly meek,
> and thus I turn the other cheek,
> when the accuser attacks me,
> I go within and merge with thee.

> **O Jesus, let the Fire of Joy,**
> **consume the devil's subtle ploy,**
> **transfigured is our planet earth,**
> **the golden age is given birth.**

6. Beloved Jesus, awaken women to see that there is a great resistance to allowing women to gain any position in the Protestant Christian churches and some male ministers are against the anointing of women as priests or bishops.

> O Jesus, ego I let die,
> surrender ev'ry earthly tie,
> the dead can bury what is dead,
> I choose to walk with you instead.

O Jesus, let the Fire of Joy,
consume the devil's subtle ploy,
transfigured is our planet earth,
the golden age is given birth.

7. Beloved Jesus, I call for the binding of the dark forces, the fallen beings and the collective entities that are behind the fact that even today, Christianity is an instrument for the suppression of women.

O Jesus, help me rise above,
the devil's test through higher love,
show me separate self unreal,
my formless self you do reveal.

O Jesus, let the Fire of Joy,
consume the devil's subtle ploy,
transfigured is our planet earth,
the golden age is given birth.

8. Beloved Jesus, I call for the binding of the collective entities that have been created by both the Catholic church and the Protestant religions, and that make men feel that they are superior, should be superior, and that women should be inferior.

O Jesus, what is that to me,
I just let go and follow thee,
with this I do pass ev'ry test,
to find with you eternal rest.

O Jesus, let the Fire of Joy,
consume the devil's subtle ploy,
transfigured is our planet earth,
the golden age is given birth.

9. Beloved Jesus, I call for the binding of the collective entities that make women accept this position so that many women who still see themselves as Christians have come to accept that women should have a secondary position.

O Jesus, fiery master mine,
my heart now melting into thine,
I love with heart and mind and soul,
the God who is my highest goal.

**O Jesus, let the Fire of Joy,
consume the devil's subtle ploy,
transfigured is our planet earth,
the golden age is given birth.**

Part 2

1. Beloved Jesus, I call for the binding of these collective entities so that people can be given an opportunity to let go of this mindset and no longer be hypnotized by it.

O Jesus, blessed brother mine,
I walk the path that you outline,
a great example to us all,
I follow now your inner call.

**O Jesus, let the Fire of Joy,
consume the devil's subtle ploy,
transfigured is our planet earth,
the golden age is given birth.**

2. Beloved Jesus, awaken those women who are the primary driving force that keeps the churches going so they can ask themselves: "Can Christianity survive in a modern developed nation? Does Christianity still have a place in these modern democracies that we live in? Does Christianity have any relevance in the very complex modern societies that we have now?"

O Jesus, open inner sight,
the ego wants to prove it's right,
but this I will no longer do,
I want to be all one with you.

**O Jesus, let the Fire of Joy,
consume the devil's subtle ploy,
transfigured is our planet earth,
the golden age is given birth.**

3. Beloved Jesus, awaken women to see that the answer to that question depends on how we look at Christianity.

O Jesus, I now clearly see,
the Key of Knowledge given me,
my Christ self I hereby embrace,
as you fill up my inner space.

**O Jesus, let the Fire of Joy,
consume the devil's subtle ploy,
transfigured is our planet earth,
the golden age is given birth.**

4. Beloved Jesus, awaken women to ask whether Christianity is a static religion that must continue to work within the boundaries defined 17 centuries ago, or 20 centuries ago, when the first scriptures were written down?

O Jesus, show me serpent's lie,
expose the beam in my own eye,
as Christ discernment you me give,
in oneness I forever live.

**O Jesus, let the Fire of Joy,
consume the devil's subtle ploy,
transfigured is our planet earth,
the golden age is given birth.**

5. Beloved Jesus, awaken women to see that Christ represents change. From a common sense, rational perspective, it makes no sense to hold on to these doctrines and rituals, this view of men and women that was created when the cultural context was entirely different.

O Jesus, I am truly meek,
and thus I turn the other cheek,

when the accuser attacks me,
I go within and merge with thee.

**O Jesus, let the Fire of Joy,
consume the devil's subtle ploy,
transfigured is our planet earth,
the golden age is given birth.**

6. Beloved Jesus, awaken women to realize that Christianity did emerge in a particular cultural context. Now that the cultural context has changed as dramatically as it has, it is necessary to make certain changes to the Christian church if it is to remain relevant.

O Jesus, ego I let die,
surrender ev'ry earthly tie,
the dead can bury what is dead,
I choose to walk with you instead.

**O Jesus, let the Fire of Joy,
consume the devil's subtle ploy,
transfigured is our planet earth,
the golden age is given birth.**

7. Beloved Jesus, awaken women to see that if a religion is to be relevant to people, it must do something for them that helps them improve their daily lives.

O Jesus, help me rise above,
the devil's test through higher love,
show me separate self unreal,
my formless self you do reveal.

**O Jesus, let the Fire of Joy,
consume the devil's subtle ploy,
transfigured is our planet earth,
the golden age is given birth.**

8. Beloved Jesus, awaken women to see that the challenges people face in their daily lives in the modern world are very different from what it was

when the Catholic church was formed, or when the Lutheran churches were formed centuries ago.

> O Jesus, what is that to me,
> I just let go and follow thee,
> with this I do pass ev'ry test,
> to find with you eternal rest.

> **O Jesus, let the Fire of Joy,**
> **consume the devil's subtle ploy,**
> **transfigured is our planet earth,**
> **the golden age is given birth.**

9. Beloved Jesus, awaken women to see that it is necessary to make changes so that Christianity can help people address the problems and concerns they have today. If people do not find anything in the Christian religion that is relevant to their daily situation, how can they feel that the Christian religion is relevant and how can the church then survive?

> O Jesus, fiery master mine,
> my heart now melting into thine,
> I love with heart and mind and soul,
> the God who is my highest goal.

> **O Jesus, let the Fire of Joy,**
> **consume the devil's subtle ploy,**
> **transfigured is our planet earth,**
> **the golden age is given birth.**

Part 3

1. Beloved Jesus, awaken women to see that the basic dualistic polarity that we can go into on a planet like earth is that in order to take embodiment on earth, we must be in a male or female body in any one embodiment.

> O Jesus, blessed brother mine,
> I walk the path that you outline,

a great example to us all,
I follow now your inner call.

**O Jesus, let the Fire of Joy,
consume the devil's subtle ploy,
transfigured is our planet earth,
the golden age is given birth.**

2. Beloved Jesus, awaken women to see that in order to take embodiment in a male body or a female body, we must create a self based on that body and that self will be based on the cultural context in which we take embodiment.

O Jesus, open inner sight,
the ego wants to prove it's right,
but this I will no longer do,
I want to be all one with you.

**O Jesus, let the Fire of Joy,
consume the devil's subtle ploy,
transfigured is our planet earth,
the golden age is given birth.**

3. Beloved Jesus, awaken women to see that the function of Christ is that no matter what kind of separate dualistic selves we have created, Christ offers us the perspective, the realization, the experience, that we are not this particular self and therefore, we can let the self die and we will not die when the self dies.

O Jesus, I now clearly see,
the Key of Knowledge given me,
my Christ self I hereby embrace,
as you fill up my inner space.

**O Jesus, let the Fire of Joy,
consume the devil's subtle ploy,
transfigured is our planet earth,
the golden age is given birth.**

4. Beloved Jesus, awaken women to see that the Christian religion will not survive in the modern democracies unless it transcends itself. Christianity must transcend this historical baggage of the Catholic church, the Jewish religion and the Old Testament.

O Jesus, show me serpent's lie,
expose the beam in my own eye,
as Christ discernment you me give,
in oneness I forever live.

O Jesus, let the Fire of Joy,
consume the devil's subtle ploy,
transfigured is our planet earth,
the golden age is given birth.

5. Beloved Jesus, awaken women to see that the Catholic religion will not survive in its present form. The question is whether the Catholic church can transform itself or whether a new form of Christianity will emerge.

O Jesus, I am truly meek,
and thus I turn the other cheek,
when the accuser attacks me,
I go within and merge with thee.

O Jesus, let the Fire of Joy,
consume the devil's subtle ploy,
transfigured is our planet earth,
the golden age is given birth.

6. Beloved Jesus, awaken women to see that if new forms of Christianity are to emerge, this will be driven primarily by women who will be able and willing to become free to tune in to the mind of the ascended master Jesus Christ.

O Jesus, ego I let die,
surrender ev'ry earthly tie,
the dead can bury what is dead,
I choose to walk with you instead.

**O Jesus, let the Fire of Joy,
consume the devil's subtle ploy,
transfigured is our planet earth,
the golden age is given birth.**

7. Beloved Jesus, awaken women so they can tune in and receive certain ideas that will allow them to suddenly have the scales fall from their eyes, and they see that it is necessary to create a new Christian church that is more focused on serving people, helping people meet the challenges they face in the modern age.

O Jesus, help me rise above,
the devil's test through higher love,
show me separate self unreal,
my formless self you do reveal.

**O Jesus, let the Fire of Joy,
consume the devil's subtle ploy,
transfigured is our planet earth,
the golden age is given birth.**

8. Beloved Jesus, awaken women to see that for people in the modern democracies, the next logical step is to follow Maslow's pyramid of needs and go into the self-actualization needs. It is possible to create a Christian church that is using the teachings and example of Christ to help people fulfill their needs for self-actualization. Awaken women to tune in to your mind and receive these ideas.

O Jesus, what is that to me,
I just let go and follow thee,
with this I do pass ev'ry test,
to find with you eternal rest.

**O Jesus, let the Fire of Joy,
consume the devil's subtle ploy,
transfigured is our planet earth,
the golden age is given birth.**

9. Beloved Jesus, awaken women to see that for a new form of Christianity to emerge, it will be necessary to take the Old Testament out of Christian scriptures. It will be necessary to incorporate some of the Gnostic Gospels, in order to get a more diversified scriptural background.

O Jesus, fiery master mine,
my heart now melting into thine,
I love with heart and mind and soul,
the God who is my highest goal.

**O Jesus, let the Fire of Joy,
consume the devil's subtle ploy,
transfigured is our planet earth,
the golden age is given birth.**

Part 4

1. Beloved Jesus, awaken women to see that it necessary to let go of the Old Testament because as long as we believe that this is the word of God and was given through some infallible revelation, we will not be able to overcome the baggage that defines women as inferior to men and as the cause of the downfall of the entire human race.

O Jesus, blessed brother mine,
I walk the path that you outline,
a great example to us all,
I follow now your inner call.

**O Jesus, let the Fire of Joy,
consume the devil's subtle ploy,
transfigured is our planet earth,
the golden age is given birth.**

2. Beloved Jesus, awaken women to see that a new form of Christianity must leave this entire mindset behind, or it will have no chance of surviving in the modern age. We must let go of this Old Testament baggage and there is no way to do it except by letting go of the Old Testament.

O Jesus, open inner sight,
the ego wants to prove it's right,
but this I will no longer do,
I want to be all one with you.

O Jesus, let the Fire of Joy,
consume the devil's subtle ploy,
transfigured is our planet earth,
the golden age is given birth.

3. Beloved Jesus, awaken women to see that a new form of Christianity is
not just a New Testament but a new attunement with the universal Christ
mind that promotes growth, that promotes self-transcendence, not a static
form of Christianity.

O Jesus, I now clearly see,
the Key of Knowledge given me,
my Christ self I hereby embrace,
as you fill up my inner space.

O Jesus, let the Fire of Joy,
consume the devil's subtle ploy,
transfigured is our planet earth,
the golden age is given birth.

4. Beloved Jesus, I call forth the judgment of Christ upon the fallen beings
who do not want a movement that is based on self-transcendence.

O Jesus, show me serpent's lie,
expose the beam in my own eye,
as Christ discernment you me give,
in oneness I forever live.

O Jesus, let the Fire of Joy,
consume the devil's subtle ploy,
transfigured is our planet earth,
the golden age is given birth.

5. Beloved Jesus, I call forth the judgment of Christ upon the fallen beings who want to maintain the kind of Christianity we have had since the formation of the Catholic church, namely a Christianity that denies our ability to self-transcend.

> O Jesus, I am truly meek,
> and thus I turn the other cheek,
> when the accuser attacks me,
> I go within and merge with thee.

> **O Jesus, let the Fire of Joy,**
> **consume the devil's subtle ploy,**
> **transfigured is our planet earth,**
> **the golden age is given birth.**

6. Beloved Jesus, I call forth the judgment of Christ upon the fallen beings who say that only the pope has direct contact with Christ. Only the ministers, the priests, are the mediators between God and men.

> O Jesus, ego I let die,
> surrender ev'ry earthly tie,
> the dead can bury what is dead,
> I choose to walk with you instead.

> **O Jesus, let the Fire of Joy,**
> **consume the devil's subtle ploy,**
> **transfigured is our planet earth,**
> **the golden age is given birth.**

7. Beloved Jesus, awaken women to see that your primary message is that no human being or human institution is the mediator between Spirit and man. Only the Christ is the mediator, and the Christ is a universal mind that is beyond any division we could possibly create on earth.

> O Jesus, help me rise above,
> the devil's test through higher love,
> show me separate self unreal,
> my formless self you do reveal.

O Jesus, let the Fire of Joy,
consume the devil's subtle ploy,
transfigured is our planet earth,
the golden age is given birth.

8. Beloved Jesus, awaken women to see that Christ is always there for all people and Christ resides in the kingdom of God that is located within us because it is a state of consciousness.

O Jesus, what is that to me,
I just let go and follow thee,
with this I do pass ev'ry test,
to find with you eternal rest.

O Jesus, let the Fire of Joy,
consume the devil's subtle ploy,
transfigured is our planet earth,
the golden age is given birth.

9. Beloved Jesus, awaken women to see that the kingdom of God is our ability to become aware that we have a limited self, our ability to decide that we are willing to let that self die in order to follow Christ, in order to come up higher in consciousness and be reborn into a higher sense of self.

O Jesus, fiery master mine,
my heart now melting into thine,
I love with heart and mind and soul,
the God who is my highest goal.

O Jesus, let the Fire of Joy,
consume the devil's subtle ploy,
transfigured is our planet earth,
the golden age is given birth.

Sealing

In the name of the I AM THAT I AM, I accept that Archangel Michael, Astrea and Shiva form an impenetrable shield around myself and all constructive people, sealing us from all fear-based energies in all four octaves. I accept that the Light of God is consuming and transforming all fear-based energies that make up the dark forces working against the liberation of women on earth!

19 | CAN WOMEN BE FULLY LIBERATED?

I am the Ascended Master Maraytaii. I hold the spiritual office of the Cosmic Mother. This is an office that is very much in line with the Office of Mother Mary, the Office of the Divine Mother. Only, whereas Mother Mary holds the office specifically for earth, I hold it at a higher level for a larger sphere than just one planet. How large is not necessary for you to know, but it is quite large. It is not confined to merely one galaxy. I have a quite broad, a quite wide, perspective compared to the perspective you have when you are in embodiment on a dense planet like earth. Naturally, in what you might call my daily activities (if there is such a thing at the cosmic level where there is no day or night) I am not attuned particularly with planet earth and with the situation of women on planet earth. I can of course do so and I am doing so now as I am anchoring my Presence here for the giving of this dictation.

When I attune my Being to the situation of so many women around the earth who are severely limited by various conditions, naturally my heart overflows with compassion. I feel a great and deep compassion for the fact that so many spiritual beings are trapped in these very limiting, very difficult, very painful situations that you see so many women on this planet being trapped in. Naturally, I also see beyond, I see what you really are, that you are not women, you are spiritual beings. Nevertheless, that does not particularly help the many women, who are in these difficult situations.

The dispensation of the Comforting Presence

What then can potentially help? Well, Mother Mary, Kuan Yin and myself have taken up counsel and we have decided to give a tool, a dispensation if you will, where we will all three anchor a certain portion of our Presences, our Beings in the earth, in the collective consciousness at the four levels of the earth. The purpose of this is to give women an opportunity to tune in to the Flame of Mother Mary, the Flame of Kuan Yin, if they are more identified in the East, or the flame or myself, which is beyond any divisions on earth and therefore as neutral as anything can be on a planet where nothing is neutral. The purpose for this is to give all women, whether they are consciously aware of it or not (but they might still sense it intuitively) an opportunity to experience a comforting presence.

When you look at the situation of many women, you see that they are often in the role of being the comforter. They comfort their own children of course when they are hurt, when they are feeling bad, when they are upset, but they also comfort sometimes the bigger children of their own husbands. Or they comfort their parents who sometimes go back to an almost childlike state in their older age. You see that many women have by various circumstances been forced to become mothers at a very early age, perhaps even in their teenage years, perhaps before they were emotionally ready to become mothers. Of course, we might ask if anybody is ever emotionally ready to become a mother, but still, at the younger age you have children, the less you are likely to be ready for this. So many women have at an early age been thrust into a situation where they now have to be the comforter of their children, of their husbands and so forth. This raises the question: "Who comforts the comforter?" Where can these women go when they need to be comforted, when they are overwhelmed by their daily lives, by their responsibility, by the chaos they experience around them, by the oppression or abuse they are exposed to? Where do they go for comfort, whether they are mothers or not, where do women go for comfort?

You will know that many women have scarcely experienced comfort even in their childhoods. So many women grow up in societies where they are, as girls, considered worthless. They do not always receive the comfort or the attention from their own mothers because their own mothers never received it, and how can you give to your own daughter what you have never received yourself—when you do not even know what it is? Well, some women *can* because they have matured in previous embodiments and now they are still able to give comfort, but many women cannot because they have never experienced it and they do not even know how to give it. One of the enduring questions on earth is: How can you give what you have not received? Once the fallen beings have managed to create a culture where for example comfort is not given, how can the people in that culture then give it?

Our purpose is to anchor our Presences so that through the Presence of Mother Mary and Kuan Yin, the greater momentum of me and my office as the Cosmic Mother can be released on earth and can therefore serve as an opportunity for women to feel comfort when there is no comfort to be found at the physical level of planet earth. Some women will be able to tune in to our Presences, many will not. Those of you who are aware of our Presences, I hope you will be able and willing to tune in, to use us in whatever way you can. Some of you will be able to just tune in to our Presences, at least after you have worked on gaining this attunement. Others may need to give a decree, to listen to one of our dictations, to read one of our dictations, to give an invocation or maybe just set aside some time and tune in. You may even just do a simple thing, such as memorize a simple verse from my decree:

O Cosmic Mother, I love you,
your love song keeps me ever true.
You fill me with your sacred tone,
and thus I never feel alone.

Four lines. Anyone can memorize this and you may give it aloud or silently whenever you feel that you are alone, and that you need comfort, and I will be there. I will manifest my Presence where you give it. Truly, all three of us would desire all women on earth to experience that Flame of Comfort. When I say comfort, this might be what people on earth would experience but in reality it is the love of the Divine Mother, which is, as we have for want of a better word called "unconditional" but really it is beyond the conditions that you normally associate with love on earth. What we desire all women to know, to experience, to accept is that you are loved for who you are. There are beings who are not in the physical realm on earth but who are nevertheless very real, and we love you for who you are. We have no conditions in that love. We accept you for who you are regardless of how you may see yourself. You may think you are not worthy of love but it is only your thinking that prevents you from experiencing the love that would actually consume all of that sense of unworthiness.

What women need to be liberated from

You see, this is the central dilemma on earth and it ties in with what other masters have said about the Christ. Christ is the universal liberator, but the thing is, what is it people need to be liberated from? They need to be liberated from the mind of anti-christ. What is the mind of anti-christ? It is the mind that defines conditions. What is the mind of Christ? It is the mind that is beyond all conditions that could be defined in duality. Once you are trapped in duality, in the mind of anti-christ, you think that in order to experience Christ, you must live up to certain conditions. Now, if you could experience Christ for a moment, that experience would change your perspective. It would awaken you from the lie that you need to live up to certain conditions in order to be worthy to receive anything from the spiritual realm. The Christ mind, the Christ experience, the Christ vibration can consume your conditions, but only if you receive it and you cannot receive it as long as you hold on to the conditions. For it is only the conditions that you have defined in your own mind (that you have taken into your own mind after they were defined by the fallen beings), it is only those conditions that prevent you from experiencing the unconditional. How can you overcome those conditions? Well, many can only overcome it through the School of Hard Knocks but it is of course our hope that many women will be able and willing to tune in to our unconditional Presence, our unconditional love and comfort, our unconditional acceptance and thereby let go of this conditionality.

The theme for this conference is the liberation of women. Is it actually possible to liberate women? As we have said before, the answer to that question is yes and no. We must recognize that liberation has two aspects; we might call it an alpha and an omega. The omega aspect of liberation is that you are oppressed by something and therefore you need to be liberated *from* something—liberated from what limits you. This is one aspect of liberation but it is not the full aspect of liberation. Let us take a woman who has grown up in one of these societies where women are put down, considered worthless, and where all of these restrictions are put upon women. Let us now say that we took such a woman and we transported her to a modern democracy and we said: "Here, now you are completely liberated from all of the circumstances and conditions in which you grew up." How would she then react? How would she deal with this new freedom? Well, in many cases such women would not be able to deal with the new freedom, they would not be able to know what to do with it because they have defined themselves, they have identified themselves, based on the cultural attitude to women so they cannot instantly make that jump from being so limited to being completely liberated.

Liberating someone from oppression can, as has been proven by history, sometimes leave them in a vacuum, in a chaotic state, in a state of confusion where they do not know what to do with themselves—they do not know what to do with their lives. The alpha aspect of liberation is the liberation *to*—the liberation to a higher awareness, a higher sense of self. How can this Alpha aspect of liberation be fulfilled? It is what we have talked about—there needs to be an awakening of women to a universal set of ideas that just living life, as comfortable as it may be in the modern democracies, is not enough in itself. Life must have a purpose. There must be a direction, and what is the most universal aspect? It is self-actualization, self-improvement and personal growth. Beyond that, the more spiritual, mystical aspects of raising your consciousness to a distinctly higher level.

How do you raise your consciousness to a higher level? There are many mystical paths, many mystical teachings, many gurus throughout the ages who have promoted a mystical path but what is the essence of this mystical path? It is that you shift your sense of identity and how do you shift your sense of identity? As Jesus explained, by letting a separate, dualistic self, die. This is how you shift your sense of identity. It may not be that much (of a shift) by letting one self, die. Many people can actually do this without even noticing it, without realizing what they are doing. Nevertheless, this is the essence of the mystical path. It is really not that mystical, nor is it that particularly glamorous. Many spiritual students want it to be some glamorous path that gives them a certain status, or perhaps some mystical path that is difficult to understand and therefore they can feel superior because they have grasped some kind of teaching. Have they really grasped the universal aspect of what the path is all about?

Mapping the liberation of women

We now come to a point where we can look at the situation of women on earth and we can see, as other masters have said, there are certain nations that have made considerable progress in improving the situation of women. If you compare some of the modern democracies, such as the Scandinavian countries, to where they were at 100 or 150 years ago, you can see a tremendous improvement in women's situation, not only in terms of legally where they have the right to vote, the right to own property, but also in how they are treated and how women are looked at. In other words, there is both the outer framework, the physical, political, legal framework, but there is also the psychological framework of the shift in the collective consciousness where there is at least a greater degree of equality between men and women. We can say that in these nations considerable progress has been made towards the liberation of women from the conditions that limited them. We can therefore use this as a standard and look at other nations around the world.

You could create a scale or a map where you could see the most liberated countries in terms of women and going down towards the less liberated where women are heavily oppressed still. When you look at this you see that when it comes to the liberation from limiting conditions, there is a range. There are the *most* liberated nations, there are the *least* liberated and then in between is a large group of nations where the liberation of women has progressed to some degree. In other words, the least liberated nations basically need to go through the same process as the more liberated nations have gone through. It will not be exactly identical because the challenges of freeing a nation from Islamic culture is not exactly the same as that of Christian culture but there are still many similarities.

As we have said before, women in the less liberated nations can certainly look to their sisters in those nations and ask for help: "What can we do?" They can look at what these nations have gone through and we also hope that women in the more liberated nations will follow Saint Germain's advice to develop this solidarity and acknowledge that "No woman is truly free until every woman is free." It is their responsibility to use their freedom to help their sisters in other nations. This is the liberation *from*.

It is clear that from an ascended perspective, we deeply honor and we are grateful for the many, many people, both men and women, who have taken action to promote this liberation of women. It is clear that this is a tremendous work that has been done, it is a necessary effort. We are in absolutely no way wanting to diminish it or make it seem unimportant. It is very important and very necessary but as we have said, what we aim to do with this conference is to do something that can help the more aware spiritual people, especially ascended master students, have an impact on the liberation of women and naturally that is why we want to give a deeper spiritual perspective. We can say that the alpha aspect of the liberation of women is that we go beyond liberating women *from* the conditions that limit them, but we liberate them *to* embracing a new direction, something positive. You are not seeking to get away from something, you are seeking to move towards a positive goal and that goal is ultimately raising your consciousness, actualizing yourself.

Liberating women from being women

This again has many levels and there are many women around the world, but especially in the more evolved nations, that have already started on this process. They have started in various ways, as we have said, through personal growth, yoga, self-awareness, mindfulness, many other things. Many women have also gone into a variety of spiritual movements. You see in all New Age movements, practically, a majority of the members being women. Many, many women have made these strides to seek for a new sense of identity; a new spiritual identity and many have made considerable progress.

It is not our intent to say that only ascended master students make progress. Naturally, there are many ways to follow the path to a higher level of consciousness and we encourage people to engage in whatever appeals to them intuitively at their present level of consciousness, always being mindful that as they move higher in consciousness they might see a higher teaching, a higher teacher and eventually come to acknowledge the ascended masters who are the, in a sense (if you want to use that word), the highest spiritual teachers available to the lifestreams on earth. This is not to set up a value judgment but simply to state that we are the beings who are in the highest level of consciousness who are working with the earth.

We are also the only beings who are beyond the four levels of the material universe, that is the nature of being ascended, and we are all united in the ascended realm. There are no divisions of ascended masters here, as some students seem to believe. When you then look at the process of liberating women *to,* what are you essentially being liberated to? You are being liberated to a higher sense of identity, a higher awareness of who you are, what kind of being you are, and what does that lead you to?

There are some who will say that this leads you to become fully empowered as a woman, to fulfill your highest potential as a woman, to express your power as a woman and these ideas are not invalid. There are women who can benefit from going through a phase where they seek to become empowered as women and they seek to have more of an impact in society. Again, we are not putting this down in any way, but for our students who acknowledge ascended masters, ascended master teachings, who have been willing to take these teachings, especially teachings on healing your spiritual traumas, overcoming all of these selves and the cosmic birth trauma, you are ready to consider the next step.

That is why I earlier said: Can women be liberated, and the answer is both a yes and a no. Women can be liberated from limiting conditions where many different cultures, always starting with the fallen beings, have put these severe limitations on what it means to be a woman. This in the world, you can be liberated from. How do you then end up seeing yourself if you have liberated yourself from all of the limitations that are put upon women on this planet? Well, if you do not put anything instead of it, you would end up in a vacuum. This cannot really happen in practicality because as you raise your consciousness, you will start building a new sense of identity. What is the identity you then begin to build? When you liberate yourself from all of the limitations put upon women on earth, do you end up being a fully liberated woman? The answer is no, my beloved. You end up being a fully liberated spiritual being who is neither male nor female.

Liberating women from the conflict of opposites

What does it mean to attain personal Christhood? We have talked about this many times, given many teachings on it, but what does it really mean in this context? Do you become a male Christ or a female Christ? Nay, there is no such thing. Christ is universal. Christ is beyond these divisions of men and women. What does that mean? You are still in embodiment on earth. You are still in a male or female body. Yes, but there is a fundamental difference between thinking that because you are in a female body in this lifetime, you are a woman, that because you are in a female body, your being is defined by you being in a female body, and then realizing that regardless of the sex of the body you are in, you are a universal spiritual being. You are not defined by the sex of your physical body and by the cultural overlay put upon that sex here on earth. There is a fundamental difference and many of you are ready to begin to contemplate this so that you are not striving to become a liberated woman, you are striving to become a Christed being who is not identified with, identifying yourself as, a woman or man.

You are still going to be in embodiment so you are going to be in a female body. The thing is, once you liberate yourself and attain the level of Christhood that I am talking about, you can look at the fact that you are in a female body and say: "So what? It's just a body. I just have to make the best of it but I am not going to let it limit me and the expression of my I AM Presence through me." You see my beloved, when you consider this process of liberating women *from,* you will see that the very concept of liberating you from something whether it is a man or a woman, the very concept that you are liberated from something is in a certain way dualistic. There is something that is limiting you and there is a state of freedom that is opposed to it and you attain it by removing the condition or removing yourself from the condition that is limiting you. There are two opposites there and for most people they see them as opposites.

There is slavery, there is freedom, there is imprisonment, there is being outside of prison; they see them as two opposites. You may know that there are certain spiritually evolved people who have been put into prison and it made no difference to them. They were still anchored in their own minds, anchored in themselves, and whether they had freedom of movement of the body, they still had the freedom of movement of the mind and they could say: "So what! That's just a situation that's there temporarily." You can come to a point where you look at, the same way, your physical body and say: "So what." Does this messenger identify himself as a man? No, he is a spiritual being who just happens to be in a male body in this lifetime and he knows full well he has been in female bodies in many lifetimes in the past, and the same for all of you. There is not one single one who is in a female body today who has always been a woman in past lifetimes.

What I am seeking to convey to you here is an idea that may require some pondering. You may have to meditate on this for a while before you fully internalize how liberating this can be. Jesus talked about the fact that when you go into duality, you have to choose one dualistic polarity and you then create a self based on that polarity. The polarity always has an opposite so you are forced to react to the opposite because when you are in one polarity you cannot escape the opposite polarity. You are forced to react to that and this creates a new self, which then has another opposite polarity, which creates another self and so forth. This is why you lose your free will because you are now in a pattern where you are reacting to something that seems opposite to the way you identify yourself. In order to deal with this, you create selves, one self here, one self there, another one, another one and pretty soon there are so many of these selves that you forget you are a spiritual being, you forget you are not confined to this earth, you forget you are not confined to these selves. You are so overwhelmed by the multiplicity of selves that you think this is who you are.

What happens here is that when you then begin to awaken, when you then begin to actually acknowledge that you are limited and that you want to be free, then you go through a phase where you are seeing: "I am a woman, I am limited by this condition in my society, for example I have to wear a burka and I want to be free from this. How can I be free from it?" How have women become free from these limiting conditions? They have done this in two ways, there are two ways to seek to do this. One is that you can genuinely transcend your own state of consciousness. There are women for example, who before women were given the right to vote in these modern democracies, they were working to create a political change but they were also willing to work with themselves and shift their sense of identity. They overcame this cultural overlay that women did not know anything about politics and therefore should not be allowed to vote, that women could not understand politics. They shifted their sense of identity in a positive way and they acknowledged, accepted, that women can indeed know as much about politics as men and that women can provide a valuable perspective in the political arena and therefore of course they should be allowed to vote, they should be allowed to run for office and so forth.

Turning the liberation of women into a dualistic struggle

There were other women who were not able or willing to make that transition so what did they do? They created a new sense of identity as a woman who was not liberated from the previous condition, but who was in opposition to it, or in some cases in opposition to men. In other words, they were not transcending themselves, their limited selves. They created another dualistic self that they defined in opposition to men, or at least a certain archetypal image of men that they had encountered. This is what you see in the more extreme feminist movements where they have a negative view of men and have created a certain image of women as being different from, superior to, that negative image of men. This is not leading to a real liberation of these women. It may lead to improved conditions in a society.

Again, we are not looking at these efforts and saying: "Oh, the whole feminist movement was wrong, they shouldn't have done this." It was necessary, given how dualistic the culture was, to create something that opposed the men and their male dominance, and could therefore shake them out of this hypnotic state they were in. This is not the highest way to do it but it is often a necessary way and, as even Jesus has expounded upon before, there are sometimes people who for a certain time can be actually in alignment with Christ in terms of doing what is necessary to bring change in a society. Then, the question is: Can they stay in alignment with Christ or will they lose it because they now go into a dualistic reaction?

What I am seeking to point out here is that those of you who are open to these teachings, you are ready to take a look at this, take a look at your own history but also your country, your culture and see that there is this element. For that matter, the men are also ready to look at this and see that men have the same pattern of creating these dualistic selves where you are in opposition to something. You see numerous examples of this in history where even the French and the Germans and the British had created selves based on being in opposition to each other and this has led to many wars in the past and even in the present.

You are ready to consider that you are not liberating yourself by creating a dualistic self that is in opposition to anything on earth. If you can truly internalize these ideas, you can then rise to a higher level where as a woman you can now take on a new role. You can be the forerunners for a new phase in the liberation of women, which is how the modern democracies can go beyond the level they are at right now and go into a new phase. You can certainly make the calls for the cutting free of other women who are ready to step up to this higher level.

What you need to look at is very simple. You need to look at your own reaction to being a woman. You may need to contemplate this; you may need to give invocations for it, you need to take some time to contemplate: What is your reaction to the fact that you are in a female body in this lifetime? Do you feel that it limits you? Do you feel that it is a disadvantage? Then, you need to consider that you probably do feel this way because in past lives you were involved with a woman's liberation movement of liberating women *from* and you created these separate selves in reaction to this, in reaction to the oppression that women are exposed to.

You can begin to gradually, one at a time, follow the process we have given you of becoming aware of a certain self and letting it die, perhaps using Mother Mary's visualization of going into the theater and seeing a past situation where you created these selves, letting them die, letting them go [See the book *Healing Your Spiritual Traumas*]. It is not a matter of liberating yourself as a woman but it is a matter of liberating yourself from being a woman, from thinking you are a woman, from seeing yourself as a woman, from identifying yourself as a woman. As long as you identify yourself as a woman, even in one of the liberated countries, you will still identify yourself based on the role that women have currently and there will be some opposition to, or resistance to, the limitations that women are still exposed to.

A higher level of the liberation of women

What you who are open to our teachings have the potential to do is rise to that next level up where you free yourself from all resistance, from all sense of opposition, from all sense of being limited. You look at the conditions that women are exposed to in your culture and society, you look at your own situation and you say: "So what! I will not identify myself based on these limitations." This can open up for an entirely new approach, not only to the overall situation in your culture, but to your personal life, including whatever relationships you are in. You may discover that you have been locked in a relationship based on a certain pattern. If you let go of the selves that have accepted this, you can come to a point where you say: "I will not be bound by this pattern anymore. I will free myself from this pattern. First of all, I will free myself in my own mind."

Then, once you have freed yourself, you will be free to talk to your partner about this and make it clear to him that you will no longer be bound by this pattern. You may be able to help him also free himself from the pattern. You may find that he has been limited by it as well. Or there may be cases where your partner will not respond and will not change. As we have said before, if you are really willing to change yourself, then either your partner will change or you will change your partner. Then you can look at this and say: "Well, if I have to change my relationship to move forward in my spiritual enfoldment, move to a higher level of Christhood, so what, this is part of the path. This is part of life."

You are on a very dense planet. You have dedicated yourself to attaining maximum spiritual growth in this lifetime. How will you attain maximum spiritual growth on a dense planet like earth? It cannot, necessarily, be done by getting married in your teenage years and following the command to live that way until death do you part. Many of you have already had more than one partner, many of you will. I am not saying *all* of you will, I am saying that when you are willing to work with yourself, then you will come to that point where you may help your partner change so the relationship can rise to a higher level. Or you may just move on and attract another partner who is willing to go to that higher level or is already there.

These are some, perhaps, deep mystical ideas that are a little bit beyond what is normally discussed in the women's liberation movement or in discussion groups between women. Nevertheless, it is important for you who are our spiritual students to have this teaching. I am not saying all of you are ready for it, but many of you are. You understand that there are two aspects of progressive revelation. One is the omega aspect where we give teachings that are easier to understand, easier to grasp than previous teachings. If you look and compare the teachings given through this messenger to teachings given through previous dispensations of the ascended masters, you will see that some of these teachings are much easier to understand. They are expressed in a more simple, everyday language much easier to grasp. You will also see that we have given some teachings here that are at a much higher level than any previous dispensation and therefore more difficult to grasp for those who are not ready for it but these are the two aspects of progressive revelation.

I know some of you have a tendency to feel sometimes that there is a huge gap between most people in the world, the people around you, the people you know (whether family or friends) and then the level of teachings that we give as ascended masters. Some of you feel that as we give more and more advanced teachings, that gap only becomes bigger. It becomes more and more difficult for you to talk to other people about the teachings that we are giving but you do not need to give other people these more advanced teachings. There are much more basic teachings that we have given and you can take these teachings and you can attempt to give them to other people. I am not saying that you need to go out and preach a specific teaching to other people. It is better to focus on giving people certain ideas.

Here you need to then come to that point where you realize that it is not a matter of what *you* want to tell other people. So many times we have students that find our teachings and now they want to go out and convert other people to believe what they now believe, to accept what they now accept. This is because you still have separate selves that are afraid of being rejected. When you go through the process I am talking about here, letting

go of these separate selves, you come to a point where you are not sharing your ideas in order to gain validation or in order to have a particular
influence on other people. You can look at other people as individuals,
look at their situation and realize this particular person is in that particular
situation. It is not a matter of me raising her up to this level that is 20 levels
of consciousness beyond where she is at right now. It is a matter of me
giving her a few ideas that can help her rise to the next level up, and then
you do that.

Perhaps over time you can give her more teachings that help her go
20 levels above where she is now, but this cannot happen in one leap just
as it did not happen for you. Do not fixate your mind on the gap. Look
at people. Tune in to what they are ready to receive. Give them one little
thing at a time. Give them some time to internalize that idea and then give
them something else. Take the long view.

In terms of yourself, do not allow your growth to be held back by
others but use the teachings in your own internal process to raise your
consciousness as much as you can, and do not let other people hold you
back. You may have relationships where you are not sharing with people
everything you are going through. This messenger has made it a point to
have people around him, some that he has known since childhood, that he
can talk to about other topics than spirituality because it helps him tune in
to how other people think and you can have the same. You do not have to
have all of your friends be spiritually interested. You can have people that
you talk to about other topics that they are able to talk about and once in
a while you give them an idea that may raise their awareness, but you are
not pushing them. You are just allowing the relationship to unfold, sharing with them a few ideas. This also applies to how you make use of the
teachings we are giving at this conference. We are not looking for people
to now go out there and try to go into women's groups for example and
say: "Here is this new fantastic teaching. This is what you should take and
use from now on." You may be able to go into such groups and take one
or two ideas and give that idea and it might resonate with them. You see,
it is all about ideas.

What changes the world is universal ideas

How was the world changed so that women in the more evolved nations
became liberated to the degree they have been liberated? It did not happen

all at once. It happened one idea at a time. How will you have an impact on changing society? *One idea at a time.* What have we said about the Christ principle? It is this interval, it is this jump that you can make. Any person that you meet is at a particular level of consciousness. There is a Christ potential for each person but the Christ potential is what? It is that this person can jump to the next level up. The person cannot jump 100 levels, cannot jump 50 levels, cannot jump ten levels cannot even jump two levels. They can jump *one* level.

What we often see with ascended master students is that they find an ascended master teaching, they open themselves to it, they feel that now they have jumped so much forward but the reality is that they still only jumped one level compared to where they were at when they found the teaching. It is just that suddenly they became conscious of a new way to look at life. You may feel it is a very dramatic movement but it was still just that one leap up. What do people do then? They are so overcome by their enthusiasm of having made this discovery, and now they go out to people they have known for years and they are essentially trying to make these people jump two, five or ten levels up all at once and nobody can do it. These people who are exposed to this impulse from ascended master students, they are overwhelmed and they must withdraw because you are asking them to do the impossible. What you need to do is tune in to where people are at and then seek to give them that one idea that will help them make that next jump, that next Christ jump, that next quantum jump to the level up from where they are at. Then, if they are willing to do that, you can give them another idea. If they are not willing to make the jump now, then you leave them alone. You do not push them. You can still talk to them, but you do not seek to give them more ideas. You give the idea time to go through the emotional, mental and identity bodies, and eventually circle back to the physical so that now, perhaps after years have passed, the person is then ready to make the shift.

This is how you deal with spreading the teachings of the ascended masters. Too many times in the past we have seen ascended master students be trapped in the same mindset that you see so many for example Christians, be trapped in. They suddenly feel that they have now found Christ and now they need to go out and make all other people do the same thing. This is not what we are asking our students to do. When you become aware of this, if you see you have the tendency to do this, you realize this comes from separate selves. If you work on letting go of these selves, you will be free of this compulsory drive to convert and convince other people.

You will simply come to a point where you are not sharing ideas with an intent to change other people, you are simply sharing ideas because you are expressing what you think and feel, how you look at things, what you experience in life and that is totally different. When you have no intent, you will find that people will respond more positively. Some will still ignore the ideas, but they will not become angry, overwhelmed or hostile. Others may respond to the ideas in a more positive way because there is no pressure put upon them from you.

This concludes the remarks I wanted to give you here but I again want to emphasize that you really have the opportunity to tune in to our Comforting Presence. I know some will say: "Well, is it only women who can tune in? What if we men need comfort?" Well, of course the offer extends to you as well for we do not see you as men and women. We aim to get you to a point where you no longer see yourselves as men and women, for this is how you can truly be united in Christ, where all are spiritual beings who are expressing yourselves through different bodies, through different personalities, different cultures, different backgrounds. You are still united by knowing that there is a core within you – which we have called the essential humanity, which we might as well call the Christ identity – and that is what unites you. You are not united by eradicating differences, you are united by overcoming the differences and realizing that these differences do not define your identity, for you have a new identity in Christ. You have, as it says in the scriptures, become reborn, you have become a new being in Christ. With this, I seal you in the comforting flame of the Cosmic Mother that I AM.

NOTE: This dictation was given May 31, 2020.

20 | INVOKING LIBERATION FROM BEING A WOMEN

In the name of the I AM THAT I AM, Jesus Christ, I use the authority that I have as a being in embodiment on earth to call upon Maraytaii to reinforce my calls and use my chakras to project the statements in this invocation into the collective consciousness and awaken people to the awareness that will liberate both men and women from all psychological and spiritual thralldom to the fallen beings. Awaken people to the reality that we are spiritual beings and that we can co-create a new future by working with the ascended masters. I especially call for …

[Make your own calls here.]

Part 1

1. Maraytaii, I invoke your Comforting Presence on behalf of all women so they will have an opportunity to experience a comforting presence.

> O Cosmic Mother, sound the gong,
> that calls me home where I belong.
> I know you love me tenderly,
> and in that knowing I am free.

**Maraytaii, I resonate
with song that opens cosmic gate.
Your melody makes me vibrate
my sense of self I recreate.**

2. Maraytaii, I invoke your Comforting Presence on behalf of all women
who need to be comforted when they are overwhelmed by their daily lives,
by their responsibility, by the chaos they experience around them, by the
oppression or abuse they are exposed to.

O Cosmic Mother, hold me tight,
I resonate with your own light.
Your music purifies my heart,
your love to all I do impart.

**Maraytaii, I resonate
with song that opens cosmic gate.
Your melody makes me vibrate
my sense of self I recreate.**

3. Maraytaii, I invoke your Comforting Presence on behalf of all women
who have not experienced comfort even in their childhoods because they
grew up in societies where girls are considered worthless.

O Cosmic Mother, we are one,
your heart is like a blazing sun.
My being can but amplify,
the sacred sound you magnify.

**Maraytaii, I resonate
with song that opens cosmic gate.
Your melody makes me vibrate
my sense of self I recreate.**

4. Maraytaii, I invoke your Comforting Presence on behalf of all women
who did not receive comfort or attention from their own mothers because
their own mothers never received it, and how can you give to your own
daughter what you have never received yourself.

O Cosmic Mother, I now hear,
the subtle sound of Sacred Sphere.
As I attune to Cosmic Hum,
the lesser self I overcome.

**Maraytaii, I resonate
with song that opens cosmic gate.
Your melody makes me vibrate
my sense of self I recreate.**

5. Maraytaii, I invoke your Comforting Presence on behalf of all women so they can receive an opportunity to feel comfort when there is no comfort to be found at the physical level of planet earth.

O Cosmic Mother, take me home,
I am in sync with Sacred OM,
The sound of sounds will raise me up,
so only light is in my cup.

**Maraytaii, I resonate
with song that opens cosmic gate.
Your melody makes me vibrate
my sense of self I recreate.**

6. Maraytaii, I invoke your Comforting Presence on behalf of all women so they can experience your Presence, experience that Flame of Comfort, experience the love of the Divine Mother, which is beyond the conditions that we normally associate with love on earth.

O Cosmic Mother, I will be,
a part of cosmic symphony.
All that I AM, an instrument,
for sound that is from heaven sent.

**Maraytaii, I resonate
with song that opens cosmic gate.
Your melody makes me vibrate
my sense of self I recreate.**

7. Maraytaii, I invoke your Comforting Presence on behalf of all women so they can know, experience and accept that they are loved for who they are. There are beings who are not in the physical realm on earth but who are nevertheless very real, and you love them for who they are.

O Cosmic Mother, I now call,
to enter sacred music hall.
I will be part of life's ascent,
towards the starry firmament.

Maraytaii, I resonate
with song that opens cosmic gate.
Your melody makes me vibrate
my sense of self I recreate.

8. Maraytaii, I invoke your Comforting Presence on behalf of all women so they can experience that there are no conditions in your love. You accept us for who we are regardless of how we may see ourselves.

O Cosmic Mother, tune my strings,
my total being with you sings.
Your song I now reverberate,
as cosmic love I celebrate.

Maraytaii, I resonate
with song that opens cosmic gate.
Your melody makes me vibrate
my sense of self I recreate.

9. Maraytaii, I invoke your Comforting Presence on behalf of all women who think they are not worthy of love, so they can realize that it is only our thinking that prevents us from experiencing the love that can consume all sense of unworthiness.

O Cosmic Mother, I love you,
your love song keeps me ever true.
You fill me with your sacred tone,
and thus I never feel alone.

**Maraytaii, I resonate
with song that opens cosmic gate.
Your melody makes me vibrate
my sense of self I recreate.**

Part 2

1. Maraytaii, I invoke your Comforting Presence on behalf of all women so they can see that they need to be liberated from the mind of anti-christ, which is the mind that defines conditions.

O Cosmic Mother, sound the gong,
that calls me home where I belong.
I know you love me tenderly,
and in that knowing I am free.

**Maraytaii, I resonate
with song that opens cosmic gate.
Your melody makes me vibrate
my sense of self I recreate.**

2. Maraytaii, I invoke your Comforting Presence on behalf of all women so they can see that the mind of Christ is beyond all conditions, and we don't need to live up to any conditions in order to experience Christ.

O Cosmic Mother, hold me tight,
I resonate with your own light.
Your music purifies my heart,
your love to all I do impart.

**Maraytaii, I resonate
with song that opens cosmic gate.
Your melody makes me vibrate
my sense of self I recreate.**

3. Maraytaii, I invoke your Comforting Presence on behalf of all women so they can experience that it is only the conditions that we have defined in our own minds that prevent us from experiencing the unconditional.

> O Cosmic Mother, we are one,
> your heart is like a blazing sun.
> My being can but amplify,
> the sacred sound you magnify.

> **Maraytaii, I resonate**
> **with song that opens cosmic gate.**
> **Your melody makes me vibrate**
> **my sense of self I recreate.**

4. Maraytaii, I invoke your Comforting Presence on behalf of all women so they can tune in to your unconditional Presence, your unconditional love and comfort, your unconditional acceptance and thereby let go of this conditionality.

> O Cosmic Mother, I now hear,
> the subtle sound of Sacred Sphere.
> As I attune to Cosmic Hum,
> the lesser self I overcome.

> **Maraytaii, I resonate**
> **with song that opens cosmic gate.**
> **Your melody makes me vibrate**
> **my sense of self I recreate.**

5. Maraytaii, awaken women to see that the omega aspect of liberation is that we are oppressed by something and therefore we need to be liberated from what limits us.

> O Cosmic Mother, take me home,
> I am in sync with Sacred OM,
> The sound of sounds will raise me up,
> so only light is in my cup.

**Maraytaii, I resonate
with song that opens cosmic gate.
Your melody makes me vibrate
my sense of self I recreate.**

6. Maraytaii, awaken women to see that many women could not handle being liberated from all of the circumstances and conditions in which they grew up.

O Cosmic Mother, I will be,
a part of cosmic symphony.
All that I AM, an instrument,
for sound that is from heaven sent.

**Maraytaii, I resonate
with song that opens cosmic gate.
Your melody makes me vibrate
my sense of self I recreate.**

7. Maraytaii, awaken women to see that many women would not be able to deal with freedom because they have defined themselves, they have identified themselves, based on the cultural attitude to women, so they cannot instantly make that jump from being so limited to being completely liberated.

O Cosmic Mother, I now call,
to enter sacred music hall.
I will be part of life's ascent,
towards the starry firmament.

**Maraytaii, I resonate
with song that opens cosmic gate.
Your melody makes me vibrate
my sense of self I recreate.**

8. Maraytaii, awaken women to see that liberating someone from oppression can leave them in a vacuum, in a chaotic state, in a state of confusion where they do not know what to do with themselves.

O Cosmic Mother, tune my strings,
my total being with you sings.
Your song I now reverberate,
as cosmic love I celebrate.

**Maraytaii, I resonate
with song that opens cosmic gate.
Your melody makes me vibrate
my sense of self I recreate.**

9. Maraytaii, awaken women to see that the alpha aspect of liberation is the liberation to a higher awareness, a higher sense of self.

O Cosmic Mother, I love you,
your love song keeps me ever true.
You fill me with your sacred tone,
and thus I never feel alone.

**Maraytaii, I resonate
with song that opens cosmic gate.
Your melody makes me vibrate
my sense of self I recreate.**

Part 3

1. Maraytaii, awaken women to see that there needs to be an awakening of women to a universal set of ideas that just living life, as comfortable as it may be in the modern democracies, is not enough in itself.

O Cosmic Mother, sound the gong,
that calls me home where I belong.
I know you love me tenderly,
and in that knowing I am free.

**Maraytaii, I resonate
with song that opens cosmic gate.**

**Your melody makes me vibrate
my sense of self I recreate.**

2. Maraytaii, awaken women to see that life must have a purpose. There must be a direction, and the most universal aspect is self-actualization, self-improvement and personal growth.

O Cosmic Mother, hold me tight,
I resonate with your own light.
Your music purifies my heart,
your love to all I do impart.

**Maraytaii, I resonate
with song that opens cosmic gate.
Your melody makes me vibrate
my sense of self I recreate.**

3. Maraytaii, awaken women to see the more spiritual and mystical aspects of raising our consciousness to a distinctly higher level.

O Cosmic Mother, we are one,
your heart is like a blazing sun.
My being can but amplify,
the sacred sound you magnify.

**Maraytaii, I resonate
with song that opens cosmic gate.
Your melody makes me vibrate
my sense of self I recreate.**

4. Maraytaii, awaken women to see that there are many mystical paths, many mystical teachings, many gurus throughout the ages who have promoted a mystical path.

O Cosmic Mother, I now hear,
the subtle sound of Sacred Sphere.
As I attune to Cosmic Hum,
the lesser self I overcome.

**Maraytaii, I resonate
with song that opens cosmic gate.
Your melody makes me vibrate
my sense of self I recreate.**

5. Maraytaii, awaken women to see that the essence of this mystical path is that we shift our sense of identity, and we do this by letting a separate, dualistic self die.

O Cosmic Mother, take me home,
I am in sync with Sacred OM,
The sound of sounds will raise me up,
so only light is in my cup.

**Maraytaii, I resonate
with song that opens cosmic gate.
Your melody makes me vibrate
my sense of self I recreate.**

6. Maraytaii, awaken women to see that in some nations women are more liberated than in others, which means the least liberated nations need to go through the same process as the more liberated nations have gone through.

O Cosmic Mother, I will be,
a part of cosmic symphony.
All that I AM, an instrument,
for sound that is from heaven sent.

**Maraytaii, I resonate
with song that opens cosmic gate.
Your melody makes me vibrate
my sense of self I recreate.**

7. Maraytaii, awaken women in the less liberated nations to ask for help from their sisters in more evolved nations.

O Cosmic Mother, I now call,
to enter sacred music hall.

I will be part of life's ascent,
towards the starry firmament.

**Maraytaii, I resonate
with song that opens cosmic gate.
Your melody makes me vibrate
my sense of self I recreate.**

8. Maraytaii, awaken women in the more liberated nations to develop this solidarity and acknowledge that "No woman is truly free until every woman is free." It is our responsibility to use our freedom to help our sisters in other nations.

O Cosmic Mother, tune my strings,
my total being with you sings.
Your song I now reverberate,
as cosmic love I celebrate.

**Maraytaii, I resonate
with song that opens cosmic gate.
Your melody makes me vibrate
my sense of self I recreate.**

9. Maraytaii, awaken women to see that the alpha aspect of the liberation of women is to go beyond liberating women *from* the conditions that limit them, but to liberate them *to* embracing a new direction, something positive.

O Cosmic Mother, I love you,
your love song keeps me ever true.
You fill me with your sacred tone,
and thus I never feel alone.

**Maraytaii, I resonate
with song that opens cosmic gate.
Your melody makes me vibrate
my sense of self I recreate.**

Part 4

1. Maraytaii, awaken women to see that there are many ways to follow the path to a higher level of consciousness, and people need to engage in whatever appeals to them intuitively at their present level of consciousness.

O Cosmic Mother, sound the gong,
that calls me home where I belong.
I know you love me tenderly,
and in that knowing I am free.

**Maraytaii, I resonate
with song that opens cosmic gate.
Your melody makes me vibrate
my sense of self I recreate.**

2. Maraytaii, awaken women to see that as they move higher in consciousness, they might see a higher teaching, a higher teacher and eventually come to acknowledge the ascended masters who are the highest spiritual teachers available on earth.

O Cosmic Mother, hold me tight,
I resonate with your own light.
Your music purifies my heart,
your love to all I do impart.

**Maraytaii, I resonate
with song that opens cosmic gate.
Your melody makes me vibrate
my sense of self I recreate.**

3. Maraytaii, awaken women to see that we need to be liberated to a higher sense of identity, a higher awareness of who we are, what kind of beings we are.

O Cosmic Mother, we are one,
your heart is like a blazing sun.

My being can but amplify,
the sacred sound you magnify.

Maraytaii, I resonate
with song that opens cosmic gate.
Your melody makes me vibrate
my sense of self I recreate.

4. Maraytaii, awaken women to see that this leads us to become fully empowered as women, to fulfill our highest potential as women, to express our power as women.

O Cosmic Mother, I now hear,
the subtle sound of Sacred Sphere.
As I attune to Cosmic Hum,
the lesser self I overcome.

Maraytaii, I resonate
with song that opens cosmic gate.
Your melody makes me vibrate
my sense of self I recreate.

5. Maraytaii, awaken women to go through a phase where we seek to become empowered as women and we seek to have more of an impact in society.

O Cosmic Mother, take me home,
I am in sync with Sacred OM,
The sound of sounds will raise me up,
so only light is in my cup.

Maraytaii, I resonate
with song that opens cosmic gate.
Your melody makes me vibrate
my sense of self I recreate.

6. Maraytaii, awaken women to see that even if we are liberated from all of the limitations that are put upon women on this planet, if we do not put anything instead of it, we would end up in a vacuum.

O Cosmic Mother, I will be,
a part of cosmic symphony.
All that I AM, an instrument,
for sound that is from heaven sent.

**Maraytaii, I resonate
with song that opens cosmic gate.
Your melody makes me vibrate
my sense of self I recreate.**

7. Maraytaii, awaken women to see that as we raise our consciousness, we will start building a new sense of identity.

O Cosmic Mother, I now call,
to enter sacred music hall.
I will be part of life's ascent,
towards the starry firmament.

**Maraytaii, I resonate
with song that opens cosmic gate.
Your melody makes me vibrate
my sense of self I recreate.**

8. Maraytaii, awaken women to see that when we liberate ourselves from all of the limitations put upon women on earth, we do not end up being a fully liberated woman. We end up being a fully liberated spiritual being who is neither male nor female.

O Cosmic Mother, tune my strings,
my total being with you sings.
Your song I now reverberate,
as cosmic love I celebrate.

**Maraytaii, I resonate
with song that opens cosmic gate.
Your melody makes me vibrate
my sense of self I recreate.**

9. Maraytaii, awaken women to see that being in a female body does not mean our being is defined by a female body. Regardless of the sex of the body we are in, we are universal spiritual beings.

> O Cosmic Mother, I love you,
> your love song keeps me ever true.
> You fill me with your sacred tone,
> and thus I never feel alone.

> **Maraytaii, I resonate**
> **with song that opens cosmic gate.**
> **Your melody makes me vibrate**
> **my sense of self I recreate.**

Part 5

1. Maraytaii, awaken women to see that we are not defined by the sex of our physical body and by the cultural overlay put upon that sex here on earth.

> O Cosmic Mother, sound the gong,
> that calls me home where I belong.
> I know you love me tenderly,
> and in that knowing I am free.

> **Maraytaii, I resonate**
> **with song that opens cosmic gate.**
> **Your melody makes me vibrate**
> **my sense of self I recreate.**

2. Maraytaii, awaken women to see that we are not striving to become liberated women, we are striving to become Christed beings who are not identifying ourselves as women or men.

> O Cosmic Mother, hold me tight,
> I resonate with your own light.

Your music purifies my heart,
your love to all I do impart.

**Maraytaii, I resonate
with song that opens cosmic gate.
Your melody makes me vibrate
my sense of self I recreate.**

3. Maraytaii, awaken women to accept that we are in female bodies and say: "So what? It's just a body. I just have to make the best of it but I am not going to let it limit me and the expression of my I AM Presence through me."

O Cosmic Mother, we are one,
your heart is like a blazing sun.
My being can but amplify,
the sacred sound you magnify.

**Maraytaii, I resonate
with song that opens cosmic gate.
Your melody makes me vibrate
my sense of self I recreate.**

4. Maraytaii, awaken women to see that the concept of liberating us from something is dualistic. There is something that is limiting us and there is a state of freedom that is opposed to it, and we attain it by removing the condition that is limiting us.

O Cosmic Mother, I now hear,
the subtle sound of Sacred Sphere.
As I attune to Cosmic Hum,
the lesser self I overcome.

**Maraytaii, I resonate
with song that opens cosmic gate.
Your melody makes me vibrate
my sense of self I recreate.**

5. Maraytaii, awaken women to see that we have all been in both male and female bodies over many lifetimes.

O Cosmic Mother, take me home,
I am in sync with Sacred OM,
The sound of sounds will raise me up,
so only light is in my cup.

Maraytaii, I resonate
with song that opens cosmic gate.
Your melody makes me vibrate
my sense of self I recreate.

6. Maraytaii, awaken women to see that we have reacted to conditions on earth by creating separate selves. These selves have caused us to forget that we are spiritual beings, that we are not confined to this earth.

O Cosmic Mother, I will be,
a part of cosmic symphony.
All that I AM, an instrument,
for sound that is from heaven sent.

Maraytaii, I resonate
with song that opens cosmic gate.
Your melody makes me vibrate
my sense of self I recreate.

7. Maraytaii, awaken women to see that as we begin to awaken, we first see that we are limited by conditions in society but the best way to become free of such conditions is to genuinely transcend our own state of consciousness.

O Cosmic Mother, I now call,
to enter sacred music hall.
I will be part of life's ascent,
towards the starry firmament.

Maraytaii, I resonate
with song that opens cosmic gate.

**Your melody makes me vibrate
my sense of self I recreate.**

8. Maraytaii, awaken women to see that those who changed society so women could vote were willing to work with themselves and shift their sense of identity, where they overcame this cultural overlay that women did not know anything about politics and therefore should not be allowed to vote, that women could not understand politics.

O Cosmic Mother, tune my strings,
my total being with you sings.
Your song I now reverberate,
as cosmic love I celebrate.

**Maraytaii, I resonate
with song that opens cosmic gate.
Your melody makes me vibrate
my sense of self I recreate.**

9. Maraytaii, awaken women to see that they shifted their sense of identity in a positive way and they accepted that women can indeed know as much about politics as men, and that women can provide a valuable perspective in the political arena and therefore should be allowed to vote and run for office.

O Cosmic Mother, I love you,
your love song keeps me ever true.
You fill me with your sacred tone,
and thus I never feel alone.

**Maraytaii, I resonate
with song that opens cosmic gate.
Your melody makes me vibrate
my sense of self I recreate.**

Part 6

1. Maraytaii, awaken women to see that some were not willing to make that transition so they created a new sense of identity as women who were not liberated from the previous condition, but who were in opposition to it, or in some cases in opposition to men.

> O Cosmic Mother, sound the gong,
> that calls me home where I belong.
> I know you love me tenderly,
> and in that knowing I am free.

> **Maraytaii, I resonate**
> **with song that opens cosmic gate.**
> **Your melody makes me vibrate**
> **my sense of self I recreate.**

2. Maraytaii, awaken women to see that they were not transcending themselves, but created another dualistic self that they defined in opposition to men, or at least a certain archetypal image of men.

> O Cosmic Mother, hold me tight,
> I resonate with your own light.
> Your music purifies my heart,
> your love to all I do impart.

> **Maraytaii, I resonate**
> **with song that opens cosmic gate.**
> **Your melody makes me vibrate**
> **my sense of self I recreate.**

3. Maraytaii, awaken women to see that people in the more extreme feminist movements have a negative view of men and have created a certain image of women as being different from, superior to, that negative image of men.

> O Cosmic Mother, we are one,
> your heart is like a blazing sun.

My being can but amplify,
the sacred sound you magnify.

**Maraytaii, I resonate
with song that opens cosmic gate.
Your melody makes me vibrate
my sense of self I recreate.**

4. Maraytaii, awaken women to see that this is not leading to a real liberation of these women. It may lead to improved conditions in a society, and it was necessary, given how dualistic the culture was, to create something that opposed men and male dominance.

O Cosmic Mother, I now hear,
the subtle sound of Sacred Sphere.
As I attune to Cosmic Hum,
the lesser self I overcome.

**Maraytaii, I resonate
with song that opens cosmic gate.
Your melody makes me vibrate
my sense of self I recreate.**

5. Maraytaii, awaken women to see that we humans have a pattern of creating these dualistic selves where we are in opposition to something.

O Cosmic Mother, take me home,
I am in sync with Sacred OM,
The sound of sounds will raise me up,
so only light is in my cup.

**Maraytaii, I resonate
with song that opens cosmic gate.
Your melody makes me vibrate
my sense of self I recreate.**

6. Maraytaii, awaken women to see that we are not liberating ourselves by creating a dualistic self that is in opposition to anything on earth.

O Cosmic Mother, I will be,
a part of cosmic symphony.
All that I AM, an instrument,
for sound that is from heaven sent.

**Maraytaii, I resonate
with song that opens cosmic gate.
Your melody makes me vibrate
my sense of self I recreate.**

7. Maraytaii, awaken women to take on a new role and be the forerunners for a new phase in the liberation of women, causing the modern democracies can go beyond the level they are at right now and go into a new phase.

O Cosmic Mother, I now call,
to enter sacred music hall.
I will be part of life's ascent,
towards the starry firmament.

**Maraytaii, I resonate
with song that opens cosmic gate.
Your melody makes me vibrate
my sense of self I recreate.**

8. Maraytaii, awaken women to look at our reaction to being a woman, to the fact that we are in a female body in this lifetime. Does it limit us, do we see it as a disadvantage?

O Cosmic Mother, tune my strings,
my total being with you sings.
Your song I now reverberate,
as cosmic love I celebrate.

**Maraytaii, I resonate
with song that opens cosmic gate.
Your melody makes me vibrate
my sense of self I recreate.**

9. Maraytaii, awaken women to see that we probably do feel this way because in past lives we were involved with a woman's liberation movement and we created these separate selves in reaction to this, in reaction to the oppression that women are exposed to.

O Cosmic Mother, I love you,
your love song keeps me ever true.
You fill me with your sacred tone,
and thus I never feel alone.

Maraytaii, I resonate
with song that opens cosmic gate.
Your melody makes me vibrate
my sense of self I recreate.

Part 7

1. Maraytaii, awaken women to see that it is not a matter of liberating ourselves as women but it is a matter of liberating ourselves from being women, from thinking we are women, from seeing ourselves as women, from identifying ourselves as women.

O Cosmic Mother, sound the gong,
that calls me home where I belong.
I know you love me tenderly,
and in that knowing I am free.

Maraytaii, I resonate
with song that opens cosmic gate.
Your melody makes me vibrate
my sense of self I recreate.

2. Maraytaii, awaken women to see that as long as we identify ourselves as women, even in one of the liberated countries, we will still identify ourselves based on the role that women have currently and there will be some opposition to the limitations that women are still exposed to.

O Cosmic Mother, hold me tight,
I resonate with your own light.
Your music purifies my heart,
your love to all I do impart.

**Maraytaii, I resonate
with song that opens cosmic gate.
Your melody makes me vibrate
my sense of self I recreate.**

3. Maraytaii, awaken women to see the potential to rise to the next level up where we free ourselves from all resistance, from all sense of opposition, from all sense of being limited. We look at the conditions that women are exposed to in our culture and say: "So what! I will not identify myself based on these limitations."

O Cosmic Mother, we are one,
your heart is like a blazing sun.
My being can but amplify,
the sacred sound you magnify.

**Maraytaii, I resonate
with song that opens cosmic gate.
Your melody makes me vibrate
my sense of self I recreate.**

4. Maraytaii, awaken women to see that we have been locked in relation-ships based on a certain pattern. If we let go of the selves that have accepted this, we can say: "I will not be bound by this pattern anymore. I will free myself from this pattern. First of all I will free myself in my own mind."

O Cosmic Mother, I now hear,
the subtle sound of Sacred Sphere.
As I attune to Cosmic Hum,
the lesser self I overcome.

**Maraytaii, I resonate
with song that opens cosmic gate.**

Your melody makes me vibrate
my sense of self I recreate.

5. Maraytaii, awaken women to see that making maximum spiritual growth cannot necessarily be done by getting married in our teenage years and following the command to live that way until death do us part.

O Cosmic Mother, take me home,
I am in sync with Sacred OM,
The sound of sounds will raise me up,
so only light is in my cup.

Maraytaii, I resonate
with song that opens cosmic gate.
Your melody makes me vibrate
my sense of self I recreate.

6. Maraytaii, awaken women to see that if we are willing to work with ourselves, then our relationships can rise to a higher level. Or we may move on and attract another partner who is willing to go higher.

O Cosmic Mother, I will be,
a part of cosmic symphony.
All that I AM, an instrument,
for sound that is from heaven sent.

Maraytaii, I resonate
with song that opens cosmic gate.
Your melody makes me vibrate
my sense of self I recreate.

7. Maraytaii, awaken both women and men to tune in to your Comforting Presence so we no longer see ourselves as men and women, but we see that we are more than these traditional roles that limit all of us.

O Cosmic Mother, I now call,
to enter sacred music hall.
I will be part of life's ascent,
towards the starry firmament.

**Maraytaii, I resonate
with song that opens cosmic gate.
Your melody makes me vibrate
my sense of self I recreate.**

8. Maraytaii, awaken both women and men to be united in Christ, where all are spiritual beings who are expressing ourselves through different bodies, through different personalities, different cultures, different backgrounds.

O Cosmic Mother, tune my strings,
my total being with you sings.
Your song I now reverberate,
as cosmic love I celebrate.

**Maraytaii, I resonate
with song that opens cosmic gate.
Your melody makes me vibrate
my sense of self I recreate.**

9. Maraytaii, awaken both women and men to see the essential humanity that unites us. We are not united by eradicating differences, we are united by overcoming the differences and realizing that these differences do not define our identity, for we have a new identity in Christ.

O Cosmic Mother, I love you,
your love song keeps me ever true.
You fill me with your sacred tone,
and thus I never feel alone.

**Maraytaii, I resonate
with song that opens cosmic gate.
Your melody makes me vibrate
my sense of self I recreate.**

Sealing

In the name of the I AM THAT I AM, I accept that Archangel Michael, Astrea and Shiva form an impenetrable shield around myself and all constructive people, sealing us from all fear-based energies in all four octaves. I accept that the Light of God is consuming and transforming all fear-based energies that make up the dark forces working against the liberation of women on earth!

21 | OVERCOMING THE CONTROL GAMES BETWEEN MEN AND WOMEN

I am the Ascended Master Liberty. My contribution to this important topic of the liberation of women is to go into what it is that the fallen beings have used to take away the liberty of both men and women. Now, as other masters have talked about, when you go into duality, there are always two polarities and they always oppose each other. This creates an inherent, an inevitable, an unavoidable tension between the two. What does this tension lead to? Well, it is not possible that one dualistic polarity can destroy the opposite dualistic polarity because they were created at the same time. It *is* possible on a planet like earth, with the density of the collective consciousness and the individual consciousness, that one dualistic polarity can overpower the other polarity on a temporary basis.

What does this mean? This means that there is a constant struggle between dualistic polarities, and this is what we might call the essence of what some psychologists have called control games. In other words, there is a struggle for who is in control, who is the stronger, who is the dominant of the two dualistic polarities.

A classical example of dualistic polarities at the overall political level is capitalism and communism, and you saw that the Cold War was essentially a control game, a struggle between the two about who would be in control, who would be in control of the world. In this case none of the two attained control, there came to be a certain status quo, a certain cease-fire between them. This is what can happen in control games also. Instead of one polarity dominating the other, the two find a certain, we might say equilibrium, where they accept the position of each other, but there is still a constant tension, a constant attempt to gain the upper hand, to undermine the other one, to take over the other one, and therefore they need to constantly be engaged in this struggle.

The oldest control game on earth

You see many times (at this overall political level, or the world level) that there is this struggle for control. You have seen this so many times in history. For example, again you saw that the Catholic church from its inception, from its creation by Constantine, was an element or a force for attaining and achieving control over society. It eventually attracted another polarity, namely Islam, and this led to the Crusades and a fight between the two. You can say that there certainly still is a tension between Christian and Muslim religions today. You can see the same between individual nations where so many nations, throughout the world, have been locked in this struggle between each other. Sometimes two nations can have been in a struggle with each other for a long time, other times it shifts and various nations join in this, what we might call the political control game.

You see in the area of the economy for example where in the 1800s in the United States, there emerged these capitalists that gained more and more money, more and more power, and that eventually gave rise to this idea that the only way to really make money was to have a monopoly. They became the forerunners of monopoly capitalism, but there was always more than one that was attempting to gain control, and so there was the inevitable control game between them.

However, what is the oldest control game that you see on earth? What is in a sense the most basic control game that you see on earth? Well, is it not precisely the control game between men and women? You can look at history and you can look at so many societies, and although you may say that these societies were clearly patriarchal societies or male-dominated societies where men had the upper hand, men had the majority of the power under control, can you really say that this meant that there was no control from the side of women? You see that in many cases, even though men in some ways had the upper hand, there was still a control game being played by women as well. There was a certain status quo that had been achieved in many societies where men had attained a certain privileged position, women were in a secondary position, but both of them had in a sense accepted the parameters for their roles, and within those parameters, they were still fighting for control in a certain way.

Now, what you realize here is that the fallen beings selected men, defined men, to be the superior sex and therefore they projected out into the collective consciousness that men should be in control. Men should be in control of society, men should be in control of the family, men should be in control of the relationship with women. This is a projection that goes way back to when the fallen beings first defined men and women as dualistic polarities that were in a struggle for dominance and control. There has been this projection for a long time, and there is this huge collective beast that has been built in the collective consciousness that men should be in control.

Now, naturally, there has been created a reaction against this from women who do not want to be in control. There are societies where women have been in control, and there has been a certain collective beast created also that says that women should take away the control of men. There is a much larger collective beast that has caused women to actually accept that men are in control of certain aspects of society or life. Yet this beast has also projected that women should seek to attain control in the areas where they *can* attain control. This has maintained then a perpetual, ongoing struggle between men and women to attain control within whatever parameters were defined in their culture and society.

Control games between men and women

As an example, we have many societies where men are the ones who are the outgoing, who are going away to work, to make money. They are the ones who are ultimately in control of where the family should live so that he can be close to his job, and he may make overall decisions like what house to buy and where to live. When it comes to the household and the raising of the children, then the woman is in control of that area. Women have accepted that the men have a certain level of control, but when it comes to the home and the relationship, they are constantly attempting to gain more and more control. There is this perpetual control game going on in the world.

Now, of course you see (when you look at the world, when you look at history) a certain shifting scenario where from time to time societies will emerge where men have more control over women, and then there are other times where they have less control. You even see a few examples of societies where women had more control than men. Generally, you see a tendency in recent centuries that, at least in the modern democracies, these societies are actually moving towards a state where there is not as strong of a control game between men and women. In other words, both men and women in these modern democracies are becoming increasingly liberated from the control games, and therefore they become free to find a new way to relate to each other as men and women. I am not saying this process is complete, but it is certainly well begun.

Now, if you look back or if you look at the psychology here, the essence of these control games, it ties in of course with what we have said before that the fallen beings have created such uncertainty and chaos on earth where people can never know what might happen to them. As you see from Maslow's pyramid of needs, at the lower levels people's needs are fear-based. Because they have a fear of what might happen in the future, they also have a need to establish a sense that they are in control of their lives. They do this in various ways, but basically we can say that they are playing a constant control game of trying to gain some psychological sense that they are in control of their situation. There are at least certain things that they can rely on, they can know how they work.

You might think that the fallen ones would be content to create this division between men and women, to project that men are the superior sex, that men therefore should be in control, and then just allow this to outplay itself, but the fallen beings are not content with this. They are in a sense also caught in a control game because they have more fear than anybody else on earth. The original inhabitants or the avatars that have come to earth have far less fear than the fallen beings. We could say that even beyond this basic control game of men and women, there is the control game that is being outplayed in the minds of the fallen beings so they are constantly seeking control. Of course, if there was only one fallen being on earth, that fallen being might attain some state of being in control, but naturally, fallen beings come in pairs, as everything else in duality and so there is always more than one and they are in a rivalry, they are opposing each other.

Men are more willing to fight for epic causes

What is the outplaying of this control game between the fallen beings? Well, it is what we have called the epic mindset where one fallen being will define a certain ideology, religion or thought system and will project that it is of some epic importance that this particular system gains control over the world. There is a reward if this happens, there is a punishment or calamity if it does not happen, so the carrot and the stick. Then, there will be another fallen being who defines another thought system (there might even be several fallen beings who are defining rivaling thought systems) and therefore there will be this constant struggle between the two.

Now, what is it that the fallen beings are doing with this? Well, you could say that they themselves are trapped in the control game, they are fighting for control. They are trying to create this sense that one fallen being is ultimately in control of this planet. They do this by using primarily men because men have a tendency to be more outgoing, more pulled into the expanding force in its perverted aspect, and therefore, they are more open, as we have said before, to the epic mindset. The fallen beings will therefore pull men into feeling that they are the ones who have to fight for this epically important cause. They are the ones who have to engage in this epic battle, even go to war and be willing to sacrifice their lives in order to win this epic battle. This of course puts men in a certain state of mind where they are often blinded by this fanatical mindset, they are hypnotized by this fanatical mindset. Therefore, they are willing to leave their families and women behind in order to go out and fight for this cause. You see this so many times in history.

Even when they are not going out and fighting for a cause, many men can still be trapped in this epic mindset where they have a certain attitude that they *have* to do this. For example, they have to pursue a career, and therefore their wife just has to support them in their career and do what is necessary to take care of the household and the children. Therefore, the man wants the wife to be in this position, wants to be able to control her so that she is there when he comes home from work, and otherwise stays out of his way and does not interfere with his career.

What is it that this tension, that is put upon men, leads to? Well, because of this mindset, whether it is fighting for some political or religious cause or whether it is pursuing a career, men have this need to feel that they are in control of their situation. Now, you understand that if you are a soldier who goes to war, what happens to you? Well, as anybody who has been in the army or knows someone who has been in the army realizes, you might make a free-will choice to join the army, but once you have joined, you have suspended your free will. You are being totally controlled by the army, by the whole apparatus of the army. You have, as some people even say: "When you learn to march in sync, you've even lost control over your own feet." There is no personal life there. This is an obvious example where men have been put in a pressured situation where they are controlled by the system.

Look at men who are pursuing a career in the business world. They have a certain goal to work their way up through the ranks to attain a certain position, but in order to do this, they have to fulfill certain requirements. They have to be more willing to sacrifice for the cause than those other middle level managers who are vying for the same position. So what does that do? Well, it puts men under tremendous pressure. You may say that men are the aggressive sex who are out there pursuing a career and women can only be at home, but the woman at home, in many cases, has much less pressure than the man who is going to work in this high-pressure environment.

The pressure on men causes them to want to own women

What I am pointing out here is that men are put under tremendous pressure by these systems created by the fallen beings. Of course, a corporation who is vying for domination of the market, perhaps even on a world scale, is an epic cause, just as a religion or political ideology who is attempting to control the world. It is the same kind of pressured environment. This means that men are under pressure, and in order to find some relief, some sense of security, some sense of equilibrium, what do they do? Well, they cannot control their work environment so they must find something else in their lives that they can control. What is it that they can control? Well, in many cultures, they can control their women.

What is the extreme outcome of this desire that men have, this collective momentum, this collective beast of men needing to have something in their lives over which they have control? Well, what is the ultimate way to have control of something? If you are borrowing your friend's car, do you have full control of that car? Well, obviously not. When do you have full control of the car? When you own it. How do you have control of your wife, or the woman in your life, or the women in your life? When you own them.

That is why you see societies that have developed a culture where women are literally the property of men. Women are essentially slaves that can be physically, legally owned by men. Men can treat them as a piece of property, could either sell them or they can subject them to very, very strict forms of control. This of course is all fed by the fallen beings and their putting men under pressure so they must find a way to relieve the pressure by feeling there is something they have control over. You see that the extreme outcome of this is when men physically, legally own women. Naturally, you see big parts of the world today where this is no longer allowed, this is no longer accepted. In fact, the majority of women in the world have more freedom than that, they are not the property of their fathers, their husbands, their sons or whatever it may be.

Ownership has a psychological component as well so it is not just a matter of physically owning a woman, it is also a matter, in many cases, that men who have no legal, political right to own their women still develop this need for controlling the women to the point where they feel that psychologically they own their wives. Their wives should be under their control and they should behave as if they are essentially the property of the man. You see many cultures where there is no legal ownership of women but there is this psychological sense of ownership. You see cultures for example where girls are considered worthless, and although they cannot necessarily be sold as slaves, they can be given away in marriages that might give the parents some kind of advantage. You see other cultures where once a woman has married, she essentially becomes the property of the man because he believes that he now has total control over her and that she should submit to this control. Of course, many women around the world have been brought up to submit themselves to this form of control and they feel that their men can own them.

What you see is that these control games of seeking ownership, where one side seeks to own the other and the other submits to it, they can outplay themselves in various ways. You even see (in some of the more developed nations where women have attained much more liberation) that there can still be these psychological control games that go on between men and women. The man can attempt to own the woman, but the woman can also develop a certain sense of ownership of her man and of her children. You will see that even in the most advanced nations in the world in terms of women's liberation, women will still talk about "my husband," "my children," men will talk about "my wife," "my children."

You see that this is a more subtle sense of psychological ownership. You can have for example these various control games that are played out. One, that was raised by someone in a question, is that some women develop this sense that their husbands are not taking care of their physical health and it is up to the woman to do something about this. She should tell him how she should take care of his health and what he should eat and this and that and the next thing. This is just an outplaying of this control game and it is often something that goes back to previous lifetimes where both the man and the woman lived in cultures where women were subjected to much harsher conditions than they are today.

You can still carry these separate selves from past lives. This means that you have this sense of control that "my husband" should behave a certain way. You have cultures for example where men are still somewhat dominant and men are often the ones who go to work, but the women in that culture feel that the physical appearance and the behavior of the men reflects back on them. If a man appears a certain way, it shows that his woman has not taken care of him and that reflects badly on her. She wants the man to appear a certain way so that nobody will criticize her for not doing her duty as a woman.

The control game of falling in and out of love

You have many, many of these control games around the world, more or less subtle, where men and women engage in this, perhaps for an entire lifetime. You see for example that there are still cultures, even some of the more developed nations in the world, where the whole game of teenagers seeking for a partner and finding a partner, and then finally getting to the point where they can say: "This is my girlfriend," "This is my boyfriend," where this entire scenario is still driven by a subtle control game. Men feel a pressure to be sexually active. Women feel a pressure to be sexually active or to have a certain status and they attain that through a relationship, but it is not really a free relationship they are engaging in. It is a control game that they are playing so that each of them can gain the status they gain by having "my girlfriend," "my boyfriend."

Being in a relationship gives you a certain status. In order to get into a relationship, you are seeking to control your potential partner and pull them into the net so to speak. This goes on from both sides. Now, once the two people have then decided that they are in a steady relationship, the control games can just keep evolving from there. Maybe they get married, maybe they move in together, maybe they have children and still they can continue to play these control games over and over again. They shift somewhat as they grow older as the children grow up, but it is still a control game.

Essentially, what you see in these more modern democracies is of course that many marriages break up. They break up because people can no longer stand the control game in many cases. They feel so trapped in this control game that they have to break out of the relationship. You also see relationships that do not break up and of course this is not in all cases, but in many cases the reason the relationship does not break up is that neither of the two partners can break free of the control games.

Now you may think that, well, those who break up a relationship, they are liberated from the control game, but not necessarily. Because what does a control game essentially do to you psychologically? You are seeing your partner as an opponent in a game and therefore it is very easy, when the relationship starts going poorly and there is more and more inharmony that creeps in, it is very easy to project that the problems are caused by your partner. Your partner is this way, your partner is that way. There eventually comes that thought: "Well, if I only had another partner who was not that way, then I would not have this situation."

Of course why are you having the experience that you are having of the relationship? Well, *your* experience takes place where? Inside your mind! Why are you having the experience you are having? It is not because of your partner. Now, your partner may be playing a control game and trying to control you but that is not what creates your *internal* experience. Your internal experience is created by *your* control game. You can break up the relationship but you still carry that control game with you. If you do not overcome those separate selves and resolve it, you might very well attract another relationship that has the same or a different control game but is still driven by these control games.

You see that this is not the case for all relationships, but it is the case for many relationships even in the nations where women have become legally and politically liberated, where there is much more equality between the sexes. There is still, at the level of individual relationships, these control games. There may not be any longer the control game at the level of society where men are seeking to own women or keep them at home or prevent them from having a job or a career, but there can still be a control game in the home, in the individual relationship.

What does this have to do with you who are ascended master students? Well, first of all, you can take a look at yourself and see if you have these control games. There is, for those of you who have come to the level where you are open to our teachings, there is no shame in this, there is no reason to feel bad about this. You need to recognize, as we have said before, you live on a very difficult, very dense planet. You have had many previous lifetimes. Look back at history. You do not have to go very far back before you would have lived in societies that were much more trapped in these control games between men and women. You might have been a man in some lifetimes, a woman in some but it is inevitable that you have developed these separate selves. It is inevitable that you carry them with you and that they will affect you and it will have affected your relationships up to this point. You need to come to the point where you can look at this and say: "So what? I had this. I live on earth, so how could I not have it? But it is time to get beyond it. It is time to liberate myself from this, and I do this by using the tools, being willing to look at these selves, identify them, let them die and stop trying to solve the problem that the control game is projecting that I have to solve."

What you can also do of course is make the calls that other women will be cut free from this, call for the binding of these collective beasts that are always created out of these control games and that are seeking to perpetuate the control games. You can call for the judgment and the binding of the fallen ones who started the entire cycle of this control game between men and women and the control game of the epic mindset, often pulling men into fighting for this epic cause. These are some of the things you can do and they are certainly some of the things that we encourage you to do and one of the reasons we are giving you this teaching.

The price you pay for feeling you are in control

Now, you will realize that what happens when you are engaged in a control game is that it is possible that you can get yourself into a state of mind where you feel like: "I am winning the game." "I have the upper hand." "I am the one who is in control." This is, in the extreme, outpicturing what the fallen beings often feel. Many people feel it, many men feel it, many women feel it, they feel they have control over a certain area of their life.

What is the price you pay for this feeling? Well, you cannot engage in a control game without being controlled by the game, or rather by the separate selves, by the collective beasts, ultimately by the fallen beings. Whenever you seek to control, you are controlled because unless you are being exposed to control, you will not engage in these control games. This goes for all people up to the level of the fallen beings where you can say that there may not be an *external* force that is exposing them to control, but there is an *internal* force, the division in their own psychology and of course other fallen beings and so forth.

You, when you are engaging in these control games, you are being controlled. Of course as an ascended master student, as a person dedicated to the path of Christhood, you do not want to be controlled. The path of Christhood is essentially the path where you free yourself from being controlled by anything on earth. Therefore, you cannot allow yourself to carry with you these separate selves that are compelling you to engage in these control games. You simply need to look at this honestly, openly, without any fear, without any shame, without any regret. Then you just identify this and you say: "Enough, I have had enough of this. I am more than this self and I can let it die because I know that I will be reborn at a higher level of Christhood. I will become a new being in Christ by letting these selves die."

Truly, if you can do this yourselves, you will make a valuable contribution, an *invaluable* contribution, to raising the collective. You will be the forerunners who will help many other people around the world, both men and women, but especially women, free themselves from these control games or at least become aware of them.

Why women are the forerunners for change

Again, why are we talking about women being the forerunners? Well, because those who have been oppressed are the ones who are most likely to start the cycle of stopping the oppression. They are the ones who are most likely to have the impetus to stop the oppression and be willing to do something about it. Now, I know that this has a certain aspect where you can say, but when people are so oppressed, they cannot free themselves. Still, as we have said, when you have experienced a certain form of oppression over many lifetimes, you gradually build that determination to free yourself. That is why you see that women in the modern democracies were the forerunners on a planetary level for speaking out against the discrimination and suppression of women and demanding greater freedom.

Someone had to be the forerunners and they are the ones who have the most experience, who have been exposed to the abuse for so long that they have built that determination to no longer take it. Many women are still not at that level and that is where your calls can come in. You can cut them free so they can receive the opportunity to see the control games, free themselves from it without having to go through another number of embodiments before they come to that point internally of building that determination.

You see here that the liberation of women is in an upward spiral. If you do nothing, if you ascended master students do not take these teachings, do not make the calls, it will take much longer before it will spread around the planet, before it will lift up other societies. If you do make the calls, and if more and more people find these teachings and make the calls, then you can accelerate the process quite significantly. Thereby, you can make it so that it will not take lifetimes or even decades before the most backwards countries in the world have set their women free from this, quite frankly, outdated medieval oppression that they are subjected to in many countries.

Truly, one of the amazing things in a way, or one of the characteristic things, of a planet like earth is this enormous range between the most developed, the most aware people and nations and the less developed, the less aware people and nations. Compare some of the modern democracies to Islamic countries, nations in Africa, South America, India, China. Compare how women are treated there and you must have the question in your mind: "How can this even exist on the same planet? How can you have people that are living the same way today that our societies lived five hundred years ago? How is this possible?"

Why is it possible, my beloved? Well, for one reason only. You have these huge collective beasts that are overpowering the minds of the people in the less developed countries so they cannot see what is so obvious to you. You may look at an Islamic country where women are wearing the burka and cannot drive and can barely go outside on their own. You may not be able to fathom how a society can function like that. How can the men accept it? How can the women accept it? It is so obvious to you that this is outdated and needs to change.

For the people living there, it is not obvious and why is it not obvious? It is not because they are stupid or not because they are less intelligent or less evolved. It is because they are hypnotized by these collective beasts.

It is the story of the emperor's new clothes where the people were literally hypnotized to think that the emperor was wearing clothes until the illusion was shattered by the little boy who cried out: "But the emperor has nothing on." Likewise, these people (in many of these countries around the world where still women are treated in medieval ways) they are hypnotized.

What can break this stalemate? Well, as I said, it will eventually be resolved by a growth in the collective consciousness but this will take a long time. What is the one thing that could really have an impact, that could really change it? It is that someone makes the calls to the ascended masters and thereby authorizes us to use the power we have to go in and bind and consume these beasts, to judge and remove the fallen beings so that this hypnotic effect can be removed and the scales fall from people's eyes and they wake up and say: "But wait a minute, why are we treating women this way? How can we be so far behind these other nations? Why are we holding on to these outdated religious doctrines and laws that define women as second grade citizens?"

You might be surprised to learn that, even in some of the seemingly most backward countries, there are many people who have over lifetimes built this desire to be free of this oppression but because of this collective beast, they cannot see it. They look at their culture, they see the problems, they see the tensions but they cannot see what can be done about it. They cannot see what can break the stalemate, what can break the spell. By enough people making the calls for the binding of these collective entities and the fallen beings behind it, suddenly people can become free. Now the momentum that they have built over these lifetimes of determination can be expressed.

Then, a society can fairly quickly shift out of this outdated mindset, out of this illusion that they have been under for so long. Suddenly, they begin to see solutions. There is a shift that happens and suddenly, a Middle Eastern country may decide to allow women to have a driver's license. This is one step in the right direction and then there can be another, and another and another.

How people in developed nations can bring change

Of course, what you can also make the calls for, hold the vision for, perhaps even take action for, is that people in the more developed nations will be cut free from the spell that they are under. Because many people in the developed nations are looking at for example Islamic nations or other nations and they see they are far behind. They see in a sense that these countries should be evolving in the same direction that they are evolving in but they cannot understand why nothing is happening and they cannot see what to do about it. They feel a certain reluctance to go in there and stir up this hornets' nest and get this negative reaction where suddenly people from Muslim countries start flying airplanes into buildings or going into offices and shooting people or blowing up bombs in busses. They do not even want to deal with this.

They do not want to put any political pressure on these nations and you can make the calls that this spell will be broken so that these nations, these more developed nations, will wake up and realize that their position comes with a responsibility where they are meant to promote the liberation of women in the rest of the world and promote many other causes and positive progress in the rest of the world. They have not only a right, but an obligation to put political pressure on these nations. You have an obligation to say: "We cannot trade with you if you continue to treat your women this way. We will not buy your oil, we will find alternatives to buying your oil."

This is also something you can make the calls on because there are people in the more developed nations who are looking at this and who are willing to apply this political pressure, but again, they are under a certain spell. They are under a collective beast that is holding them back from saying: "This is our responsibility." Of course, it cannot happen by just one nation. It does not do any good if Denmark puts pressure on Saudi Arabia, but if the EU puts pressure on Saudi Arabia, now that would be something different and much more difficult to ignore.

You can make the calls that these spells will be broken, these collective beasts will be bound or consumed or reduced in strength so that people can be free in their outer minds to take the actions that they are actually prepared to take in the emotional, mental and identity body. Often it is a blockage in the emotional body that prevents people from acting on what they already see in their mental bodies. That is primarily where these beasts can come in and block people so that they have all the right insights, they see what is going on, they know what should be done, but somehow they cannot get themselves to act it out because they are blocked at the emotional level from taking action based on their understanding.

This was the teaching I wanted to give you here. I am grateful for your willingness, around the world as you are, to be the open doors whereby I can use your chakras, *we* can use your chakras, to project this into the collective consciousness with much greater impulse than it otherwise could have been done. So I seal you in the Flame of Liberty that I AM and that I hold for this planet.

NOTE: This dictation was given May 31, 2020.

22 | INVOKING FREEDOM FROM CONTROL GAMES (PART 1)

In the name of the I AM THAT I AM, Jesus Christ, I use the authority that I have as a being in embodiment on earth to call upon Mother Liberty to reinforce my calls and use my chakras to project the statements in this invocation into the collective consciousness and awaken people to the awareness that will liberate both men and women from all psychological and spiritual thralldom to the fallen beings. Awaken people to the reality that we are spiritual beings and that we can co-create a new future by working with the ascended masters. I especially call for …

[Make your own calls here.]

Part 1

1. Liberty, awaken women to see that when we go into duality, there are always two polarities, and they always oppose each other. This creates a tension between the two.

O Liberty now set me free
from devil's curse of poverty.
I blame not Mother for my lack,
O Blessed Mother, take me back.

O Cosmic Mother Liberty,
conduct Abundance Symphony.
My highest service I now see,
abundance is now real for me.

2. Liberty, awaken women to see that it is *not* possible that one dualistic polarity can destroy the opposite dualistic polarity because they were created at the same time. It *is* possible that one dualistic polarity can overpower the other polarity on a temporary basis.

O Liberty, from distant shore,
I come with longing to be More.
I see abundance is a flow,
abundance consciousness I grow.

O Cosmic Mother Liberty,
conduct Abundance Symphony.
My highest service I now see,
abundance is now real for me.

3. Liberty, awaken women to see that there is a constant struggle between dualistic polarities, and this is the essence of control games. There is a struggle for who is in control, who is the stronger, who is the dominant of the two polarities.

O Liberty, expose the lie,
that limitations can me tie.
The Ma-ter light is not my foe,
true opulence it does bestow.

O Cosmic Mother Liberty,
conduct Abundance Symphony.
My highest service I now see,
abundance is now real for me.

4. Liberty, awaken women to see that the Cold War was essentially a control game, a struggle between the two about who would be in control of the world.

> O Liberty, expose the plot,
> projected by the fallen lot.
> O Cosmic Mother, I now see,
> that Mother's not my enemy.

> **O Cosmic Mother Liberty,**
> **conduct Abundance Symphony.**
> **My highest service I now see,**
> **abundance is now real for me.**

5. Liberty, awaken women to see that instead of one polarity dominating the other, the two can find a certain equilibrium where they accept the position of each other, but there is still a constant tension.

> O Liberty, with opened eyes,
> I now reject the devil's lies.
> I now embrace the Mother realm,
> for I see Father at the helm.

> **O Cosmic Mother Liberty,**
> **conduct Abundance Symphony.**
> **My highest service I now see,**
> **abundance is now real for me.**

6. Liberty, awaken women to see that the Catholic church was from its creation by Constantine, a force for attaining control over society.

> O Liberty, a chalice pure,
> my lower bodies are for sure.
> Release through me your symphony,
> your gift of Cosmic Liberty.

> **O Cosmic Mother Liberty,**
> **conduct Abundance Symphony.**

**My highest service I now see,
abundance is now real for me.**

7. Liberty, awaken women to see that this attracted another polarity, namely Islam, and this led to the Crusades and a fight between the two.

O Liberty, the open door,
I am for Symphony of More.
In chakras mine light you release,
the flow of love shall never cease.

**O Cosmic Mother Liberty,
conduct Abundance Symphony.
My highest service I now see,
abundance is now real for me.**

8. Liberty, awaken women to see that many nations have been locked in this struggle between each other. Sometimes two nations can be in a struggle with each other for a long time, other times various nations join the political control game.

O Liberty, release the flow,
of opulence that you bestow.
For I am willing to receive,
the Golden Fleece that you now weave.

**O Cosmic Mother Liberty,
conduct Abundance Symphony.
My highest service I now see,
abundance is now real for me.**

9. Liberty, awaken women to see that the oldest control game we see on earth is the control game between men and women.

O Liberty, release the cure,
to free the tired and the poor.
The huddled masses are set free,
by loving Song of Liberty.

**O Cosmic Mother Liberty,
conduct Abundance Symphony.
My highest service I now see,
abundance is now real for me.**

Part 2

1. Liberty, awaken women to see that many societies were patriarchal societies where men had the majority of the power under control, but there was still a control game being played by women.

O Liberty now set me free
from devil's curse of poverty.
I blame not Mother for my lack,
O Blessed Mother, take me back.

**O Cosmic Mother Liberty,
conduct Abundance Symphony.
My highest service I now see,
abundance is now real for me.**

2. Liberty, awaken women to see that in many societies a certain status quo had been achieved where men had attained a privileged position, women were in a secondary position, but both of them had accepted the parameters for their roles, and within those parameters, they were still fighting for control.

O Liberty, from distant shore,
I come with longing to be More.
I see abundance is a flow,
abundance consciousness I grow.

**O Cosmic Mother Liberty,
conduct Abundance Symphony.
My highest service I now see,
abundance is now real for me.**

3. Liberty, awaken women to see that the fallen beings selected men to be the superior sex and therefore they projected into the collective consciousness that men should be in control. Men should be in control of society, the family and the relationship with women.

O Liberty, expose the lie,
that limitations can me tie.
The Ma-ter light is not my foe,
true opulence it does bestow.

O Cosmic Mother Liberty,
conduct Abundance Symphony.
My highest service I now see,
abundance is now real for me.

4. Liberty, awaken women to see that this is a projection that goes back to when the fallen beings first defined men and women as dualistic polarities that were in a struggle for dominance and control.

O Liberty, expose the plot,
projected by the fallen lot.
O Cosmic Mother, I now see,
that Mother's not my enemy.

O Cosmic Mother Liberty,
conduct Abundance Symphony.
My highest service I now see,
abundance is now real for me.

5. Liberty, I call forth the judgment and binding of the collective beast that has been built in the collective consciousness based on the idea that men should be in control.

O Liberty, with opened eyes,
I now reject the devil's lies.
I now embrace the Mother realm,
for I see Father at the helm.

**O Cosmic Mother Liberty,
conduct Abundance Symphony.
My highest service I now see,
abundance is now real for me.**

6. Liberty, awaken women to see that there has been a reaction against this from women who do not want to be controlled.

O Liberty, a chalice pure,
my lower bodies are for sure.
Release through me your symphony,
your gift of Cosmic Liberty.

**O Cosmic Mother Liberty,
conduct Abundance Symphony.
My highest service I now see,
abundance is now real for me.**

7. Liberty, I call forth the judgment and binding of the collective beast that says that women should take away the control of men.

O Liberty, the open door,
I am for Symphony of More.
In chakras mine light you release,
the flow of love shall never cease.

**O Cosmic Mother Liberty,
conduct Abundance Symphony.
My highest service I now see,
abundance is now real for me.**

8. Liberty, I call forth the judgment and binding of the collective beast that has caused women to accept that men are in control of certain aspects of society or life.

O Liberty, release the flow,
of opulence that you bestow.
For I am willing to receive,
the Golden Fleece that you now weave.

O Cosmic Mother Liberty,
conduct Abundance Symphony.
My highest service I now see,
abundance is now real for me.

9. Liberty, I call forth the judgment and binding of the collective beast that has projected that women should seek to attain control in the areas where they can attain control.

O Liberty, release the cure,
to free the tired and the poor.
The huddled masses are set free,
by loving Song of Liberty.

O Cosmic Mother Liberty,
conduct Abundance Symphony.
My highest service I now see,
abundance is now real for me.

Part 3

1. Liberty, awaken women to see that this has maintained an ongoing struggle between men and women to attain control within whatever parameters were defined in their culture and society.

O Liberty now set me free
from devil's curse of poverty.
I blame not Mother for my lack,
O Blessed Mother, take me back.

O Cosmic Mother Liberty,
conduct Abundance Symphony.
My highest service I now see,
abundance is now real for me.

2. Liberty, awaken women to see that the essence of these control games is that the fallen beings have created such uncertainty and chaos on earth where people can never know what might happen to them.

> O Liberty, from distant shore,
> I come with longing to be More.
> I see abundance is a flow,
> abundance consciousness I grow.

> **O Cosmic Mother Liberty,**
> **conduct Abundance Symphony.**
> **My highest service I now see,**
> **abundance is now real for me.**

3. Liberty, awaken women to see that because people have a fear of what might happen in the future, they have a need to be in control of their lives, causing them to play a constant control game of trying to gain some psychological sense that they are in control of their situation.

> O Liberty, expose the lie,
> that limitations can me tie.
> The Ma-ter light is not my foe,
> true opulence it does bestow.

> **O Cosmic Mother Liberty,**
> **conduct Abundance Symphony.**
> **My highest service I now see,**
> **abundance is now real for me.**

4. Liberty, awaken women to see that the fallen beings are not content to create this division between men and women, to project that men are the superior sex, that men should be in control.

> O Liberty, expose the plot,
> projected by the fallen lot.
> O Cosmic Mother, I now see,
> that Mother's not my enemy.

O Cosmic Mother Liberty,
conduct Abundance Symphony.
My highest service I now see,
abundance is now real for me.

5. Liberty, awaken women to see that the fallen beings are also caught in a control game because they have more fear than anybody else on earth.

O Liberty, with opened eyes,
I now reject the devil's lies.
I now embrace the Mother realm,
for I see Father at the helm.

O Cosmic Mother Liberty,
conduct Abundance Symphony.
My highest service I now see,
abundance is now real for me.

6. Liberty, awaken women to see that beyond this basic control game of men and women, there is the control game that is being outplayed in the minds of the fallen beings so they are constantly seeking control.

O Liberty, a chalice pure,
my lower bodies are for sure.
Release through me your symphony,
your gift of Cosmic Liberty.

O Cosmic Mother Liberty,
conduct Abundance Symphony.
My highest service I now see,
abundance is now real for me.

7. Liberty, awaken women to see that fallen beings come in pairs, as everything else in duality and there is always more than one and they are in a rivalry, they are opposing each other.

O Liberty, the open door,
I am for Symphony of More.

In chakras mine light you release,
the flow of love shall never cease.

**O Cosmic Mother Liberty,
conduct Abundance Symphony.
My highest service I now see,
abundance is now real for me.**

8. Liberty, awaken women to see that the outplaying of this control game between the fallen beings is the epic mindset where one fallen being will define a certain ideology, religion or thought system and will project that it is of epic importance that this particular system gains control over the world.

O Liberty, release the flow,
of opulence that you bestow.
For I am willing to receive,
the Golden Fleece that you now weave.

**O Cosmic Mother Liberty,
conduct Abundance Symphony.
My highest service I now see,
abundance is now real for me.**

9. Liberty, awaken women to see that another fallen being defines another thought system and therefore there will be this constant struggle between two or more systems.

O Liberty, release the cure,
to free the tired and the poor.
The huddled masses are set free,
by loving Song of Liberty.

**O Cosmic Mother Liberty,
conduct Abundance Symphony.
My highest service I now see,
abundance is now real for me.**

Part 4

1. Liberty, awaken women to see that they are trying to create this sense that one fallen being is ultimately in control of this planet. They do this by using men because men have a tendency to be more open to the epic mindset.

> O Liberty now set me free
> from devil's curse of poverty.
> I blame not Mother for my lack,
> O Blessed Mother, take me back.

> **O Cosmic Mother Liberty,**
> **conduct Abundance Symphony.**
> **My highest service I now see,**
> **abundance is now real for me.**

2. Liberty, awaken women to see that the fallen beings will pull men into feeling that they are the ones who have to fight for this epically important cause. They are the ones who have to engage in this epic battle, even go to war and be willing to sacrifice their lives in order to win this epic battle.

> O Liberty, from distant shore,
> I come with longing to be More.
> I see abundance is a flow,
> abundance consciousness I grow.

> **O Cosmic Mother Liberty,**
> **conduct Abundance Symphony.**
> **My highest service I now see,**
> **abundance is now real for me.**

3. Liberty, awaken women to see that this puts men in a certain state of mind where they are blinded by this fanatical mindset. They are willing to leave their families and women behind in order to go out and fight for this cause.

O Liberty, expose the lie,
that limitations can me tie.
The Ma-ter light is not my foe,
true opulence it does bestow.

**O Cosmic Mother Liberty,
conduct Abundance Symphony.
My highest service I now see,
abundance is now real for me.**

4. Liberty, awaken women to see that many men are trapped in the epic mindset where they think they have to pursue a career, and therefore their wife just has to support them in their career and do what is necessary to take care of the household and the children.

O Liberty, expose the plot,
projected by the fallen lot.
O Cosmic Mother, I now see,
that Mother's not my enemy.

**O Cosmic Mother Liberty,
conduct Abundance Symphony.
My highest service I now see,
abundance is now real for me.**

5. Liberty, awaken women to see that a man in the epic mindset wants his wife to be in this position, wants to be able to control her so that she is there when he comes home from work, and otherwise stays out of his way and does not interfere with his career.

O Liberty, with opened eyes,
I now reject the devil's lies.
I now embrace the Mother realm,
for I see Father at the helm.

**O Cosmic Mother Liberty,
conduct Abundance Symphony.
My highest service I now see,
abundance is now real for me.**

6. Liberty, awaken women to see that the tension that is put upon men leads to this need to feel that they are in control of their situation. Yet men who join the army lose control over their situation.

O Liberty, a chalice pure,
my lower bodies are for sure.
Release through me your symphony,
your gift of Cosmic Liberty.

**O Cosmic Mother Liberty,
conduct Abundance Symphony.
My highest service I now see,
abundance is now real for me.**

7. Liberty, awaken women to see that men who are pursuing a career in the business world have to be willing to sacrifice for the cause and this puts men under tremendous pressure.

O Liberty, the open door,
I am for Symphony of More.
In chakras mine light you release,
the flow of love shall never cease.

**O Cosmic Mother Liberty,
conduct Abundance Symphony.
My highest service I now see,
abundance is now real for me.**

8. Liberty, awaken women to see that men are put under tremendous pressure by these systems created by the fallen beings.

O Liberty, release the flow,
of opulence that you bestow.
For I am willing to receive,
the Golden Fleece that you now weave.

**O Cosmic Mother Liberty,
conduct Abundance Symphony.**

**My highest service I now see,
abundance is now real for me.**

9. Liberty, awaken women to see that a corporation that is vying for domination of the market, perhaps even on a world scale, is an epic cause, just as a religion or political ideology that is attempting to control the world.

O Liberty, release the cure,
to free the tired and the poor.
The huddled masses are set free,
by loving Song of Liberty.

**O Cosmic Mother Liberty,
conduct Abundance Symphony.
My highest service I now see,
abundance is now real for me.**

Part 5

1. Liberty, I call forth the judgment and binding of the collective beast that puts men are under pressure, where they need some sense of equilibrium and therefore they must control their women.

O Liberty now set me free
from devil's curse of poverty.
I blame not Mother for my lack,
O Blessed Mother, take me back.

**O Cosmic Mother Liberty,
conduct Abundance Symphony.
My highest service I now see,
abundance is now real for me.**

2. Liberty, I call forth the judgment and binding of the collective beast of men needing to have something in their lives over which they have control.

O Liberty, from distant shore,
I come with longing to be More.
I see abundance is a flow,
abundance consciousness I grow.

**O Cosmic Mother Liberty,
conduct Abundance Symphony.
My highest service I now see,
abundance is now real for me.**

3. Liberty, I call forth the judgment and binding of the collective beast behind the belief that the ultimate way to have control of something is to own it, making men want to own the women in their lives.

O Liberty, expose the lie,
that limitations can me tie.
The Ma-ter light is not my foe,
true opulence it does bestow.

**O Cosmic Mother Liberty,
conduct Abundance Symphony.
My highest service I now see,
abundance is now real for me.**

4. Liberty, awaken women to see that this is why some societies have developed a culture where women are literally the property of men. Women are essentially slaves that can be physically, legally owned by men.

O Liberty, expose the plot,
projected by the fallen lot.
O Cosmic Mother, I now see,
that Mother's not my enemy.

**O Cosmic Mother Liberty,
conduct Abundance Symphony.
My highest service I now see,
abundance is now real for me.**

5. Liberty, I call forth the judgment and binding of the fallen beings who are putting men under pressure so they must find a way to relieve the pressure by feeling there is something they can control.

O Liberty, with opened eyes,
I now reject the devil's lies.
I now embrace the Mother realm,
for I see Father at the helm.

**O Cosmic Mother Liberty,
conduct Abundance Symphony.
My highest service I now see,
abundance is now real for me.**

6. Liberty, I call forth the judgment and binding of the collective beast behind the idea that men physically, legally own women.

O Liberty, a chalice pure,
my lower bodies are for sure.
Release through me your symphony,
your gift of Cosmic Liberty.

**O Cosmic Mother Liberty,
conduct Abundance Symphony.
My highest service I now see,
abundance is now real for me.**

7. Liberty, I call forth the judgment and binding of the collective beast behind men feeling that beyond the legal, political right to own their women, they need to control the women to the point where they feel they psychologically own their wives.

O Liberty, the open door,
I am for Symphony of More.
In chakras mine light you release,
the flow of love shall never cease.

**O Cosmic Mother Liberty,
conduct Abundance Symphony.**

My highest service I now see,
abundance is now real for me.

8. Liberty, I call forth the judgment and binding of the collective beast behind the cultures where there is no legal ownership of women but there is this psychological sense of ownership.

O Liberty, release the flow,
of opulence that you bestow.
For I am willing to receive,
the Golden Fleece that you now weave.

O Cosmic Mother Liberty,
conduct Abundance Symphony.
My highest service I now see,
abundance is now real for me.

9. Liberty, I call forth the judgment and binding of the collective beast behind cultures where girls are considered worthless, and although they cannot necessarily be sold as slaves, they can be given away in marriages that might give the parents some kind of advantage.

O Liberty, release the cure,
to free the tired and the poor.
The huddled masses are set free,
by loving Song of Liberty.

O Cosmic Mother Liberty,
conduct Abundance Symphony.
My highest service I now see,
abundance is now real for me.

Sealing

In the name of the I AM THAT I AM, I accept that Archangel Michael, Astrea and Shiva form an impenetrable shield around myself and all constructive people, sealing us from all fear-based energies in all four octaves. I accept that the Light of God is consuming and transforming all fear-based energies that make up the dark forces working against the liberation of women on earth!

23 | INVOKING FREEDOM FROM CONTROL GAMES (PART 2)

In the name of the I AM THAT I AM, Jesus Christ, I use the authority that I have as a being in embodiment on earth to call upon Mother Liberty to reinforce my calls and use my chakras to project the statements in this invocation into the collective consciousness and awaken people to the awareness that will liberate both men and women from all psychological and spiritual thralldom to the fallen beings. Awaken people to the reality that we are spiritual beings and that we can co-create a new future by working with the ascended masters. I especially call for …

[Make your own calls here.]

Part 1

1. Liberty, I call forth the judgment and binding of the collective beast behind the cultures where once a woman has married, she essentially becomes the property of the man because he believes that he now has total control over her and that she should submit to this control.

O Liberty now set me free
from devil's curse of poverty.
I blame not Mother for my lack,
O Blessed Mother, take me back.

**O Cosmic Mother Liberty,
conduct Abundance Symphony.
My highest service I now see,
abundance is now real for me.**

2. Liberty, I call forth the judgment and binding of the collective beast behind the fact that women around the world have been brought up to submit themselves to this form of control and feel that their men can own them.

O Liberty, from distant shore,
I come with longing to be More.
I see abundance is a flow,
abundance consciousness I grow.

**O Cosmic Mother Liberty,
conduct Abundance Symphony.
My highest service I now see,
abundance is now real for me.**

3. Liberty, awaken women to see that these control games of seeking ownership, where one side seeks to own the other and the other submits to it, they can outplay themselves in various ways.

O Liberty, expose the lie,
that limitations can me tie.
The Ma-ter light is not my foe,
true opulence it does bestow.

**O Cosmic Mother Liberty,
conduct Abundance Symphony.
My highest service I now see,
abundance is now real for me.**

4. Liberty, awaken women to see that even in the more developed nations where women have attained much more liberation, there can still be these psychological control games that go on between men and women.

> O Liberty, expose the plot,
> projected by the fallen lot.
> O Cosmic Mother, I now see,
> that Mother's not my enemy.

> **O Cosmic Mother Liberty,**
> **conduct Abundance Symphony.**
> **My highest service I now see,**
> **abundance is now real for me.**

5. Liberty, awaken women to see that the man can attempt to own the woman, but the woman can also develop a certain sense of ownership of her man and of her children. Even in the most advanced nations in the world, women will still talk about "my husband," "my children," men talk about "my wife," "my children."

> O Liberty, with opened eyes,
> I now reject the devil's lies.
> I now embrace the Mother realm,
> for I see Father at the helm.

> **O Cosmic Mother Liberty,**
> **conduct Abundance Symphony.**
> **My highest service I now see,**
> **abundance is now real for me.**

6. Liberty, awaken women to see that some women carry these separate selves from past lives, and they have this sense of control that "my husband" should behave a certain way.

> O Liberty, a chalice pure,
> my lower bodies are for sure.
> Release through me your symphony,
> your gift of Cosmic Liberty.

**O Cosmic Mother Liberty,
conduct Abundance Symphony.
My highest service I now see,
abundance is now real for me.**

7. Liberty, I call forth the judgment and binding of the collective beast behind cultures where men are still dominant, but the women in that culture feel that the physical appearance and the behavior of men reflect back on them.

O Liberty, the open door,
I am for Symphony of More.
In chakras mine light you release,
the flow of love shall never cease.

**O Cosmic Mother Liberty,
conduct Abundance Symphony.
My highest service I now see,
abundance is now real for me.**

8. Liberty, I call forth the judgment and binding of the collective beast that makes women feel that if the man appears a certain way, it shows that his woman has not taken care of him and that reflects badly on her.

O Liberty, release the flow,
of opulence that you bestow.
For I am willing to receive,
the Golden Fleece that you now weave.

**O Cosmic Mother Liberty,
conduct Abundance Symphony.
My highest service I now see,
abundance is now real for me.**

9. Liberty, I call forth the judgment and binding of the collective beast behind the control game of teenagers seeking for a partner.

O Liberty, release the cure,
to free the tired and the poor.

The huddled masses are set free,
by loving Song of Liberty.

O Cosmic Mother Liberty,
conduct Abundance Symphony.
My highest service I now see,
abundance is now real for me.

Part 2

1. Liberty, I call forth the judgment and binding of the collective beast behind men feeling a pressure to be sexually active and women feeling a pressure to be sexually active or to have a certain status through a relationship but it is not a free relationship but a control game.

O Liberty now set me free
from devil's curse of poverty.
I blame not Mother for my lack,
O Blessed Mother, take me back.

O Cosmic Mother Liberty,
conduct Abundance Symphony.
My highest service I now see,
abundance is now real for me.

2. Liberty, awaken women to see that being in a relationship gives you a certain status, and in order to get into a relationship you are seeking to control your potential partner and pull them into the net.

O Liberty, from distant shore,
I come with longing to be More.
I see abundance is a flow,
abundance consciousness I grow.

O Cosmic Mother Liberty,
conduct Abundance Symphony.

My highest service I now see,
abundance is now real for me.

3. Liberty, awaken women to see that once partners enter a relationship because of a control game, they can continue to play these control games over and over again. They shift somewhat as they grow older but it is still a control game.

O Liberty, expose the lie,
that limitations can me tie.
The Ma-ter light is not my foe,
true opulence it does bestow.

O Cosmic Mother Liberty,
conduct Abundance Symphony.
My highest service I now see,
abundance is now real for me.

4. Liberty, awaken women to see that many marriages break up because people can no longer stand the control game. They feel so trapped in this control game that they have to break out of the relationship.

O Liberty, expose the plot,
projected by the fallen lot.
O Cosmic Mother, I now see,
that Mother's not my enemy.

O Cosmic Mother Liberty,
conduct Abundance Symphony.
My highest service I now see,
abundance is now real for me.

5. Liberty, awaken women to see that in many cases the reason the relationship does not break up is that neither of the two partners can break free of the control games.

O Liberty, with opened eyes,
I now reject the devil's lies.

I now embrace the Mother realm,
for I see Father at the helm.

O Cosmic Mother Liberty,
conduct Abundance Symphony.
My highest service I now see,
abundance is now real for me.

6. Liberty, awaken women to see that those who break up a relationship are not necessarily liberated from the control game.

O Liberty, a chalice pure,
my lower bodies are for sure.
Release through me your symphony,
your gift of Cosmic Liberty.

O Cosmic Mother Liberty,
conduct Abundance Symphony.
My highest service I now see,
abundance is now real for me.

7. Liberty, awaken women to see that when a relationship starts going poorly, it is very easy to project that the problems are caused by your partner, making people feel: "Well, if I only had another partner who was not that way, then I would not have this situation."

O Liberty, the open door,
I am for Symphony of More.
In chakras mine light you release,
the flow of love shall never cease.

O Cosmic Mother Liberty,
conduct Abundance Symphony.
My highest service I now see,
abundance is now real for me.

8. Liberty, awaken women to see that *our* experience of a relationship takes place inside our minds! We are not having the experience we are having because of our partners.

O Liberty, release the flow,
of opulence that you bestow.
For I am willing to receive,
the Golden Fleece that you now weave.

O Cosmic Mother Liberty,
conduct Abundance Symphony.
My highest service I now see,
abundance is now real for me.

9. Liberty, awaken women to see that our partner may be playing a control game and trying to control us but that is not what creates our *internal* experience. Our internal experience is created by *our* control game.

O Liberty, release the cure,
to free the tired and the poor.
The huddled masses are set free,
by loving Song of Liberty.

O Cosmic Mother Liberty,
conduct Abundance Symphony.
My highest service I now see,
abundance is now real for me.

Part 3

1. Liberty, awaken women to see that we can break up the relationship but we still carry that control game with us, and if we do not overcome those separate selves and resolve it, we might attract another relationship driven by control games.

O Liberty now set me free
from devil's curse of poverty.
I blame not Mother for my lack,
O Blessed Mother, take me back.

O Cosmic Mother Liberty,
conduct Abundance Symphony.
My highest service I now see,
abundance is now real for me.

2. Liberty, awaken women to see that even if women have become legally and politically liberated, there is still, at the level of individual relationships, these control games.

O Liberty, from distant shore,
I come with longing to be More.
I see abundance is a flow,
abundance consciousness I grow.

O Cosmic Mother Liberty,
conduct Abundance Symphony.
My highest service I now see,
abundance is now real for me.

3. Liberty, help me see if I personally have these control games. Help me look at this and say: "So what? I had this. I live on earth, so how could I not have it? But it is time to get beyond it. It is time to liberate myself from this. And I do this by using the tools, being willing to look at these selves, identify them, let them die and stop trying to solve the problem that the control game is projecting that I have to solve."

O Liberty, expose the lie,
that limitations can me tie.
The Ma-ter light is not my foe,
true opulence it does bestow.

O Cosmic Mother Liberty,
conduct Abundance Symphony.
My highest service I now see,
abundance is now real for me.

4. Liberty, cut all women free from these control games and bind the collective beasts that are seeking to perpetuate the control games.

O Liberty, expose the plot,
projected by the fallen lot.
O Cosmic Mother, I now see,
that Mother's not my enemy.

**O Cosmic Mother Liberty,
conduct Abundance Symphony.
My highest service I now see,
abundance is now real for me.**

5. Liberty, I call for the judgment and the binding of the fallen beings who started the entire cycle of this control game between men and women and the control game of the epic mindset, often pulling men into fighting for this epic cause.

O Liberty, with opened eyes,
I now reject the devil's lies.
I now embrace the Mother realm,
for I see Father at the helm.

**O Cosmic Mother Liberty,
conduct Abundance Symphony.
My highest service I now see,
abundance is now real for me.**

6. Liberty, awaken women to see that when we are engaged in a control game, we can get the feeling that we are winning the game. Yet there is a price we pay for this feeling.

O Liberty, a chalice pure,
my lower bodies are for sure.
Release through me your symphony,
your gift of Cosmic Liberty.

**O Cosmic Mother Liberty,
conduct Abundance Symphony.
My highest service I now see,
abundance is now real for me.**

7. Liberty, awaken women to see that we cannot engage in a control game without being controlled by the game, or rather by the separate selves, by the collective beasts, ultimately by the fallen beings.

O Liberty, the open door,
I am for Symphony of More.
In chakras mine light you release,
the flow of love shall never cease.

O Cosmic Mother Liberty,
conduct Abundance Symphony.
My highest service I now see,
abundance is now real for me.

8. Liberty, awaken women to see that whenever we seek to control, we are controlled because unless we are being exposed to control, we will not engage in these control games.

O Liberty, release the flow,
of opulence that you bestow.
For I am willing to receive,
the Golden Fleece that you now weave.

O Cosmic Mother Liberty,
conduct Abundance Symphony.
My highest service I now see,
abundance is now real for me.

9. Liberty, help me look at this honestly and say: "Enough, I have had enough of this. I am more than this self and I can let it die because I know that I will be reborn at a higher level of Christhood. I will become a new being in Christ by letting these selves die."

O Liberty, release the cure,
to free the tired and the poor.
The huddled masses are set free,
by loving Song of Liberty.

**O Cosmic Mother Liberty,
conduct Abundance Symphony.
My highest service I now see,
abundance is now real for me.**

Part 4

1. Liberty, cut free both men and women, but especially women, to free themselves from these control games or at least become aware of them.

O Liberty now set me free
from devil's curse of poverty.
I blame not Mother for my lack,
O Blessed Mother, take me back.

**O Cosmic Mother Liberty,
conduct Abundance Symphony.
My highest service I now see,
abundance is now real for me.**

2. Liberty, awaken women to see that women can be the forerunners because those who have been oppressed are the ones who are most likely to start the cycle of stopping the oppression.

O Liberty, from distant shore,
I come with longing to be More.
I see abundance is a flow,
abundance consciousness I grow.

**O Cosmic Mother Liberty,
conduct Abundance Symphony.
My highest service I now see,
abundance is now real for me.**

3. Liberty, awaken women to see that when we have experienced a certain form of oppression over many lifetimes, we gradually build that determination to free ourselves.

O Liberty, expose the lie,
that limitations can me tie.
The Ma-ter light is not my foe,
true opulence it does bestow.

O Cosmic Mother Liberty,
conduct Abundance Symphony.
My highest service I now see,
abundance is now real for me.

4. Liberty, awaken women to see that this is why women in the modern democracies were the forerunners on a planetary level for speaking out against the discrimination and suppression of women and demanding greater freedom.

O Liberty, expose the plot,
projected by the fallen lot.
O Cosmic Mother, I now see,
that Mother's not my enemy.

O Cosmic Mother Liberty,
conduct Abundance Symphony.
My highest service I now see,
abundance is now real for me.

5. Liberty, cut women free so we can receive the opportunity to see the control games, free ourselves from them without having to go through another number of embodiments before we build enough determination.

O Liberty, with opened eyes,
I now reject the devil's lies.
I now embrace the Mother realm,
for I see Father at the helm.

O Cosmic Mother Liberty,
conduct Abundance Symphony.
My highest service I now see,
abundance is now real for me.

6. Liberty, awaken women to see that the liberation of women is in an upward spiral. Cut women free so it will not take lifetimes or even decades before the most backwards countries in the world have set their women free from this outdated medieval oppression that they are subjected to.

O Liberty, a chalice pure,
my lower bodies are for sure.
Release through me your symphony,
your gift of Cosmic Liberty.

O Cosmic Mother Liberty,
conduct Abundance Symphony.
My highest service I now see,
abundance is now real for me.

7. Liberty, awaken women to see that the enormous range between the most developed nations and the less developed is possible only because of these huge collective beasts that are overpowering the minds of the people in the less developed countries so they cannot see what is so obvious to us.

O Liberty, the open door,
I am for Symphony of More.
In chakras mine light you release,
the flow of love shall never cease.

O Cosmic Mother Liberty,
conduct Abundance Symphony.
My highest service I now see,
abundance is now real for me.

8. Liberty, cut women in Islamic countries free from being hypnotized by these collective beasts. I hereby authorize the ascended masters to use the power you have to go in and bind and consume these beasts, to judge and remove the fallen beings so that this hypnotic effect can be removed.

O Liberty, release the flow,
of opulence that you bestow.
For I am willing to receive,
the Golden Fleece that you now weave.

O Cosmic Mother Liberty,
conduct Abundance Symphony.
My highest service I now see,
abundance is now real for me.

9. Liberty, awaken people so that the scales fall from their eyes and they wake up and say: "But wait a minute, why are we treating women this way? How can we be so far behind these other nations? Why are we holding on to these outdated religious doctrines and laws that define women as second grade citizens?"

O Liberty, release the cure,
to free the tired and the poor.
The huddled masses are set free,
by loving Song of Liberty.

O Cosmic Mother Liberty,
conduct Abundance Symphony.
My highest service I now see,
abundance is now real for me.

Part 5

1. Liberty, bind these collective entities and the fallen beings behind them so people can become free to express the momentum of determination they have built over many lifetimes.

O Liberty now set me free
from devil's curse of poverty.
I blame not Mother for my lack,
O Blessed Mother, take me back.

O Cosmic Mother Liberty,
conduct Abundance Symphony.
My highest service I now see,
abundance is now real for me.

2. Liberty, awaken women to see that once people are determined, a society can quickly shift out of this outdated mindset and begin to see solutions.

O Liberty, from distant shore,
I come with longing to be More.
I see abundance is a flow,
abundance consciousness I grow.

**O Cosmic Mother Liberty,
conduct Abundance Symphony.
My highest service I now see,
abundance is now real for me.**

3. Liberty, I call forth the judgment and binding of the collective beast that is creating the spell women are under, where they do not want to put any political pressure on these less developed nations.

O Liberty, expose the lie,
that limitations can me tie.
The Ma-ter light is not my foe,
true opulence it does bestow.

**O Cosmic Mother Liberty,
conduct Abundance Symphony.
My highest service I now see,
abundance is now real for me.**

4. Liberty, help women in the developed nations realize that our position comes with a responsibility where we are meant to promote the liberation of women in the rest of the world and promote many other causes and positive progress.

O Liberty, expose the plot,
projected by the fallen lot.
O Cosmic Mother, I now see,
that Mother's not my enemy.

**O Cosmic Mother Liberty,
conduct Abundance Symphony.**

**My highest service I now see,
abundance is now real for me.**

5. Liberty, awaken women to see that we have not only a right, but an obligation to put political pressure on these nations. We have an obligation to say: "We cannot trade with you if you continue to treat your women this way. We will not buy your oil, we will find alternatives to buying your oil."

O Liberty, with opened eyes,
I now reject the devil's lies.
I now embrace the Mother realm,
for I see Father at the helm.

**O Cosmic Mother Liberty,
conduct Abundance Symphony.
My highest service I now see,
abundance is now real for me.**

6. Liberty, cut free the people in the more developed nations who are willing to apply this political pressure. I call for the binding of the collective beast that is holding us back from saying: "This is our responsibility."

O Liberty, a chalice pure,
my lower bodies are for sure.
Release through me your symphony,
your gift of Cosmic Liberty.

**O Cosmic Mother Liberty,
conduct Abundance Symphony.
My highest service I now see,
abundance is now real for me.**

7. Liberty, I call for these spells to be broken, for these collective beasts to be bound or consumed or reduced in strength so that people can be free in their outer minds to take the actions that they are actually prepared to take in the emotional, mental and identity body.

O Liberty, the open door,
I am for Symphony of More.

In chakras mine light you release,
the flow of love shall never cease.

O Cosmic Mother Liberty,
conduct Abundance Symphony.
My highest service I now see,
abundance is now real for me.

8. Liberty, cut people free from the blockage in the emotional body that prevents them from acting on what they already see in their mental bodies.

O Liberty, release the flow,
of opulence that you bestow.
For I am willing to receive,
the Golden Fleece that you now weave.

O Cosmic Mother Liberty,
conduct Abundance Symphony.
My highest service I now see,
abundance is now real for me.

9. Liberty, I call for the binding of these beasts that block people so that they have all the right insights, they know what should be done, but they cannot get themselves to act it out because they are blocked at the emotional level from taking action based on their understanding.

O Liberty, release the cure,
to free the tired and the poor.
The huddled masses are set free,
by loving Song of Liberty.

O Cosmic Mother Liberty,
conduct Abundance Symphony.
My highest service I now see,
abundance is now real for me.

Sealing

In the name of the I AM THAT I AM, I accept that Archangel Michael, Astrea and Shiva form an impenetrable shield around myself and all constructive people, sealing us from all fear-based energies in all four octaves. I accept that the Light of God is consuming and transforming all fear-based energies that make up the dark forces working against the liberation of women on earth!

24 | HAVE YOU HAD ENOUGH OF VIOLENCE AGAINST WOMEN?

I am the Ascended Master Mother Mary. My first point that I want to bring out in this release is that I want to continue, based on what the Ascended Master Liberty said, about the control games between men and women. One of the more insidious and widespread control games is of course that men attempt to control women through money, or rather by denying them money or access to money. You have seen societies where women could not have a job, could not really work, could not earn a living, and therefore were totally dependent on getting married and staying married in order to survive physically. You see many societies today where this is still the case, and it is truly a form of control, a control game, that men are playing. The fallen beings have created these beasts that overpower men's minds where they somehow think that women should not have money or they are not capable of using money wisely. Therefore, men must keep women away from money and keep money away from women so that the men are in control. In many cases the men are so blinded by this collective beast that they cannot see how illogical it is, how untrue it is. They cannot see that even though they consider this to be necessary, it is simply a control game that they are caught in and, as we said, if you are controlling others, *you* are controlled yourself.

There are many, many men who even today feel that since they are the one who is primarily earning the money or exclusively earning the money, they should be in control of how it is spent. The fact of the matter is that if men have this attitude and they deliberately keep their women out of the decision making process relating to money, then the men cannot stay in attunement with the flow of life. They cannot therefore multiply the money they are making, and that is why many of these men are living in poverty and will not get out of poverty precisely because they have that attitude. If instead they would give more equal value to their wives so that their wives were involved in the process of making money, then men and women together could add their momentum and this would result in a higher level of abundance for the couple, for the family. Either the man would make more money, get a better job or the woman would get an income and therefore the entire family would be better off financially than they are when men have this attitude of allowing themselves to be caught in this control game of limiting women through money.

It is clear that one of the major aspects of the progress we have seen in the more developed nations is that women have been able to get an education, women have been able to get jobs, to get reasonably paid jobs, and to get equal pay with men in the jobs that they do get. This is an extremely important development in terms of giving women more independence, more freedom and the ability to remove themselves from an abusive relationship because they can survive financially.

We have great compassion for the many women around the world who feel trapped in an abusive relationship but they know they cannot get out of that relationship because they could not survive themselves or they could not keep their children alive if they were not in that relationship. They endure the abuse but it has profound effects on the soul of these women and it really sets the stage for them going into a downward spiral where often they come into their next embodiment being at a lower level of consciousness, perhaps again attracting an abusive relationship or another abusive situation. Even if they come in as men in their next embodiment, they are still in that downward spiral of feeling they are not worthy to have money, not worthy to earn money, and therefore they subconsciously push abundance away from them. It is very important for you to keep the vision, to make the calls that women throughout the world will be cut free from this financial dependence on men. You can call for the binding of these beasts behind these control games, for the binding of these beasts that want to keep money away from women and keep women dependent on men for the money they need in order to survive.

Do you know where your clothes is made?

Now again, there is this possibility that you can call so that women in the West will wake up, women in the affluent nations will wake up, and they will take a hard look at their clothes-buying habits. They will say: "When I look at the clothes in my closet, do I actually know where it was made?" Most of the clothes you have in your closet were probably made by women who work in garment factories, but do you know in which nation it was made, and do you know under which conditions these women worked? Do you know what pay they were given? Was it just a very low income that allowed them barely to survive, and was it so that the factory was owned by men and that men were skimming off the majority of the profit? Is it so that the store where you bought the clothes is owned by men, or a corporation owned by men? Is it so that the importers, the middle men, are also men who are making money? When you see the price that you pay in the store in a modern country and you see what a particular woman made from making that particular dress, you can see there is a huge gap between the two, and the woman who did the actual work got almost nothing out of it.

Well again, you can look at this and say: "Is this a sustainable situation?" Could there not spring up, and of course there *can*, a movement of women in affluent nations who express solidarity with their sisters in less affluent nations, and who demand to know: "Where are my clothes made? You who are owning a particular store, or a chain of stores, where is the clothes made you are selling for women? Who made it? Was it made by women? What were they paid relative to the price that I pay in the store? What were they paid relative to the cost of living in their countries? What conditions were they working under? Were they working in these sweatshops or in unsafe conditions around the world? If that is the case, I will not buy in your store. We, as a force of women, will boycott the stores that are not open and forward about where the clothes are made and under which conditions these women are working."

This could then promote a movement where these factories were forced to change, even give women better pay. You could even see the springing up of factories owned and run by women, as a cooperative, not as this traditional one owner or one corporation skimming off all the profits, but where there was a shared ownership where women shared in the income of the business, those who did the work. This is some of the potentials that you see whereby women in the Western world could put political pressure on not only companies but even nations where entire nations could be forced to change. For example, the nation of Bangladesh where there is an extensive garment industry, but the same in China, Vietnam and other nations, they would be forced to take a look at this and say: "We cannot continue to sell our products in the modern nations unless we give the women working in the garment industry reasonable working conditions and reasonable pay, and therefore we must make sure that this happens."

In other words what you have today, is you have an entire clothing industry, garment industry, that is driven by profit and you have a large population of women in the affluent nations who are buying clothes and often buying more clothes than they need, but they look often at price, they look for the cheapest possible clothes that they can find and they do not care where it is made and under which conditions. This could change so that you saw a shift where women go for quality, they do not buy more than they need, and they have concerns about the conditions under which the clothes was made and they will not support this exploitation of women. It truly *is* an exploitation of women and an abuse of women and a violence against women that is going on in the garment industry, in other industries as well. Therefore, it can spread from there to other industries where women in the affluent nations, they are willing of course to support businesses in the less affluent nations that give work to women, but they demand that women get reasonable conditions and reasonable pay.

Explaining violence against women

Now, my next agenda here is to talk about a slightly different topic. We have talked about violence against women. Goddess of Liberty, the Ascended Master Liberty, talked about the control games where women are being controlled by men. There are many of these control games where men are using violence to control women, but when you look at women's situations, when you look at what women are exposed to around the planet, you cannot explain all violence against women by control games. Some violence is driven by control games where men are simply using violence as a way to control the women in their lives, but not all violence can be explained by this.

What needs to happen, what you can make the calls for, is that women in the more developed nations, women who are liberated to the greatest possible degree, will start using their freedom to consider the issue of violence against women. It may not be such a big problem in their own countries, but again you need to show this solidarity and look at women in other countries and the violence against women there. Even in the most developed nations, there is some violence against women that cannot be explained by control games. Women can come to look at this and they can look at some of the worst instances of violence against women and they can see that when men rape women, you cannot explain this in most cases as a control game. There is, when you look at a man or even a group of men who are raping a woman, there is more to it.

What can you see if you look at these situations? I know that most women do not want to look at this, but nevertheless it is necessary that you look at this in order to improve conditions. You cannot improve conditions without being willing to look at a problem. When you look at men who are raping women, the first thing you can see is that there is more to this than just sexual desire, it is not just a matter of fulfilling some sexual desire. There is an anger, there is even a stronger feeling of a hatred that is directed against women.

You can look at men that are beating up women, and in some cases beating them up so much that they either die or have permanent damage as a result. Some women have been exposed to this, but many women of course have not experienced it directly. If you could look into the eyes of a man who is beating up a woman beyond any kind of *rational* explanation, you need to look for an *irrational* explanation. If you could look in the man's eyes, you would see this anger, this hatred directed against the woman. There may be some men that are using violence, that are beating up women, because they want to punish the women for some reason. An aspect of control games is that you want to punish those that will not allow themselves to be controlled and so you have this desire for punishment, but violence against women cannot be explained by punishment either. There is an anger, there is a hatred. This goes in many other situations where women are abused in various ways.

If you go to a Muslim country where you have these fundamentalist Muslim preachers or imams who are promoting this Sharia Law and who are supporting the suppression of women, the limitation of women, if you could get them to talk openly and freely about their attitude to women, about why they support this suppression of women, you would also see in their eyes something that cannot be explained rationally. There is that anger, there is that hatred that is shining through them. I say it is shining *through* them because the question really is: Does it come from the man or has the man been taken over by it?

Here is where we first will see that in many cases, it does not actually come from the man. It comes because the man has had his mind, the four levels of his mind (his physical, emotional, mental and identity body) taken over by a collective entity. That collective entity is created over a very long time, and it is an entity of anger against women. There is another one of hatred against women and there are other entities that I will talk about later. There are these collective entities of anger directed against women, hatred against women and they can take over men's minds when they are weak. When men are weak, it means that they have gotten themselves into a frustrated state of mind. They feel they are living under deep pressure, they are insecure, they are uncertain about their future. They feel this enormous pressure upon them and they are overwhelmed by this, and in order to get some kind of relief, they need to take out their anger against someone and who is closer than their wives? They get taken over by this anger entity and they direct the anger against their wives and for a brief period of time they may feel empowered by having taken their anger out. Of course, it does not last very long where they then go even deeper, often start self-loathing and now they are feeling even more frustrated, even more disempowered, even more under pressure and then, even though they had a certain release, the pressure starts building and the cycle repeats all over again.

Of course you can make the calls for the binding and the consuming of these collective entities, for men to be cut free from them, and for women to be cut free from the collective entities that overpower women's minds so that they actually endure this kind of violence. In many cases the reason they endure it, as I said, is they have nowhere to go financially because they cannot sustain themselves and their children without the money coming from their husbands. Still, there is more to it than that.

Explaining why women endure violence

If again you could take some of these women who are continually abused by men, who are beaten up by men for example, and if you could look in their eyes, you could see that there is also something there that you cannot explain rationally. It is because these women have been taken over by the collective entities that have been created that cause women to submit to this kind of abuse. They feel that they have no alternative, that they cannot object, that they cannot say no, that they cannot walk away. They see no option for themselves other than to endure it for the time that it lasts and then move on with life as if nothing had happened.

You can see these women who are trapped in this situation where they never actually get to a point where they can mount the determination to attempt to do something about it, whatever that could be in their situation. I understand many women do not have that much they can do, but they could potentially talk to their husbands, draw a line and say no, they could potentially help their husbands in various ways but this they cannot see how to do because they are so trapped. They cannot see either that they potentially could remove themselves from their husbands and still survive because they think there is no way out for them. This is because their minds are blinded so this is also something of course to make calls on.

A deeper explanation for violence against women

What we see is that there is a certain segment of men who are violent against women but who do so because their minds are overtaken, overpowered by these collective entities. I am not saying in any way that this frees these men from responsibility or frees them from making karma. Naturally, it is because these men have not taken responsibility for themselves psychologically, they are not on the spiritual path, they know nothing about the spiritual path and therefore they are trapped. Even though they are trapped, they are still responsible for their actions because you can feel trapped without beating up your wife, as many men prove. I am not excusing this, I am simply stating that there are certain men who are violent against women because of these collective entities.

However, when you look at the male population and when you espe-cially look at the segment of the male population who are violent against women, you will see that there are some men where you cannot fully explain their violence by saying that their minds are taken over by these collective entities. Now, this is somewhat subtle because any man who is violent against women, *has* his mind taken over by these collective entities that are directing anger and hatred against women. What I am pointing out is that there are those men who are only violent because their minds are taken over. In other words, the man is acting without realizing what he is doing. There is still an anger energy, a hatred energy that is flowing through this man, but it is not really in his own forcefield, in his own aura. In his emotional and mental mind he does not have this hatred or anger against women. It is coming *through* him when he is opened up to it, but it is not really coming *from* him. The other segment of the male population that I am talking about, even though their anger is reinforced by these enti-ties, it is not exclusively coming from the entities, it is not coming through these people only, because these men have it inside themselves.

They have created these separate selves that are angry with women, that hate women. This is a segment of the male population where you can make the calls for the binding of these entities, but even if these entities were completely removed from the earth tomorrow, this particular seg-ment of men would still be angry and would still express hatred against women, not to the degree they are doing it when their minds are reinforced by the entities, but they would still do it. In other words, you could remove the entities, and the majority of men who are violent against women would stop the violence, but there will still be a small (relatively small compared to the population of earth but far too large anyway) segment of men who will still have that anger and hatred against women, and it will spill over into violence. There are even some of these men who are not physically violent with women, but who still have the anger and the hatred internal-ized. What you see here is this: There are certain men who from their own beings direct anger and hatred against women. You then need to consider where this comes from and you need to recognize that this goes back to the fallen beings. It started with the fallen beings but I am not thereby saying that all these men are fallen beings. They have been affected by the fallen beings.

Fallen beings who hate women

Let us look at the situation of fallen beings. We have said that when you go into duality you are creating/generating one dualistic polarity but there will always be an opposite. The other way to look at duality is to say that when you do something from the dualistic mindset, there is a consequence, there is a price to pay. You can do something but when you do that, you exclude something else. There are certain other things you cannot do. What the fallen beings chose to do was that they chose to elevate men to the position of superiority. They chose to elevate or to create this male God, this male personal God, such as the Old Testament God, and in doing so, they opened up the possibility of suppressing women.

Now, the fallen beings have in their beings a clear anger against God. They are angry with God. They would like to express that anger but they find it difficult to do so on earth because they have created this male God and elevated this to being supposedly the Supreme God of the universe. It is therefore difficult for the fallen beings to get men to feel or even dare to express anger against this God. In other words, they can get men to accept the male God, to worship and obey the commands of the male God, but they cannot get most men to express anger or feel anger against this God. The fallen beings now have an anger, it is an anger against God, but they cannot express it. Of course, even if you cannot express anger against the object of your anger, you can divert your anger to express it against another object. So, what have the fallen beings done?

They have expressed anger against women, against the feminine energy and polarity, even against the entire matter realm, which can be said to be the female polarity to the spiritual realm. This is what has given rise to a concept, we have talked about before, that we have called "hatred of the mother." In other words, hatred of the mother realm. It even goes all the way to hatred of women, whether they are mothers or not.

There is that hatred of the matter realm, hatred of the mother realm, hatred of the physical matter world, hatred of the human body. The fallen beings have then created these false religions, false spiritual movements, and they have created false gurus. You see many of them in India who are promoting this view that the matter realm and the physical body and the lusts and the desires of the body, are an enemy of spirituality, an enemy of men attaining their spiritual goals. They are a temptation for men, just as you see in Genesis that Eve was the one who fell for temptation, and then tempted Adam into going along with her. You see even in the East, parallels to this where it is always the women that are less spiritual or are susceptible to temptation, and where the desires of the body are a temptation for the men, tempting them away from pursuing a more spiritual lifestyle, however it is defined.

What you actually have is this enormous anger against women, against the mother realm, against the matter world, that originally comes from the fallen beings. It has been expressed on this planet for so long that it has filtered its way into many aspects of society. It has caused many, many men who are not fallen beings, to take into their beings this anger and hatred against the matter realm, against their own physical bodies and against women.

Now, I have talked about men who are violent against women because they have internalized this anger and hatred against women. They want to express that anger, they desire to punish women, to hurt them, to put them down. This is what we might call raw destruction, simply raw physical destruction. There are some men where it may seem as if they are trying to control women psychologically, but it is actually beyond the control game because it is simply that these men are using psychological means to express anger and hatred towards women. Thereby, they also punish them, hurt them, destroy their souls if they can because they have such a hatred that they actually want to destroy these women.

Then of course there is a certain segment of men who have taken this into a greater extreme, who have become more overpowered by the fallen beings. They are the ones who serve in various positions where they promote ideas that suppress women, ideas that are actually a form of violence against women, that have no real rational explanation. They are simply ideas that are only created to justify this anger and hatred against women. They are of course often very cleverly disguised by various means. Truly, the driving force behind it is not rational. If you take the Sharia law promoted by fundamentalist Islam, there is no rationality behind it. You may be able to see certain arguments, certain reasoning, but if you really look at this, it is not rational. It is not consistent. It is not logical. It is not based on any reality. It is camouflaged as some religious scripture or doctrine, but the driving force behind it is simply pure anger and hatred against women. What rational reason could there be for the fact that millions of women live in very, very hot climates, but they have to wear black clothing that covers their entire body, except for a narrow slit over the eyes, possibly even a veil over the eyes. What rational explanation could there be for this? It is anger and hatred against women.

You take Genesis and the fall of Eve and the fall of Adam, and how they were cast out from Paradise by the angry God, saying that the entire downfall of the human race and that all of the unpleasant conditions seen on earth is caused by women. What rational explanation could there be for this? It is nothing but an expression of pure anger and hatred against women, camouflaged as a religious scripture and doctrine, but nevertheless, nothing but hatred, hatred of the mother, hatred of women.

There is a group of men on earth that are simply violent against women out of this raw anger and hatred. There is another group of men on earth who have an even greater anger and hatred against women, but they are camouflaging it as some "benign" reason, often a religion. Even among materialists, you can find this. You can find materialists who are absolutely convinced that women are biologically different than men, that the female brain is wired in a different way. This is caused by evolution where women were given a certain role and therefore have evolved to be a certain way. It may seem benign, to some it even seems scientific, but it is again an expression of this pure anger and hatred against women, hatred of the mother. There are of course many more examples of this, many more than I want to describe here. Nevertheless, what you can do as our ascended master students is you can make the calls for this through the invocations that will be made based on these dictations and it can have a tremendous impact.

Some men need to be removed from earth

Now, one thing I want to emphasize here. I have talked about two groups of men. The ones that are violent, physically violent out of this anger and hatred and the ones that are psychologically, even attempting to be spiritually, violent against women also out of hatred. Now, these men, most of them in embodiment, are not fallen beings. They did not fall in a previous sphere, they originated in this sphere. Some of them are the original inhabitants of the earth, some of them have come from other lower planets.

These men have had this anger and hatred for so long. They have been the driving force behind all of this suppression, discrimination and violence against women that you see on this planet. They have been the physical anchor point for it by being in physical embodiment. They have had this for so long in their consciousness that they are not likely to be willing to give this up and start the upward path towards Christhood. What is the solution to this? Well, there is only one solution: They need to be removed from the planet.

This does not mean that I am asking you to call for their death, or to even envision that they should die or wish that they should die. I am simply asking you, who are our ascended master students, to make the decision that as far as you are concerned, this anger and hatred is no longer acceptable on planet earth. I am asking you to also make the calls to us to thereby use our authority to take the steps necessary to remove the outlet for this anger and hatred by confronting these people with the need to either change or to be removed from the earth.

We cannot expect that women in general will be able to do this so therefore, we need you who are our ascended master students to make this decision and make these calls. Now, when you do this, then more and more women can awaken from this hypnotic state. They can look at this, they can identify this anger and hatred, and they can also decide that it is unacceptable for them. This can then gradually spread to the point where all of these men can be confronted with the choice, as it even says in the Bible: "I have put before you life and death, choose life." If they will not choose life, then they must go somewhere else, to another planet where they can continue in their current state of consciousness but that planet is even denser than the earth.

A new cycle in the liberation of women

Clearly, as we have expressed in this conference, there is an upward spiral on earth and it is one of the effects of this spiral that women are becoming increasingly liberated. We have simply reached the point in this spiral where women deserve to be liberated from this anger and hatred and that is why these men must be confronted with that choice to either be willing to lose their mortal selves and follow Christ towards eternal life or to lose their opportunity to embody on this planet. This is simply the stark reality of the turning of cycles in this upward spiral towards liberating planet earth from the influence of the fallen beings.

I know, my beloved, that this is a heavy topic but nevertheless I trust that those of you who are familiar with our teachings will not feel overly burdened by it. You will simply make the calls and then let us deal with the energy and with the lifestreams that need to be dealt with. We are not asking you of course to feel any kind of anger or hatred against these people. We are asking you to look at this realistically and decide whether you want this to continue on this planet, or whether you want it to end. I am not saying you *shall* decide, you *must* decide that it should end, it is your free-will choice. I trust of course that most of you who are familiar with our teachings will want this to end. With this, I have completed this somewhat heavy address but it was necessary to bring this out in order to have a more complete coverage of this topic of the liberation of women. How can you talk about the liberation of women without talking about some of these very destructive forces that are seeking to keep women in bondage?

This of course is where we have determined that you, our student body, are ready to be aware of these issues so that you can be the forerunners for this awareness to spread so that more and more women can become aware of this. For truly, you have the saying, inspired upon Albert Einstein, that if you continue to do the same thing and expect different results, you are insane. You can look at women's situation, you can see what has been done, what progress has been made. You can acknowledge, as we have said, that real progress has been made. You can also acknowledge that there are certain problems that have not gone away. Therefore, you must say: "Can we, if we continue to do the same thing that we have done so far, can we expect that these very severe abuses of women will go away by doing the same thing?"

If not, then we must look for something different, and that something different really has not been available on this planet before in the physical octave. By the teachings we have given and will be giving for the rest of this conference, we are now making that something else available in the physical so that women can begin to find it, implement it so that these ideas can even spread in the collective consciousness and women can begin to rise up and make that determination: Enough is enough, we will no longer allow this abuse of women on planet earth.

You understand that when those who have been abused by a certain force come to that point where they decide that enough is enough, this is also a way to authorize the ascended masters to step in and use our power to remove these forces from the earth. Your direct calls is one way but this determination that we have had enough of this is another way, and that means there is a certain critical mass of women that need to come to this point before we can fully remove these forces. By you doing your work, we will more quickly move to that turning point so that these forces can be removed. When they are removed, all of a sudden, it is as if these problems just evaporate into thin air. They melt away, and the heavy consciousness surrounding these problems will also melt away. Suddenly, women can stand up more straight, they can feel more free and there is a new day dawning and a new opportunity. This truly is what we desire to see as many women as possible feel: that there is a new day, a new cycle, a new opportunity, an opportunity to redefine what it means to be a woman on planet earth. With this I seal you in my Mother Flame of the most tender, comforting love you could possibly feel.

NOTE: This dictation was given May 31, 2020.

25 | INVOKING AN END TO VIOLENCE AGAINST WOMEN (PART 1)

In the name of the I AM THAT I AM, Jesus Christ, I use the authority that I have as a being in embodiment on earth to call upon Mother Mary to reinforce my calls and use my chakras to project the statements in this invocation into the collective consciousness and awaken people to the awareness that will liberate both men and women from all psychological and spiritual thralldom to the fallen beings. Awaken people to the reality that we are spiritual beings and that we can co-create a new future by working with the ascended masters. I especially call for …

[Make your own calls here.]

Part 1

1. Mother Mary, I call forth the judgment of the Divine Mother upon the dark forces behind the control game where men attempt to control women through money, or rather by denying them money or access to money.

O blessed Mary, Mother mine,
there is no greater love than thine,
as we are one in heart and mind,
my place in hierarchy I find.

O Mother Mary, generate,
the song that does accelerate,
the earth into a higher state,
all matter does now scintillate.

2. Mother Mary, I call forth the judgment of the Divine Mother upon the dark forces behind societies where women cannot have a job, cannot earn a living, and therefore are totally dependent on getting married and staying married in order to survive physically.

I came to earth from heaven sent,
as I am in embodiment,
I use Divine authority,
commanding you to set earth free.

O Mother Mary, generate,
the song that does accelerate,
the earth into a higher state,
all matter does now scintillate.

3. Mother Mary, I call forth the judgment of the Divine Mother upon the fallen beings who have created these beasts that overpower men's minds so they think women should not have money or they are not capable of using money wisely.

I call now in God's sacred name,
for you to use your Mother Flame,
to burn all fear-based energy,
restoring sacred harmony.

O Mother Mary, generate,
the song that does accelerate,
the earth into a higher state,
all matter does now scintillate.

4. Mother Mary, I call forth the judgment of the Divine Mother upon the dark forces that make men think they must keep women away from money and keep money away from women so that the men are in control.

> Your sacred name I hereby praise,
> collective consciousness you raise,
> no more of fear and doubt and shame,
> consume it with your Mother Flame.

> **O Mother Mary, generate,**
> **the song that does accelerate,**
> **the earth into a higher state,**
> **all matter does now scintillate.**

5. Mother Mary, I call forth the judgment of the Divine Mother upon the collective beast that prevents men from seeing how illogical it is, how untrue it is that women cannot be trusted with money.

> All darkness from the earth you purge,
> your light moves as a mighty surge,
> no force of darkness can now stop,
> the spiral that goes only up.

> **O Mother Mary, generate,**
> **the song that does accelerate,**
> **the earth into a higher state,**
> **all matter does now scintillate.**

6. Mother Mary, I call forth the judgment of the Divine Mother upon the dark forces that prevent men from seeing that this is simply a control game that they are caught in, and if you are controlling others, *you* are controlled yourself.

> All elemental life you bless,
> removing from them man-made stress,
> the nature spirits are now free,
> outpicturing Divine decree.

O Mother Mary, generate,
the song that does accelerate,
the earth into a higher state,
all matter does now scintillate.

7. Mother Mary, I call forth the judgment of the Divine Mother upon the dark forces who make men feel that since they are the ones who are earning the money, they should be in control of how it is spent.

I raise my voice and take my stand,
a stop to war I do command,
no more shall warring scar the earth,
a golden age is given birth.

O Mother Mary, generate,
the song that does accelerate,
the earth into a higher state,
all matter does now scintillate.

8. Mother Mary, I call forth the judgment of the Divine Mother upon men who have this attitude and deliberately keep their women out of the decision making process relating to money.

As Mother Earth is free at last,
disasters belong to the past,
your Mother Light is so intense,
that matter is now far less dense.

O Mother Mary, generate,
the song that does accelerate,
the earth into a higher state,
all matter does now scintillate.

9. Mother Mary, I call forth the judgment of the Divine Mother upon the dark forces that prevent men from seeing that with this attitude they cannot multiply the money they are making, and that is why many of these men are living in poverty and will not get out of poverty precisely because they have that attitude.

In Mother Light the earth is pure,
the upward spiral will endure,
prosperity is now the norm,
God's vision manifest as form.

O Mother Mary, generate,
the song that does accelerate,
the earth into a higher state,
all matter does now scintillate.

Part 2

1. Mother Mary, awaken men to see that if they would give more equal value to their wives so that their wives were involved in the process of making and spending money, then men and women together could add their momentum and this would result in a higher level of abundance for the family.

O blessed Mary, Mother mine,
there is no greater love than thine,
as we are one in heart and mind,
my place in hierarchy I find.

O Mother Mary, generate,
the song that does accelerate,
the earth into a higher state,
all matter does now scintillate.

2. Mother Mary, awaken men to see that if they work with their wives, then either the man would make more money or the woman would get an income and therefore the entire family would be better off financially than when men are caught in this control game of limiting women through money.

I came to earth from heaven sent,
as I am in embodiment,

I use Divine authority,
commanding you to set earth free.

O Mother Mary, generate,
the song that does accelerate,
the earth into a higher state,
all matter does now scintillate.

3. Mother Mary, awaken people to see that one of the major aspects of the progress we have seen in the more developed nations is that women have been able to get an education, to get reasonably paid jobs, and to get equal pay with men.

I call now in God's sacred name,
for you to use your Mother Flame,
to burn all fear-based energy,
restoring sacred harmony.

O Mother Mary, generate,
the song that does accelerate,
the earth into a higher state,
all matter does now scintillate.

4. Mother Mary, awaken people to see that this is an extremely important development in terms of giving women more independence, more freedom and the ability to remove themselves from an abusive relationship because they can survive financially.

Your sacred name I hereby praise,
collective consciousness you raise,
no more of fear and doubt and shame,
consume it with your Mother Flame.

O Mother Mary, generate,
the song that does accelerate,
the earth into a higher state,
all matter does now scintillate.

5. Mother Mary, cut free the women around the world who feel trapped in an abusive relationship. Help them know how they can get out of that relationship and keep themselves and their children alive if they are not in that relationship.

All darkness from the earth you purge,
your light moves as a mighty surge,
no force of darkness can now stop,
the spiral that goes only up.

O Mother Mary, generate,
the song that does accelerate,
the earth into a higher state,
all matter does now scintillate.

6. Mother Mary, cut free women who endure abuse so they will not go into a downward spiral, but will be able to change their situation in this lifetime or the next.

All elemental life you bless,
removing from them man-made stress,
the nature spirits are now free,
outpicturing Divine decree.

O Mother Mary, generate,
the song that does accelerate,
the earth into a higher state,
all matter does now scintillate.

7. Mother Mary, I call forth the judgment of the Divine Mother upon the dark forces who make women feel they are not worthy to have money, not worthy to earn money, and therefore they subconsciously push abundance away from them.

I raise my voice and take my stand,
a stop to war I do command,
no more shall warring scar the earth,
a golden age is given birth.

O Mother Mary, generate,
the song that does accelerate,
the earth into a higher state,
all matter does now scintillate.

8. Mother Mary, cut free women throughout the world from this financial dependence on men so they can change their personal situation and change their societies.

As Mother Earth is free at last,
disasters belong to the past,
your Mother Light is so intense,
that matter is now far less dense.

O Mother Mary, generate,
the song that does accelerate,
the earth into a higher state,
all matter does now scintillate.

9. Mother Mary, I call forth the judgment and binding of the beasts that want to keep money away from women and keep women dependent on men for the money they need in order to survive.

In Mother Light the earth is pure,
the upward spiral will endure,
prosperity is now the norm,
God's vision manifest as form.

O Mother Mary, generate,
the song that does accelerate,
the earth into a higher state,
all matter does now scintillate.

Part 3

1. Mother Mary, awaken women in the affluent nations so they will take a hard look at their clothes-buying habits and find out where the clothes

is made and under what conditions people work in order to produce the clothes.

O blessed Mary, Mother mine,
there is no greater love than thine,
as we are one in heart and mind,
my place in hierarchy I find.

O Mother Mary, generate,
the song that does accelerate,
the earth into a higher state,
all matter does now scintillate.

2. Mother Mary, awaken women in the affluent nations to refuse buying clothes that was made in factories where men take advantage of women and make them work under poor conditions for low pay while skimming off all of the profit.

I came to earth from heaven sent,
as I am in embodiment,
I use Divine authority,
commanding you to set earth free.

O Mother Mary, generate,
the song that does accelerate,
the earth into a higher state,
all matter does now scintillate.

3. Mother Mary, awaken women in the affluent nations to refuse buying clothes from stores that are owned by men, from corporations owned by men or from importers owned by men so that men make all the money.

I call now in God's sacred name,
for you to use your Mother Flame,
to burn all fear-based energy,
restoring sacred harmony.

O Mother Mary, generate,
the song that does accelerate,

**the earth into a higher state,
all matter does now scintillate.**

4. Mother Mary, awaken women in the affluent nations to refuse buying clothes if there is a huge gap between what a particular woman made from making that particular dress, and what men made from her labor.

Your sacred name I hereby praise,
collective consciousness you raise,
no more of fear and doubt and shame,
consume it with your Mother Flame.

**O Mother Mary, generate,
the song that does accelerate,
the earth into a higher state,
all matter does now scintillate.**

5. Mother Mary, awaken women in the affluent nations to create a movement of women who express solidarity with their sisters in less affluent nations, and who demand to know how their clothes was made and who made the profit.

All darkness from the earth you purge,
your light moves as a mighty surge,
no force of darkness can now stop,
the spiral that goes only up.

**O Mother Mary, generate,
the song that does accelerate,
the earth into a higher state,
all matter does now scintillate.**

6. Mother Mary, awaken women in the affluent nations to demand that the women making their clothes work under good conditions and are paid well according to the cost of living in their countries.

All elemental life you bless,
removing from them man-made stress,

the nature spirits are now free,
outpicturing Divine decree.

O Mother Mary, generate,
the song that does accelerate,
the earth into a higher state,
all matter does now scintillate.

7. Mother Mary, awaken women in the affluent nations to form a force of women who will boycott the stores that are not open and forward about where the clothes are made and under which conditions these women are working.

I raise my voice and take my stand,
a stop to war I do command,
no more shall warring scar the earth,
a golden age is given birth.

O Mother Mary, generate,
the song that does accelerate,
the earth into a higher state,
all matter does now scintillate.

8. Mother Mary, awaken people to create factories owned and run by women, as a cooperative, not as a traditional business, but where there is a shared ownership and women share in the income of the business.

As Mother Earth is free at last,
disasters belong to the past,
your Mother Light is so intense,
that matter is now far less dense.

O Mother Mary, generate,
the song that does accelerate,
the earth into a higher state,
all matter does now scintillate.

9. Mother Mary, awaken women in the affluent nations to put political pressure on not only companies but even nations where entire nations could be forced to change.

> In Mother Light the earth is pure,
> the upward spiral will endure,
> prosperity is now the norm,
> God's vision manifest as form.

> **O Mother Mary, generate,**
> **the song that does accelerate,**
> **the earth into a higher state,**
> **all matter does now scintillate.**

Part 4

1. Mother Mary, I call forth the judgment of the Divine Mother upon the dark forces behind the garment industry in Bangladesh, China, Vietnam and other nations.

> O blessed Mary, Mother mine,
> there is no greater love than thine,
> as we are one in heart and mind,
> my place in hierarchy I find.

> **O Mother Mary, generate,**
> **the song that does accelerate,**
> **the earth into a higher state,**
> **all matter does now scintillate.**

2. Mother Mary, awaken people to see that they cannot continue to sell their products in the modern nations unless they give the women working in the garment industry reasonable working conditions and reasonable pay.

> I came to earth from heaven sent,
> as I am in embodiment,

I use Divine authority,
commanding you to set earth free.

O Mother Mary, generate,
the song that does accelerate,
the earth into a higher state,
all matter does now scintillate.

3. Mother Mary, I call forth the judgment of the Divine Mother upon the dark forces behind the garment industry that is driven by profit and the women in the affluent nations who look for the cheapest possible clothes and they don't care where it is made and under which conditions.

I call now in God's sacred name,
for you to use your Mother Flame,
to burn all fear-based energy,
restoring sacred harmony.

O Mother Mary, generate,
the song that does accelerate,
the earth into a higher state,
all matter does now scintillate.

4. Mother Mary, awaken women to go for quality, to not buy more than they need, and to be concerned about the conditions under which the clothes was made so they do not support this exploitation of women.

Your sacred name I hereby praise,
collective consciousness you raise,
no more of fear and doubt and shame,
consume it with your Mother Flame.

O Mother Mary, generate,
the song that does accelerate,
the earth into a higher state,
all matter does now scintillate.

5. Mother Mary, I call forth the judgment of the Divine Mother upon the dark forces that prevent people from seeing that it truly *is* an exploitation

of women, an abuse of women and a violence against women that is going
on in the garment industry and in other industries as well.

> All darkness from the earth you purge,
> your light moves as a mighty surge,
> no force of darkness can now stop,
> the spiral that goes only up.

> **O Mother Mary, generate,**
> **the song that does accelerate,**
> **the earth into a higher state,**
> **all matter does now scintillate.**

6. Mother Mary, awaken women in the affluent nations so they are willing
to support businesses in the less affluent nations that give work to women,
but they demand that women get reasonable conditions and reasonable
pay.

> All elemental life you bless,
> removing from them man-made stress,
> the nature spirits are now free,
> outpicturing Divine decree.

> **O Mother Mary, generate,**
> **the song that does accelerate,**
> **the earth into a higher state,**
> **all matter does now scintillate.**

7. Mother Mary, I call forth the judgment of the Divine Mother upon the
dark forces behind the control games where men are using violence to
control women.

> I raise my voice and take my stand,
> a stop to war I do command,
> no more shall warring scar the earth,
> a golden age is given birth.

> **O Mother Mary, generate,**
> **the song that does accelerate,**

the earth into a higher state,
all matter does now scintillate.

8. Mother Mary, awaken people to see that we cannot explain all violence against women by control games. Some violence is driven by control games, where men are using violence as a way to control the women in their lives, but not all violence can be explained by this.

As Mother Earth is free at last,
disasters belong to the past,
your Mother Light is so intense,
that matter is now far less dense.

O Mother Mary, generate,
the song that does accelerate,
the earth into a higher state,
all matter does now scintillate.

9. Mother Mary, awaken women in the more developed nations to use their freedom to consider the issue of violence against women, to show solidarity and look at women in other countries and the violence against women there.

In Mother Light the earth is pure,
the upward spiral will endure,
prosperity is now the norm,
God's vision manifest as form.

O Mother Mary, generate,
the song that does accelerate,
the earth into a higher state,
all matter does now scintillate.

Part 5

1. Mother Mary, awaken people to see that even in the most developed nations, there is some violence against women that cannot be explained by control games.

> O blessed Mary, Mother mine,
> there is no greater love than thine,
> as we are one in heart and mind,
> my place in hierarchy I find.
>
> **O Mother Mary, generate,**
> **the song that does accelerate,**
> **the earth into a higher state,**
> **all matter does now scintillate.**

2. Mother Mary, I call forth the judgment of the Divine Mother upon the dark forces behind men who are using violence because they want to punish women.

> I came to earth from heaven sent,
> as I am in embodiment,
> I use Divine authority,
> commanding you to set earth free.
>
> **O Mother Mary, generate,**
> **the song that does accelerate,**
> **the earth into a higher state,**
> **all matter does now scintillate.**

3. Mother Mary, awaken people to see that an aspect of control games is that you want to punish those that will not allow themselves to be controlled. But violence against women cannot be explained by punishment alone.

> I call now in God's sacred name,
> for you to use your Mother Flame,

to burn all fear-based energy,
restoring sacred harmony.

O Mother Mary, generate,
the song that does accelerate,
the earth into a higher state,
all matter does now scintillate.

4. Mother Mary, awaken people to see that when men rape women, we cannot explain this in most cases as a control game. When we look at a man or even a group of men who are raping a woman, there is more to it.

Your sacred name I hereby praise,
collective consciousness you raise,
no more of fear and doubt and shame,
consume it with your Mother Flame.

O Mother Mary, generate,
the song that does accelerate,
the earth into a higher state,
all matter does now scintillate.

5. Mother Mary, awaken people to see that we cannot improve conditions without being willing to look at a problem. When we look at men who are raping women, we see that there is more to this than just sexual desire. There is an anger, there is even a stronger feeling of a hatred that is directed against women.

All darkness from the earth you purge,
your light moves as a mighty surge,
no force of darkness can now stop,
the spiral that goes only up.

O Mother Mary, generate,
the song that does accelerate,
the earth into a higher state,
all matter does now scintillate.

6. Mother Mary, awaken people to see that when a man is beating up a woman, there is no *rational* explanation so we need to look for an *irrational* explanation.

> All elemental life you bless,
> removing from them man-made stress,
> the nature spirits are now free,
> outpicturing Divine decree.

> **O Mother Mary, generate,**
> **the song that does accelerate,**
> **the earth into a higher state,**
> **all matter does now scintillate.**

7. Mother Mary, I call forth the judgment of the Divine Mother upon the dark forces causing the anger and hatred that is seen in many situations where women are abused in various ways.

> I raise my voice and take my stand,
> a stop to war I do command,
> no more shall warring scar the earth,
> a golden age is given birth.

> **O Mother Mary, generate,**
> **the song that does accelerate,**
> **the earth into a higher state,**
> **all matter does now scintillate.**

8. Mother Mary, I call forth the judgment of the Divine Mother upon the dark forces behind the fundamentalist Muslim preachers or imams who are promoting Sharia Law and who are supporting the suppression of women, the limitation of women.

> As Mother Earth is free at last,
> disasters belong to the past,
> your Mother Light is so intense,
> that matter is now far less dense.

O Mother Mary, generate,
the song that does accelerate,
the earth into a higher state,
all matter does now scintillate.

9. Mother Mary, I call forth the judgment of the Divine Mother upon the Muslim clergy whose attitude to women, and whose support for the suppression of women, is driven by anger and hatred that does not come from the man because the man has been taken over by it.

In Mother Light the earth is pure,
the upward spiral will endure,
prosperity is now the norm,
God's vision manifest as form.

O Mother Mary, generate,
the song that does accelerate,
the earth into a higher state,
all matter does now scintillate.

Sealing

In the name of the I AM THAT I AM, I accept that Archangel Michael, Astrea and Shiva form an impenetrable shield around myself and all constructive people, sealing us from all fear-based energies in all four octaves. I accept that the Light of God is consuming and transforming all fear-based energies that make up the dark forces working against the liberation of women on earth!

26 | INVOKING AN END TO VIOLENCE AGAINST WOMEN (PART 2)

In the name of the I AM THAT I AM, Jesus Christ, I use the authority that I have as a being in embodiment on earth to call upon Mother Mary to reinforce my calls and use my chakras to project the statements in this invocation into the collective consciousness and awaken people to the awareness that will liberate both men and women from all psychological and spiritual thralldom to the fallen beings. Awaken people to the reality that we are spiritual beings and that we can co-create a new future by working with the ascended masters. I especially call for …

[Make your own calls here.]

Part 1

1. Mother Mary, I call forth the judgment of the Divine Mother upon the men who have allowed their minds, the four levels of the mind, to be taken over by a collective entity of anger against women.

O blessed Mary, Mother mine,
there is no greater love than thine,
as we are one in heart and mind,
my place in hierarchy I find.

**O Mother Mary, generate,
the song that does accelerate,
the earth into a higher state,
all matter does now scintillate.**

2. Mother Mary, I call forth the judgment of the Divine Mother upon the collective entity of anger against women.

I came to earth from heaven sent,
as I am in embodiment,
I use Divine authority,
commanding you to set earth free.

**O Mother Mary, generate,
the song that does accelerate,
the earth into a higher state,
all matter does now scintillate.**

3. Mother Mary, I call forth the judgment of the Divine Mother upon the collective entity of hatred against women.

I call now in God's sacred name,
for you to use your Mother Flame,
to burn all fear-based energy,
restoring sacred harmony.

**O Mother Mary, generate,
the song that does accelerate,
the earth into a higher state,
all matter does now scintillate.**

4. Mother Mary, I call forth the judgment of the Divine Mother upon the collective entities of anger against women, hatred against women, who have taken over men's minds when they are weak.

Your sacred name I hereby praise,
collective consciousness you raise,
no more of fear and doubt and shame,
consume it with your Mother Flame.

O Mother Mary, generate,
the song that does accelerate,
the earth into a higher state,
all matter does now scintillate.

5. Mother Mary, I call forth the judgment of the Divine Mother upon the dark forces causing men to be in a frustrated state of mind, feeling they are living under deep pressure, they are insecure, they are uncertain about their future.

All darkness from the earth you purge,
your light moves as a mighty surge,
no force of darkness can now stop,
the spiral that goes only up.

O Mother Mary, generate,
the song that does accelerate,
the earth into a higher state,
all matter does now scintillate.

6. Mother Mary, I call forth the judgment of the Divine Mother upon the dark forces causing men to feel this enormous pressure upon them, being overwhelmed by this, and in order to get some kind of relief, they take out their anger against their wives.

All elemental life you bless,
removing from them man-made stress,
the nature spirits are now free,
outpicturing Divine decree.

O Mother Mary, generate,
the song that does accelerate,
the earth into a higher state,
all matter does now scintillate.

7. Mother Mary, I call forth the judgment of the Divine Mother upon the men who are taken over by this anger entity and they direct the anger against their wives.

> I raise my voice and take my stand,
> a stop to war I do command,
> no more shall warring scar the earth,
> a golden age is given birth.

> **O Mother Mary, generate,**
> **the song that does accelerate,**
> **the earth into a higher state,**
> **all matter does now scintillate.**

8. Mother Mary, I call forth the judgment of the Divine Mother upon the men who abuse their wives and then start self-loathing and now they are feeling even more frustrated, and then the pressure starts building and the cycle repeats all over again.

> As Mother Earth is free at last,
> disasters belong to the past,
> your Mother Light is so intense,
> that matter is now far less dense.

> **O Mother Mary, generate,**
> **the song that does accelerate,**
> **the earth into a higher state,**
> **all matter does now scintillate.**

9. Mother Mary, I call for the binding and the consuming of these collective entities, for men to be cut free from them, and for women to be cut free from the collective entities that overpower women's minds so that they endure this kind of violence.

> In Mother Light the earth is pure,
> the upward spiral will endure,
> prosperity is now the norm,
> God's vision manifest as form.

O Mother Mary, generate,
the song that does accelerate,
the earth into a higher state,
all matter does now scintillate.

Part 2

1. Mother Mary, awaken people to see that when women are continually abused by men, these women have been taken over by collective entities that cause women to submit to this kind of abuse.

O blessed Mary, Mother mine,
there is no greater love than thine,
as we are one in heart and mind,
my place in hierarchy I find.

O Mother Mary, generate,
the song that does accelerate,
the earth into a higher state,
all matter does now scintillate.

2. Mother Mary, I call forth the judgment of the Divine Mother upon the dark forces who make women feel that they have no alternative, that they cannot object, that they cannot say no, that they cannot walk away. They see no option for themselves other than to endure it for the time that it lasts and then move on with life as if nothing happened.

I came to earth from heaven sent,
as I am in embodiment,
I use Divine authority,
commanding you to set earth free.

O Mother Mary, generate,
the song that does accelerate,
the earth into a higher state,
all matter does now scintillate.

3. Mother Mary, cut free women who are trapped in this situation so they can mount the determination to a do something about it, such as talk to their husbands and draw a line and say no.

> I call now in God's sacred name,
> for you to use your Mother Flame,
> to burn all fear-based energy,
> restoring sacred harmony.

> **O Mother Mary, generate,**
> **the song that does accelerate,**
> **the earth into a higher state,**
> **all matter does now scintillate.**

4. Mother Mary, cut free women to see how they could potentially help their husbands, or how they could remove themselves from their husbands and still survive.

> Your sacred name I hereby praise,
> collective consciousness you raise,
> no more of fear and doubt and shame,
> consume it with your Mother Flame.

> **O Mother Mary, generate,**
> **the song that does accelerate,**
> **the earth into a higher state,**
> **all matter does now scintillate.**

5. Mother Mary, I call forth the judgment of the Divine Mother upon the segment of men who are violent against women because their minds are overpowered by these collective entities.

> All darkness from the earth you purge,
> your light moves as a mighty surge,
> no force of darkness can now stop,
> the spiral that goes only up.

> **O Mother Mary, generate,**
> **the song that does accelerate,**

the earth into a higher state,
all matter does now scintillate.

6. Mother Mary, I call forth the judgment of the Divine Mother upon men who have not taken responsibility for themselves psychologically, who know nothing about the spiritual path and therefore feel trapped.

All elemental life you bless,
removing from them man-made stress,
the nature spirits are now free,
outpicturing Divine decree.

O Mother Mary, generate,
the song that does accelerate,
the earth into a higher state,
all matter does now scintillate.

7. Mother Mary, awaken people to see that for some men we cannot fully explain their violence by saying that their minds are taken over by collective entities. Their anger is reinforced by the entities, but it is not exclusively coming from the entities because these men have it inside themselves.

I raise my voice and take my stand,
a stop to war I do command,
no more shall warring scar the earth,
a golden age is given birth.

O Mother Mary, generate,
the song that does accelerate,
the earth into a higher state,
all matter does now scintillate.

8. Mother Mary, I call forth the judgment of the Divine Mother upon men who have created these separate selves that are angry with women, that hate women.

As Mother Earth is free at last,
disasters belong to the past,

your Mother Light is so intense,
that matter is now far less dense.

**O Mother Mary, generate,
the song that does accelerate,
the earth into a higher state,
all matter does now scintillate.**

9. Mother Mary, I call forth the judgment of the Divine Mother upon men who are not physically violent with women, but from their own beings they direct anger and hatred against women.

In Mother Light the earth is pure,
the upward spiral will endure,
prosperity is now the norm,
God's vision manifest as form.

**O Mother Mary, generate,
the song that does accelerate,
the earth into a higher state,
all matter does now scintillate.**

Part 3

1. Mother Mary, I call forth the judgment of the Divine Mother upon the fallen beings who started this anger and hatred against women and who have spread it to men who are not fallen beings.

O blessed Mary, Mother mine,
there is no greater love than thine,
as we are one in heart and mind,
my place in hierarchy I find.

**O Mother Mary, generate,
the song that does accelerate,
the earth into a higher state,
all matter does now scintillate.**

2. Mother Mary, I call forth the judgment of the Divine Mother upon the fallen beings who chose to elevate men to the position of superiority. They chose to create this male personal God, such as the Old Testament God, and in doing so, they opened up the possibility of suppressing women.

I came to earth from heaven sent,
as I am in embodiment,
I use Divine authority,
commanding you to set earth free.

O Mother Mary, generate,
the song that does accelerate,
the earth into a higher state,
all matter does now scintillate.

3. Mother Mary, I call forth the judgment of the Divine Mother upon the fallen beings who have anger against God but who cannot express it on earth because they have created this male God who is supposedly the Supreme God of the universe.

I call now in God's sacred name,
for you to use your Mother Flame,
to burn all fear-based energy,
restoring sacred harmony.

O Mother Mary, generate,
the song that does accelerate,
the earth into a higher state,
all matter does now scintillate.

4. Mother Mary, I call forth the judgment of the Divine Mother upon the fallen beings who cannot get men to express anger against God and who have gotten men to express anger against women, against the feminine energy and polarity, even against the entire matter realm.

Your sacred name I hereby praise,
collective consciousness you raise,
no more of fear and doubt and shame,
consume it with your Mother Flame.

O Mother Mary, generate,
the song that does accelerate,
the earth into a higher state,
all matter does now scintillate.

5. Mother Mary, I call forth the judgment of the Divine Mother upon the fallen beings who have given rise to the concept of "hatred of the mother," hatred of the mother realm, hatred of women, whether they are mothers or not.

All darkness from the earth you purge,
your light moves as a mighty surge,
no force of darkness can now stop,
the spiral that goes only up.

O Mother Mary, generate,
the song that does accelerate,
the earth into a higher state,
all matter does now scintillate.

6. Mother Mary, I call forth the judgment of the Divine Mother upon the fallen beings who have created false religions and gurus that promote hatred of the matter realm, hatred of the mother realm, hatred of the physical matter world, hatred of the human body.

All elemental life you bless,
removing from them man-made stress,
the nature spirits are now free,
outpicturing Divine decree.

O Mother Mary, generate,
the song that does accelerate,
the earth into a higher state,
all matter does now scintillate.

7. Mother Mary, I call forth the judgment of the Divine Mother upon the false gurus in India who are promoting the view that the matter realm and the physical body and the lusts and the desires of the body, are an enemy of spirituality, an enemy of men attaining their spiritual goals.

I raise my voice and take my stand,
a stop to war I do command,
no more shall warring scar the earth,
a golden age is given birth.

O Mother Mary, generate,
the song that does accelerate,
the earth into a higher state,
all matter does now scintillate.

8. Mother Mary, I call forth the judgment of the Divine Mother upon the fallen beings and false religions who promote the view that women are a temptation for men, that women are less spiritual or are susceptible to temptation, using the desires of the body as a temptation for men, tempting them away from a more spiritual lifestyle.

As Mother Earth is free at last,
disasters belong to the past,
your Mother Light is so intense,
that matter is now far less dense.

O Mother Mary, generate,
the song that does accelerate,
the earth into a higher state,
all matter does now scintillate.

9. Mother Mary, I call forth the judgment of the Divine Mother upon the dark forces behind the anger against women, against the mother realm, against the matter world, that originally comes from the fallen beings.

In Mother Light the earth is pure,
the upward spiral will endure,
prosperity is now the norm,
God's vision manifest as form.

O Mother Mary, generate,
the song that does accelerate,
the earth into a higher state,
all matter does now scintillate.

Part 4

1. Mother Mary, I call forth the judgment of the Divine Mother upon men who are not fallen beings, but who have taken into their beings this anger and hatred against the matter realm, against their own physical bodies and against women.

O blessed Mary, Mother mine,
there is no greater love than thine,
as we are one in heart and mind,
my place in hierarchy I find.

**O Mother Mary, generate,
the song that does accelerate,
the earth into a higher state,
all matter does now scintillate.**

2. Mother Mary, I call forth the judgment of the Divine Mother upon men who are violent against women because they have internalized this anger and hatred against women, men who have a desire to punish women, to hurt them, to put them down as raw physical destruction.

I came to earth from heaven sent,
as I am in embodiment,
I use Divine authority,
commanding you to set earth free.

**O Mother Mary, generate,
the song that does accelerate,
the earth into a higher state,
all matter does now scintillate.**

3. Mother Mary, I call forth the judgment of the Divine Mother upon men who may seem as if they are trying to control women psychologically, but beyond the control game these men are using psychological means to express anger and hatred towards women.

I call now in God's sacred name,
for you to use your Mother Flame,
to burn all fear-based energy,
restoring sacred harmony.

O Mother Mary, generate,
the song that does accelerate,
the earth into a higher state,
all matter does now scintillate.

4. Mother Mary, I call forth the judgment of the Divine Mother upon men who seek to punish women, hurt them, destroy their souls if they can because they have such a hatred that they actually want to destroy women.

Your sacred name I hereby praise,
collective consciousness you raise,
no more of fear and doubt and shame,
consume it with your Mother Flame.

O Mother Mary, generate,
the song that does accelerate,
the earth into a higher state,
all matter does now scintillate.

5. Mother Mary, I call forth the judgment of the Divine Mother upon men who have taken this into a greater extreme, who serve in various positions where they promote ideas that suppress women, ideas that are a form of violence against women and that have no rational explanation.

All darkness from the earth you purge,
your light moves as a mighty surge,
no force of darkness can now stop,
the spiral that goes only up.

O Mother Mary, generate,
the song that does accelerate,
the earth into a higher state,
all matter does now scintillate.

6. Mother Mary, I call forth the judgment of the Divine Mother upon the fallen beings behind ideas that are only created to justify this anger and hatred against women even though they are cleverly disguised.

All elemental life you bless,
removing from them man-made stress,
the nature spirits are now free,
outpicturing Divine decree.

O Mother Mary, generate,
the song that does accelerate,
the earth into a higher state,
all matter does now scintillate.

7. Mother Mary, awaken people to see that the Sharia law promoted by fundamentalist Islam has no rationality behind it. There may be certain arguments, certain reasoning, but it is not rational, consistent or logical.

I raise my voice and take my stand,
a stop to war I do command,
no more shall warring scar the earth,
a golden age is given birth.

O Mother Mary, generate,
the song that does accelerate,
the earth into a higher state,
all matter does now scintillate.

8. Mother Mary, awaken people to see that Sharia law is not based on any reality. It is camouflaged as a religious scripture or doctrine, but the driving force behind it is anger and hatred against women.

As Mother Earth is free at last,
disasters belong to the past,
your Mother Light is so intense,
that matter is now far less dense.

O Mother Mary, generate,
the song that does accelerate,

the earth into a higher state,
all matter does now scintillate.

9. Mother Mary, awaken people to see that there is no rational reason for the fact that millions of women live in very hot climates, but they have to wear black clothing that covers their entire body. It is anger and hatred against women.

In Mother Light the earth is pure,
the upward spiral will endure,
prosperity is now the norm,
God's vision manifest as form.

O Mother Mary, generate,
the song that does accelerate,
the earth into a higher state,
all matter does now scintillate.

Part 5

1. Mother Mary, awaken people to see that there is no rational reason for saying that the entire downfall of the human race and that all of the unpleasant conditions seen on earth is caused by women. It is nothing but an expression of pure anger and hatred against women, camouflaged as a religious scripture and doctrine.

O blessed Mary, Mother mine,
there is no greater love than thine,
as we are one in heart and mind,
my place in hierarchy I find.

O Mother Mary, generate,
the song that does accelerate,
the earth into a higher state,
all matter does now scintillate.

2. Mother Mary, I call forth the judgment of the Divine Mother upon men who are violent against women out of this raw anger and hatred. I call forth the judgment of the Divine Mother upon men who have an even greater anger and hatred against women, but they are camouflaging it as some benign reason, often a religion.

I came to earth from heaven sent,
as I am in embodiment,
I use Divine authority,
commanding you to set earth free.

O Mother Mary, generate,
the song that does accelerate,
the earth into a higher state,
all matter does now scintillate.

3. Mother Mary, I call forth the judgment of the Divine Mother upon materialists who are absolutely convinced that women are biologically different than men, that the female brain is wired in a different way and that evolution has given women a certain role.

I call now in God's sacred name,
for you to use your Mother Flame,
to burn all fear-based energy,
restoring sacred harmony.

O Mother Mary, generate,
the song that does accelerate,
the earth into a higher state,
all matter does now scintillate.

4. Mother Mary, I call forth the judgment of the Divine Mother upon men who are physically violent out of anger and hatred and men that are psychologically or spiritually violent against women also out of hatred.

Your sacred name I hereby praise,
collective consciousness you raise,
no more of fear and doubt and shame,
consume it with your Mother Flame.

O Mother Mary, generate,
the song that does accelerate,
the earth into a higher state,
all matter does now scintillate.

5. Mother Mary, I call forth the judgment of the Divine Mother upon men who have had this anger and hatred for a long time and who have been the driving force behind all of the suppression, discrimination and violence against women by being the physical anchor point for it.

All darkness from the earth you purge,
your light moves as a mighty surge,
no force of darkness can now stop,
the spiral that goes only up.

O Mother Mary, generate,
the song that does accelerate,
the earth into a higher state,
all matter does now scintillate.

6. Mother Mary, I call forth the judgment of the Divine Mother upon men who have had this anger for so long that they are not likely to be willing to give this up and start the upward path towards Christhood. Therefore, they need to be removed from the planet.

All elemental life you bless,
removing from them man-made stress,
the nature spirits are now free,
outpicturing Divine decree.

O Mother Mary, generate,
the song that does accelerate,
the earth into a higher state,
all matter does now scintillate.

7. Mother Mary, as an ascended master student, I hereby make the decision that as far as I am concerned, this anger and hatred is no longer acceptable on planet earth.

I raise my voice and take my stand,
a stop to war I do command,
no more shall warring scar the earth,
a golden age is given birth.

O Mother Mary, generate,
the song that does accelerate,
the earth into a higher state,
all matter does now scintillate.

8. Mother Mary, I call forth the judgment of the Divine Mother and I give you the authority to take the steps necessary to remove the outlet for this anger and hatred by confronting these people with the need to either change or to be removed from the earth.

As Mother Earth is free at last,
disasters belong to the past,
your Mother Light is so intense,
that matter is now far less dense.

O Mother Mary, generate,
the song that does accelerate,
the earth into a higher state,
all matter does now scintillate.

9. Mother Mary, cut free more and more women to awaken from this hypnotic state, identify this anger and hatred, and decide that it is unacceptable for them.

In Mother Light the earth is pure,
the upward spiral will endure,
prosperity is now the norm,
God's vision manifest as form.

O Mother Mary, generate,
the song that does accelerate,
the earth into a higher state,
all matter does now scintillate.

Part 6

1. Mother Mary, I call forth the judgment of the Divine Mother and I give you the authority to confront these men with the reality that if they will not choose life, then they must go to another planet.

O blessed Mary, Mother mine,
there is no greater love than thine,
as we are one in heart and mind,
my place in hierarchy I find.

O Mother Mary, generate,
the song that does accelerate,
the earth into a higher state,
all matter does now scintillate.

2. Mother Mary, awaken women to see that there is an upward spiral on earth and women are becoming increasingly liberated. We have reached the point where women deserve to be liberated from this anger and hatred from this small group of men.

I came to earth from heaven sent,
as I am in embodiment,
I use Divine authority,
commanding you to set earth free.

O Mother Mary, generate,
the song that does accelerate,
the earth into a higher state,
all matter does now scintillate.

3. Mother Mary, I call forth the judgment of the Divine Mother upon these men so they can be confronted with the choice to either be willing to lose their mortal selves and follow Christ towards eternal life or to lose their opportunity to embody on this planet.

I call now in God's sacred name,
for you to use your Mother Flame,

to burn all fear-based energy,
restoring sacred harmony.

O Mother Mary, generate,
the song that does accelerate,
the earth into a higher state,
all matter does now scintillate.

4. Mother Mary, cut free women from feeling any kind of anger or hatred against these people but to neutrally decide that it is time for this to end on our planet.

Your sacred name I hereby praise,
collective consciousness you raise,
no more of fear and doubt and shame,
consume it with your Mother Flame.

O Mother Mary, generate,
the song that does accelerate,
the earth into a higher state,
all matter does now scintillate.

5. Mother Mary, cut free women to see that we cannot truly talk about the liberation of women without talking about some of these very destructive forces that are seeking to keep women in bondage.

All darkness from the earth you purge,
your light moves as a mighty surge,
no force of darkness can now stop,
the spiral that goes only up.

O Mother Mary, generate,
the song that does accelerate,
the earth into a higher state,
all matter does now scintillate.

6. Mother Mary, cut free women to see that if we continue to do the same thing and expect different results, we are insane. Although much progress has been made, certain problems have not gone away. We cannot continue

to do the same thing and expect that these very severe abuses of women will go away.

All elemental life you bless,
removing from them man-made stress,
the nature spirits are now free,
outpicturing Divine decree.

O Mother Mary, generate,
the song that does accelerate,
the earth into a higher state,
all matter does now scintillate.

7. Mother Mary, cut free women to see that we need to look for something different, namely the knowledge of dark forces that spread anger and hatred against women beyond any rational explanation.

I raise my voice and take my stand,
a stop to war I do command,
no more shall warring scar the earth,
a golden age is given birth.

O Mother Mary, generate,
the song that does accelerate,
the earth into a higher state,
all matter does now scintillate.

8. Mother Mary, cut free women to rise up and make the determination: enough is enough, thereby authorizing the ascended masters to step in and use your power to remove these forces from the earth.

As Mother Earth is free at last,
disasters belong to the past,
your Mother Light is so intense,
that matter is now far less dense.

O Mother Mary, generate,
the song that does accelerate,

**the earth into a higher state,
all matter does now scintillate.**

9. Mother Mary, cut free a critical mass of women to awaken to the determination that we have had enough of this, and it is time that this entire phenomenon of violence against women is removed from the earth. Help women accept that there is a new opportunity to redefine what it means to be a woman on planet earth.

In Mother Light the earth is pure,
the upward spiral will endure,
prosperity is now the norm,
God's vision manifest as form.

**O Mother Mary, generate,
the song that does accelerate,
the earth into a higher state,
all matter does now scintillate.**

Sealing

In the name of the I AM THAT I AM, I accept that Archangel Michael, Astrea and Shiva form an impenetrable shield around myself and all constructive people, sealing us from all fear-based energies in all four octaves. I accept that the Light of God is consuming and transforming all fear-based energies that make up the dark forces working against the liberation of women on earth!

27 | MOST MEN ARE ADDICTED TO SEX

I am the Elohim Astrea, Elohim of the Fourth Ray. The Fourth Ray has often been considered the ray of purity, but we have also given you the teaching that it is the ray of acceleration. It is also said that the masters on the fourth ray are quite direct, quite outspoken and, to use an American expression, we are no-nonsense. What I aim to do in this discourse is give you the no-nonsense view on sex because sex is obviously one of the factors that have been used to suppress and abuse women.

What is the no-nonsense view on sex? Well, here is my starting remark: For over 90% of the men on this planet, sex is an addiction. What then is an addiction? Well, you go out in the world and you see how science has attempted to explain addictions. They have come up with some rather convoluted intellectual explanations, but have they really helped people overcome addictions? Have they allowed societies to stop the rise in addictions that many societies are seeing?

You can look at these, what we have called the more evolved nations, the modern democracies, and you can see that there has been considerable progress in these nations. In many ways you can look at these societies and see that there has been tremendous progress compared to 100 or several hundred years ago. You can also see that there are certain areas where there has not been progress and certain problems even are accelerating. One of these problems is obviously addictions. You go back 100 years and there were far fewer people who were addicted to drugs for example. You can also go back 100 years and see that there were far fewer people who were addicted to sex.

No materialistic explanations for addictions

You must ask yourself, if you are willing to look at this neutrally and with a no-nonsense perspective: Why do these societies see a rise in addictions when they see so much progress in other areas? You can even take the perspective of saying: What has happened in these modern democracies over the last 100 years? Well, in many ways, politically and economically, people have become more free, but is an addiction something that makes people more free? Obviously not. An addiction is something that takes away people's freedom. Here you have societies that are seeing a rise in people's *political* and *economic* freedom but at the same time, they are seeing a decrease in people's *psychological* freedom, even in some ways their *physical* freedom because an addiction can force people into certain actions that clearly take away their freedom. How do you explain this? Well, you simply cannot explain it if you insist on doing what science has been insisting on doing now for a long time, and that is provide a materialistic explanation for everything.

You can study the body. You can study the brain. You can study the genes and you can try and come up with a gene that is linked to addiction. You can try and come up with certain aspects of brain chemistry that supposedly lead to addiction. You can try and look at hormones or the nervous system or whatever you want, but you will never be able to explain addiction, nor will you ever be able to help people free themselves from addiction. You cannot do this through a materialistic approach. *It cannot be done.*

We have before used the old story of Zeno's paradox that shows that you can divide the distance indefinitely into smaller and smaller increments. Scientists know this very well. You can analyze the body from a purely materialistic viewpoint. You can try and find smaller and smaller units in the body or in the molecules and the atoms. You can try and find how these microcosmic elements of the body can explain addictive behavior and you will see that despite this tradition, started by Aristotle, you will never be able to explain macrocosmic phenomena through microcosmic elements. *It cannot be done.*

Human beings are not objects

A human being is not a collection of cells, molecules, atoms or subatomic particles. Of course, the human body is made up of subatomic particles, atoms, molecules and cells, but the human *being* is more than a collection of these parts. The whole is more than the sum of the parts because a human being is a *being,* not a *machine,* not a device, not an object. How will you explain addictive behavior by only looking at human beings as an object? Well, you cannot. *You cannot.* In fact, even science and many modern democracies are at the point where a large group of people are very close to breaking through to where they can begin to look at how human beings have been objectified.

Obviously, this relates to the topic of sex and how sex has been used to abuse, limit and trap women. What is it that happens in this process? Well, it is that women are objectified. They become sexual objects but is this the only example of objectification? Of course not. Take another obvious example—soldiers who go to war. They are not looked at as individual people or human beings. They are just objects that can be moved around and sacrificed in order to achieve some supposedly epically important goal of winning a battle or winning a war. What have I said about science when science takes a materialistic approach? What is it doing? Well, when science uses the materialistic approach to investigate anything that relates to human beings, then science is objectifying human beings. There is absolutely no other way to put it. The materialistic approach to science has been and is still objectifying human beings and this is, in the modern democracies, the very foundation for all other areas where human beings are objectified, including the objectification of women as sexual objects.

What is an addiction?

If you cannot explain the addiction to sex through a materialistic approach, how can you explain it? Well, let us first consider what an addiction is. In a certain way, we can start with a more universally acceptable explanation. We can look at the effects of an addiction. What does it do to the person who is addicted? Well, as I said, it takes away that person's freedom and it does this first of all at the psychological level. The person, let us say it is a man who is addicted to sex, loses his psychological freedom because there is something in his psyche that compels him to have sex. It is not something he freely, neutrally chooses to do. He is compelled to do it by some force that overtakes his conscious will. He cannot choose to say stop. This is the same with alcoholics or drug addicts, they have lost their freedom of will.

This is something that should be a great concern to all modern democracies who take pride in seeing themselves as free societies that give people the greatest possible personal freedom. How can you see the rise in political, economic freedom and at the same time see the rise in this psychological addiction that takes away people's freedom? This is cognitive dissonance. Why is it that this happens? Well, this is where materialistic science falls short. It comes up against the limitations of the materialistic approach. Yes, you can look at the body. Yes, you can analyze hormones, the nervous system, brain chemistry, genetic material and you may be able to come up with some correlations. There may be certain genes that can be linked to alcohol abuse in the sense that you find that in people who are alcoholics, certain genes are activated, or you find certain states of brain chemistry or certain electromagnetic patterns in the brain. Sure, you can find this, but are those things you discover in the body the cause of addiction or are they just a side effect at the physical level of a deeper cause? Of course, they are just side effects.

What is the teaching we have given you who are ascended master students? Well, we have said that the physical universe is not all there is. The physical octave, the physical level is actually the lowest level of a continuum of energy vibrations. Above the physical is the emotional level. Above that is the mental. Above that is the identity level. A human being is an energy system, and as has been known for thousands of years in the East, you have an energy field around the body. Now, many see that the body produces the energy field, but we have told you this is not the case. The body is actually the lowest vibrating extension of the total energy field of a human being. Energy flows through this energy system from the spiritual realm into the identity body, then into the mental body, then into the emotional body and then into the physical. This means that everything that happens at the physical level is not a cause in and of itself. It is the effect of causes at the emotional, mental and identity level. If you do not understand this very, very basic reality, you cannot explain addiction.

What happens in an addiction is not purely physical. Something happens at the emotional level, the emotional body. It is what happens at the emotional level that overpowers the person's conscious will. In other words, in an addiction, there is such a surge of a particular form of energy that comes from the emotional body of that person into the conscious mind that it overpowers, it colors the conscious mind and it neutralizes the conscious will. It simply overrides the conscious will, and the person has no power to stop this emotional impulse and it must act upon it.

Now, of course the emotional level is not the highest level of the human energy system, for there is also a mental component and even an identity level component. When you are looking at addiction, it starts at the identity level by the way the person looks at itself and what kind of being it is. It then also has a component at the mental level where it looks at how it relates to the world, what it can do, what it is allowed to do and not do. This then sets the matrix for the production, we might say, of certain energies in the emotional body, which can then overpower the conscious mind at the physical level. Unless you understand this, you cannot explain an addiction.

An energetic view of addiction

The next level that you need to consider is that the human energy field is a very complex structure. There is already technology available that can actually make the human energy field visible—if scientists would be willing to use it and interpret the results. If you could make the human energy field visible (as some clairvoyants have been able to see it for thousands of years), then you would see that there are certain centers in the human energy field, which are what have traditionally been called chakras. These are centers that are, we might say, portals, portals through which energy can flow.

As we have said, there are certain chakras at the identity level. We have focused on the seven main ones, even though in reality there are 144 chakras, but there are seven main chakras at the identity level. At the identity level, energy can flow from the spiritual realm, from the ascended masters, from your I AM Presence through these chakras into the identity body. Nothing can flow back through the chakras at the identity level to the spiritual realm, no energy, because the energies are lower and cannot flow into the spiritual realm. Now through the chakras, at the identity level, light can flow from there, energy can flow from there, into the chakras at the mental level. Then the energy flows through those chakras at the mental level, but energy can also flow the other way from the mental level into the identity body. In other words, at the identity level, the chakras are portals that go both ways and of course the same at the emotional level where the chakras are also portals that are two-way portals so that energy can flow from the physical through the chakras at the emotional level, to the mental level and from there back up to the identity level.

This is how it is possible that a human being, or rather a *spiritual* being, the Conscious You, can have its sense of identity at the identity level affected by what it experiences at the physical level. We can say that if you are in command of yourself and your energy system, then you will be consciously aware of what you allow to flow back up through your chakras. Therefore, you will not allow anything that happens at the physical level to reprogram your sense of identity beyond what you are willing to see happen. What of course happens to most people, and certainly this is the case for the vast majority of people in embodiment today, is that they have no awareness of this. The ideal of walking the spiritual path or the path to Christhood is that you gradually take back command over your four lower bodies and over your chakras, so that you are in command of what flows back up through the chakras. Ideally, you come to that point where you have self-mastery, where really nothing is flowing back up through the chakras. There is just an energy in the one direction from the spiritual realm, through the chakras into the four levels of the material universe. That is when you become a spiritually self-sufficient, independent person or being.

We now look at the chakras. We have given you a model that they can be put on a vertical line and that the lowest chakra is centered over the genitals and the others go up from there until you have the crown chakra at the top with the heart chakra in the middle. If you are to explain addiction, you need to look at the chakras and if you are to explain sexual addiction, you need to be aware that the base chakra or the mother chakra is located in line with the genitals because this is where the life energy streams through and can then be directed into the sexual organs and expressed as sexual energy. Therefore, when a person (and it can be of course both a man and a woman) is addicted to sex, it is because something has happened in that person's base chakra. There is a disturbance and imbalance in the base chakra, which means that the person's sexual desires have been multiplied beyond what we might call a natural limit. This is causing, in many cases, the base chakra to spin in the opposite direction of what is natural. It is causing a certain pollution in the base chakra. Now, we have given you the model (which is different from many of the models you will find out there in the New Age, spiritual community) that the base chakra is meant to be white because it is corresponding to the Fourth Ray, which is the white ray of purity. In its natural state, the base chakra appears white and it radiates white light, but when it is polluted by these inordinate or unbalanced sexual desires and energies, it can glow red, very bright red. This is in fact what many clairvoyants see because that is how it is for most people who have a polluted base chakra. It glows red and some think this is the natural state, but it is not.

You can then observe, you can even use these instruments that have been developed to observe, that many people have a red base chakra. You can even, if you were willing to do this, observe that as a person's sexual desire grows, the base chakra begins to pulsate with this red light and this can then cause the person at the conscious level to feel this irrepressible urge to have sex. This is what you could observe scientifically if you were willing to do so by using the technology that is already available or can quickly be developed. Now, this of course is not necessarily an explanation because why does the base chakra glow red? It is like saying: "There's a certain gene that can be linked to alcoholism." Is it really the cause? The base chakra glowing red is not the cause of sexual addiction. It is an effect of sexual addiction.

The real cause of sexual addiction

What is the cause of sexual addiction? Well, this is again where you cannot get anywhere with the materialist approach. You can only understand any addiction when you are recognizing that it is possible for human beings to create these semi-conscious (they are conscious but not self-aware) entities that human beings have created collectively over time. There are these entities both in the emotional realm, in the mental realm and in the identity realm. In the emotional realm, there are these collective entities that are created in relation to sex. When people are vulnerable to this, these collective entities can invade a person's energy field. For example, the sex entity can invade a person's base chakra.

Now, what you need to understand about a collective entity is that it is created over a long period of time by individual human beings feeding energy into it. Again, you have a very strong anger entity that is created, going very, very far back in time by people becoming angry. Thereby, they are radiating anger energy, which the entity can then absorb and as it does so, it becomes stronger and stronger. Now the sex entity is not created by the *pure* sexual drive, as I will talk about later, but it is created by a *perverted* sexual drive, which has also been going on for a very long time on this planet.

What happens is that when a collective entity reaches a certain strength, a certain amount of accumulated energy, then the collective entity is able to overpower many people's energy field and chakras. The created sex entity has such a tremendous pool of energy that it can direct this energy at an individual person's base chakra. Most people have no defense against this, they are not aware that these entities exist, they are not aware that their chakras can be subjected to this very strong energy. They do not even know that this is happening, but even if they did know, they would not necessarily be able to defend themselves against it because of what I will talk about later.

You have a situation here where this entity can single out a specific person, direct a tremendous energy burst at that person's base chakra and it totally disturbs the functioning of the base chakra. Now the chakra begins to spin in an opposite direction. It begins to have this pollution of this red-hot energy that is almost like molten lava that interferes with the base chakra. All of a sudden the person's sexual desires now become amplified so that the person feels this very strong compulsion to have sex. As the person then engages in this energy (it can be by fantasizing about sex, it can be by masturbating, or it can be by having sex), then of course the person is expressing energy through its base chakra. Now, you see here, if the energy expressed through this process was only the same energy that the entity had directed into the person's base chakra, then the entity would not gain anything. What happens is that most people still have some flow of energy from their I AM Presences. When they then engage in this sexual expression that is initiated by the collective entity, some of their, we might say *vital* energy or their own energy, is then expressed through this sexual activity and this energy can then feed the entity.

In other words, the entity is directing some of its energy into a person's base chakra, but as the person then acts upon this energy, even through fantasy, the entity gains back more energy than it sent. Therefore, the entity is literally stealing, siphoning off, vital energy from the person. The entity itself cannot get this energy from the spiritual realm. That is why the entity in order to survive, in order to multiply itself, must then get human beings to misqualify the energy with a lower vibration, a fear-based vibration that the entity can absorb. You see, you can also say that when an entity directs energy into the person's base chakra, some of the energy that is in the base chakra goes into a reactionary pattern, an interference pattern with the energy that comes from the outside. This means the energy in a person's base chakra is lowered in vibration to the more base sexual desires and then expressed that way, and it is this energy that the entity can absorb.

What happens to the person? Well, you are depleted of energy and you can feel depleted of energy. Now, you can over time then replace that energy by what is still streaming from your I AM Presence, but you will be able to notice (if you are just normally sensitive and aware of this) that many, many people after they engage in sex can feel depleted of energy. Not just physical energy, but even on a deeper level feel depleted of energy. This is really what is behind an addiction—at the emotional level, at least. You can look at the same pattern for every addiction. It can relate to the other chakras as well but I am focusing here on sex and sexual addiction, which relates to the base chakra. These entities, collective entities, exist at the emotional level. We have said before that they have a certain rudimentary form of consciousness, but they are not self-aware. An example of this can be an animal. An animal has consciousness, but it is not self-aware. A cow has some level of consciousness, but it cannot choose to look at itself and decide to change its behavior. That is what human beings can do and that is unique to human beings, which is what we call self-awareness or a spiritual spark or divine spark.

It is what we now call the Conscious You that enables you to step back, look at yourself and consciously choose to change your behavior. This is also what enables you to free yourself from an addiction, but it requires that you are able and willing to step back, look at the addictive behavior, identify that it takes away your freedom, that you do not want this and therefore make the decision to change it. This is truly what explains an addiction at the emotional level. Of course, you might say: Well, could any human being on earth be overpowered by the collective sex entity? The answer is no. As I said, more than 90% of men on the planet have been overpowered by the sex entity and are addicted to sex, but there are men who are not and there are many more women who are not addicted to sex.

Why is it that some people (even though this collective entity is very, very strong) are not overpowered by the sex entity? Well, it is because they do not allow that lower sexual energy to enter their base chakra. Why do they not allow this? Well, they do not allow it because they have some awareness, some understanding at the mental level and they have a sense of identity at the identity level that blocks the emotional energy from gaining entrance into their base chakra. You might say that in order for the sex entity at the emotional level to invade a person's base chakra, there has to be an opening. That means there has to be some energy in the person's base chakra that the entity can use. Where does that energy at the base chakra come from? Well, it comes from the mental level. The person has certain beliefs about sex and sexuality at the mental level, has certain understanding and it has a certain identity at the identity level, seeing itself a certain way, perhaps as a sexual being and feeling at the mental level that it is necessary for a man to be sexually active, it is okay for a man to be sexually active and it is okay for a man to get satisfaction of his sexual desires in any way he can.

People's attitude to sex

This now leads us to go beyond this and say that even though there is this sex entity at the emotional level, it cannot explain sex addiction in its totality because we also need to look at the mental level and look at the beliefs and attitudes that people have about sex. When we look at this, we can look at the influence of various thought systems. The first one we can look at is of course the Christian religion, which has influenced many of what we today call the modern democracies. What is the Christian religion's attitude to sex, the view of sex being projected by the Christian religion?

Well, it is of course (at least for some Christian churches,who believe that it was sexual desire that caused the fall of Adam and Eve) that the forbidden fruit was related to sexual desire. This is of course not correct as we have given teachings about this. Nevertheless, this is what many Christians believe. Some Christians believe that original sin was engaging in sexual activity. You have, throughout the centuries since the formation of the Catholic church, had this schizophrenic, ambivalent view of sex or attitude to sex in the population. First of all, of course all people have a sex drive, but the Christian religion has portrayed this as being wrong or sinful, therefore as something that should be restricted. Now, today many people in the modern democracies look at this as being completely primitive and belonging to an old age.

You have seen what has been called the sexual revolution, which has supposedly set people free from the restrictions of the Christian religion, set them free to explore and enjoy their sexuality. Let us just look at this from the perspective that there has been, even far before the Christian religion, a collective sex entity at the emotional level. What was the effect of the Christian religion's portrayal of sex in terms of whether it made people more or less vulnerable to the sex entity? The fact is that it had a double effect, it had a two-sided effect. Many people use the Christian teachings to try to forcefully suppress their sexual activity. Some forcefully try to suppress their sexual desires at the emotional level, or they try to suppress any beliefs that sex was okay or sex was natural at the mental level. The Christian religion caused a quite considerable suppression of the sex drive and sexual energies and this created a pressure in many people's base chakras. It caused many people to try to suppress their sex drive, but suppression, forceful suppression, of the sex drive just means that energies keep accumulating.

Eventually, these people would become vulnerable to the sex entity. They would give in to their sexual desires, they would have sex and then they would feel very bad about it afterwards, which actually created another collective entity particular to the Christian religion. There are other religions that also have these repressive sex entities that make people feel guilty or shamed for having sex.

It is by no means the intent here to say that the Christian religion had a positive influence, but there were a considerable number of people who grew up in this Christian environment who could use the teachings to not so forcefully repress their sexual desires, but to, even at the mental level, not give in to them so they did not allow the energy to build up in their base chakras. This meant that these people were not as vulnerable, and some were even completely invulnerable, to the collective sex entity at the emotional level. If you look at the modern democracies, you can go back and see that a hundred years ago or 200 years ago when the Christian influence was stronger, there were fewer people back then who were addicted to sex. There were also fewer instances of the sexual abuse of women through for example rape. There were fewer instances of what you today call sexual harassment where women were subjected to these very low, base, lewd comments from men, or touch, unwanted touch from men.

Overall, you must actually say, if you look at this neutrally, that the sexual harassment and abuse of women was lower in these Christian environments. It does not mean that it was not there, but it was lower.

Did the sexual revolution benefit women?

What happened when societies became less dominated by the Christian view of sex, when you had the so-called sexual revolution that some people say liberated women to express their sexual desires? Well, it certainly also liberated men, did it not? What you actually see is that you have an increase in sexual addiction because now all of a sudden people feel free to express their sexual desires, but what have you seen accompany this so-called sexual revolution? Well, you have seen a rise in many, many things that seek to actually magnify the sex drive. It can be anything from direct pornography, to all kinds of devices that are supposed to help people have more satisfying sex, to even Viagra or other means of chemically boosting men's ability to have sex.

You have seen a rise in these drugs that are used as rape drugs where they put women in this passive state of barely being conscious where they can be raped by men, sometimes even not being aware of it. You have seen a rise in prostitution. You have seen a rise in human trafficking. You can see a rise in women being lured into or even sold into prostitution, being forced into drug addiction in order to make them willing to do prostitution to feed their drug addiction and so forth and so on. The net result in the modern democracies of the so-called sexual revolution is an increase of sexual addiction.

A sexual addiction takes away men's freedom because now they cannot choose whether they want to have sex or not. They feel *compelled* by the addiction to have sex. What does this do? Well, it causes men to look at women (as many psychologists have become more aware of and have certainly raised consciousness of) as sexual objects. In other words, what we can say here is—very, very clearly: What is the *real* cause, or at least the *immediate* cause of the sexual objectification of women? Well, it is this increase in sexual addiction in men.

When a man is not addicted to sex, does he look at women as sexual objects? The answer is no. He looks at women as individuals and as human beings. When a man is not sexually addicted, he does not want to have sex with any woman under any circumstance. For a man who is not addicted to sex, sex is not just a physical act of physical gratification. It is not just an emotional gratification he is seeking. He is seeking a deeper connection with another human being who has a different energetic polarity, than he has, which then can balance his own sexual or energetic polarity.

There is a deeper purpose to sex. When a man is not addicted to sex, he primarily seeks a connection with a woman. You cannot have a connection, my beloved, with an object. You can only have a genuine connection with another human being and you can only have that when you look at that other person as a human being, which means you are sensitive to the other person's needs and desires. You would never force a woman to have sex in order to get a deeper connection with that woman because when there is force involved, the connection is gone.

You see here that sexual addiction in men is the immediate cause of the sexual objectification of women. When men are addicted to sex, they are compelled by the addiction. You cannot say they *want* to have sex, but they are *compelled* to have sex and that is why they are looking for an object who can fulfill that physical or emotional gratification, which is a temporary gratification. When you have a deeper connection with a woman as a man, it happens at the mental and identity level. It does not happen at the emotional and physical level, at least not for most men. You can have a deeper emotional connection with a woman, but not when you are addicted, not when your base chakra is disturbed by a lower sexual energy. Unless you understand this and unless you address this, you will not be able to overcome the sexual objectification of women.

The sexual objectification of women

You can look at the modern democracies and you can look at how they pride themselves on having given women rights, and yes, women have more political rights, they have more economic opportunities and rights. At the same time you see an increase in the sexual objectification of women, which is clearly abusive and clearly a form of violence against women. How do you explain this in these modern democracies? Again, you cannot explain it through the materialistic paradigm. Neither can you explain it through the Christian paradigm. These paradigms are useless to explain what you see growing in these societies.

If you are willing to look at this honestly and objectively, you can look at the trends. You can even create statistics for the number of rapes, the amount of pornography, the amount of sexual harassment of women and you can see that the trend is clearly growing. Therefore, if you project into the future, you can see that unless the modern democracies address this problem and do something about it, there will come a point where all of the political and economic liberation of women that has happened over the last hundred years will be nullified by this sexual objectification of women.

Is it not obvious that there must come this point where there is this rude awakening where the modern democracies realize: We have a problem here that we must do something about, but what we have so far done, the Christian paradigm, the materialist paradigm has not diminished the problem. Therefore, we must reason we cannot solve it through these paradigms. Either we declare that we are powerless to solve the problem and admit that we are powerless to protect our women against sexual exploitation or we must find another approach.

Of course, we do not expect nations to do this at the official level, at the governmental level or even at the scientific level. What can happen is certainly that you who are our ascended master students can make the calls so that women will be cut free to see that there is something here that needs to be addressed. We need to find a different way to look at it so we can explain why this is happening. This is of course why we are giving you this teaching. We are not seeking to overwhelm you by now feeling that you have the responsibility for changing your entire society, but you can make the calls that can set the foundation for this process to begin. In order to give you a deeper understanding, let us go on.

Should women be sexually attractive to men?

The sexual exploitation of women through the objectification of women can be said to have a clearly emotional component. There is the fact that men become addicted to sex. That is why they are willing to go to prostitutes where women clearly are objectified. They are willing to look at pornography where women are also objectified. They are willing to rape women, which is clearly also an objectification of women. What you see is that the 90 plus percent of men who are addicted to sex in their emotional bodies, they look at women as sexual objects and really nothing else. They may have periods where they are not so overpowered by the unbalanced energies in their base chakras, where they can have a more nuanced view of women but nevertheless, they have that objectification of women in their base chakras at the emotional level.

Where does the emotional level energy or view come from? As we said, it comes from the mental. So, what is it at the mental level? Here you find a variety of activities that all are aimed at objectifying women. You will find various ideas and thoughts out there that are not necessarily a real philosophy or ideology, but you will see many of these ideas floating around. For example, you see in the advertising industry, how women are portrayed in sexually challenging, explicit positions, with revealing dress, with makeup, with a certain expression on their faces, with certain movements that clearly are aimed at arousing men's sexual desire. This is clearly an objectification of women. You even have this entire idea that women should be sexually appealing to men. It is not really a philosophy, but it is certainly floating around. There is this belief, and it is held by both men and women, that women should be attractive, that they should be evaluated based on their sexual attractiveness. Of course this ties in with the entire beauty industry that has created this standard for how a beautiful woman looks. It is then projected, and there are beasts created at the mental and emotional level that are projecting at women, that they should live up to this other-worldly standard of beauty.

You know very well that there is no woman in embodiment who lives up to this standard for beauty. You may take some of these models that are used, or these actresses that are used time and again in advertisement, and you may look at an ad in a magazine that makes this woman look very, very beautiful. If you looked at the actual woman, you would see that she is not so beautiful in reality, the difference is what you could call the Photoshop effect where computer software can manipulate a photograph. The camera never lies it used to be said, but the computer certainly does. There is an entire industry that is based on projecting this belief that women should look a certain way and that it is perfectly normal and acceptable that women should dress like what they see in the advertisement, or what they see in movies or TV series. They should appear sexually attractive to men, they should appeal to men's sex drive, and this supposedly gives a woman a certain status in the eyes of many people.

You can then go up to the identity level and see that there are also certain beliefs floating around that cause women to identify themselves based on their sexual attractiveness. They identify themselves as sexual beings who should be attractive to men, who maybe even should be available to men. This gives them a certain self-image that makes them feel superior, makes them feel good, or in some cases even make women feel powerful because they feel that they could make any man want to have sex with them. Then, by denying the sex after the man wants it, they gain a certain perverted sense of power. You have examples in the history of women, often actresses who have gained this sense of identity of being able to make any man want them, and it has given them this sense of power. You even have examples of women who have used this to gain political positions and political influence. You have created this identity at the identity level that projects that women should be like this, they should live up to this ideal. There are even some in the women's liberation movement who believe that women should use any means to gain power in a male-dominated society and if sex works, then why not use it?

You have, even among women, the acceptance of these mental and identity level ideas and beliefs that cause the objectification of women. There are women who have objectified themselves in order to gain influence in a male-dominated society. The effect of all this is that, starting at the identity level, there is an objectification of women. If you believe that a woman should be beautiful according to a standard of beauty defined in your particular society and culture, which is very temporary and very artificial, then already there at the identity level you are objectifying women. You are saying that a woman should ideally live up to some standard for beauty.

The industry of controlling women's appearance

What is the problem with this? Well, is a woman in control of her physical appearance? There is an entire industry out there that will project at women that of course you can be in control of your physical appearance. As the vast majority of women realize, there is a limit to how much you can improve your physical appearance with these means that are available because you cannot change your genetic inheritance. You realize here that what this does is it objectifies women.

It creates an image, and an image is an object. It projects this image onto all women and it projects that you should strive to live up to it and if you cannot, you should feel bad about this. It also projects that you should live up to this image that makes you attractive to men. You know as a woman that you cannot fully live up to the image, but what is the psychological effect of this? It is: "But I should have men making advances towards me." Many men may not do this, but suddenly here is a man who does so. In order not to miss out, I must give in to this. I do not need to look at what kind of person this man is. Is he really the kind of man I want to have a relationship with? No! I feel compelled to give in to his advances just so I can gain the illusion that I live up to this image that I believe I should live up to.

This is why you see many, many women who get into relationships that are abusive. They do not see it ahead of time because they are not looking. They are so compelled by this image that is projected at women, to give in to the first man that comes and makes advances towards them without evaluating: "Is this the kind of man I want a relationship with? Is this the kind of man I even want to have sex with? Is this the kind of man I want to have a long-term relationship with? Is this the kind of man I want to start a family with and that I potentially want to live with the rest of my life? Women are put into this position where they cannot make good decisions about relationships.

Of course, on a greater level, women are put in a position where they are constantly subjected to this sexual aggression from men. In many cases they do not feel they can defend themselves against it, at least not on the overall level. If you look at the situation in even some of the modern democracies, women feel increasingly powerless to stop this sexual harassment, to stop this sexual exploitation, these aggressive advances from men. They do not know what to do with it because on the one hand, they have this ideal that they should be sexually attractive to men. On the other hand, they very clearly experience that they do not want these low, base comments or advances from men but they do not know how to balance those two drives. They do not know how to say stop, and society does not know how to say stop so they are letting this juggernaut run down the hill as a snowball gathering strength. Nobody in society has said: "We need to stop this. This has gone too far."

Male and female archetypes

Now I have already given you an overwhelming message that at least would overwhelm those who are not ascended master students but I will not stop here because there is more to say about this. Other masters have already talked about the fallen beings and how they, at a very early stage after coming to this planet, decided to make men the superior sex and women the inferior sex. In this process of manipulating men and women this way, they have of course used the sex drive. They have done everything they could to put out these ideas, even philosophies and religions, that manipulate the sex drive of men, inflate the sex drive of men artificially, to project that men should be sexual conquerors, that they should have sex with as many women as possible. This is something they have projected out there.

Obviously, not all men are vulnerable to this, but many men are and have been throughout history. You see this male archetype that has been created of this strong masculine man who is the sexual conqueror, who can make any woman give in to his advances or even make any woman want to have sex with him, because he is the alpha male and he is the one that she wants to have children with. That is an archetype that is portrayed out there—completely false, completely artificially created, only created to manipulate men and women.

What this also does is project a female archetype that the woman is the passive recipient of the man's sexual advances, that she should accept this in order to carry on the human race because she should be available to have children and therefore propagate the race. These are some very subtle ideas that you can find even in the Christian religion, as repressive as it is of sex. You can still find these ideas among many Christians. You have this projection from the fallen beings. What I want to say here is simply this. It has no reality to it whatsoever. There is no spiritual reality to it. There is not even a physical, evolutionary reality to it—even if you look at the evolutionary theory, as incomplete as it is.

Look at animals. Do they have sex all the time, year-round? No. All animals have a certain period where they are sexually active. The male is sexually active, the female is receptive to this, but once the female has been impregnated, the male sex drive disappears. I can assure you that a male lion is not going around, year-round, having sexual fantasies. When certain hormones kick in, in a male lion's body, he becomes sexually active, so he goes looking for a female lion who also has her hormones activated and is receptive. When the female is impregnated and the rutting season is over the male lion does not have any more sexual desire or fantasies. It just disappears. Now he is focused on what he is normally focused on, which is mostly eating and sleeping. Quite similar to some men but that is beside the point.

What you have here is, when you look at evolution, that animals are only sexually active for the purpose of having offspring and then the rest of the year, sex does not even enter their minds, so why is it not that way in humans? Well, if you look at humans as biological animals it *should* be that way and therefore you must say, first of all, humans cannot be biological animals because then they would have the same approach to sex that all animals have. Since human beings clearly do not, human beings must be more than this, which means then that you can see that if human beings are not exclusively driven by their biological drives, then your human sexual activity cannot be exclusively a biological activity. What is it then driven by? Well something in the psychology and then that opens up to the teachings I have given that people can be manipulated and the sex drive can be artificially accelerated and multiplied to the point where the sex drive controls people's behavior and takes away the unique aspect of being human, namely that you have free conscious will.

Manipulating people in order to create chaos

This is what is unique to humans: the freedom of will, the conscious will to make decisions about your actions, about your feelings, about your mental beliefs and about your sense of identity. If you do not have that, you are not really a human, you are not living up to the potential for a human being, but neither are you an animal, you are something in between. You are in a sense, a mechanized creation or a more conscious animal, but still not self-aware, fully self-aware.

This of course can only be understood when you understand that there are fallen beings, there are narcissistic beings, who are only seeking to manipulate the rest of the population. You really need to understand that they do not exist just in the physical realm in embodiment, but they also exist in the other three realms and they have a very complex agenda of manipulating human beings. This is what is behind all forms of human manipulation, but especially the way they have used sex and the sexual tension between men and women. They have artificially inflated that tension, partly in order to control people, partly in order to just create chaos and conflict.

You need to recognize here that when you look at the modern democracies and the increase in sexual exploitation of women and sexual harassment and so forth, there is no epic agenda behind it necessarily, but there are certain fallen beings who are using this to just create chaos. They did not want the modern democracies to emerge. They preferred a more dictatorial form of government as we have talked about in our books on dictatorships, fanaticism and elitism. They are angry with the democracies and they are using anything they *can* to create chaos and disorder that might break down these societies. It is not that there is a rational or logical agenda behind this, but there is a very destructive agenda.

This is what women need to become aware of. They need to become aware that there is no rational, biological or spiritual reason that women should allow themselves to become sexual objects. It is simply a destructive movement, a destructive drive, and you need to become aware of this and you need to resist it. Women need to stand up and say: "Enough! We have had enough of being appointed as sexual objects and we will not stand for this anymore." It will require a very determined effort to break through this. I wish to say something, even though it has been a long discourse, I still wish to say something about why it will be very difficult to change this in the modern democracies.

The archetype of the powerful man

Now, you will know, if you look at politicians in many countries (and especially in the United States when you look at Washington, D.C.) that there has been a lot of sexual scandals. You have seen how even presidents in the United States had multiple extramarital affairs with secretaries or interns or whatever you call them. You will know that many congressmen and senators have a mistress in Washington D.C. and then they have a wife who is their trophy wife in their big home out in the country, in their state wherever they live. What has happened here is that, throughout the world, in a way that has really never been written down or publicized, you have had this emergence of an attitude, which certainly is attached to these collective entities or is driven by these collective entities.

It is an attitude that starts at the identity level, filters into the mental and even the emotional. It relates to the creation of a sort of archetype for the powerful man, the man who is able to lead. This is a very complex archetype, but one component of it is that this powerful man is and should be sexually active. It is not necessarily that he should sleep with as many women as possible, but he certainly should not be confining his sexual activity to just one woman so having a mistress is perfectly acceptable. Well, of course there are many men who may objectify their own wives. Certainly, if a man has a mistress, he has objectified both his wife and the mistress. It can be no other way. What you actually see when you look at this male archetype of the powerful man who is the leader, he, in this archetype's mind, objectifies women. Women are simply objects for men's sexual exploitation, to satisfy men's sexual desire.

What I am saying here is this: When you look at society, you will see that the majority of politicians, the majority of people in the media, many scientists, many actors, writers, in other words, you look at the most influential people in the world, and the majority of them believe in and accept, even at the identity level, this archetype for the male leader: the important man, the powerful man. They all believe in it in one form or another.

An aspect of this male archetype is the objectification of women, the sexual objectification of women. The challenge that you face, even in the modern democracies where women have gained some political freedoms, some economic freedom and equality, is that in order to change the sexual objectification of women, you need to get the decision makers, most of whom are men, to agree to this. How can you get them to agree to this when they are clouded, when their minds are taken over by this male archetype that wants to objectify women? How are you going to get a congressman or a senator who has a mistress to agree to legislation or even promote legislation that works against the objectification of women? Well, in some cases you can force them or pressure them into agreeing with this, but it is an uphill battle and it will take a considerable fight to stop this.

Naturally, there are women in embodiment who are able to go through this process and to promote this process. I am not saying that you should necessarily consider yourselves among them as ascended master students. I am not saying you should not, if this is what is in your Divine plan, but what I am calling you to do, both men and women who are ascended master students, is make the calls for this. Use the invocations that we will create. Use our decrees, perhaps even look into these issues as they relate to you personally and then make the calls based on the knowledge that you gain. Perhaps you can also serve to make other women and other men aware of these issues and these problems.

Again, I know very well that whenever we have a conference, we are giving you a lot of teachings and it can seem overwhelming. As we have said before, you do not have to act upon everything we tell you. You find something that appeals to you personally and then you focus on that topic, you make the calls on that. If you are a woman and an ascended master student, there must be something from this conference that appeals to you personally, so focus on that. Avoid becoming overwhelmed and realize that you can have a tremendous impact by focusing on one area, making the calls so that other women will be free to take action. Then you will see that in this coming decade there will be many, many shifts in society, there will be a raising of awareness. There will be women who suddenly begin to speak out about topics they have never spoken out about before. There will be men who respond to this. Suddenly, there can be a new movement and new women's liberation movement that goes much, much deeper and demands more than political and economic freedom, more than equality, but also demands psychological freedom.

Because truly, what is it that happens when a woman is made a sexual object? Well, if she accepts this, her psychological freedom is taken away. What is it that happens to a man who is sexually addicted and therefore wants to objectify women? Well, his psychological freedom is taken away as well. We are of course not looking just to liberate women psychologically, but also to liberate men. What we are seeing is that this time is a historic opportunity for women to be the driving force in the liberation of society at the psychological level and creating a new revolution in society that is aimed at bringing psychological freedom.

With this, my beloved, I am immensely grateful for your attention, your willingness to endure this long discourse, to allow your chakras to be used as broadcasting stations and therefore, I seal you in the accelerating, the *ever-accelerating* joy, of the Fourth Ray. Astrea I AM.

NOTE: This dictation was given June 1, 2020.

28 | LIBERATING WOMEN FROM SEXUAL EXPLOITATION (PART 1)

In the name of the I AM THAT I AM, Jesus Christ, I use the authority that I have as a being in embodiment on earth to call upon Elohim Astrea to reinforce my calls and use my chakras to project the statements in this invocation into the collective consciousness and awaken people to the awareness that will liberate both men and women from all psychological and spiritual thralldom to the fallen beings. Awaken people to the reality that we are spiritual beings and that we can co-create a new future by working with the ascended masters. I especially call for …

[Make your own calls here.]

Part 1

1. Astrea, awaken people to see that for over 90% of the men on this planet, sex is an addiction.

Astrea, loving Being white,
your Presence is my pure delight,

your sword and circle white and blue,
the astral plane is cutting through.

Astrea, come accelerate,
with purity I do vibrate,
release the fire so blue and white,
my aura filled with vibrant light.

2. Astrea, awaken people to see that even though the modern democracies have made considerable progress, certain problems are accelerating and one of these problems is addictions.

Astrea, calm the raging storm,
so purity will be the norm,
my aura filled with blue and white,
with shining armor, like a knight.

Astrea, come accelerate,
with purity I do vibrate,
release the fire so blue and white,
my aura filled with vibrant light.

3. Astrea, awaken people to the need to ask why these societies see a rise in addictions when they see so much progress in other areas.

Astrea, come and cut me free,
from every binding entity,
let astral forces all be bound,
true freedom I have surely found.

Astrea, come accelerate,
with purity I do vibrate,
release the fire so blue and white,
my aura filled with vibrant light.

4. Astrea, awaken people to see that over the last hundred years people have become more free politically and economically, but an addiction does not make people more free. An addiction takes away people's freedom.

Astrea, I sincerely urge,
from demons all, do me purge,
consume them all and take me higher,
I will endure your cleansing fire.

Astrea, come accelerate,
with purity I do vibrate,
release the fire so blue and white,
my aura filled with vibrant light.

5. Astrea, awaken people to see that many societies are seeing a rise in people's political and economic freedom but at the same time, they are seeing a decrease in people's psychological freedom, even in some ways their physical freedom because an addiction can take away their freedom.

Astrea, do all spirits bind,
so that I am no longer blind,
I see the spirit and its twin,
the victory of Christ I win.

Astrea, come accelerate,
with purity I do vibrate,
release the fire so blue and white,
my aura filled with vibrant light.

6. Astrea, awaken people to see that we cannot explain this if we insist on doing what science has been insisting on doing, namely providing a materialistic explanation for everything.

Astrea, clear my every cell,
from energies of death and hell,
my body is now free to grow,
each cell emits an inner glow.

Astrea, come accelerate,
with purity I do vibrate,
release the fire so blue and white,
my aura filled with vibrant light.

7. Astrea, awaken people to see that we will never be able to explain addiction, nor will we be able to help people free themselves from addiction, through a materialistic approach.

> Astrea, clear my feeling mind,
> in purity my peace I find,
> with higher feeling you release,
> I co-create in perfect peace.

> **Astrea, come accelerate,**
> **with purity I do vibrate,**
> **release the fire so blue and white,**
> **my aura filled with vibrant light.**

8. Astrea, awaken people to see that we can analyze the body from a purely materialistic viewpoint, but we will never be able to explain macrocosmic phenomena through microcosmic elements.

> Astrea, clear my mental realm,
> my Christ self always at the helm,
> I see now how to manifest,
> the matrix that for all is best.

> **Astrea, come accelerate,**
> **with purity I do vibrate,**
> **release the fire so blue and white,**
> **my aura filled with vibrant light.**

9. Astrea, awaken people to see that a human being is not a collection of cells, molecules, atoms or subatomic particles. A human being is more than a collection of parts. The whole is more than the sum of the parts because a human being is a *being,* not a machine, not a device, not an object.

> Astrea, with great clarity,
> I claim a new identity,
> etheric blueprint I now see,
> I co-create more consciously.

Astrea, come accelerate,
with purity I do vibrate,
release the fire so blue and white,
my aura filled with vibrant light.

Part 2

1. Astrea, awaken people to see that we cannot explain addictive behavior by only looking at human beings as objects. Cut free the large group of people who are close to breaking through so they can look at how human beings have been objectified.

Astrea, loving Being white,
your Presence is my pure delight,
your sword and circle white and blue,
the astral plane is cutting through.

Astrea, come accelerate,
with purity I do vibrate,
release the fire so blue and white,
my aura filled with vibrant light.

2. Astrea, awaken people to see that sex has been used to abuse, limit and trap women because women are objectified. They become sexual objects.

Astrea, calm the raging storm,
so purity will be the norm,
my aura filled with blue and white,
with shining armor, like a knight.

Astrea, come accelerate,
with purity I do vibrate,
release the fire so blue and white,
my aura filled with vibrant light.

3. Astrea, awaken people to see that soldiers who go to war are not looked at as individual people or human beings. They are just objects that can be

moved around and sacrificed in order to achieve some epically important goal.

> Astrea, come and cut me free,
> from every binding entity,
> let astral forces all be bound,
> true freedom I have surely found.

> **Astrea, come accelerate,**
> **with purity I do vibrate,**
> **release the fire so blue and white,**
> **my aura filled with vibrant light.**

4. Astrea, awaken people to see that when science takes a materialistic approach, science is objectifying human beings. The materialistic approach to science has been and is still objectifying human beings.

> Astrea, I sincerely urge,
> from demons all, do me purge,
> consume them all and take me higher,
> I will endure your cleansing fire.

> **Astrea, come accelerate,**
> **with purity I do vibrate,**
> **release the fire so blue and white,**
> **my aura filled with vibrant light.**

5. Astrea, awaken people to see that in the modern democracies, this is the foundation for all other areas where human beings are objectified, including seeing women as sexual objects.

> Astrea, do all spirits bind,
> so that I am no longer blind,
> I see the spirit and its twin,
> the victory of Christ I win.

> **Astrea, come accelerate,**
> **with purity I do vibrate,**

release the fire so blue and white,
my aura filled with vibrant light.

6. Astrea, awaken people to see that an addiction takes away a person's freedom and it does this first of all at the psychological level.

Astrea, clear my every cell,
from energies of death and hell,
my body is now free to grow,
each cell emits an inner glow.

Astrea, come accelerate,
with purity I do vibrate,
release the fire so blue and white,
my aura filled with vibrant light.

7. Astrea, awaken people to see that when a man is addicted to sex, he loses his psychological freedom because there is something in his psyche that compels him to have sex.

Astrea, clear my feeling mind,
in purity my peace I find,
with higher feeling you release,
I co-create in perfect peace.

Astrea, come accelerate,
with purity I do vibrate,
release the fire so blue and white,
my aura filled with vibrant light.

8. Astrea, awaken people to see that this is not something he freely, neutrally chooses to do. He is compelled to do it by some force that overtakes his conscious will. He cannot choose to say stop. This is the same with alcoholics or drug addicts, they have lost their freedom of will.

Astrea, clear my mental realm,
my Christ self always at the helm,
I see now how to manifest,
the matrix that for all is best.

Astrea, come accelerate,
with purity I do vibrate,
release the fire so blue and white,
my aura filled with vibrant light.

9. Astrea, awaken people to see that this should be a great concern to all modern democracies who take pride in seeing themselves as free societies that give people the greatest possible personal freedom.

Astrea, with great clarity,
I claim a new identity,
etheric blueprint I now see,
I co-create more consciously.

Astrea, come accelerate,
with purity I do vibrate,
release the fire so blue and white,
my aura filled with vibrant light.

Part 3

1. Astrea, awaken people to see that it is cognitive dissonance that we see the rise in political, economic freedom and at the same time see the rise in this psychological addiction that takes away people's freedom.

Astrea, loving Being white,
your Presence is my pure delight,
your sword and circle white and blue,
the astral plane is cutting through.

Astrea, come accelerate,
with purity I do vibrate,
release the fire so blue and white,
my aura filled with vibrant light.

2. Astrea, awaken people to see that materialistic science cannot explain this because it comes up against the limitations of the materialistic approach.

We can analyze hormones, the nervous system, brain chemistry, genetic material but what we discover are a side effect at the physical level of a deeper cause.

> Astrea, calm the raging storm,
> so purity will be the norm,
> my aura filled with blue and white,
> with shining armor, like a knight.

> **Astrea, come accelerate,**
> **with purity I do vibrate,**
> **release the fire so blue and white,**
> **my aura filled with vibrant light.**

3. Astrea, awaken people to see that a human being is an energy system and we have an energy field around the body. Energy flows through this energy system from the spiritual realm into the identity body, then into the mental body, then into the emotional body and then into the physical.

> Astrea, come and cut me free,
> from every binding entity,
> let astral forces all be bound,
> true freedom I have surely found.

> **Astrea, come accelerate,**
> **with purity I do vibrate,**
> **release the fire so blue and white,**
> **my aura filled with vibrant light.**

4. Astrea, awaken people to see that everything that happens at the physical level is not a cause in and of itself. It is the effect of causes at the emotional, mental and identity level. If we do not understand this basic reality, we cannot explain addiction.

> Astrea, I sincerely urge,
> from demons all, do me purge,
> consume them all and take me higher,
> I will endure your cleansing fire.

Astrea, come accelerate,
with purity I do vibrate,
release the fire so blue and white,
my aura filled with vibrant light.

5. Astrea, awaken people to see that what happens in an addiction is not purely physical. Something happens at the emotional level that overpowers the person's conscious will.

Astrea, do all spirits bind,
so that I am no longer blind,
I see the spirit and its twin,
the victory of Christ I win.

Astrea, come accelerate,
with purity I do vibrate,
release the fire so blue and white,
my aura filled with vibrant light.

6. Astrea, awaken people to see that in an addiction, there is such a surge of a particular form of energy that comes from the emotional body of that person into the conscious mind that it overpowers the conscious mind and it neutralizes the conscious will.

Astrea, clear my every cell,
from energies of death and hell,
my body is now free to grow,
each cell emits an inner glow.

Astrea, come accelerate,
with purity I do vibrate,
release the fire so blue and white,
my aura filled with vibrant light.

7. Astrea, awaken people to see that the surge of energy overrides the conscious will, and the person has no power to stop this emotional impulse and it must act upon it.

Astrea, clear my feeling mind,
in purity my peace I find,
with higher feeling you release,
I co-create in perfect peace.

Astrea, come accelerate,
with purity I do vibrate,
release the fire so blue and white,
my aura filled with vibrant light.

8. Astrea, awaken people to see that the emotional level is not the highest
level of the human energy system, for there is also a mental component
and an identity level component.

Astrea, clear my mental realm,
my Christ self always at the helm,
I see now how to manifest,
the matrix that for all is best.

Astrea, come accelerate,
with purity I do vibrate,
release the fire so blue and white,
my aura filled with vibrant light.

9. Astrea, awaken people to see that an addiction starts at the identity level
by the way the person looks at itself and what kind of being it is. It then
also has a component at the mental level where it looks at how it relates to
the world, what it can do, what it is allowed to do and not do.

Astrea, with great clarity,
I claim a new identity,
etheric blueprint I now see,
I co-create more consciously.

Astrea, come accelerate,
with purity I do vibrate,
release the fire so blue and white,
my aura filled with vibrant light.

Part 4

1. Astrea, awaken people to see that this sets the matrix for the production of certain energies in the emotional body, which can then overpower the conscious mind at the physical level. Unless we understand this, we cannot explain an addiction.

> Astrea, loving Being white,
> your Presence is my pure delight,
> your sword and circle white and blue,
> the astral plane is cutting through.

> **Astrea, come accelerate,**
> **with purity I do vibrate,**
> **release the fire so blue and white,**
> **my aura filled with vibrant light.**

2. Astrea, awaken the people who can develop the technology that can make the human energy field visible and who can interpret the measurements made.

> Astrea, calm the raging storm,
> so purity will be the norm,
> my aura filled with blue and white,
> with shining armor, like a knight.

> **Astrea, come accelerate,**
> **with purity I do vibrate,**
> **release the fire so blue and white,**
> **my aura filled with vibrant light.**

3. Astrea, awaken people to see that the human energy field has certain centers that allow energy to flow through the four lower bodies.

> Astrea, come and cut me free,
> from every binding entity,
> let astral forces all be bound,
> true freedom I have surely found.

Astrea, come accelerate,
with purity I do vibrate,
release the fire so blue and white,
my aura filled with vibrant light.

4. Astrea, awaken people to see that if we are to explain sexual addiction, we need to be aware that the base chakra is located in line with the genitals because this is where the life energy streams through and can then be directed into the sexual organs and expressed as sexual energy.

Astrea, I sincerely urge,
from demons all, do me purge,
consume them all and take me higher,
I will endure your cleansing fire.

Astrea, come accelerate,
with purity I do vibrate,
release the fire so blue and white,
my aura filled with vibrant light.

5. Astrea, awaken people to see that when a person is addicted to sex, it is because something has happened in that person's base chakra. There is a disturbance and imbalance in the base chakra.

Astrea, do all spirits bind,
so that I am no longer blind,
I see the spirit and its twin,
the victory of Christ I win.

Astrea, come accelerate,
with purity I do vibrate,
release the fire so blue and white,
my aura filled with vibrant light.

6. Astrea, awaken people to see that this means that the person's sexual desires have been multiplied beyond a natural limit. This can cause the base chakra to spin in the opposite direction of what is natural. It is causing a pollution in the base chakra.

Astrea, clear my every cell,
from energies of death and hell,
my body is now free to grow,
each cell emits an inner glow.

**Astrea, come accelerate,
with purity I do vibrate,
release the fire so blue and white,
my aura filled with vibrant light.**

7. Astrea, awaken people to see that as a person's sexual desire grows, the base chakra begins to pulsate with red light and this can cause the person at the conscious level to feel this irrepressible urge to have sex.

Astrea, clear my feeling mind,
in purity my peace I find,
with higher feeling you release,
I co-create in perfect peace.

**Astrea, come accelerate,
with purity I do vibrate,
release the fire so blue and white,
my aura filled with vibrant light.**

8. Astrea, awaken people to see that the cause of sexual addiction is that it is possible for human beings to create semi-conscious entities that we have created collectively over time.

Astrea, clear my mental realm,
my Christ self always at the helm,
I see now how to manifest,
the matrix that for all is best.

**Astrea, come accelerate,
with purity I do vibrate,
release the fire so blue and white,
my aura filled with vibrant light.**

9. Astrea, awaken people to see that there are entities both in the emotional realm, in the mental realm and in the identity realm. In the emotional realm, there are these collective entities that are created in relation to sex.

> Astrea, with great clarity,
> I claim a new identity,
> etheric blueprint I now see,
> I co-create more consciously.

> **Astrea, come accelerate,**
> **with purity I do vibrate,**
> **release the fire so blue and white,**
> **my aura filled with vibrant light.**

Part 5

1. Astrea, awaken people to see that when people are vulnerable to this, these collective entities can invade a person's energy field, the sex entity can invade a person's base chakra.

> Astrea, loving Being white,
> your Presence is my pure delight,
> your sword and circle white and blue,
> the astral plane is cutting through.

> **Astrea, come accelerate,**
> **with purity I do vibrate,**
> **release the fire so blue and white,**
> **my aura filled with vibrant light.**

2. Astrea, awaken people to see that a collective entity is created over a long period of time by individual human beings feeding energy into it. The sex entity is not created by the *pure* sexual drive, it is created by a *perverted* sexual drive, which has also been going on for a very long time on this planet.

Astrea, calm the raging storm,
so purity will be the norm,
my aura filled with blue and white,
with shining armor, like a knight.

Astrea, come accelerate,
with purity I do vibrate,
release the fire so blue and white,
my aura filled with vibrant light.

3. Astrea, awaken people to see that when a collective entity reaches a certain strength, a certain amount of accumulated energy, then the entity is able to overpower many people's energy field and chakras.

Astrea, come and cut me free,
from every binding entity,
let astral forces all be bound,
true freedom I have surely found.

Astrea, come accelerate,
with purity I do vibrate,
release the fire so blue and white,
my aura filled with vibrant light.

4. Astrea, awaken people to see that the sex entity has such a tremendous pool of energy that it can direct this energy at an individual person's base chakra. Most people have no defense against this, they are not aware that these entities exist, they are not aware that their chakras can be subjected to this very strong energy.

Astrea, I sincerely urge,
from demons all, do me purge,
consume them all and take me higher,
I will endure your cleansing fire.

Astrea, come accelerate,
with purity I do vibrate,
release the fire so blue and white,
my aura filled with vibrant light.

5. Astrea, awaken people to see that the entity can single out a specific person, direct a tremendous energy burst at that person's base chakra and it disturbs the functioning of the base chakra. The chakra begins to spin in an opposite direction and have this red-hot energy that interferes with the base chakra.

> Astrea, do all spirits bind,
> so that I am no longer blind,
> I see the spirit and its twin,
> the victory of Christ I win.

> **Astrea, come accelerate,**
> **with purity I do vibrate,**
> **release the fire so blue and white,**
> **my aura filled with vibrant light.**

6. Astrea, awaken people to see that all of a sudden the person's sexual desires become amplified so that the person feels this very strong compulsion to have sex. As the person engages in this energy, then the person is expressing energy through its base chakra.

> Astrea, clear my every cell,
> from energies of death and hell,
> my body is now free to grow,
> each cell emits an inner glow.

> **Astrea, come accelerate,**
> **with purity I do vibrate,**
> **release the fire so blue and white,**
> **my aura filled with vibrant light.**

7. Astrea, awaken people to see that when we engage in this sexual expression that is initiated by the collective entity, some of our *vital* energy can feed the entity.

> Astrea, clear my feeling mind,
> in purity my peace I find,
> with higher feeling you release,
> I co-create in perfect peace.

Astrea, come accelerate,
with purity I do vibrate,
release the fire so blue and white,
my aura filled with vibrant light.

8. Astrea, awaken people to see that the entity is directing some of its energy into a person's base chakra, but as the person then acts upon this energy, the entity gains back more energy than it sent. The entity is literally stealing vital energy from the person.

Astrea, clear my mental realm,
my Christ self always at the helm,
I see now how to manifest,
the matrix that for all is best.

Astrea, come accelerate,
with purity I do vibrate,
release the fire so blue and white,
my aura filled with vibrant light.

9. Astrea, awaken people to see that in order to survive and multiply itself, the entity must get human beings to misqualify the energy with a lower vibration, a fear-based vibration that the entity can absorb.

Astrea, with great clarity,
I claim a new identity,
etheric blueprint I now see,
I co-create more consciously.

Astrea, come accelerate,
with purity I do vibrate,
release the fire so blue and white,
my aura filled with vibrant light.

Sealing

In the name of the I AM THAT I AM, I accept that Archangel Michael, Astrea and Shiva form an impenetrable shield around myself and all constructive people, sealing us from all fear-based energies in all four octaves. I accept that the Light of God is consuming and transforming all fear-based energies that make up the dark forces working against the liberation of women on earth!

29 | LIBERATING WOMEN FROM SEXUAL EXPLOITATION (PART 2)

In the name of the I AM THAT I AM, Jesus Christ, I use the authority that I have as a being in embodiment on earth to call upon Elohim Astrea to reinforce my calls and use my chakras to project the statements in this invocation into the collective consciousness and awaken people to the awareness that will liberate both men and women from all psychological and spiritual thralldom to the fallen beings. Awaken people to the reality that we are spiritual beings and that we can co-create a new future by working with the ascended masters. I especially call for ...

[Make your own calls here.]

Part 1

1. Astrea, awaken people to acknowledge that they often feel depleted of energy after they engage in sex.

> Astrea, loving Being white,
> your Presence is my pure delight,

your sword and circle white and blue,
the astral plane is cutting through.

Astrea, come accelerate,
with purity I do vibrate,
release the fire so blue and white,
my aura filled with vibrant light.

2. Astrea, awaken people to see that we have the Conscious You, which enables us to step back, look at ourselves and consciously choose to change our behavior. This is what enables us to free ourselves from an addiction.

Astrea, calm the raging storm,
so purity will be the norm,
my aura filled with blue and white,
with shining armor, like a knight.

Astrea, come accelerate,
with purity I do vibrate,
release the fire so blue and white,
my aura filled with vibrant light.

3. Astrea, awaken people to see that freeing ourselves requires that we are able and willing to step back, look at the addictive behavior, identify that it takes away our freedom, that we do not want this and therefore make the decision to change it.

Astrea, come and cut me free,
from every binding entity,
let astral forces all be bound,
true freedom I have surely found.

Astrea, come accelerate,
with purity I do vibrate,
release the fire so blue and white,
my aura filled with vibrant light.

4. Astrea, awaken people to see that some people are not overpowered by the sex entity because they do not allow lower sexual energy to enter their base chakra.

> Astrea, I sincerely urge,
> from demons all, do me purge,
> consume them all and take me higher,
> I will endure your cleansing fire.

> **Astrea, come accelerate,**
> **with purity I do vibrate,**
> **release the fire so blue and white,**
> **my aura filled with vibrant light.**

5. Astrea, awaken people to see that they do not allow it because they have some awareness at the mental level and they have a sense of identity at the identity level that blocks the emotional energy from gaining entrance into their base chakra.

> Astrea, do all spirits bind,
> so that I am no longer blind,
> I see the spirit and its twin,
> the victory of Christ I win.

> **Astrea, come accelerate,**
> **with purity I do vibrate,**
> **release the fire so blue and white,**
> **my aura filled with vibrant light.**

6. Astrea, awaken people to see that in order for the sex entity at the emotional level to invade a person's base chakra, there has to be an opening, there has to be some energy in the person's base chakra that the entity can use.

> Astrea, clear my every cell,
> from energies of death and hell,
> my body is now free to grow,
> each cell emits an inner glow.

Astrea, come accelerate,
with purity I do vibrate,
release the fire so blue and white,
my aura filled with vibrant light.

7. Astrea, awaken people to see that the energy in the base chakra comes from the mental level. The person has certain beliefs about sex and sexuality at the mental level and it has a certain identity at the identity level.

Astrea, clear my feeling mind,
in purity my peace I find,
with higher feeling you release,
I co-create in perfect peace.

Astrea, come accelerate,
with purity I do vibrate,
release the fire so blue and white,
my aura filled with vibrant light.

8. Astrea, awaken people to see that we are vulnerable to the sex entity when we are seeing ourselves a certain way, perhaps as sexual beings and feeling at the mental level that it is necessary for a man to be sexually active to get satisfaction of his sexual desires in any way he can.

Astrea, clear my mental realm,
my Christ self always at the helm,
I see now how to manifest,
the matrix that for all is best.

Astrea, come accelerate,
with purity I do vibrate,
release the fire so blue and white,
my aura filled with vibrant light.

9. Astrea, awaken people to see that in order to explain sex addiction, we also need to look at the mental level and the beliefs and attitudes that people have about sex.

Astrea, with great clarity,
I claim a new identity,
etheric blueprint I now see,
I co-create more consciously.

Astrea, come accelerate,
with purity I do vibrate,
release the fire so blue and white,
my aura filled with vibrant light.

Part 2

1. Astrea, awaken people to see that the Christian religion has projected this schizophrenic, ambivalent view of sex into the population. The Christian religion has portrayed sex as being wrong or sinful, therefore as something that should be restricted.

Astrea, loving Being white,
your Presence is my pure delight,
your sword and circle white and blue,
the astral plane is cutting through.

Astrea, come accelerate,
with purity I do vibrate,
release the fire so blue and white,
my aura filled with vibrant light.

2. Astrea, awaken people to see that today many people in the modern democracies look at this as being primitive and belonging to an old age, thinking the sexual revolution has set people free from restrictions.

Astrea, calm the raging storm,
so purity will be the norm,
my aura filled with blue and white,
with shining armor, like a knight.

Astrea, come accelerate,
with purity I do vibrate,
release the fire so blue and white,
my aura filled with vibrant light.

3. Astrea, awaken people to see that even before the Christian religion, there has been a collective sex entity at the emotional level. Christianity has had a two-sided effect in terms of making people more or less vulnerable to the sex entity.

Astrea, come and cut me free,
from every binding entity,
let astral forces all be bound,
true freedom I have surely found.

Astrea, come accelerate,
with purity I do vibrate,
release the fire so blue and white,
my aura filled with vibrant light.

4. Astrea, awaken people to see that the Christian religion has caused a considerable suppression of the sex drive and sexual energies and this created a pressure in many people's base chakras. It caused many people to try to suppress their sex drive, but forceful suppression means that energies keep accumulating.

Astrea, I sincerely urge,
from demons all, do me purge,
consume them all and take me higher,
I will endure your cleansing fire.

Astrea, come accelerate,
with purity I do vibrate,
release the fire so blue and white,
my aura filled with vibrant light.

5. Astrea, awaken people to see that eventually these people would become vulnerable to the sex entity. They would give in to their sexual desires and

then they would feel very bad about it afterwards, which created another collective entity particular to the Christian religion.

> Astrea, do all spirits bind,
> so that I am no longer blind,
> I see the spirit and its twin,
> the victory of Christ I win.

> **Astrea, come accelerate,**
> **with purity I do vibrate,**
> **release the fire so blue and white,**
> **my aura filled with vibrant light.**

6. Astrea, awaken people to see that the Christian religion enabled some people to not so forcefully repress their sexual desires, but to, even at the mental level, not give in to them so they did not allow the energy to build up in their base chakras.

> Astrea, clear my every cell,
> from energies of death and hell,
> my body is now free to grow,
> each cell emits an inner glow.

> **Astrea, come accelerate,**
> **with purity I do vibrate,**
> **release the fire so blue and white,**
> **my aura filled with vibrant light.**

7. Astrea, awaken people to see that when the Christian influence was stronger fewer people were addicted to sex. There were also fewer instances of the sexual abuse of women through rape or sexual harassment.

> Astrea, clear my feeling mind,
> in purity my peace I find,
> with higher feeling you release,
> I co-create in perfect peace.

> **Astrea, come accelerate,**
> **with purity I do vibrate,**

**release the fire so blue and white,
my aura filled with vibrant light.**

8. Astrea, awaken people to see that when societies became less dominated by the Christian view of sex, when we had the so-called sexual revolution, we see an increase in sexual addiction because now people feel free to express their sexual desires.

Astrea, clear my mental realm,
my Christ self always at the helm,
I see now how to manifest,
the matrix that for all is best.

**Astrea, come accelerate,
with purity I do vibrate,
release the fire so blue and white,
my aura filled with vibrant light.**

9. Astrea, awaken people to see that the sexual revolution has given rise to many things that seek to magnify the sex drive, such as pornography, Viagra or drugs that are used to rape women.

Astrea, with great clarity,
I claim a new identity,
etheric blueprint I now see,
I co-create more consciously.

**Astrea, come accelerate,
with purity I do vibrate,
release the fire so blue and white,
my aura filled with vibrant light.**

Part 3

1. Astrea, awaken people to see that we have seen a rise in prostitution, human trafficking, women being lured into or sold into prostitution, or

being forced into drug addiction in order to make them willing to do prostitution.

> Astrea, loving Being white,
> your Presence is my pure delight,
> your sword and circle white and blue,
> the astral plane is cutting through.

> **Astrea, come accelerate,**
> **with purity I do vibrate,**
> **release the fire so blue and white,**
> **my aura filled with vibrant light.**

2. Astrea, awaken people to see that the net result in the modern democracies of the so-called sexual revolution is an increase of sexual addiction.

> Astrea, calm the raging storm,
> so purity will be the norm,
> my aura filled with blue and white,
> with shining armor, like a knight.

> **Astrea, come accelerate,**
> **with purity I do vibrate,**
> **release the fire so blue and white,**
> **my aura filled with vibrant light.**

3. Astrea, awaken people to see that a sexual addiction takes away men's freedom because now they cannot choose whether they want to have sex or not. They feel compelled by the addiction to have sex.

> Astrea, come and cut me free,
> from every binding entity,
> let astral forces all be bound,
> true freedom I have surely found.

> **Astrea, come accelerate,**
> **with purity I do vibrate,**
> **release the fire so blue and white,**
> **my aura filled with vibrant light.**

4. Astrea, awaken people to see that this causes men to look at women as sexual objects. The immediate cause of the sexual objectification of women is this increase in sexual addiction in men.

> Astrea, I sincerely urge,
> from demons all, do me purge,
> consume them all and take me higher,
> I will endure your cleansing fire.

> **Astrea, come accelerate,**
> **with purity I do vibrate,**
> **release the fire so blue and white,**
> **my aura filled with vibrant light.**

5. Astrea, awaken people to see that when a man is not addicted to sex, he does not look at women as sexual objects. He looks at women as individuals and as human beings.

> Astrea, do all spirits bind,
> so that I am no longer blind,
> I see the spirit and its twin,
> the victory of Christ I win.

> **Astrea, come accelerate,**
> **with purity I do vibrate,**
> **release the fire so blue and white,**
> **my aura filled with vibrant light.**

6. Astrea, awaken people to see that when a man is not sexually addicted, he does not want to have sex with any woman under any circumstance. He is seeking a deeper connection with another human being who has a different energetic polarity than he has, which then can balance his own energetic polarity.

> Astrea, clear my every cell,
> from energies of death and hell,
> my body is now free to grow,
> each cell emits an inner glow.

Astrea, come accelerate,
with purity I do vibrate,
release the fire so blue and white,
my aura filled with vibrant light.

7. Astrea, awaken people to see that there is a deeper purpose to sex. When a man is not addicted to sex, he primarily seeks a connection with a woman and we cannot have a connection with an object.

Astrea, clear my feeling mind,
in purity my peace I find,
with higher feeling you release,
I co-create in perfect peace.

Astrea, come accelerate,
with purity I do vibrate,
release the fire so blue and white,
my aura filled with vibrant light.

8. Astrea, awaken people to see that we can only have a genuine connection with another human being, and we can only have that when we look at that other person as a human being, which means we are sensitive to the other person's needs and desires.

Astrea, clear my mental realm,
my Christ self always at the helm,
I see now how to manifest,
the matrix that for all is best.

Astrea, come accelerate,
with purity I do vibrate,
release the fire so blue and white,
my aura filled with vibrant light.

9. Astrea, awaken people to see that men would never force a woman to have sex in order to get a deeper connection with that woman because when there is force involved, the connection is gone.

Astrea, with great clarity,
I claim a new identity,
etheric blueprint I now see,
I co-create more consciously.

Astrea, come accelerate,
with purity I do vibrate,
release the fire so blue and white,
my aura filled with vibrant light.

Part 4

1. Astrea, awaken people to see that sexual addiction in men is the immediate cause of the sexual objectification of women. When men are addicted to sex, they are compelled by the addiction.

Astrea, loving Being white,
your Presence is my pure delight,
your sword and circle white and blue,
the astral plane is cutting through.

Astrea, come accelerate,
with purity I do vibrate,
release the fire so blue and white,
my aura filled with vibrant light.

2. Astrea, awaken people to see that we cannot say they *want* to have sex, but they are *compelled* to have sex and that is why they are looking for an object who can fulfill that physical or emotional gratification, which is a temporary gratification.

Astrea, calm the raging storm,
so purity will be the norm,
my aura filled with blue and white,
with shining armor, like a knight.

Astrea, come accelerate,
with purity I do vibrate,
release the fire so blue and white,
my aura filled with vibrant light.

3. Astrea, awaken people to see that when men have a deeper connection with a woman, it happens at the mental and identity level. It does not happen at the emotional and physical level.

Astrea, come and cut me free,
from every binding entity,
let astral forces all be bound,
true freedom I have surely found.

Astrea, come accelerate,
with purity I do vibrate,
release the fire so blue and white,
my aura filled with vibrant light.

4. Astrea, awaken people to see that men cannot have a deeper emotional connection with women when they are addicted, when their base chakras are disturbed by a lower sexual energy.

Astrea, I sincerely urge,
from demons all, do me purge,
consume them all and take me higher,
I will endure your cleansing fire.

Astrea, come accelerate,
with purity I do vibrate,
release the fire so blue and white,
my aura filled with vibrant light.

5. Astrea, awaken people to see that unless we understand this and unless we address this, we will not be able to overcome the sexual objectification of women.

Astrea, do all spirits bind,
so that I am no longer blind,

I see the spirit and its twin,
the victory of Christ I win.

Astrea, come accelerate,
with purity I do vibrate,
release the fire so blue and white,
my aura filled with vibrant light.

6. Astrea, awaken people to see that in the modern democracies women have more political rights and economic opportunities, but at the same time we see an increase in the sexual objectification of women, which is abusive and a form of violence against women.

Astrea, clear my every cell,
from energies of death and hell,
my body is now free to grow,
each cell emits an inner glow.

Astrea, come accelerate,
with purity I do vibrate,
release the fire so blue and white,
my aura filled with vibrant light.

7. Astrea, awaken people to see that the number of rapes, the amount of pornography, the amount of sexual harassment of women is growing, and unless we address this problem, the political and economic liberation of women will be nullified by this sexual objectification of women.

Astrea, clear my feeling mind,
in purity my peace I find,
with higher feeling you release,
I co-create in perfect peace.

Astrea, come accelerate,
with purity I do vibrate,
release the fire so blue and white,
my aura filled with vibrant light.

8. Astrea, awaken people to realize: We have a problem here that we must do something about, but what we have done so far, the Christian paradigm, the materialist paradigm has not diminished the problem. Therefore, we must reason we cannot solve it through these paradigms.

Astrea, clear my mental realm,
my Christ self always at the helm,
I see now how to manifest,
the matrix that for all is best.

Astrea, come accelerate,
with purity I do vibrate,
release the fire so blue and white,
my aura filled with vibrant light.

9. Astrea, awaken people to see that either we declare that we are powerless to solve the problem and admit that we are powerless to protect our women against sexual exploitation or we must find another approach.

Astrea, with great clarity,
I claim a new identity,
etheric blueprint I now see,
I co-create more consciously.

Astrea, come accelerate,
with purity I do vibrate,
release the fire so blue and white,
my aura filled with vibrant light.

Part 5

1. Astrea, cut women free to see that there is something here that needs to be addressed. We need to find a different way to look at it so we can explain why this is happening.

Astrea, loving Being white,
your Presence is my pure delight,

your sword and circle white and blue,
the astral plane is cutting through.

**Astrea, come accelerate,
with purity I do vibrate,
release the fire so blue and white,
my aura filled with vibrant light.**

2. Astrea, awaken people to see that the sexual exploitation of women
through the objectification of women has an emotional component. When
men go to prostitutes, look at pornography or rape women, there is an
objectification of women.

Astrea, calm the raging storm,
so purity will be the norm,
my aura filled with blue and white,
with shining armor, like a knight.

**Astrea, come accelerate,
with purity I do vibrate,
release the fire so blue and white,
my aura filled with vibrant light.**

3. Astrea, awaken people to see that the 90 plus percent of men who are
addicted to sex in their emotional bodies, they look at women as sexual
objects and really nothing else.

Astrea, come and cut me free,
from every binding entity,
let astral forces all be bound,
true freedom I have surely found.

**Astrea, come accelerate,
with purity I do vibrate,
release the fire so blue and white,
my aura filled with vibrant light.**

4. Astrea, awaken people to see that the emotional level view comes from the mental. At the mental level we find a variety of activities that are aimed at objectifying women.

Astrea, I sincerely urge,
from demons all, do me purge,
consume them all and take me higher,
I will endure your cleansing fire.

Astrea, come accelerate,
with purity I do vibrate,
release the fire so blue and white,
my aura filled with vibrant light.

5. Astrea, I call forth the judgment of Christ upon the dark forces behind ideas and thoughts that in subtle ways promote the objectification of women.

Astrea, do all spirits bind,
so that I am no longer blind,
I see the spirit and its twin,
the victory of Christ I win.

Astrea, come accelerate,
with purity I do vibrate,
release the fire so blue and white,
my aura filled with vibrant light.

6. Astrea, I call forth the judgment of Christ upon the dark forces behind the advertising industry, how women are portrayed in ways aimed at arousing men's sexual desire.

Astrea, clear my every cell,
from energies of death and hell,
my body is now free to grow,
each cell emits an inner glow.

Astrea, come accelerate,
with purity I do vibrate,

**release the fire so blue and white,
my aura filled with vibrant light.**

7. Astrea, I call forth the judgment of Christ upon the dark forces behind
the idea that women should be sexually appealing to men, that women
should be evaluated based on their sexual attractiveness.

Astrea, clear my feeling mind,
in purity my peace I find,
with higher feeling you release,
I co-create in perfect peace.

**Astrea, come accelerate,
with purity I do vibrate,
release the fire so blue and white,
my aura filled with vibrant light.**

8. Astrea, I call forth the judgment of Christ upon the dark forces behind
the beauty industry that has created this standard for how a beautiful
woman looks.

Astrea, clear my mental realm,
my Christ self always at the helm,
I see now how to manifest,
the matrix that for all is best.

**Astrea, come accelerate,
with purity I do vibrate,
release the fire so blue and white,
my aura filled with vibrant light.**

9. Astrea, I call for the binding of the beasts created at the mental and
emotional level that are projecting at women that they should live up to
this other-worldly standard of beauty.

Astrea, with great clarity,
I claim a new identity,
etheric blueprint I now see,
I co-create more consciously.

Astrea, come accelerate,
with purity I do vibrate,
release the fire so blue and white,
my aura filled with vibrant light.

Sealing

In the name of the I AM THAT I AM, I accept that Archangel Michael, Astrea and Shiva form an impenetrable shield around myself and all constructive people, sealing us from all fear-based energies in all four octaves. I accept that the Light of God is consuming and transforming all fear-based energies that make up the dark forces working against the liberation of women on earth!

30 | LIBERATING WOMEN FROM SEXUAL EXPLOITATION (PART 3)

In the name of the I AM THAT I AM, Jesus Christ, I use the authority that I have as a being in embodiment on earth to call upon Elohim Astrea to reinforce my calls and use my chakras to project the statements in this invocation into the collective consciousness and awaken people to the awareness that will liberate both men and women from all psychological and spiritual thralldom to the fallen beings. Awaken people to the reality that we are spiritual beings and that we can co-create a new future by working with the ascended masters. I especially call for …

[Make your own calls here.]

Part 1

1. Astrea, I call forth the judgment of Christ upon the dark forces behind the use of computer technology to make women artificially set a standard of beauty that no real woman could live up to.

Astrea, loving Being white,
your Presence is my pure delight,
your sword and circle white and blue,
the astral plane is cutting through.

Astrea, come accelerate,
with purity I do vibrate,
release the fire so blue and white,
my aura filled with vibrant light.

2. Astrea, I call forth the judgment of Christ upon the dark forces behind the industry that is based on projecting this belief that women should look a certain way and that it is perfectly normal and acceptable that women should dress like what they see in the advertisements, movies or TV series.

Astrea, calm the raging storm,
so purity will be the norm,
my aura filled with blue and white,
with shining armor, like a knight.

Astrea, come accelerate,
with purity I do vibrate,
release the fire so blue and white,
my aura filled with vibrant light.

3. Astrea, I call forth the judgment of Christ upon the dark forces behind the industry that is projecting that women should appear sexually attractive to men, they should appeal to men's sex drive, and this supposedly gives a woman a certain status in the eyes of many people.

Astrea, come and cut me free,
from every binding entity,
let astral forces all be bound,
true freedom I have surely found.

Astrea, come accelerate,
with purity I do vibrate,
release the fire so blue and white,
my aura filled with vibrant light.

4. Astrea, I call forth the judgment of Christ upon the dark forces behind the ideas at the identity level that cause women to identify themselves based on their sexual attractiveness. They identify themselves as sexual beings who should be attractive to men, who should be available to men.

> Astrea, I sincerely urge,
> from demons all, do me purge,
> consume them all and take me higher,
> I will endure your cleansing fire.

> **Astrea, come accelerate,**
> **with purity I do vibrate,**
> **release the fire so blue and white,**
> **my aura filled with vibrant light.**

5. Astrea, I call forth the judgment of Christ upon the dark forces that give women a certain self-image that makes them feel superior because of their sex-appeal.

> Astrea, do all spirits bind,
> so that I am no longer blind,
> I see the spirit and its twin,
> the victory of Christ I win.

> **Astrea, come accelerate,**
> **with purity I do vibrate,**
> **release the fire so blue and white,**
> **my aura filled with vibrant light.**

6. Astrea, I call forth the judgment of Christ upon the dark forces that make some women feel powerful because they could make any man want to have sex with them. Then, by denying the sex after the man wants it, they gain a perverted sense of power.

> Astrea, clear my every cell,
> from energies of death and hell,
> my body is now free to grow,
> each cell emits an inner glow.

**Astrea, come accelerate,
with purity I do vibrate,
release the fire so blue and white,
my aura filled with vibrant light.**

7. Astrea, I call forth the judgment of Christ upon the dark forces behind women who have used sex appeal to gain a sense of power or gain political positions and political influence.

Astrea, clear my feeling mind,
in purity my peace I find,
with higher feeling you release,
I co-create in perfect peace.

**Astrea, come accelerate,
with purity I do vibrate,
release the fire so blue and white,
my aura filled with vibrant light.**

8. Astrea, I call forth the judgment of Christ upon the dark forces who use the women's liberation movement to make some women believe that women should use any means to gain power in a male-dominated society and if sex works, then why not use it?

Astrea, clear my mental realm,
my Christ self always at the helm,
I see now how to manifest,
the matrix that for all is best.

**Astrea, come accelerate,
with purity I do vibrate,
release the fire so blue and white,
my aura filled with vibrant light.**

9. Astrea, I call forth the judgment of Christ upon the dark forces behind causing women to objectify themselves in order to gain influence in a male-dominated society.

Astrea, with great clarity,
I claim a new identity,
etheric blueprint I now see,
I co-create more consciously.

Astrea, come accelerate,
with purity I do vibrate,
release the fire so blue and white,
my aura filled with vibrant light.

Part 2

1. Astrea, awaken people to see that if we believe that a woman should be beautiful according to a standard defined in our particular society and culture, then already there at the identity level we are objectifying women.

Astrea, loving Being white,
your Presence is my pure delight,
your sword and circle white and blue,
the astral plane is cutting through.

Astrea, come accelerate,
with purity I do vibrate,
release the fire so blue and white,
my aura filled with vibrant light.

2. Astrea, I call forth the judgment of Christ upon the dark forces behind the industry that is projecting at women that they can be in control of their physical appearance.

Astrea, calm the raging storm,
so purity will be the norm,
my aura filled with blue and white,
with shining armor, like a knight.

Astrea, come accelerate,
with purity I do vibrate,

release the fire so blue and white,
my aura filled with vibrant light.

3. Astrea, help all women realize there is a limit to how much we can improve our physical appearance with these means that are available because we cannot change your genetic inheritance. Thus, this belief objectifies women.

Astrea, come and cut me free,
from every binding entity,
let astral forces all be bound,
true freedom I have surely found.

Astrea, come accelerate,
with purity I do vibrate,
release the fire so blue and white,
my aura filled with vibrant light.

4. Astrea, awaken people to see that the beauty industry creates an image, and an image is an object. It projects this image onto all women and it projects that they should strive to live up to it, and if they cannot, they should feel bad about this.

Astrea, I sincerely urge,
from demons all, do me purge,
consume them all and take me higher,
I will endure your cleansing fire.

Astrea, come accelerate,
with purity I do vibrate,
release the fire so blue and white,
my aura filled with vibrant light.

5. Astrea, I call forth the judgment of Christ upon the dark forces behind the projection that women should live up to this image that makes them attractive to men.

Astrea, do all spirits bind,
so that I am no longer blind,

I see the spirit and its twin,
the victory of Christ I win.

**Astrea, come accelerate,
with purity I do vibrate,
release the fire so blue and white,
my aura filled with vibrant light.**

6. Astrea, I call forth the judgment of Christ upon the dark forces that make women feel they should have men making advances towards them and feeling they should give in to this.

Astrea, clear my every cell,
from energies of death and hell,
my body is now free to grow,
each cell emits an inner glow.

**Astrea, come accelerate,
with purity I do vibrate,
release the fire so blue and white,
my aura filled with vibrant light.**

7. Astrea, cut women free so they do not get into relationships that are abusive because they are so compelled to give in to the first man that comes and makes advances towards them.

Astrea, clear my feeling mind,
in purity my peace I find,
with higher feeling you release,
I co-create in perfect peace.

**Astrea, come accelerate,
with purity I do vibrate,
release the fire so blue and white,
my aura filled with vibrant light.**

8. Astrea, cut women free to evaluate: "Is this the kind of man I want a relationship with? Is this the kind of man I even want to have sex with? Is this the kind of man I want to have a long-term relationship with? Is this

the kind of man I want to start a family with and that I potentially want to live with the rest of my life?"

Astrea, clear my mental realm,
my Christ self always at the helm,
I see now how to manifest,
the matrix that for all is best.

Astrea, come accelerate,
with purity I do vibrate,
release the fire so blue and white,
my aura filled with vibrant light.

9. Astrea, I call forth the judgment of Christ upon the dark forces behind women being put in a position where they are constantly subjected to this sexual aggression from men, often feeling they cannot defend themselves against it.

Astrea, with great clarity,
I claim a new identity,
etheric blueprint I now see,
I co-create more consciously.

Astrea, come accelerate,
with purity I do vibrate,
release the fire so blue and white,
my aura filled with vibrant light.

Part 3

1. Astrea, I call forth the judgment of Christ upon the dark forces behind women feeling increasingly powerless to stop this sexual harassment, to stop this sexual exploitation, these aggressive advances from men.

Astrea, loving Being white,
your Presence is my pure delight,

your sword and circle white and blue,
the astral plane is cutting through.

**Astrea, come accelerate,
with purity I do vibrate,
release the fire so blue and white,
my aura filled with vibrant light.**

2. Astrea, cut free a critical mass of women from the ideal that they should be sexually attractive to men, so they can say: "We need to stop this. This has gone too far."

Astrea, calm the raging storm,
so purity will be the norm,
my aura filled with blue and white,
with shining armor, like a knight.

**Astrea, come accelerate,
with purity I do vibrate,
release the fire so blue and white,
my aura filled with vibrant light.**

3. Astrea, I call forth the judgment of Christ upon the fallen beings who in the process of manipulating men and women have used the sex drive.

Astrea, come and cut me free,
from every binding entity,
let astral forces all be bound,
true freedom I have surely found.

**Astrea, come accelerate,
with purity I do vibrate,
release the fire so blue and white,
my aura filled with vibrant light.**

4. Astrea, I call forth the judgment of Christ upon the fallen beings who have put out these ideas, even philosophies and religions, that inflate the sex drive of men artificially, to project that men should be sexual conquerors, that they should have sex with as many women as possible.

Astrea, I sincerely urge,
from demons all, do me purge,
consume them all and take me higher,
I will endure your cleansing fire.

Astrea, come accelerate,
with purity I do vibrate,
release the fire so blue and white,
my aura filled with vibrant light.

5. Astrea, I call forth the judgment of Christ upon the fallen beings who created the male archetype of this strong masculine man who is the sexual conqueror who can make any woman give in to his advances or even make any woman want to have sex with him, because he is the alpha male and he is the one that she wants to have children with.

Astrea, do all spirits bind,
so that I am no longer blind,
I see the spirit and its twin,
the victory of Christ I win.

Astrea, come accelerate,
with purity I do vibrate,
release the fire so blue and white,
my aura filled with vibrant light.

6. Astrea, I call forth the judgment of Christ upon the fallen beings who created the female archetype that the woman is the passive recipient of the man's sexual advances, that she should accept this in order to carry on the human race because she should be available to have children and therefore propagate the race.

Astrea, clear my every cell,
from energies of death and hell,
my body is now free to grow,
each cell emits an inner glow.

Astrea, come accelerate,
with purity I do vibrate,

release the fire so blue and white,
my aura filled with vibrant light.

7. Astrea, cut people free to see that this has no reality to it whatsoever. There is no spiritual reality to it. There is not even a physical, evolutionary reality to it because animals do not have sex all the time.

Astrea, clear my feeling mind,
in purity my peace I find,
with higher feeling you release,
I co-create in perfect peace.

Astrea, come accelerate,
with purity I do vibrate,
release the fire so blue and white,
my aura filled with vibrant light.

8. Astrea, cut people free to see that animals are only sexually active for the purpose of having offspring and then the rest of the year, sex does not even enter their minds, so why is it not that way in humans?

Astrea, clear my mental realm,
my Christ self always at the helm,
I see now how to manifest,
the matrix that for all is best.

Astrea, come accelerate,
with purity I do vibrate,
release the fire so blue and white,
my aura filled with vibrant light.

9. Astrea, cut people free to see that if humans were biological animals, then we would have the same approach to sex that all animals have. Since human beings clearly do not, human beings must be more than animals.

Astrea, with great clarity,
I claim a new identity,
etheric blueprint I now see,
I co-create more consciously.

**Astrea, come accelerate,
with purity I do vibrate,
release the fire so blue and white,
my aura filled with vibrant light.**

Part 4

1. Astrea, cut people free to see that if human beings are not exclusively driven by their biological drives, then human sexual activity cannot be exclusively a biological activity.

Astrea, loving Being white,
your Presence is my pure delight,
your sword and circle white and blue,
the astral plane is cutting through.

**Astrea, come accelerate,
with purity I do vibrate,
release the fire so blue and white,
my aura filled with vibrant light.**

2. Astrea, cut people free to see that sex is driven by something in the psychology, meaning that people can be manipulated and the sex drive can be artificially accelerated and multiplied to the point where the sex drive controls people's behavior and takes away the unique aspect of being human, namely that we have free conscious will.

Astrea, calm the raging storm,
so purity will be the norm,
my aura filled with blue and white,
with shining armor, like a knight.

**Astrea, come accelerate,
with purity I do vibrate,
release the fire so blue and white,
my aura filled with vibrant light.**

3. Astrea, cut people free to see that what is unique to humans is the freedom of will, the conscious will to make decisions about our actions, about our feelings, about our mental beliefs and about our sense of identity.

> Astrea, come and cut me free,
> from every binding entity,
> let astral forces all be bound,
> true freedom I have surely found.

> **Astrea, come accelerate,**
> **with purity I do vibrate,**
> **release the fire so blue and white,**
> **my aura filled with vibrant light.**

4. Astrea, cut people free to see that without freedom of will, we are not really humans, we are not living up to the potential for a human being, but neither are we animals, we are something in between. We are a mechanized creation or a more conscious animal, but still not fully self-aware.

> Astrea, I sincerely urge,
> from demons all, do me purge,
> consume them all and take me higher,
> I will endure your cleansing fire.

> **Astrea, come accelerate,**
> **with purity I do vibrate,**
> **release the fire so blue and white,**
> **my aura filled with vibrant light.**

5. Astrea, cut people free to see there are fallen beings, there are narcissistic beings, who are only seeking to manipulate the rest of the population. They do not exist just in the physical realm, but they also exist in the other three realms and they have a very complex agenda of manipulating human beings.

> Astrea, do all spirits bind,
> so that I am no longer blind,
> I see the spirit and its twin,
> the victory of Christ I win.

Astrea, come accelerate,
with purity I do vibrate,
release the fire so blue and white,
my aura filled with vibrant light.

6. Astrea, cut people free to see that these fallen beings are behind all forms of human manipulation, but especially the use of sex and the sexual tension between men and women. They have artificially inflated that tension, partly in order to control people, partly in order to just create chaos and conflict.

Astrea, clear my every cell,
from energies of death and hell,
my body is now free to grow,
each cell emits an inner glow.

Astrea, come accelerate,
with purity I do vibrate,
release the fire so blue and white,
my aura filled with vibrant light.

7. Astrea, cut people free to see that concerning the increase in sexual exploitation of women and sexual harassment, there is no epic agenda behind it, but there are certain fallen beings who are using this to just create chaos.

Astrea, clear my feeling mind,
in purity my peace I find,
with higher feeling you release,
I co-create in perfect peace.

Astrea, come accelerate,
with purity I do vibrate,
release the fire so blue and white,
my aura filled with vibrant light.

8. Astrea, cut people free to see that the fallen beings did not want the modern democracies to emerge. They preferred a more dictatorial form

of government, and they are using anything they *can* to create chaos and disorder that might break down these societies.

Astrea, clear my mental realm,
my Christ self always at the helm,
I see now how to manifest,
the matrix that for all is best.

Astrea, come accelerate,
with purity I do vibrate,
release the fire so blue and white,
my aura filled with vibrant light.

9. Astrea, cut people free to see that there is no rational, biological or spiritual reason that women should allow themselves to become sexual objects. It is simply a destructive movement, a destructive drive and we need to become aware of this and resist it.

Astrea, with great clarity,
I claim a new identity,
etheric blueprint I now see,
I co-create more consciously.

Astrea, come accelerate,
with purity I do vibrate,
release the fire so blue and white,
my aura filled with vibrant light.

Part 5

1. Astrea, cut women free to stand up and say: "Enough! We have had enough of being appointed as sexual objects and we will not stand for this anymore."

Astrea, loving Being white,
your Presence is my pure delight,

your sword and circle white and blue,
the astral plane is cutting through.

**Astrea, come accelerate,
with purity I do vibrate,
release the fire so blue and white,
my aura filled with vibrant light.**

2. Astrea, bind the fallen beings and consume the collective entities behind
the creation of the archetype for the powerful man, the man who is able to
lead, as a man who is sexually active, and should not be confining his sexual activity to just one woman so having a mistress is perfectly acceptable.

Astrea, calm the raging storm,
so purity will be the norm,
my aura filled with blue and white,
with shining armor, like a knight.

**Astrea, come accelerate,
with purity I do vibrate,
release the fire so blue and white,
my aura filled with vibrant light.**

3. Astrea, cut people free to see that this archetype of the powerful man
who is the leader, objectifies women. Women are simply objects for men's
sexual exploitation, to satisfy men's sexual desire.

Astrea, come and cut me free,
from every binding entity,
let astral forces all be bound,
true freedom I have surely found.

**Astrea, come accelerate,
with purity I do vibrate,
release the fire so blue and white,
my aura filled with vibrant light.**

4. Astrea, cut people free to see that the majority of politicians, people
in the media, many scientists, many actors, writers and other influential

people believe in and accept this archetype for the male leader: the important man, the powerful man.

Astrea, I sincerely urge,
from demons all, do me purge,
consume them all and take me higher,
I will endure your cleansing fire.

Astrea, come accelerate,
with purity I do vibrate,
release the fire so blue and white,
my aura filled with vibrant light.

5. Astrea, cut people free to see that in order to change the sexual objectification of women, we need to get the decision makers, most of whom are men, to agree to this. We cannot get them to agree to this when their minds are taken over by this male archetype that wants to objectify women.

Astrea, do all spirits bind,
so that I am no longer blind,
I see the spirit and its twin,
the victory of Christ I win.

Astrea, come accelerate,
with purity I do vibrate,
release the fire so blue and white,
my aura filled with vibrant light.

6. Astrea, cut free the women in embodiment who are able to promote this process and drive the shifts in society, so there will be a raising of awareness. Cut free women to begin to speak out about topics they have never spoken out about before. Cut free men to respond to this.

Astrea, clear my every cell,
from energies of death and hell,
my body is now free to grow,
each cell emits an inner glow.

Astrea, come accelerate,
with purity I do vibrate,
release the fire so blue and white,
my aura filled with vibrant light.

7. Astrea, cut people free to create a new women's liberation movement that goes much deeper and demands more than political and economic freedom, more than equality, but also demands psychological freedom.

Astrea, clear my feeling mind,
in purity my peace I find,
with higher feeling you release,
I co-create in perfect peace.

Astrea, come accelerate,
with purity I do vibrate,
release the fire so blue and white,
my aura filled with vibrant light.

8. Astrea, cut people free to see that when a woman is made a sexual object, her psychological freedom is taken away. When a man is sexually addicted and therefore wants to objectify women, his psychological freedom is taken away as well.

Astrea, clear my mental realm,
my Christ self always at the helm,
I see now how to manifest,
the matrix that for all is best.

Astrea, come accelerate,
with purity I do vibrate,
release the fire so blue and white,
my aura filled with vibrant light.

9. Astrea, cut people free to see the need to not only liberate women psychologically, but also to liberate men. There is a historic opportunity for women to be the driving force in the liberation of society at the psychological level and creating a new revolution in society that is aimed at bringing psychological freedom.

Astrea, with great clarity,
I claim a new identity,
etheric blueprint I now see,
I co-create more consciously.

Astrea, come accelerate,
with purity I do vibrate,
release the fire so blue and white,
my aura filled with vibrant light.

Sealing

In the name of the I AM THAT I AM, I accept that Archangel Michael, Astrea and Shiva form an impenetrable shield around myself and all constructive people, sealing us from all fear-based energies in all four octaves. I accept that the Light of God is consuming and transforming all fear-based energies that make up the dark forces working against the liberation of women on earth!

31 | WHY THE POWER ELITE WANTS TO SUPPRESS WOMEN

I am the Ascended Master Mother Mary. I wish to continue the remarks made by Astrea on sex because there is more to be said about the topic. What you see in the world today is that sex has been turned into something that, if we look at the Fourth Ray of purity associated with the base chakra, we can say that sex has become a very dirty, a very impure activity in many cases. You see perversions of sex, degradations of sex, you see how the entire concept of sexuality has been pulled down to a much lower level than it was a generation or two ago. I am not saying this is purely caused by the sexual revolution, but it should give pause that it has accompanied the sexual revolution. Supposedly, the more free people have become to express their sexuality, the more "dirty" the expression of that sexuality has become and the more abusive it has become, especially towards women.

Why is this? Well, you cannot understand this unless you understand that there are some very narcissistic, self-centered, insensitive beings who are manipulating everything on earth to the extent that they are able to do so—to the extent that they can get human beings or the population to go along with this manipulation or to not be aware of this manipulation. The fallen beings have deliberately done everything they could to pull sex down to, first, being a purely physical activity, then being a lower activity that most people will see as something impure. Many, many people around the world can see that many of the sexual activities that are being promoted out there are impure.

Why has this happened? Well, it has happened for two main reasons: One is actually that the more impure an activity becomes (the more base, the more gross, the more primitive it becomes) the more addictive it can become for at least some people. Of course, the more impure an activity becomes, the more it can force people who engage in the activity to release energy, to release light through that activity. We have said before, for example that one of the most (we might say) efficient ways to force people to release light is through torture, which is obviously a very impure activity. The fallen beings and the collective entities in the emotional realm have absolutely no sensitivity to life, no compunctions about forcing people to release the energy that they need in order to survive and in order to do what they want to do.

The other thing that is part of the entire phenomenon of sexual addiction is that the fallen beings want to detract people from their higher goals in life. The fallen beings want to control the population, and they can do that best if the people are not activating their higher chakras, from the heart chakra and above. These are the chakras that primarily express the higher qualities, what you might call the more spiritual or creative qualities. You have the teaching given by Astrea that you have the seven chakras on a vertical line, and the lowest of the chakras is the base chakra and the energy descends first to the base chakra.

There is actually a reason for this, and it is that the base chakra is not only the center of the sexual function and the sexual organs, but of the life force that is needed to drive the physical body, to keep the physical body alive. When you are in a physical body, you might say that the basic need that you have is to keep the physical body alive because that is the foundation for your spiritual growth. That is why the energy first descends there; it upholds the physical body, upholds the nervous system, upholds the brain. Then, when these basic functions of the physical body are taken care of, the energy that is left over can rise up through the higher chakras, first the heart chakra, then throat, third eye, and crown chakra. As these centers are activated, people become more aware, they become more spiritual, they become more connected, more intuitive, more connected to the whole.

The fallen beings want to stop Christhood

This is what the fallen beings want to prevent because people who are spiritual and who are walking the path to Christhood (which you can only do when all seven chakras are activated) are a threat to the fallen beings. They cannot be controlled by the fallen beings and they might show people a way out of the control. They want to get as many people as possible to concentrate the energy in the base chakra as a diversion so there is not enough energy left over to rise up. When a man is addicted to sex for example and spends most of his attention on sex and his time and energy engaging in sex or fantasizing about it, then this pulls his energy out through the base chakra and there is very little left to rise up to activate the other chakras.

There are of course many agendas that the fallen beings have. You have the entire concept, as Astrea said, that some religions believe that it was sexual activity that caused the fall of man. You have today, where you see sexual activity becoming more and more dirty, and all of this works together to create an attitude that is very much out there in the collective consciousness, but often is unspoken or not written down. You can find it written down in some specifically eastern religions and also in the Christian religion, and it is that sex is contrary to your spiritual growth, is an enemy of your spiritual goals, the limitation of your spiritual growth. You can therefore find the whole ideal that you see outpictured in the Catholic church where priests are not allowed to marry and they, therefore, supposedly should not have sex, which of course you all know is largely a lie. At least some priests do manage to be celibate for a lifetime. You have many eastern religions, gurus, the whole concept of monks and nuns and sages and spiritual people who are living a life of renunciation. They are living as recluses and they are abstaining from sexual activity and many other physical activities.

You have this ideal that has been created that spiritual growth means that you have to not have sex. What is one of the purposes of this? It is to prevent as many people as possible from following the spiritual path so they do not become a threat to the fallen beings. The fallen beings have at the same time sought to inflate the sexual desire of most people, both men and women. People are forced with this choice, they think, between giving up sex, having sex or pursuing the spiritual path. In other words they think they have to give up sex in order to really pursue a spiritual path, so many people do not want to pursue a spiritual path. They either do not know about it or, if they are confronted with it, they do not want to give up sex in order to grow spiritually.

Sex is not inherently anti-spiritual

The first thing I want to address here is that, from a spiritual, ascended master perspective, there is nothing inherently impure or anti-spiritual about sex. You are in a physical body on earth. One of the activities you can do with this physical body is to have sex. There is, from an ascended master perspective, nothing inherently impure about many bodily activities. Now, this does not mean that I say sex is always pure because, as I have said, sex can become one of the most dirty and debased of human activities, but that goes for any activity. There is nothing inherently impure about it. It is entirely possible to be sexually active and walk the spiritual path, including the path to Christhood or Buddhahood while being sexually active.

Why do you then have this ideal, going far back? Well, partly because of the fallen beings, partly because there is of course a certain reality here. As I have said, there is a certain amount of energy. Dependent on your level of consciousness, there is a certain amount of energy that descends from your I AM Presence into your four lower bodies. In order to make spiritual progress, there has to be some of that energy that rises up to the higher chakras and activates those chakras. The question simply is: How much of the amount of energy that you are receiving at any given time is used in what we might call physical, bodily activities in the physical octave, and how much of it is left over to activate the higher chakras? It is simply not necessary, as Gautama Buddha also discovered after living as an ascetic for six years, to renounce all worldly or physical activities in order to pursue spiritual growth. You have to find a way so that all of the energy you receive from your I AM Presence is not spent on physical activities, so there is something left over to rise to the higher chakras and activate them. This of course means that you have to look at the activities you engage in, and you have to look at how much energy you are spending on these activities and this includes sex.

It is perfectly possible, and in fact, we have said several times that the ideal for the Aquarian Age is not that spiritual people live an ascetic lifestyle, but that you live an active life in society (have a family, have a relationship), but you are still pursuing spiritual growth. You need to evaluate then that you do not need to refrain from having sex, but obviously you cannot go into the extreme that men, who are addicted to sex are into, of spending most of their time and energy on sexual activity. Then, there is nothing left over. You need to find a more balanced approach to this and this is what you really can do only when you live in a committed relationship with one partner and you are dedicated to fulfilling each others needs, both sexual and otherwise. You can help each other with the physical needs and to deal with these needs, to take care of these needs, in such a way that you both have energy left over to rise up to the other chakras. In other words, this is simply a spiritual reality. It is so to speak the economics of spiritual growth. There has to be a balance between the money coming in and the money going out—basic economic theory.

This is what has then been perverted by the fallen beings into these ideas that sex is an enemy of your spiritual growth, will stop your spiritual growth, or even prevent it entirely, even prevent your salvation, which some believe. We are not saying that you cannot make spiritual growth by renouncing sex. For some people it can be the fastest way to make spiritual growth and they may still want to do it. What we are saying is that for the majority of people in this age and cycle we are in, it is not necessary to do this. You can actually in many cases make faster spiritual growth by living an active life in society, living in a relationship, because this brings out your reactionary patterns so you have a chance to see them.

There are people, both in the past and now, who have lived the life of a recluse where they sit in an isolated, controlled environment and meditate all day. While it can lead to some growth, it will not in many cases lead to the fastest growth because when you are in a controlled environment, what stirs up your reactionary patterns, your separate selves? You can very easily get yourself in a state of mind where you think you are spiritual, you think you are in harmony but it is simply because nothing stirs up your unresolved psychology so you do not see it. You believe you do not even have it. There are people who have sat there for years and decades in a meditative environment and made hardly any progress in that time. That is why an active life is what we recommend for most people in this age. There can be exceptions and you need to follow your intuition on this.

What I wanted to say here is this (just as a conclusion): sex is not in itself an impure activity, it can *become* a very pure activity. If two partners are dedicated to helping each other grow spiritually, they can purify their sexual desires, they can purify their base chakras, they can protect themselves, cut themselves free from these collective entities. They can resolve their separate selves relating to sex because all of you (all of us who have been in embodiment) will have such separate selves related to sex because of the manipulation that has been going on for so long. Once you do this, you can actually be sexually active in a way that does not detract from your spiritual growth.

The physical world is not an enemy of spiritual growth

The other thing is again sexual activity or many bodily activities are not the enemies of your spiritual growth. Why is this? Because, why are you in physical embodiment in the first place? If you look at some of these spiritual ideas that are floating around out there about spiritual growth and about not only sex, but even the matter realm or the physical body being an enemy of your spiritual growth, what are they actually saying without anybody really realizing what they are saying? They are saying that the purpose of life in the material realm is to get out of here as quickly as possible. They might even be saying that it was almost a mistake that you came here. But, what have we attempted to say in our books, from *Healing your Spiritual Traumas* and forward?

Why did you come to earth? Because your I AM Presence had a positive goal and wanted to experience something on earth and it wanted to experience itself in this environment. The purpose is not to get out of here as quickly as possible. The purpose is to have certain experiences on earth because they actually advance the spiritual growth of your I AM Presence, not necessarily of your outer self, your soul, your four lower bodies, but they do advance the spiritual growth of your I AM Presence. Now, there can be some people who have been on earth for a long time and who are in (what they in their Divine plans define as) their last embodiment. Their goal is to make their ascension after this lifetime and of course you have to then be more focused on fulfilling that goal, but you will most likely also have fulfilled many of the desires to have experiences on earth.

Where objectification of people came from

I now want to shift gears. I am going to continue to talk about what Astrea said about the objectification of women. If we now step back through the layers of insight that Astrea gave us, we can ask the question: Where does objectification in general come from? This entire concept, idea, behavior, attitude to life that human beings can be looked at as mere objects, where does it come from? Do human beings naturally have this tendency to objectify other human beings, thereby implicitly objectifying themselves? The reality is that they do not. Before fallen beings came to earth, human beings did not objectify each other. They can theoretically do it by going into duality because, by going into duality, you are to some degree objectifying everything. As we have said, you are looking at an object, you are looking at yourself as a subject, and there is an object that is external to you and that object is actually objectified.

What you saw on earth before the fallen beings came is that beyond this general objectification of everything, there was not the kind of objectification you see today. There was still what we have called the basic humanity, the essential humanity, where even though you see yourself as a subject and you see that you are surrounded by objects, you are still aware that human beings are not objects as for example rocks or trees. Human beings are also conscious self-aware beings, they have thoughts, they have feelings, and when you are connected to the basic humanity, you realize that what you do to another person will generate certain thoughts and feelings in that person and therefore you are open to what is the by-word, the motto of all spiritual, religious teachings: "Do unto others as you want them to do to you." You are aware that if you do to others what does not harm them, then others will not do something to you that harms you and this is in everybody's best interest.

Now, you have the situation where the fallen beings come to earth and the fallen beings, because they have fallen, they have rebelled against the upward movement of self-transcendence. You can say, what is the essence of self-transcendence? Well, when you transcend yourself you are moving out of any tendency to look at yourself as a fixed entity, as something that is clearly defined, unchangeable. You are letting a self die, you are in a sense freeing yourself from any tendency to look at that self as an object, therefore looking at yourself as an object. The fallen beings rebelled against this process and in doing so they objectified themselves because they objectified the self that they would not give up, that they would not let die in order to follow Christ. Therefore, they objectified everything else, they objectified the ascended masters, they objectified God, they objectified everything around them. Now the fallen beings come to earth and they come in with a mindset that the human beings on earth are just objects for them. Fallen beings are completely self-centered, they are what you today call narcissists or psychopaths or sociopaths because they are completely focused on themselves and what they want, completely insensitive to what they do to others, how that affects those other people.

This is the total objectification: Human beings are just objects for the fallen beings, they have an agenda, they have certain desires. First of all, they want to have power, they want to set themselves up as having as much power as can possibly be gained on earth. What does that mean? That means they have to get the human population on earth to submit to them as their leaders so that people will blindly follow the command of the leader. This is what you see in dictatorial nations throughout the ages. You see this tendency that this one person sets himself up as a dictator, he is completely insensitive to those who are under him and he will command them to go to war and millions of them are killed and he has absolutely no compassion or any kind of problem with this happening. For the fallen beings, human beings are nothing but objects. You are only objects to the fallen beings.

The suppression of women comes from the power elite

I know very well that it is not quite realistic in the short term to make the general population aware of fallen beings and accept this idea. I can assure you that there are many, many women in all countries, but especially there are many in the more developed nations, the modern democracies, who are ready to take a step up in their recognition of their own situation. There are many women who are ready to see, and by you making the calls they can come to see, that it simply is not realistic, and it is not actually reasonable or fair, to blame the suppression of women on men in general. There was a time when the women's liberation movement was very negative, or many people were very negative towards men in general. This was a, we might say, necessary step to break through the resistance to women getting more equal rights but it is not constructive anymore and many women have actually already moved out of it.

What can happen is that there can be this awakening, this shift in awareness, where women begin to realize that we need to be more nuanced; we need to be more discerning, we need to be smarter and not say that women are suppressed by men in general. Instead, we need to identify that throughout history and even today, women are suppressed by a specific group of people. Most of these people are men but there can be a few women among them if you look at history. The vast majority are men and what is their characteristic? They have power, they form an elite; they set themselves up as an elite because they think they are better, more capable, have more authority, have more power and therefore are better able to lead the population than the average person. They have an elitist mindset, they have an almost unlimited desire for power and for privilege, and once they have that power and that privilege, they are very reluctant to give it up. This is the force on earth that has historically and today, suppressed women: the power elite.

In order to truly liberate women, you need to liberate women from the influence of the power elite. You may say: "But aren't there some modern democracies where, because we have a democracy, there is no longer such a big influence by the power elite, there is no longer such a power elite as there used to be?" I would say: "Is that so?" Is it so that the modern democracies do not have a power elite? Well, you do not have a power elite like you saw in the feudal societies of the Middle Ages in Europe. You do not have a small group of landlords and noblemen and a king or emperor who has physical, military and political control over the population—*that* is true. You still have a power elite that has a less obvious control of the population. First of all, you have in most nations a financial power elite, an economic power elite that has control over the financial system of the earth. We have said before that in the United States more and more money, a greater and greater percentage of the wealth, is concentrated in the hands of fewer and fewer people. You see the same tendency worldwide.

You see that there is a power elite, but now they are not using military or political power in an open way, they are using it indirectly by the influence they have because they control the money and the money system. They control the big businesses and therefore they can, behind the surface, put pressure on even a democratically elected government. What have you seen, my beloved, in this Corona virus crisis? Democratic governments, what have they felt a need to do? Stimulate the economy by creating money or by borrowing money. Where have they given that money out? Well, primarily to the financial institutions and the financial elite. Why not give it, as we have said, directly to the people? Why not indeed? So this proves to you that there is a power elite. Even in the so-called most advanced democratic nations, there is still a power elite.

You also need to recognize that there is a political power elite. As Astrea has talked about in America, you have many of the leaders both in the political arena and in the economic arena, and among actors, writers and other people who believe they are opinion makers in society, who have this very elitist mindset. What women have the potential to recognize is that the members of this power elite, they have a very derogatory attitude to women.

Astrea mentioned how many of these people have a mistress and they are not about to do anything too active about the sexual harassment or exploitation of women in modern democracies because it would limit their sexual freedom as they see it. It goes beyond this, it goes beyond to where you can actually look at history and you can look at the power elites, and you can say, what is characteristic of these power elites? Well, they have a certain goal that they want to achieve and the people in their nation are simply objects for achieving that goal. You are not real human beings, you are just objects.

What the power elite wants from women

Men might be objects who can be forced into military service so the power elite can wage war against a rivaling power elite in another country and therefore strive towards this fantasy goal of world domination. Now look at how the power elites of history, and even today, have looked at women. Women are also objects. They have not traditionally, only in recent decades, put women into military service but women have still been objects because what are they needed for? First of all, they are needed to produce children that can continue to ensure that the power elite has, number one, soldiers that they can use in war, number two, workers, both men and women who can do all the dirty work for them because you never see the power elite being out there doing the dirty work on a factory or in the fields on a hot day.

The power elite, they want soldiers to wage war and they want workers to do all the practical work for them. That gives them a privileged position and that gives them an economic benefit so that they can reap most of the money or the wealth that is produced by the people's labor. You see traditionally that many among this power elite, they look at women as primarily there to raise children. They have created these, even religions, even political ideologies, but even these subtle beliefs that are floating around in the collective consciousness without being recognized, that say that women should stay at home, they should focus on being mothers and taking care of their husbands and so on. You will see even today if you look at the business elite in many countries that they are running a business, they are on an epic cause to grow that business to the biggest possible size and to take over the competitors. In order to do this, they need to have some men who are willing to spend 60-80 hours a week on the job so they can be more efficient than the competing business. How can they have men who can do this unless they have women at home taking care of all the practical aspects of the household and the children? This is the role that this power elite, even today and historically, wants women to be confined to.

Of course, the power elite also wants women to be available for sexual exploitation, not necessarily by themselves, but they also want the men who are working for them or the men who are soldiers to have a way to have their sexual needs fulfilled, therefore women can be forced into that role. You saw for example how the Japanese Empire when it occupied Korea, forced many women into prostitution as they use this nice word "comfort women" for Japanese soldiers, but they were not comfort women. They were forced into prostitution and exploited by the power elite of Japan. You see the same throughout the world and throughout history.

You see that women are in a unique position because you are the most likely to be open to these ideas, to be open to see the need to liberate yourself, and thereby also liberate men and society from this narcissistic power elite. Again, can the general population of women accept the idea of fallen beings? Probably not but they can certainly, many of them, come to accept the idea of a narcissistic power elite that has ruled this planet as far as we can look back in history. It is high time to do something about this and liberate women from being confined to these roles where they are simply objects serving this cause of the power elite.

Women can bring real change in society

Why is it that women are in a unique position to do this? Because women can more easily see through the epic mindset than men can. Men have traditionally (and this is, as we have said before, an aspect of the perverted male psychology that has been created on earth) been more likely to be pulled into fighting for these epic causes, espousing an epic cause, being willing to sacrifice their lives or being willing to kill other people to promote this epic cause. Women have often looked at these epic causes, and looked at how the men are all fired up to go out and fight in the crusades or this or that, and they have quietly shaken their heads, knowing they could not really say anything and just waited for how things would outplay themselves. There is of course a growing awareness among women of the need for them to simply say "Stop!" when their husbands cannot say stop, and say: "Why are you working so much? Is it really worth it? Do we need that money? Do you really need that promotion? Do you really need to spend your entire life working in this corporate environment and then you die two years after you retire, like this person and that person did before you?"

Women are not as easily caught up in this, partly because they are more focused on the family, their children, but also because women are more open to spiritual growth in general than men. Men are, in general, more focused on physical activities and women are more open to spiritual activities. This is a very important turning point in history we are approaching where women can really shift the focus of society, shift the focus of relationships. What women can be the forerunners for is a sort of movement that steps back and looks at society and says: "Where are we going? What are we doing? If we continue doing what we are doing now, where will that take us? And is that really where we want to go?"

When you look at the last hundred years in the modern democracies, the economy has been improved, most people have had their economic situation improved, they have had greater political and economic freedom, women have been given greater freedom, there is more and more equality. Is this a goal in itself? Is economic growth a goal in itself? Should we just then continue to try to get richer and richer? We already have more material goods than we need, so should we just continue, mindlessly accumulating material goods indefinitely? Or does there come a point where we say: "What's the purpose of having a comfortable material lifestyle? What can we do with it?" That is where there can be, and there already is on the way, an awakening among women who say: "Well, there has to be a higher purpose for this. It can't be in order to just be more and more comfortable, or to travel, or to have bigger cars, or more summer houses, or this or that, there must be a real purpose here." That purpose is, as we have said before, self-actualization, self-improvement, personal growth, a raising of consciousness. This can really have an impact on some of these modern democracies.

There can be a shift in focus of the entire country where there is a shift that says: "It isn't the purpose of our society to provide more and more material wealth and goods. The purpose is to have a better quality of life and we get that only through learning about the human psychology, what makes us happy, what makes us feel fulfilled, and focusing on this." We have said before that the rise in mental illness in many of these modern nations is a sign that many people are ready to pursue self-actualization, but they do not know what to do with it, society does not give them any help. This is why you see this rise in mental illness that is forcing society to change something because otherwise it will take the social safety nets and the health-care systems down. Women can be the forerunners for this shift to focus on personal growth, quality of life and gaining some sense of purpose in life.

A new era in male-female relationships

It can also be a purpose to reach beyond yourselves and, as we have said, use the privileged position you have to help those less fortunate in other nations. This can have an important impact on the next topic I want to cover here and that is male-female relationships.

So far, if you look at what I have said about the power elite that wants women to have a certain role that they fulfill, what has been the purpose of relationships? Men in many cases have seen their wives as objects. Many of the men who are caught in the corporate rat race are looking at their wives as objects: "The wife is there so that whenever I come home, when I need sex, she's there for me. She is there to give me children, which I somehow think I need even though I never see them because I'm always at work. But she's there to take care of the children and raise them so that sometime in the future I can have the feeling that I have raised some good children and been a good father for them, even though I was never really there. The woman has to take care of this. She has to make sure that I have clothes to wear to work so I can look the way I need to look in my professional environment. As long as she fulfills all of these needs, she can have the money, she can do with it whatever she wants, she can do whatever she wants with her time when I'm not there. As long as my needs are taken care of, everything is fine."

That is objectifying your wife. You are not really having a partner that you can share something with. You are having one person who fulfills the functions that you would otherwise have to hire several other people to do. There might be a mother, there might be a prostitute, there might be a cleaner, there might be a cook, and so on. You see indeed that the power elite who have unlimited money, they have hired various people to fulfill these functions. They may still have a wife but they may still go to pros-titutes or have a mistress. So women have, in the traditional relationship, been objectified.

This means women can then come to a point when they say, to them-selves first, to their husbands next and then to society: "This simply isn't enough for us. Enough is enough, but this is not enough. And we have had enough of not having enough. We want more in a relationship." There has to be a purpose for our relationship, and what can it be, if it is not to accumulate material possessions? It is spirit. It is personal growth, self-actualization, which really is also spiritual growth. Most people may not be ready to call it that so they can see that there has to be a purpose of improving ourselves. The real purpose of a relationship is that you help each other improve yourselves. You grow together, you stimulate each others growth, you help each other, you support each other, *that* is the higher purpose of a relationship.

Many women are ready to see this (some already have of course) and to embrace it and this can be a completely earth-shattering revolution in societies. It is something that the fallen beings will not know what to do about. The power elite will not know what to do about this. When it breaks through to a certain level, it will begin to have an impact on society and the power elite cannot stop it because they cannot wrap their minds around this and why someone would want this. Really, this can have a major impact, first on the modern democracies and then it can spread to other nations.

Spiritualizing personal relationships

Having talked about all of these general overall things about society and changes in society, I want to bring this down to a more personal level. I want to talk to you who are women, who are ascended master students, and I want to even talk broader to women who may find these teachings in the future, or even speak into the collective consciousness. What can you do about your personal relationships? If you are a woman, what can you do about the relationship to the man in your life? First of all, you can make a shift. You can make a shift so you realize that (and some of you have already done this but many more can do it) the purpose of your personal life is your personal growth, your spiritual growth, your raising of your consciousness towards a higher level. You can simply look at yourself as an individual being, not as a woman, not as a wife, not as a partner, you are just looking at yourself as an individual being, your goal is spiritual growth, a higher level of awareness.

You then need to make this shift (which we have promoted many times in various teachings) to realize that there is a force in this world, which in Buddhism is called the demons of Mara or Maya and illusion and which Jesus called the prince of this world or Satan. It is again primarily the fallen beings but it is also the mass consciousness and the entities, the collective entities in it. There is a force that wants to stop spiritual growth, that wants to prevent anyone on earth from reaching a higher level of consciousness, especially personal Christhood. What is the primary weapon used by this force to stop peoples' spiritual growth? It is this: It is the projection that your personal spiritual growth depends upon circumstances outside yourself. It may depend on your society, your religion, your profession, your wealth, your this, your that, your health. In this context, many women still believe, even though they are open to spiritual teachings, that their spiritual growth depends on their male partner. You need to make the shift where you realize this is not true—unless you make it true and become a self-fulfilling prophecy. There is absolutely no real force, no spiritual force, that has made your personal growth dependent on anything outside yourself. It is only a process that takes place inside your aura, your four lower bodies, your mind your psychology. It depends only on your willingness to look at your psychology, to work with your psychology, to resolve the things that need to be resolved so you can let an old sense of self die and be reborn in Christ as a new being in Christ. By doing this, you can accomplish two things.

First of all, you can take any pressure off your husband that you might be putting on him now, that he should also grow spiritually, that he should respond, that he should this, that he should that. Then, you can make yourself an independent, a truly independent person, where you say: "My inner growth depends on a process inside myself." Now, you can still be a practical realist. You may be in a relationship that you feel has some ongoing quality, you may have children, you may have a job, you may have a career, you may have all of these outer things that are pulling on you. You can say: "I can find a personal balance here, where I render unto Caesar, meaning the worldly activities, that which is Caesar's, and unto God that which is God's." In other words, I find ways to pursue my spiritual growth while still fulfilling all of these daily obligations that I may have. You do not need to set them aside; you do not need to resent them. You just do what you need to do and then you use whatever time and energy you have leftover, and there will in most cases be something left over to pursue your spiritual growth, work on your psychology, resolving things in your psychology.

What need is my man fulfilling?

When you have made this shift, you can make another shift and you can realize something we have said in our book on dictatorships, that even the worst dictator seen in history actually fulfilled the needs of the people he was dictating to. The people subjected themselves to that dictator because they had some kind of need that the dictator was fulfilling. You can therefore use this to look at your outer situation, you can especially look at your husband, or the man in your life and you can say: "That man must be fulfilling some need that I have, otherwise I would not have magnetized myself to this situation. I am in this situation because this man fulfilled some need that I have." You can then begin to look at what that need might be.

You have a common realization in psychological circles that women who are abused by men, if they are freed from the abuse of the relationship to one man, they often attract another man who is equally abusive or even more abusive. This is because even an abusive man fulfills some need that the woman has. It is obviously not a higher need, but there is a separate self that the woman has, that has a certain need. Perhaps it feels unworthy and the man reaffirms that. Perhaps it does not want to make decisions and the man reaffirms that. You can look at yourself (even when you are not in an abusive relationship) and you can say: "Is there some need that I have, some psychological need that I have, that the man in my life is actually fulfilling?" Then, you can look at that psychological need, you can use our tools about the separate self to see if it actually comes from a separate self. In other words: "Is it me who has this need or is it a separate self that has this need?" Then, you can use the tools to identify that separate self, see the decision behind it, let it go, let it die and you are free of the need.

In other cases you may actually come to the realization that you have a certain need that is a legitimate need that your husband is fulfilling. It might be for example in some cases that you want to stay at home, focus on your spiritual growth, and therefore your husband is fulfilling this need by going out, making the money so you can still survive in a materially comfortable position. There is nothing inherently wrong about such a need but you can then look at this, acknowledge the need, and then acknowledge that your husband is actually doing what you want him to do. Once you get rid of these selves that give you some kind of need, it is possible you can come to the realization that this man is not really what you need anymore, he is not able to fulfill the needs that you now have for personal growth or spiritual growth. In that case the relationship might end and you might move on, you might find a new relationship, you might live alone for a while, whatever the case may be. I am not saying you *should* or *should not*.

What I am saying is that if you have these needs that come from a wound in a past life that are really clearly what Maslow calls "deficit needs," then once you overcome them, you can be free to move on. In many cases it is not necessary to change your partner, you may actually move into another phase where you can relate to your partner in a different way. If you have one of these deficit needs, then there will be a tension between you and your partner. If you overcome these needs, then you can remove that tension, you can move beyond the tension, and then you will be able to talk to your partner in a more open way. You will be able to look beyond your own needs and perhaps look at: "Well, what if I had needs that my husband was fulfilling, is it possible he has needs that I have been either fulfilling or not fulfilling? What are his needs?" You can then look at that and you can say: "Is that a legitimate need he has? Can I fulfill it better than I have done so far?" Or you can even perhaps help him see that he is actually trapped in this need and that he could grow from moving beyond it.

Changing yourself will change a relationship

What I am saying is this. When you focus on working on yourself, resolving your psychology, overcoming these separate selves, over a period of time you healing your psychology will change the dynamic of your relationship. You will be able to communicate with the man in your life in a more open way, a more direct way and in many cases, this man will respond positively to this. He has also perhaps felt a certain tension in your relationship but not knowing what to do with it. If you can resolve it, if you can ease the tension, he might relax, he might become open, he might be more willing to look at himself, actually even look at his feelings, which many men are brought up to suppress, and recognize what his needs and wants are in life, where he wants to go. This can in many, many cases, lead to a relationship that I talked about where both of you are aware that you want to improve yourselves, you want to experience personal growth and self-actualization, even spiritual growth, and you are supporting each other in doing this, based on who you are, where you are at on your personal path. This can shift the dynamic of a relationship. In some cases, you may need to find another relationship before you can experience this but then this will also be part of your Divine plan.

The next revolution for women starts at home, and with "at home" I do not mean the house and the household, I mean the psyche. The next revolution of women will be, *must be, can only be,* a psychological revolution. It starts with women, as many have done, looking at themselves, seeking to improve their own psychology. Many women have so far been doing this in a somewhat superficial way where they take what is popularly available. They might go to yoga without really looking into the spiritual background of yoga, they might practice mindfulness without looking into it. When you who are our direct students make your calls for many of these things we have brought to your attention at this conference, things will open up and many more women will be able to find a higher approach, a deeper approach to this and start to pursue spiritual growth, whatever they may call it.

It is not our goal to make all women ascended master students, but to put all women on a positive path of personal growth and of course we also have a goal to put men on that path. We are just starting at the most realistic goal first and that is to get women to shift into this. This can mean in the long run (in a little longer run) that the modern democracies shift into not being so focused on material welfare, but being focused on psychological, spiritual, psycho-spiritual welfare. This is our real goal because this is the only way that human beings are to become happy, fulfilled, have peace of mind, have a sense of purpose and see that life actually is a process that moves them somewhere.

Life is a gift. It is not something to be resented or resisted; it is not something to be lived mindlessly, it is truly a gift. That is what we really desire to see on this planet. That is what the fallen beings absolutely do not want to see on this planet. When you realize that your inner growth does not depend on or cannot be stopped by anything outside yourself, what can the fallen beings do? The prince of this world will come and have nothing in you and therefore they will lose their power over society and over women and over men.

With this I have fulfilled my purpose for this discourse. I thank you for your attention for this discourse, for all of the discourses we have given at this conference, for the decrees and invocations you have given and we are all very, very grateful for your willingness to be part of this initial process of starting a second feminist or at least female revolution that will make the decades of the 2020s a real breakthrough for women around the planet.

NOTE: This dictation was given June 1, 2020.

32 | FREEING WOMEN FROM THE POWER ELITE (PART 1)

In the name of the I AM THAT I AM, Jesus Christ, I use the authority that I have as a being in embodiment on earth to call upon Mother Mary to reinforce my calls and use my chakras to project the statements in this invocation into the collective consciousness and awaken people to the awareness that will liberate both men and women from all psychological and spiritual thralldom to the fallen beings. Awaken people to the reality that we are spiritual beings and that we can co-create a new future by working with the ascended masters. I especially call for ...

[Make your own calls here.]

Part 1

1. Mother Mary, I call forth the judgment of the Divine Mother upon the fallen beings and collective entities behind the trend that sex has become a dirty and impure activity with many perversions and degradations.

O blessed Mary, Mother mine,
there is no greater love than thine,

as we are one in heart and mind,
my place in hierarchy I find.

O Mother Mary, generate,
the song that does accelerate,
the earth into a higher state,
all matter does now scintillate.

2. Mother Mary, I call forth the judgment of the Divine Mother upon the fallen beings and collective entities behind the fact that the entire concept of sexuality has been pulled down to a much lower level than it was a generation ago.

I came to earth from heaven sent,
as I am in embodiment,
I use Divine authority,
commanding you to set earth free.

O Mother Mary, generate,
the song that does accelerate,
the earth into a higher state,
all matter does now scintillate.

3. Mother Mary, I call forth the judgment of the Divine Mother upon the fallen beings and collective entities behind the fact that the more free people have become to express their sexuality, the more "dirty" the expression of that sexuality has become and the more abusive it has become, especially towards women.

I call now in God's sacred name,
for you to use your Mother Flame,
to burn all fear-based energy,
restoring sacred harmony.

O Mother Mary, generate,
the song that does accelerate,
the earth into a higher state,
all matter does now scintillate.

4. Mother Mary, I call forth the judgment of the Divine Mother upon the fallen beings and collective entities who have deliberately done everything they could to pull sex down to being a purely physical activity, and being a lower activity.

Your sacred name I hereby praise,
collective consciousness you raise,
no more of fear and doubt and shame,
consume it with your Mother Flame.

O Mother Mary, generate,
the song that does accelerate,
the earth into a higher state,
all matter does now scintillate.

5. Mother Mary, I call forth the judgment of the Divine Mother upon the fallen beings and collective entities that have pulled sex down because the more impure an activity becomes, the more addictive it becomes.

All darkness from the earth you purge,
your light moves as a mighty surge,
no force of darkness can now stop,
the spiral that goes only up.

O Mother Mary, generate,
the song that does accelerate,
the earth into a higher state,
all matter does now scintillate.

6. Mother Mary, I call forth the judgment of the Divine Mother upon the fallen beings and collective entities that have pulled sex down because the more impure an activity becomes, the more it can force people to release energy.

All elemental life you bless,
removing from them man-made stress,
the nature spirits are now free,
outpicturing Divine decree.

O Mother Mary, generate,
the song that does accelerate,
the earth into a higher state,
all matter does now scintillate.

7. Mother Mary, I call forth the judgment of the Divine Mother upon the fallen beings and collective entities who have no sensitivity to life, no compunctions about forcing people to release the energy that they need in order to survive and in order to do what they want to do.

I raise my voice and take my stand,
a stop to war I do command,
no more shall warring scar the earth,
a golden age is given birth.

O Mother Mary, generate,
the song that does accelerate,
the earth into a higher state,
all matter does now scintillate.

8. Mother Mary, I call forth the judgment of the Divine Mother upon the fallen beings and collective entities who want to detract people from their higher goals in life, who want to control the population by preventing people from activating the higher chakras.

As Mother Earth is free at last,
disasters belong to the past,
your Mother Light is so intense,
that matter is now far less dense.

O Mother Mary, generate,
the song that does accelerate,
the earth into a higher state,
all matter does now scintillate.

9. Mother Mary, I call forth the judgment of the Divine Mother upon the fallen beings and collective entities who want to prevent people from walking the path to Christhood and become a threat to the fallen beings.

In Mother Light the earth is pure,
the upward spiral will endure,
prosperity is now the norm,
God's vision manifest as form.

O Mother Mary, generate,
the song that does accelerate,
the earth into a higher state,
all matter does now scintillate.

Part 2

1. Mother Mary, I call forth the judgment of the Divine Mother upon the fallen beings and collective entities who want to get as many people as possible to concentrate the energy in the base chakra as a diversion so there is not enough energy to rise to the higher chakras.

O blessed Mary, Mother mine,
there is no greater love than thine,
as we are one in heart and mind,
my place in hierarchy I find.

O Mother Mary, generate,
the song that does accelerate,
the earth into a higher state,
all matter does now scintillate.

2. Mother Mary, I call forth the judgment of the Divine Mother upon the fallen beings and collective entities who want to get men to spend most of their attention on sex and their time and energy engaging in sex or fantasizing about it, pulling the energy out through the base chakra so there is very little left to activate the other chakras.

I came to earth from heaven sent,
as I am in embodiment,
I use Divine authority,
commanding you to set earth free.

O Mother Mary, generate,
the song that does accelerate,
the earth into a higher state,
all matter does now scintillate.

3. Mother Mary, I call forth the judgment of the Divine Mother upon the fallen beings and collective entities who are promoting the idea that sex is contrary to our spiritual growth, is an enemy of our spiritual goals, the limitation of our spiritual growth.

I call now in God's sacred name,
for you to use your Mother Flame,
to burn all fear-based energy,
restoring sacred harmony.

O Mother Mary, generate,
the song that does accelerate,
the earth into a higher state,
all matter does now scintillate.

4. Mother Mary, I call forth the judgment of the Divine Mother upon the fallen beings and collective entities behind the fact that Catholic priests are not allowed to marry and therefore should not have sex.

Your sacred name I hereby praise,
collective consciousness you raise,
no more of fear and doubt and shame,
consume it with your Mother Flame.

O Mother Mary, generate,
the song that does accelerate,
the earth into a higher state,
all matter does now scintillate.

5. Mother Mary, I call forth the judgment of the Divine Mother upon the fallen beings and collective entities behind the fact that in many religions monks, nuns and spiritual people live a life of renunciation.

All darkness from the earth you purge,
your light moves as a mighty surge,
no force of darkness can now stop,
the spiral that goes only up.

**O Mother Mary, generate,
the song that does accelerate,
the earth into a higher state,
all matter does now scintillate.**

6. Mother Mary, I call forth the judgment of the Divine Mother upon the fallen beings and collective entities behind the ideal that spiritual growth means that you cannot have sex.

All elemental life you bless,
removing from them man-made stress,
the nature spirits are now free,
outpicturing Divine decree.

**O Mother Mary, generate,
the song that does accelerate,
the earth into a higher state,
all matter does now scintillate.**

7. Mother Mary, I call forth the judgment of the Divine Mother upon the fallen beings and collective entities who seek to prevent as many people as possible from following the spiritual path so they do not become a threat to the fallen beings.

I raise my voice and take my stand,
a stop to war I do command,
no more shall warring scar the earth,
a golden age is given birth.

**O Mother Mary, generate,
the song that does accelerate,
the earth into a higher state,
all matter does now scintillate.**

8. Mother Mary, I call forth the judgment of the Divine Mother upon the fallen beings and collective entities who have sought to inflate the sexual desire of most people in order to force them into the choice between having sex or pursuing the spiritual path.

As Mother Earth is free at last,
disasters belong to the past,
your Mother Light is so intense,
that matter is now far less dense.

O Mother Mary, generate,
the song that does accelerate,
the earth into a higher state,
all matter does now scintillate.

9. Mother Mary, I call forth the judgment of the Divine Mother upon the fallen beings and collective entities who get people to think they have to give up sex in order to pursue spiritual growth, so many people do not want to walk the spiritual path.

In Mother Light the earth is pure,
the upward spiral will endure,
prosperity is now the norm,
God's vision manifest as form.

O Mother Mary, generate,
the song that does accelerate,
the earth into a higher state,
all matter does now scintillate.

Part 3

1. Mother Mary, awaken people to see that from a spiritual, ascended master perspective, there is nothing inherently impure or anti-spiritual about sex. We are in physical bodies on earth and one of the activities we can do with these physical bodies is to have sex.

O blessed Mary, Mother mine,
there is no greater love than thine,
as we are one in heart and mind,
my place in hierarchy I find.

O Mother Mary, generate,
the song that does accelerate,
the earth into a higher state,
all matter does now scintillate.

2. Mother Mary, awaken people to see that from an ascended master perspective, there is nothing inherently impure about many bodily activities. Although sex can become a dirty activity, there is nothing inherently impure about it.

I came to earth from heaven sent,
as I am in embodiment,
I use Divine authority,
commanding you to set earth free.

O Mother Mary, generate,
the song that does accelerate,
the earth into a higher state,
all matter does now scintillate.

3. Mother Mary, awaken people to see that it is entirely possible to be sexually active and walk the spiritual path, including the path to Christhood or Buddhahood.

I call now in God's sacred name,
for you to use your Mother Flame,
to burn all fear-based energy,
restoring sacred harmony.

O Mother Mary, generate,
the song that does accelerate,
the earth into a higher state,
all matter does now scintillate.

4. Mother Mary, awaken people to see that dependent on our level of consciousness, there is a certain amount of energy that descends from our I AM Presences into our four lower bodies. In order to make spiritual progress, some of that energy must rises up and activate the higher chakras.

Your sacred name I hereby praise,
collective consciousness you raise,
no more of fear and doubt and shame,
consume it with your Mother Flame.

O Mother Mary, generate,
the song that does accelerate,
the earth into a higher state,
all matter does now scintillate.

5. Mother Mary, awaken people to see that the question is how much of the energy we are receiving is used in physical activities and how much of is left over to activate the higher chakras.

All darkness from the earth you purge,
your light moves as a mighty surge,
no force of darkness can now stop,
the spiral that goes only up.

O Mother Mary, generate,
the song that does accelerate,
the earth into a higher state,
all matter does now scintillate.

6. Mother Mary, awaken people to see that it is not necessary to renounce all worldly or physical activities in order to pursue spiritual growth. We have to find a balance so some of the energy can rise to the higher chakras and activate them.

All elemental life you bless,
removing from them man-made stress,
the nature spirits are now free,
outpicturing Divine decree.

**O Mother Mary, generate,
the song that does accelerate,
the earth into a higher state,
all matter does now scintillate.**

7. Mother Mary, awaken people to see that the ideal for the Aquarian Age is not that spiritual people live an ascetic lifestyle, but that we live an active life in society while still pursuing spiritual growth.

I raise my voice and take my stand,
a stop to war I do command,
no more shall warring scar the earth,
a golden age is given birth.

**O Mother Mary, generate,
the song that does accelerate,
the earth into a higher state,
all matter does now scintillate.**

8. Mother Mary, awaken people to find a balanced approach so they take care of the physical needs in such a way that they have energy left over that can rise to the other chakras.

As Mother Earth is free at last,
disasters belong to the past,
your Mother Light is so intense,
that matter is now far less dense.

**O Mother Mary, generate,
the song that does accelerate,
the earth into a higher state,
all matter does now scintillate.**

9. Mother Mary, awaken people to see that many of us can make faster spiritual growth by living an active life in society, living in a relationship, because this brings out our reactionary patterns so we have a chance to see them.

In Mother Light the earth is pure,
the upward spiral will endure,
prosperity is now the norm,
God's vision manifest as form.

O Mother Mary, generate,
the song that does accelerate,
the earth into a higher state,
all matter does now scintillate.

Part 4

1. Mother Mary, awaken people from the state of mind where we think we are spiritual, we think we are in harmony but it is simply because nothing stirs up our unresolved psychology so we do not see it.

O blessed Mary, Mother mine,
there is no greater love than thine,
as we are one in heart and mind,
my place in hierarchy I find.

O Mother Mary, generate,
the song that does accelerate,
the earth into a higher state,
all matter does now scintillate.

2. Mother Mary, awaken people to see that partners who are dedicated to helping each other grow spiritually, can purify their sexual desires, can purify their base chakras so they can protect themselves, cut themselves free from these collective entities.

I came to earth from heaven sent,
as I am in embodiment,
I use Divine authority,
commanding you to set earth free.

**O Mother Mary, generate,
the song that does accelerate,
the earth into a higher state,
all matter does now scintillate.**

3. Mother Mary, awaken people to see that partners can resolve their separate selves relating to sex, because all of us will have such separate selves because of the manipulation by the fallen beings. Thereby we can be sexually active in a way that does not detract from our spiritual growth.

I call now in God's sacred name,
for you to use your Mother Flame,
to burn all fear-based energy,
restoring sacred harmony.

**O Mother Mary, generate,
the song that does accelerate,
the earth into a higher state,
all matter does now scintillate.**

4. Mother Mary, awaken people to see that we came to earth because our I AM Presences had a positive goal and wanted to experience something on earth and wanted to experience themselves in this environment.

Your sacred name I hereby praise,
collective consciousness you raise,
no more of fear and doubt and shame,
consume it with your Mother Flame.

**O Mother Mary, generate,
the song that does accelerate,
the earth into a higher state,
all matter does now scintillate.**

5. Mother Mary, awaken people to see that the purpose is not to get out of here as quickly as possible. The purpose is to have certain experiences on earth because they actually advance the spiritual growth of our I AM Presences.

All darkness from the earth you purge,
your light moves as a mighty surge,
no force of darkness can now stop,
the spiral that goes only up.

O Mother Mary, generate,
the song that does accelerate,
the earth into a higher state,
all matter does now scintillate.

6. Mother Mary, awaken people to see that the entire, idea that human beings can be looked at as mere objects, comes from the fallen beings.

All elemental life you bless,
removing from them man-made stress,
the nature spirits are now free,
outpicturing Divine decree.

O Mother Mary, generate,
the song that does accelerate,
the earth into a higher state,
all matter does now scintillate.

7. Mother Mary, awaken people to see that before fallen beings came to earth, human beings did not objectify each other. People had the basic humanity, the essential humanity, where even though we see ourselves as a subject surrounded by objects, we are still aware that human beings are not objects.

I raise my voice and take my stand,
a stop to war I do command,
no more shall warring scar the earth,
a golden age is given birth.

O Mother Mary, generate,
the song that does accelerate,
the earth into a higher state,
all matter does now scintillate.

8. Mother Mary, awaken people to see that when we realize that what we do to another person will generate certain thoughts and feelings in that person, we are open to the motto of all spiritual teachings: "Do unto others as you want them to do to you."

As Mother Earth is free at last,
disasters belong to the past,
your Mother Light is so intense,
that matter is now far less dense.

O Mother Mary, generate,
the song that does accelerate,
the earth into a higher state,
all matter does now scintillate.

9. Mother Mary, I call forth the judgment of the Divine Mother upon the fallen beings who have rebelled against the upward movement of self-transcendence, where we are moving out of any tendency to look at ourselves as fixed entities.

In Mother Light the earth is pure,
the upward spiral will endure,
prosperity is now the norm,
God's vision manifest as form.

O Mother Mary, generate,
the song that does accelerate,
the earth into a higher state,
all matter does now scintillate.

Part 5

1. Mother Mary, I call forth the judgment of the Divine Mother upon the fallen beings who rebelled against this process and in doing so objectified themselves, because they objectified the self that they would not give up, that they would not let die in order to follow Christ.

O blessed Mary, Mother mine,
there is no greater love than thine,
as we are one in heart and mind,
my place in hierarchy I find.

O Mother Mary, generate,
the song that does accelerate,
the earth into a higher state,
all matter does now scintillate.

2. Mother Mary, I call forth the judgment of the Divine Mother upon the fallen beings who objectified everything else, they objectified the ascended masters, they objectified God, they objectified everything around them.

I came to earth from heaven sent,
as I am in embodiment,
I use Divine authority,
commanding you to set earth free.

O Mother Mary, generate,
the song that does accelerate,
the earth into a higher state,
all matter does now scintillate.

3. Mother Mary, I call forth the judgment of the Divine Mother upon the fallen beings who came to earth with a mindset that the human beings on earth are just objects for them.

I call now in God's sacred name,
for you to use your Mother Flame,
to burn all fear-based energy,
restoring sacred harmony.

O Mother Mary, generate,
the song that does accelerate,
the earth into a higher state,
all matter does now scintillate.

4. Mother Mary, I call forth the judgment of the Divine Mother upon the fallen beings who are completely self-centered, they are narcissists, psychopaths or sociopaths because they are completely focused on themselves and what they want, completely insensitive to what they do to others, how that affects other people.

Your sacred name I hereby praise,
collective consciousness you raise,
no more of fear and doubt and shame,
consume it with your Mother Flame.

O Mother Mary, generate,
the song that does accelerate,
the earth into a higher state,
all matter does now scintillate.

5. Mother Mary, I call forth the judgment of the Divine Mother upon the fallen beings who have created a total objectification of human beings. They have an agenda, they have certain desires and they want to have power, they want to set themselves up as having as much power as can possibly be gained on earth.

All darkness from the earth you purge,
your light moves as a mighty surge,
no force of darkness can now stop,
the spiral that goes only up.

O Mother Mary, generate,
the song that does accelerate,
the earth into a higher state,
all matter does now scintillate.

6. Mother Mary, I call forth the judgment of the Divine Mother upon the fallen beings who want to get the human population to submit to them as their leaders so that people will blindly follow the command of the leader.

All elemental life you bless,
removing from them man-made stress,

the nature spirits are now free,
outpicturing Divine decree.

**O Mother Mary, generate,
the song that does accelerate,
the earth into a higher state,
all matter does now scintillate.**

7. Mother Mary, I call forth the judgment of the Divine Mother upon the fallen beings who are completely insensitive to whether millions of people are killed because they have absolutely no compassion or any kind of problem with this happening. For the fallen beings, human beings are nothing but objects.

I raise my voice and take my stand,
a stop to war I do command,
no more shall warring scar the earth,
a golden age is given birth.

**O Mother Mary, generate,
the song that does accelerate,
the earth into a higher state,
all matter does now scintillate.**

8. Mother Mary, awaken women in the modern democracies to see that it is not realistic, nor reasonable to blame the suppression of women on men in general. Help these women move out of being negative towards men in general.

As Mother Earth is free at last,
disasters belong to the past,
your Mother Light is so intense,
that matter is now far less dense.

**O Mother Mary, generate,
the song that does accelerate,
the earth into a higher state,
all matter does now scintillate.**

9. Mother Mary, awaken women to realize that we need to be more nuanced, we need to be more discerning, we need to be smarter and not say that women are suppressed by men in general.

In Mother Light the earth is pure,
the upward spiral will endure,
prosperity is now the norm,
God's vision manifest as form.

O Mother Mary, generate,
the song that does accelerate,
the earth into a higher state,
all matter does now scintillate.

Sealing

In the name of the I AM THAT I AM, I accept that Archangel Michael, Astrea and Shiva form an impenetrable shield around myself and all constructive people, sealing us from all fear-based energies in all four octaves. I accept that the Light of God is consuming and transforming all fear-based energies that make up the dark forces working against the liberation of women on earth!

33 | FREEING WOMEN FROM THE POWER ELITE (PART 2)

In the name of the I AM THAT I AM, Jesus Christ, I use the authority that I have as a being in embodiment on earth to call upon Mother Mary to reinforce my calls and use my chakras to project the statements in this invocation into the collective consciousness and awaken people to the awareness that will liberate both men and women from all psychological and spiritual thralldom to the fallen beings. Awaken people to the reality that we are spiritual beings and that we can co-create a new future by working with the ascended masters. I especially call for …

[Make your own calls here.]

Part 1

1. Mother Mary, awaken women to the need to identify that throughout history and even today, women are suppressed by a specific group of people who form an elite who think they are better able to lead the population than the average person.

O blessed Mary, Mother mine,
there is no greater love than thine,

as we are one in heart and mind,
my place in hierarchy I find.

O Mother Mary, generate,
the song that does accelerate,
the earth into a higher state,
all matter does now scintillate.

2. Mother Mary, awaken women to see that we have been suppressed by a small elite who have an elitist mindset, they have an almost unlimited desire for power and for privilege, and once they have that power and privilege, they are very reluctant to give it up.

I came to earth from heaven sent,
as I am in embodiment,
I use Divine authority,
commanding you to set earth free.

O Mother Mary, generate,
the song that does accelerate,
the earth into a higher state,
all matter does now scintillate.

3. Mother Mary, awaken women to see that the force on earth that has historically and today suppressed women is the power elite.

I call now in God's sacred name,
for you to use your Mother Flame,
to burn all fear-based energy,
restoring sacred harmony.

O Mother Mary, generate,
the song that does accelerate,
the earth into a higher state,
all matter does now scintillate.

4. Mother Mary, awaken women to see that in order to truly liberate women, we need to liberate women from the influence of the power elite.

Your sacred name I hereby praise,
collective consciousness you raise,
no more of fear and doubt and shame,
consume it with your Mother Flame.

O Mother Mary, generate,
the song that does accelerate,
the earth into a higher state,
all matter does now scintillate.

5. Mother Mary, awaken women to see that even the modern democracies have a power elite that has a less obvious control of the population, for example as an economic power elite that has control over the financial system.

All darkness from the earth you purge,
your light moves as a mighty surge,
no force of darkness can now stop,
the spiral that goes only up.

O Mother Mary, generate,
the song that does accelerate,
the earth into a higher state,
all matter does now scintillate.

6. Mother Mary, awaken women to see that there is a power elite, but they are not using military or political power in an open way, they are using it indirectly by the influence they have because they control the money and the money system.

All elemental life you bless,
removing from them man-made stress,
the nature spirits are now free,
outpicturing Divine decree.

O Mother Mary, generate,
the song that does accelerate,
the earth into a higher state,
all matter does now scintillate.

7. Mother Mary, awaken women to see that many among the opinion makers in society have an elitist mindset and the members of this power elite have a very derogatory attitude to women.

I raise my voice and take my stand,
a stop to war I do command,
no more shall warring scar the earth,
a golden age is given birth.

O Mother Mary, generate,
the song that does accelerate,
the earth into a higher state,
all matter does now scintillate.

8. Mother Mary, awaken women to see that power elites have a certain goal that they want to achieve and the people in their nation are simply objects for achieving that goal. We are not real human beings, we are just objects.

As Mother Earth is free at last,
disasters belong to the past,
your Mother Light is so intense,
that matter is now far less dense.

O Mother Mary, generate,
the song that does accelerate,
the earth into a higher state,
all matter does now scintillate.

9. Mother Mary, awaken women to see that the power elites of history, and even today, have looked at women as objects who are there to produce children that can become soldiers and workers who can do all the dirty work for the elite.

In Mother Light the earth is pure,
the upward spiral will endure,
prosperity is now the norm,
God's vision manifest as form.

O Mother Mary, generate,
the song that does accelerate,
the earth into a higher state,
all matter does now scintillate.

Part 2

1. Mother Mary, awaken women to see that members of the power elite want soldiers to wage war and they want workers to do all the practical work for them. That gives them a privileged position and that gives them an economic benefit so that they can reap most of the wealth that is produced by people's labor.

O blessed Mary, Mother mine,
there is no greater love than thine,
as we are one in heart and mind,
my place in hierarchy I find.

O Mother Mary, generate,
the song that does accelerate,
the earth into a higher state,
all matter does now scintillate.

2. Mother Mary, awaken women to see that many among this power elite, they look at women as primarily there to raise children. They have created these religions, political ideologies and more subtle beliefs that say that women should stay at home, they should focus on being mothers and taking care of their husbands.

I came to earth from heaven sent,
as I am in embodiment,
I use Divine authority,
commanding you to set earth free.

O Mother Mary, generate,
the song that does accelerate,

the earth into a higher state,
all matter does now scintillate.

3. Mother Mary, awaken women to see that the business elite in many countries are on an epic cause to grow that business to the biggest possible size and to take over the competitors.

I call now in God's sacred name,
for you to use your Mother Flame,
to burn all fear-based energy,
restoring sacred harmony.

O Mother Mary, generate,
the song that does accelerate,
the earth into a higher state,
all matter does now scintillate.

4. Mother Mary, awaken women to see that the elite needs men who are willing to work hard, and these men need women at home taking care of the household and children. This is the role that this power elite wants women to be confined to.

Your sacred name I hereby praise,
collective consciousness you raise,
no more of fear and doubt and shame,
consume it with your Mother Flame.

O Mother Mary, generate,
the song that does accelerate,
the earth into a higher state,
all matter does now scintillate.

5. Mother Mary, awaken women to see that the power elite also wants women to be available for sexual exploitation, not necessarily by themselves, but also for the men who are working for them.

All darkness from the earth you purge,
your light moves as a mighty surge,

no force of darkness can now stop,
the spiral that goes only up.

O Mother Mary, generate,
the song that does accelerate,
the earth into a higher state,
all matter does now scintillate.

6. Mother Mary, awaken women to see that women are in a unique position, because we are the most likely to be open to these ideas, to be open to see the need to liberate ourselves, and thereby also liberate men and society from this narcissistic power elite.

All elemental life you bless,
removing from them man-made stress,
the nature spirits are now free,
outpicturing Divine decree.

O Mother Mary, generate,
the song that does accelerate,
the earth into a higher state,
all matter does now scintillate.

7. Mother Mary, awaken women to accept the idea of a narcissistic power elite that has ruled this planet as far as we can look back in history. Help women see that it is high time to do something about this and liberate women from being confined to these roles where they are simply objects serving this cause of the power elite.

I raise my voice and take my stand,
a stop to war I do command,
no more shall warring scar the earth,
a golden age is given birth.

O Mother Mary, generate,
the song that does accelerate,
the earth into a higher state,
all matter does now scintillate.

8. Mother Mary, awaken women to see that we can see through the epic mindset, whereas men are more likely to be pulled into fighting for these epic causes, being willing to sacrifice their lives or being willing to kill other people to promote an epic cause.

As Mother Earth is free at last,
disasters belong to the past,
your Mother Light is so intense,
that matter is now far less dense.

O Mother Mary, generate,
the song that does accelerate,
the earth into a higher state,
all matter does now scintillate.

9. Mother Mary, awaken women to see that men cannot free this planet from the epic mindset and the epic causes, and therefore women have a historic opportunity to lift society beyond warfare and conflict.

In Mother Light the earth is pure,
the upward spiral will endure,
prosperity is now the norm,
God's vision manifest as form.

O Mother Mary, generate,
the song that does accelerate,
the earth into a higher state,
all matter does now scintillate.

Part 3

1. Mother Mary, awaken women to the need for us to simply say "Stop!" when our husbands cannot say stop, and say: "Why are you working so much? Is it really worth it? Do we need that money? Do you really need that promotion? Do you need really need to spend your entire life working in this corporate environment and then you die two years after you retire?"

O blessed Mary, Mother mine,
there is no greater love than thine,
as we are one in heart and mind,
my place in hierarchy I find.

O Mother Mary, generate,
the song that does accelerate,
the earth into a higher state,
all matter does now scintillate.

2. Mother Mary, awaken women to see that we are more open to spiritual growth than men. Men are more focused on physical activities and women are more open to spiritual activities.

I came to earth from heaven sent,
as I am in embodiment,
I use Divine authority,
commanding you to set earth free.

O Mother Mary, generate,
the song that does accelerate,
the earth into a higher state,
all matter does now scintillate.

3. Mother Mary, awaken women to see that we are approaching a very important turning point in history where women can really shift the focus of society, shift the focus of relationships.

I call now in God's sacred name,
for you to use your Mother Flame,
to burn all fear-based energy,
restoring sacred harmony.

O Mother Mary, generate,
the song that does accelerate,
the earth into a higher state,
all matter does now scintillate.

4. Mother Mary, awaken women to be the forerunners for a movement that steps back and looks at society and says: "Where are we going? What are we doing? If we continue doing what we are doing now, where will that take us? And is that really where we want to go?"

Your sacred name I hereby praise,
collective consciousness you raise,
no more of fear and doubt and shame,
consume it with your Mother Flame.

O Mother Mary, generate,
the song that does accelerate,
the earth into a higher state,
all matter does now scintillate.

5. Mother Mary, awaken women to ask if economic growth is a goal in itself? Should we just continue to try to get richer and richer, should we continue mindlessly accumulating material goods indefinitely?

All darkness from the earth you purge,
your light moves as a mighty surge,
no force of darkness can now stop,
the spiral that goes only up.

O Mother Mary, generate,
the song that does accelerate,
the earth into a higher state,
all matter does now scintillate.

6. Mother Mary, awaken women to say: "What's the purpose of having a comfortable material lifestyle? What can we do with it?"

All elemental life you bless,
removing from them man-made stress,
the nature spirits are now free,
outpicturing Divine decree.

O Mother Mary, generate,
the song that does accelerate,

**the earth into a higher state,
all matter does now scintillate.**

7. Mother Mary, awaken women to say: "Well, there has to be a higher purpose for this. It can't be in order to just be more and more comfortable, or to travel, or to have bigger cars, or more summer houses, there must be a real purpose here."

I raise my voice and take my stand,
a stop to war I do command,
no more shall warring scar the earth,
a golden age is given birth.

**O Mother Mary, generate,
the song that does accelerate,
the earth into a higher state,
all matter does now scintillate.**

8. Mother Mary, awaken women to see that the purpose is self-actualization, self-improvement, personal growth, a raising of consciousness.

As Mother Earth is free at last,
disasters belong to the past,
your Mother Light is so intense,
that matter is now far less dense.

**O Mother Mary, generate,
the song that does accelerate,
the earth into a higher state,
all matter does now scintillate.**

9. Mother Mary, awaken women to shift the focus of an entire country to say: "It isn't the purpose of our society to provide more and more material wealth and goods. The purpose is to have a better quality of life and we get that only through learning about the human psychology, what makes us happy, what makes us feel fulfilled."

In Mother Light the earth is pure,
the upward spiral will endure,

prosperity is now the norm,
God's vision manifest as form.

O Mother Mary, generate,
the song that does accelerate,
the earth into a higher state,
all matter does now scintillate.

Part 4

1. Mother Mary, awaken women to see that the rise in mental illness in many modern nations is a sign that many people are ready to pursue self-actualization, but they do not know what to do with it, society does not give them any help.

O blessed Mary, Mother mine,
there is no greater love than thine,
as we are one in heart and mind,
my place in hierarchy I find.

O Mother Mary, generate,
the song that does accelerate,
the earth into a higher state,
all matter does now scintillate.

2. Mother Mary, awaken women to be the forerunners for this shift and to focus on personal growth, quality of life and gaining some sense of purpose in life.

I came to earth from heaven sent,
as I am in embodiment,
I use Divine authority,
commanding you to set earth free.

O Mother Mary, generate,
the song that does accelerate,

the earth into a higher state,
all matter does now scintillate.

3. Mother Mary, awaken women to see that many of the men who are caught in the corporate rat race are looking at their wives as objects who are there to give them sex and raise the children.

I call now in God's sacred name,
for you to use your Mother Flame,
to burn all fear-based energy,
restoring sacred harmony.

O Mother Mary, generate,
the song that does accelerate,
the earth into a higher state,
all matter does now scintillate.

4. Mother Mary, awaken women to say: "This simply isn't enough for us. Enough is enough, but this is not enough. And we have had enough of not having enough. We want more in a relationship."

Your sacred name I hereby praise,
collective consciousness you raise,
no more of fear and doubt and shame,
consume it with your Mother Flame.

O Mother Mary, generate,
the song that does accelerate,
the earth into a higher state,
all matter does now scintillate.

5. Mother Mary, awaken women to see that there has to be a purpose for a relationship and it is not to accumulate material possessions. It is personal growth, self-actualization.

All darkness from the earth you purge,
your light moves as a mighty surge,
no force of darkness can now stop,
the spiral that goes only up.

**O Mother Mary, generate,
the song that does accelerate,
the earth into a higher state,
all matter does now scintillate.**

6. Mother Mary, awaken women to see that the real purpose of a relationship is to help each other improve ourselves. We grow together, we stimulate each others growth, we help each other, we support each other, *that* is the higher purpose of a relationship.

All elemental life you bless,
removing from them man-made stress,
the nature spirits are now free,
outpicturing Divine decree.

**O Mother Mary, generate,
the song that does accelerate,
the earth into a higher state,
all matter does now scintillate.**

7. Mother Mary, awaken women to see that this can be a completely earth-shattering revolution in societies, something the power elite will not know what to do about.

I raise my voice and take my stand,
a stop to war I do command,
no more shall warring scar the earth,
a golden age is given birth.

**O Mother Mary, generate,
the song that does accelerate,
the earth into a higher state,
all matter does now scintillate.**

8. Mother Mary, awaken women to see that when this breaks through to a certain level, it will have an impact on society, and the power elite cannot stop it because they cannot wrap their minds around why someone would want this.

As Mother Earth is free at last,
disasters belong to the past,
your Mother Light is so intense,
that matter is now far less dense.

O Mother Mary, generate,
the song that does accelerate,
the earth into a higher state,
all matter does now scintillate.

9. Mother Mary, awaken women to see that there is a force that wants to stop spiritual growth, that wants to prevent anyone on earth from reaching a higher level of consciousness, especially personal Christhood.

In Mother Light the earth is pure,
the upward spiral will endure,
prosperity is now the norm,
God's vision manifest as form.

O Mother Mary, generate,
the song that does accelerate,
the earth into a higher state,
all matter does now scintillate.

Part 5

1. Mother Mary, awaken women to see that the primary weapon used by this force is the projection that our personal spiritual growth depends upon circumstances outside ourselves.

O blessed Mary, Mother mine,
there is no greater love than thine,
as we are one in heart and mind,
my place in hierarchy I find.

O Mother Mary, generate,
the song that does accelerate,

the earth into a higher state,
all matter does now scintillate.

2. Mother Mary, awaken women from the illusion that our spiritual growth depends on a male partner. Help women see that there is no real force, no spiritual force, that has made our personal growth dependent on anything outside ourselves.

I came to earth from heaven sent,
as I am in embodiment,
I use Divine authority,
commanding you to set earth free.

O Mother Mary, generate,
the song that does accelerate,
the earth into a higher state,
all matter does now scintillate.

3. Mother Mary, awaken women to see that personal growth takes place inside our minds and depends only on our willingness to look at our psychology and resolve what needs to be resolved.

I call now in God's sacred name,
for you to use your Mother Flame,
to burn all fear-based energy,
restoring sacred harmony.

O Mother Mary, generate,
the song that does accelerate,
the earth into a higher state,
all matter does now scintillate.

4. Mother Mary, awaken women to make ourselves truly independent persons and say: "My inner growth depends on a process inside myself, and I can find a balance between growth and my daily life.

Your sacred name I hereby praise,
collective consciousness you raise,

no more of fear and doubt and shame,
consume it with your Mother Flame.

**O Mother Mary, generate,
the song that does accelerate,
the earth into a higher state,
all matter does now scintillate.**

5. Mother Mary, awaken women to look at the man in their lives and say: "That man must be fulfilling some need that I have, otherwise I would not have magnetized myself to this situation. I am in this situation because this man fulfilled some need that I have."

All darkness from the earth you purge,
your light moves as a mighty surge,
no force of darkness can now stop,
the spiral that goes only up.

**O Mother Mary, generate,
the song that does accelerate,
the earth into a higher state,
all matter does now scintillate.**

6. Mother Mary, awaken women to see their psychological needs and use practical tools to either resolve those needs or make peace with having them.

All elemental life you bless,
removing from them man-made stress,
the nature spirits are now free,
outpicturing Divine decree.

**O Mother Mary, generate,
the song that does accelerate,
the earth into a higher state,
all matter does now scintillate.**

7. Mother Mary, awaken women to overcome all deficit needs so they can relate to their partners in a different way and overcome tension so they can talk to their partners more openly.

> I raise my voice and take my stand,
> a stop to war I do command,
> no more shall warring scar the earth,
> a golden age is given birth.

> **O Mother Mary, generate,**
> **the song that does accelerate,**
> **the earth into a higher state,**
> **all matter does now scintillate.**

8. Mother Mary, awaken women to look at the needs of their partners and either fulfill them or help their partners grow beyond them.

> As Mother Earth is free at last,
> disasters belong to the past,
> your Mother Light is so intense,
> that matter is now far less dense.

> **O Mother Mary, generate,**
> **the song that does accelerate,**
> **the earth into a higher state,**
> **all matter does now scintillate.**

9. Mother Mary, awaken women to see that by focusing on healing their psychology, they will change the dynamic of their relationships and overcome the tension that blocks open communication.

> In Mother Light the earth is pure,
> the upward spiral will endure,
> prosperity is now the norm,
> God's vision manifest as form.

> **O Mother Mary, generate,**
> **the song that does accelerate,**

the earth into a higher state,
all matter does now scintillate.

Part 6

1. Mother Mary, awaken women so they can create relationships where both partners are aware that they want to improve themselves, they want to experience self-actualization and are supporting each other in doing this.

O blessed Mary, Mother mine,
there is no greater love than thine,
as we are one in heart and mind,
my place in hierarchy I find.

O Mother Mary, generate,
the song that does accelerate,
the earth into a higher state,
all matter does now scintillate.

2. Mother Mary, awaken women to see that the next revolution for women starts at home, meaning the psyche. The next revolution of women will be, *must be, can only be,* a psychological revolution.

I came to earth from heaven sent,
as I am in embodiment,
I use Divine authority,
commanding you to set earth free.

O Mother Mary, generate,
the song that does accelerate,
the earth into a higher state,
all matter does now scintillate.

3. Mother Mary, awaken women to start looking at ourselves, seeking to improve our own psychology, finding a higher approach, a deeper approach to this and start to pursue spiritual growth.

I call now in God's sacred name,
for you to use your Mother Flame,
to burn all fear-based energy,
restoring sacred harmony.

O Mother Mary, generate,
the song that does accelerate,
the earth into a higher state,
all matter does now scintillate.

4. Mother Mary, awaken women to get on a positive path of personal growth and then help to put men on that path.

Your sacred name I hereby praise,
collective consciousness you raise,
no more of fear and doubt and shame,
consume it with your Mother Flame.

O Mother Mary, generate,
the song that does accelerate,
the earth into a higher state,
all matter does now scintillate.

5. Mother Mary, awaken women to help the modern democracies shift into not being so focused on material welfare, but being focused on psychological, spiritual, psycho-spiritual welfare.

All darkness from the earth you purge,
your light moves as a mighty surge,
no force of darkness can now stop,
the spiral that goes only up.

O Mother Mary, generate,
the song that does accelerate,
the earth into a higher state,
all matter does now scintillate.

6. Mother Mary, awaken women to see that this is the only way that human beings can become happy, fulfilled, have peace of mind, have a sense of purpose and see that life actually is a process that moves us somewhere.

All elemental life you bless,
removing from them man-made stress,
the nature spirits are now free,
outpicturing Divine decree.

O Mother Mary, generate,
the song that does accelerate,
the earth into a higher state,
all matter does now scintillate.

7. Mother Mary, awaken women to see that life is a gift. It is not something to be resented or resisted; it is not something to be lived mindlessly, it is truly a gift.

I raise my voice and take my stand,
a stop to war I do command,
no more shall warring scar the earth,
a golden age is given birth.

O Mother Mary, generate,
the song that does accelerate,
the earth into a higher state,
all matter does now scintillate.

8. Mother Mary, awaken women to free modern societies from the heavy burden created by the power elite that for ordinary people life is a struggle to be endured, not enjoyed.

As Mother Earth is free at last,
disasters belong to the past,
your Mother Light is so intense,
that matter is now far less dense.

O Mother Mary, generate,
the song that does accelerate,

**the earth into a higher state,
all matter does now scintillate.**

9. Mother Mary, awaken women to see that it is time for women to rise over the roles that turn our lives into a struggle so we can truly embrace and enjoy life and make maximum use of our opportunity to transcend ourselves.

In Mother Light the earth is pure,
the upward spiral will endure,
prosperity is now the norm,
God's vision manifest as form.

**O Mother Mary, generate,
the song that does accelerate,
the earth into a higher state,
all matter does now scintillate.**

Sealing

In the name of the I AM THAT I AM, I accept that Archangel Michael, Astrea and Shiva form an impenetrable shield around myself and all constructive people, sealing us from all fear-based energies in all four octaves. I accept that the Light of God is consuming and transforming all fear-based energies that make up the dark forces working against the liberation of women on earth!

34 | GIVING ALL WOMEN A BETTER LIFE

I AM the Ascended Master, Gautama Buddha. Some might say: "What does the Buddha know about women?" I would reply: "Nothing, I know nothing about women, for I know nothing from a distance." What is the Buddhic consciousness? It is that you reach that level where there is no more the intellectual, linear, rational mind. There is no more the mind that knows from a distance. You know by being one with, by experiencing from within, *that* is the Buddhic consciousness. So, I can project (as *you* would say) my mind anywhere in space. *I* would not say I project my mind anywhere in space, I would say that my mind *is* everywhere in space, the space that I hold for earth. So I experience, I know from within, the situation of every human being on earth. I know your minds by experiencing them. I can focus anywhere in the space of earth and experience the consciousness that is there. Does this mean I know women? Well, *that* is the question I would expound upon.

What does it mean to know?

Again, what does it mean to know? There was an ancient temple where above the door it said: "Man, know thyself." Of course that was back then in the male chauvinist times. Let us just say then that it said: "Human, know thyself." What would it mean for a human to know itself? In a sense, you could say that we have given you many, many teachings through many different spiritual movements, in helping you know things about yourself, know your psychology, know the different stages of spiritual growth, know your reactionary patterns, your attachments, your separate selves, so that you can resolve all of this. If you took all of these teachings, studied them, applied them, would you know your self? Well, that depends on what state of mind you are in. If you are in this linear state of mind that most human beings on this planet are in, you *can* know yourself—but you will see that in this sentence there is a *you* and there is a *self*.

The you is supposedly knowing the self, but is the you the same as the self? If the you really knows itself, what is it knowing—a self? Is the you the same as the self? Is there a subject and an object, is there a subject-object duality? For most people on earth, even for many of the spiritual gurus and teachers that have come, there is still a subject-object duality. A spiritual teacher may have made some progress, may have raised his or her consciousness, may even claim to know itself. But if you see yourself as a subject, knowing your self as an object, you do not have true self-knowledge.

Based on this, you might say that I do not know women as most women know themselves because most women see themselves through this subject-object duality. That is why they become deceived, seduced by the lies of the fallen beings that are defined from that subject-object duality that the fallen beings cannot escape. Therefore, what the fallen beings define can only reinforce that subject-object duality. What the fallen beings have attempted to create is all of these roles or archetypes for what it means to be a woman.

For example, you can even see in spiritual circles where you have people who look at their astrology to see what kind of person they are. There are other spiritual movements that have created all of these divisions, saying that there is this type of person, there is that type of person, there is the next type of person and here are some criteria you can use to find out which type of person you are. The same of course with women, you see in women's magazines where they can have these surveys or tests you can take, to see whether you are in this category or that category. You even see some spiritual teachings, or some feminist teachings, that talk about different kinds of women. Of course, you have the whole division between women and men. Are women different from men? What have we said? The Conscious You is neither male nor female. It is pure, undifferentiated awareness. Your I AM Presence is neither male nor female. It is beyond these divisions that are defined on earth.

Only separate selves can be male or female

When the Conscious You first is sent from the I AM Presence into the four levels of the material realm on earth, it is neither male nor female. Over time, as it takes embodiment in both male and female bodies, it creates certain selves. Unfortunately, these selves are often created in reaction to the fallen beings and various forms of manipulation or violence that people are exposed to on earth. This means you create certain selves that define how you see being a woman and how you see being a man. The Conscious You of a man is not different from the Conscious You of a woman, but the separate selves of a man are different from the separate selves of a woman. So, are men different from women? In the eyes of most men they are, in the eyes of most women they are.

There are some that will say that such distinctions or divisions are necessary, even beneficial. You might say, at a certain level of consciousness, that a lifestream is not ready to acknowledge the freedom to define itself any way it wants. It can be helpful to go into a predefined role, play out that role as you do when you are an actor who goes into a theater, puts on a costume and acts out a role written by some playwright. Very few actors are ready to go up on stage without any predefined role, without any script and feel confident that they could capture the attention of the audience. So it is with many human beings on earth—they need some kind of predefined role. Even the roles that have been defined by the fallen beings can be helpful for a time, they can help you gain experiences on earth. Given that these roles are defined from duality and are defined deliberately to make it possible for the fallen beings to manipulate you, then it is obvious that these roles will also imprison you.

We have talked about the liberation of women from certain outer oppressions, and the liberation of men too. In order to fully liberate women, you must be liberated from the roles for women defined on this planet. You must be liberated to see and identify yourself as a spiritual being, as a spiritual being that is not androgynous or gender neutral, but is beyond gender. That is how you can gain freedom to look at the predefined roles for women that you were brought up to take on (or that you have chosen to take on) and evaluate: "Do I want to continue to act out that role?" Now, in some cases you may decide that you want to continue this for some time for various reasons. There is nothing to say you should not. When you are making the deliberate choice to continue the role rather than having been brought up – programmed – to take it on, then you are no longer identified fully with the role. You are not trapped in it, you do not think the role defines you as a spiritual being.

Transcending the roles defined for women

Now, of course once you see through the role, you also have the option to transcend it. At that point (and many of you who are ascended master students have the potential to do this and it is in your Divine plan to do it) you can begin to redefine what it means to be a woman on earth. You might define a different role for what it means to be a woman. You might act out that role for a time. There can even come a stage where you are no longer defining any role, you are no longer acting out any role, you are no longer being a woman, you are being a spiritual being who happens to be in a female body.

These are of course subtle topics, esoteric topics, mystical topics, beyond what the average woman on earth is ready to deal with, but in order to give a more full picture of what it means to liberate women, this needs to be expressed. You who are ascended master students, some of you will be able to ponder this, internalize it, live it. Therefore, you can again break new ground in the collective consciousness that over time will enable other women to begin to break free of these roles that have been defined on earth.

Some might say: "Well, aren't there any roles for women on earth, that are natural, that are okay, that are spiritual, that are not affected by the fallen beings?" The answer is simply: "No." The fallen beings have manipulated every aspect of life on this planet and there is no role for men or women that is not affected by the fallen beings. There are many spiritual people who have in their minds a certain image, a certain role for what it means to be a spiritual teacher or guru. Those images are also affected by the fallen beings, often in subtle ways that can be very difficult to recognize. This messenger has for years worked on this particular issue, which is why he does not present himself in a certain way. He simply does not want to be trapped in one of these predefined roles for spiritual teachers that exist on this planet. This is very legitimate. Jesus did the same when he was in embodiment, I did the same when I was in embodiment, other spiritual teachers have done the same because the goal of the ascended masters is to help people escape these roles. How could we do this if we, while in embodiment, acted out such a role affected by the fallen beings?

Now, the difficulty is of course that when you do act out as a spiritual teacher of some kind, the students who study your teaching may have a role in their minds and they may project it upon you. What can you do about that? Well, sometimes you can counteract that role, you can expose it, you can challenge it, you can do the opposite of what the students expect. You can also seek to help the students see this, see how unnecessary it is and realize that as you grow towards the 144th level of consciousness, you shed the snakeskin of these predefined roles. Therefore, you do not follow a set pattern for what it means to be a spiritual person, a spiritual teacher, or a christed being. Even ascended master students, especially in previous dispensations, attempted to define a certain role for what it meant to be a Christed being. What would Jesus say to some students who came to him and wanted to project such an image upon him? Well, he would say what he said to Peter: "Get thee behind me, Satan." What is the role of the Christ? What is the role of the Buddha? What is the role of any person who attains to these higher levels of consciousness? Well, of course it is to demonstrate that there is a way out of these human roles. How can you demonstrate that if you validate a role and image projected upon you by certain people?

Women want a better life

Truly, when I project my awareness into the minds of women on earth, (and I can do this for every woman on earth at the same time, as I am doing now), at first there seems to be so many different situations that women are in. So many different outer situations, so many states of consciousness and psychology. Can you really say anything general about women, or the situation of women on earth? When you experience the differences of their individual minds, can you say anything general? Well, you *can* say certain things. Women in general want a better life, they want a better life than they are having right now. It does not matter whether they live in one of the poorest circumstances on earth, or whether they live in a mansion somewhere, having servants at their beck and call, they still want a better life. They feel a tension because they know (they do not always know why they know but somewhere within them they know) that the outer circumstances they experience could be better or higher than what they are, they feel that it is not right, that they have not improved.

Why is this so? Because women are attuned to the Mother Flame, to the Mother consciousness. What is the Mother consciousness? It is the consciousness that gives birth to something new. Other masters have said that there is a certain Christ principle that defines the intervals for growth and the process of growth, this upward spiral of growth for an unascended sphere. The Mother is attuned to this but the Mother is also attuned to the practical reality in the physical octave. Therefore, the Mother consciousness knows that there is a certain process, a certain upward spiral for improvements that could have happened on earth in very practical, concrete outer improvements that could have happened on earth. The Mother Flame knows that at this particular time, there was a potential that this particular new circumstance could have been born. It is comparable to knowing that a child could have been born on that day but it was not, it was delayed. The Mother senses this and when the Mother senses this, there is a certain tension: "My child has not been born, therefore I can't nourish it and see it grow." Almost all women on earth sense this. Even if many are not consciously aware of what it is they sense, they sense the tension. For many women, this is not a pleasant thing, it is in fact very unpleasant because they feel that something is wrong, something is missing, they are deprived of something, this is unfair, this is unjust, they should not be in these conditions. It gives them a certain (we might say) tense or negative view of life, attitude to life. Sometimes they take it out on their husbands, blaming their husbands for the fact that they do not have better conditions, other times they blame themselves, but there is no reason to really blame. Of course, saying this does not really help the many women who are not aware that I even exist, but it can help some. *Some* will understand.

What you see is that when you look at women in general, women are not satisfied with status quo. In fact, you could say that from the moment the fallen beings came to earth and chose that men would be the superior sex, and women would be suppressed, from that moment women have not been satisfied with status quo. In many cases, many men have been satisfied with status quo, especially those who are part of the power elite, who have gained this privileged position where they have other people serving them. They do not want to change status quo and that is often why the new has not been born.

Women must stop waiting for men to change

What is the greatest potential for improvement on this planet? It is that women become more aware of what they feel, what they sense intuitively, what they know intuitively: that things could and should be better than what they are, that we are behind the potential, the possibility that there is something that has not been born. Instead of blaming men in general (and in fact even instead of blaming the power elite but simply placing responsibility on the power elite) what would be really constructive was that women would say: "Listen, we are not waiting for the men anymore. We are not waiting for the men to make change happen. We are making change happen ourselves. If the men want to be part of it—fine. But if they do not, we women will come together and make change happen. We will use our attunement to know that things should have been improved and we will improve them, no matter what the men say or do about it. We simply will not let them hold us back, let anything on earth hold us back anymore. We will use our inner attunement. We will acknowledge it, acknowledge its validity, and we will make change happen."

It is not a matter of demanding that the men should make change happen. It is a matter of women deciding to make change happen according to their vision and their attunement. Of course, there are also men who have this intuition and who know that things could be better. The men and the women who have this (are consciously aware of it), can of course come together and work together on making change happen. If they can do this, they can achieve more than any of them could achieve alone because, as we have said, in the cosmic perspective, the non-dualistic perspective, the outgoing and the contracting force are the two aspects of creation. Men and women on earth, have the potential to lock in to these basic creative forces and therefore in a sense, balance, supplement and magnify each other so that they can achieve more together than they could alone. Ultimately, of course you can come to the point where you no longer identify yourselves as men or women, you know you are spiritual beings, you just happen to be in a male or female body but you are working together as spiritual beings.

As such, it could be said that from this perspective it is not women who are the key to growth, it is awakened beings who have moved beyond the identification with the body. This conference has been, from our perspective as ascended masters, a tremendous step forward. We have been able to release everything that we had planned to release at this conference and even more. In other words, despite the fact that you have not been physically together in one location, you as a group of students have achieved more than the highest potential for this conference. You have exceeded our expectations. It is partly because you have been in your home locations around the world so the momentum of your decrees and your attention has rolled around the planet as a wave that has been magnified by us so that it gained more and more momentum during this conference. This momentum can continue almost indefinitely as you or other people study these teachings and use the tools to drive that momentum forward.

This is of course what we hope to see. A conference that we give is not meant to be a one-time event but a continual process. You can relate to this through the Mother flame, which does not simply give birth to a child in order to give birth to the child. It gives birth to the child in order to see it grow and mature and it is the same here. This conference has given birth to a child that we hope to see grow and mature, take on a life of its own, and many people will use these teachings and tools to make the calls and thereby create a movement that can move on, gain a life of it's own. It will serve to liberate women first, but also in a little longer perspective liberate men as well. Therefore, it can free this planet, liberate this planet from the influence of this power elite, of the fallen beings or the men who are trapped in the mindset of the fallen beings, and cannot or will not see how this mindset is abusing and trapping not only women, but men as well. Truly, in order to do something to others, you must already have done it to yourself. In other words, in order to abuse someone else, you must have created a self in your own being based on that consciousness, that abusive matrix. A man may think that he is raping a woman and it only affects the woman. But he has a self based on the consciousness of rape and it stays in his four lower bodies. It affects him every second of every day. He is not conscious of it but it still affects him.

You are affected by what you do not now

There are so many things in this world that demonstrate that even if you are not conscious of something, you can still be affected by it. There was a time when humankind was not aware of what you know today, that there is a force of gravity that pulls you towards the center of the earth. You know very well that people were not floating around in space back then. They were still pulled towards the earth by gravity, even though they were not consciously aware of it. What men do to women is also affecting themselves even if they are not willing to acknowledge it. That means men are actually even more trapped than women on this planet.

You may say that in this conference, we have focused on how women have been trapped and need to be liberated. The reality is that even though women are trapped, are imprisoned, are being abused, men are even more trapped than women, they are more trapped in these roles and this mind-set. They also have a certain tension that they feel, but most men are not consciously aware of it and so they project out that the tension is caused by external circumstances. In reality, the tension is *internal,* is inside the psyche. It is caused by your reaction to external circumstances.

If a particular external circumstance (that you feel is oppressing you) was removed, it does not mean the psychological reactionary pattern was removed, you would just find another external circumstance to react to. This is the essence of the teaching I gave 2,500 years ago about the cause of suffering being wrong desire, wrong expectations, being these attachments. The key to liberation was to overcome attachments, psychological attachments. Human psychology has not changed in those 2,500 years. The basic dynamic on the planet has not changed in those 2,500 years, even though there has been a raising of the collective consciousness. Why did I not, 2,500 years ago, talk more about women and the need to liberate women? Why did I not set the stage for a spiritual movement that could give full equality to women?

When you look at Buddhism today, you see that there may be some sects that have more of a liberation or equality between men and women. There are also many Buddhist sects that have a clear discrimination against women. Some consider Tibet to be a spiritually advanced country but look at the status of women in Tibet. Could I not have done more? Well, in a way yes, in a way no. Because the collective consciousness was at the level it was at 2,500 years ago, and it would have been very difficult for people to even begin to contemplate what you today call the liberation of women. They could not really have dealt with the concept. What I did instead was give a universal teaching that could be applied equally by both men and women. It could lead men and women to reach those higher levels of consciousness where they would no longer identify themselves as men or women but as spiritual beings.

What did I say: "Everything is the Buddha nature." That means that women also have the Buddha nature within them and therefore have the potential to walk the path towards Buddhahood. When you do, you come to that point where you have overcome your attachments to being in a female body. It no longer matters, it no longer limits, it no longer defines you that you are in a female body. That is then the ultimate liberation of a woman. When the woman is no longer a woman, *then* you are liberated. When the man is no longer a man, *then* you are liberated. When the human being is no longer a human being but a spiritual being, *then* you are liberated.

That is the liberation I desire to see, not for everyone because it is not realistic at this time. But at least for some of you who are ascended master students, who have been very willing to open yourself and apply these teachings, who have been very diligent in your practice, some of you for decades. I desire to see you take those last steps and attain that state of liberation that I experienced. Because I experienced it, you can experience it as well today. What one has done, all can do. Sometimes there is one person who must be the one who breaks the resistance and manifests and demonstrates a new level of consciousness. Once one person has manifested that level of consciousness, others can more easily manifest it as well, that is the entire principle of the Great White Brotherhood, of the ascended masters, of the path to Christhood, of the path to Buddhahood, of the spiritual path. "What one has done, all can do." One has manifested the Buddhic consciousness, one has manifested the Christ Consciousness on earth, so you too can manifest it as well.

This is my wish for you, my vision for you. It is my great joy to seal this conference, to seal you who have participated in this conference in this very, very joyful flame of the Buddha. Who looks at the students and sees their progress, sees how they are coming closer to liberation and often sees better than themselves how close they are to that liberation, but has the patience to let them walk those last steps until it breaks through and they are able to know from within: I Am the Christ, I Am The Buddha. For how else can you know it but knowing it from within? If someone needs to tell you, you are not there. So, the answer to the question about "where am I at in consciousness, am I there yet?" is always no. Because as long as you have the question, you are not there.

I visualize, I hold the vision that you will come to the point where the question fades away, as your attachments and your separate selves have faded away. So with this I seal you, I seal this conference in the joy flame of the Buddha. Gautama, I AM.

NOTE: This dictation was given June 1, 2020.

35 | INVOKING OUR SPIRITUAL LIBERATION

In the name of the I AM THAT I AM, Jesus Christ, I use the authority that I have as a being in embodiment on earth to call upon Gautama Buddha to reinforce my calls and use my chakras to project the statements in this invocation into the collective consciousness and awaken people to the awareness that will liberate both men and women from all psychological and spiritual thralldom to the fallen beings. Awaken people to the reality that we are spiritual beings and that we can co-create a new future by working with the ascended masters. I especially call for ...

[Make your own calls here.]

Part 1

1. Gautama Buddha, help people awaken to see that when the Conscious You is sent from the I AM Presence into the four levels of the material realm, it is neither male nor female.

> Gautama, show my mental state
> that does give rise to love and hate,

your exposé I do endure,
so my perception will be pure.

**Gautama, Flame of Cosmic Peace,
unruly thoughts do hereby cease,
we radiate from you and me
the peace to still Samsara's Sea.**

2. Gautama Buddha, help people awaken to see that over time, as the Conscious You takes embodiment in both male and female bodies, it creates certain selves.

Gautama, in your Flame of Peace,
the struggling self I now release,
the Buddha Nature I now see,
it is the core of you and me.

**Gautama, Flame of Cosmic Peace,
unruly thoughts do hereby cease,
we radiate from you and me
the peace to still Samsara's Sea.**

3. Gautama Buddha, help people awaken to see that these selves are often created in reaction to the fallen beings and various forms of manipulation or violence that people are exposed to on earth.

Gautama, I am one with thee,
Mara's demons do now flee,
your Presence like a soothing balm,
my mind and senses ever calm.

**Gautama, Flame of Cosmic Peace,
unruly thoughts do hereby cease,
we radiate from you and me
the peace to still Samsara's Sea.**

4. Gautama Buddha, help people awaken to see that we create certain selves that define how we see being a woman and how we see being a man.

Gautama, I now take the vow,
to live in the eternal now,
with you I do transcend all time,
to live in present so sublime.

**Gautama, Flame of Cosmic Peace,
unruly thoughts do hereby cease,
we radiate from you and me
the peace to still Samsara's Sea.**

5. Gautama Buddha, help people awaken to see that the Conscious You of a man is not different from the Conscious You of a woman, but the separate selves of a man are different from the separate selves of a woman.

Gautama, I have no desire,
to nothing earthly I aspire,
in non-attachment I now rest,
passing Mara's subtle test.

**Gautama, Flame of Cosmic Peace,
unruly thoughts do hereby cease,
we radiate from you and me
the peace to still Samsara's Sea.**

6. Gautama Buddha, help people awaken to see that at a certain level of consciousness, where a lifestream is not ready to acknowledge the freedom to define itself any way it wants, it can be helpful to go into a predefined role and play out that role as an actor in a theater.

Gautama, I melt into you,
my mind is one, no longer two,
immersed in your resplendent glow,
Nirvana is all that I know.

**Gautama, Flame of Cosmic Peace,
unruly thoughts do hereby cease,
we radiate from you and me
the peace to still Samsara's Sea.**

7. Gautama Buddha, help people awaken to see that even the roles that have been defined by the fallen beings can be helpful for a time, but given that these roles are defined from duality and are defined deliberately to make it possible for the fallen beings to manipulate us, then these roles will also imprison us.

> Gautama, in your timeless space,
> I am immersed in Cosmic Grace,
> I know the God beyond all form,
> to world I will no more conform.

> **Gautama, Flame of Cosmic Peace,**
> **unruly thoughts do hereby cease,**
> **we radiate from you and me**
> **the peace to still Samsara's Sea.**

8. Gautama Buddha, help women awaken to see that in order to fully liberate women, we must be liberated from the roles for women defined on this planet.

> Gautama, I am now awake,
> I clearly see what is at stake,
> and thus I claim my sacred right
> to be on earth the Buddhic Light.

> **Gautama, Flame of Cosmic Peace,**
> **unruly thoughts do hereby cease,**
> **we radiate from you and me**
> **the peace to still Samsara's Sea.**

9. Gautama Buddha, help women awaken to see that we must be liberated to see and identify ourselves as spiritual beings that are not androgynous or gender neutral, but are beyond gender.

> Gautama, with your thunderbolt,
> we give the earth a mighty jolt,
> I know that some will understand,
> and join the Buddha's timeless band.

**Gautama, Flame of Cosmic Peace,
unruly thoughts do hereby cease,
we radiate from you and me
the peace to still Samsara's Sea.**

Part 2

1. Gautama Buddha, help women awaken to see that this is how we can gain freedom to look at the predefined roles for women that we were brought up to take on and evaluate: "Do I want to continue to act out that role?"

Gautama, show my mental state
that does give rise to love and hate,
your exposé I do endure,
so my perception will be pure.

**Gautama, Flame of Cosmic Peace,
unruly thoughts do hereby cease,
we radiate from you and me
the peace to still Samsara's Sea.**

2. Gautama Buddha, help women awaken to see that when we are making the deliberate choice to continue the role, rather than having been programmed to take it on, then we are no longer identified fully with the role. We are not trapped in it, we do not think the role defines us as spiritual beings.

Gautama, in your Flame of Peace,
the struggling self I now release,
the Buddha Nature I now see,
it is the core of you and me.

**Gautama, Flame of Cosmic Peace,
unruly thoughts do hereby cease,
we radiate from you and me
the peace to still Samsara's Sea.**

　　　　　　　　　　　　　　The Spiritual Liberation of Women

3. Gautama Buddha, help women awaken to see that once we see through the role, we have the option to transcend it and redefine what it means to be a woman on earth.

> Gautama, I am one with thee,
> Mara's demons do now flee,
> your Presence like a soothing balm,
> my mind and senses ever calm.

> **Gautama, Flame of Cosmic Peace,**
> **unruly thoughts do hereby cease,**
> **we radiate from you and me**
> **the peace to still Samsara's Sea.**

4. Gautama Buddha, help women awaken to see that we might define a different role for what it means to be a woman and act out that role for a time.

> Gautama, I now take the vow,
> to live in the eternal now,
> with you I do transcend all time,
> to live in present so sublime.

> **Gautama, Flame of Cosmic Peace,**
> **unruly thoughts do hereby cease,**
> **we radiate from you and me**
> **the peace to still Samsara's Sea.**

5. Gautama Buddha, help women awaken to see that there is a stage where we are no longer defining any role, we are no longer acting out any role, we are no longer being women, we are spiritual beings who happen to be in female bodies.

> Gautama, I have no desire,
> to nothing earthly I aspire,
> in non-attachment I now rest,
> passing Mara's subtle test.

Gautama, Flame of Cosmic Peace,
unruly thoughts do hereby cease,
we radiate from you and me
the peace to still Samsara's Sea.

6. Gautama Buddha, help women awaken to see the potential to break new ground in the collective consciousness so that other women can begin to break free of these roles that have been defined on earth.

Gautama, I melt into you,
my mind is one, no longer two,
immersed in your resplendent glow,
Nirvana is all that I know.

Gautama, Flame of Cosmic Peace,
unruly thoughts do hereby cease,
we radiate from you and me
the peace to still Samsara's Sea.

7. Gautama Buddha, help people awaken to see that there are no roles for women on earth that are natural. The fallen beings have manipulated every aspect of life on this planet and there is no role for men or women that is not affected by the fallen beings.

Gautama, in your timeless space,
I am immersed in Cosmic Grace,
I know the God beyond all form,
to world I will no more conform.

Gautama, Flame of Cosmic Peace,
unruly thoughts do hereby cease,
we radiate from you and me
the peace to still Samsara's Sea.

8. Gautama Buddha, help women awaken to see that women in general want a better life, we want a better life than we are having right now. We feel a tension because we know that the outer circumstances we experience could be better than what they are, we feel that it is not right that they have not improved.

Gautama, I am now awake,
I clearly see what is at stake,
and thus I claim my sacred right
to be on earth the Buddhic Light.

Gautama, Flame of Cosmic Peace,
unruly thoughts do hereby cease,
we radiate from you and me
the peace to still Samsara's Sea.

9. Gautama Buddha, help women awaken to see that we are attuned to the
Mother Flame, to the Mother consciousness. This is the consciousness
that gives birth to something new.

Gautama, with your thunderbolt,
we give the earth a mighty jolt,
I know that some will understand,
and join the Buddha's timeless band.

Gautama, Flame of Cosmic Peace,
unruly thoughts do hereby cease,
we radiate from you and me
the peace to still Samsara's Sea.

Part 3

1. Gautama Buddha, help people awaken to see that the Mother is attuned
to the Christ principle that defines the intervals for growth and the process
of growth. She is also attuned to the practical reality in the physical octave.

Gautama, show my mental state
that does give rise to love and hate,
your exposé I do endure,
so my perception will be pure.

Gautama, Flame of Cosmic Peace,
unruly thoughts do hereby cease,

we radiate from you and me
the peace to still Samsara's Sea.

2. Gautama Buddha, help people awaken to see that the Mother consciousness knows that there is a certain process, a certain upward spiral for improvements that could have happened on earth in very practical, concrete outer improvements.

Gautama, in your Flame of Peace,
the struggling self I now release,
the Buddha Nature I now see,
it is the core of you and me.

Gautama, Flame of Cosmic Peace,
unruly thoughts do hereby cease,
we radiate from you and me
the peace to still Samsara's Sea.

3. Gautama Buddha, help people awaken to see that the Mother Flame knows that at this particular time, there was a potential that this particular new circumstance could have been born. It is comparable to knowing that a child could have been born on that day but it was delayed.

Gautama, I am one with thee,
Mara's demons do now flee,
your Presence like a soothing balm,
my mind and senses ever calm.

Gautama, Flame of Cosmic Peace,
unruly thoughts do hereby cease,
we radiate from you and me
the peace to still Samsara's Sea.

4. Gautama Buddha, help women awaken to see that almost all of us sense this, even if many are not consciously aware of what it is we sense.

Gautama, I now take the vow,
to live in the eternal now,

with you I do transcend all time,
to live in present so sublime.

**Gautama, Flame of Cosmic Peace,
unruly thoughts do hereby cease,
we radiate from you and me
the peace to still Samsara's Sea.**

5. Gautama Buddha, help women awaken to see that for many of us, this is not a pleasant thing because we feel that something is wrong, something is missing, we are deprived of something, we should not be in these conditions.

Gautama, I have no desire,
to nothing earthly I aspire,
in non-attachment I now rest,
passing Mara's subtle test.

**Gautama, Flame of Cosmic Peace,
unruly thoughts do hereby cease,
we radiate from you and me
the peace to still Samsara's Sea.**

6. Gautama Buddha, help women awaken to see that this gives many of us a tense or negative attitude to life. Sometimes we blame our husbands for the fact that we do not have better conditions, other times we blame ourselves, but there is no reason to blame.

Gautama, I melt into you,
my mind is one, no longer two,
immersed in your resplendent glow,
Nirvana is all that I know.

**Gautama, Flame of Cosmic Peace,
unruly thoughts do hereby cease,
we radiate from you and me
the peace to still Samsara's Sea.**

7. Gautama Buddha, help women awaken to see that in general we are not satisfied with status quo. From the moment the fallen beings came to earth and chose that men would be the superior sex, and women would be suppressed, from that moment women have not been satisfied with status quo.

Gautama, in your timeless space,
I am immersed in Cosmic Grace,
I know the God beyond all form,
to world I will no more conform.

**Gautama, Flame of Cosmic Peace,
unruly thoughts do hereby cease,
we radiate from you and me
the peace to still Samsara's Sea.**

8. Gautama Buddha, help people awaken to see that many men have been satisfied with status quo, especially those who are part of the power elite, who have gained this privileged position. They do not want to change status quo and that is often why the new has not been born.

Gautama, I am now awake,
I clearly see what is at stake,
and thus I claim my sacred right
to be on earth the Buddhic Light.

**Gautama, Flame of Cosmic Peace,
unruly thoughts do hereby cease,
we radiate from you and me
the peace to still Samsara's Sea.**

9. Gautama Buddha, help women awaken to see that the greatest potential for improvement on this planet is that women become more aware of what we know intuitively: that things could and should be better than what they are, that we are behind the potential, that there is a possibility that something has not been born.

Gautama, with your thunderbolt,
we give the earth a mighty jolt,

I know that some will understand,
and join the Buddha's timeless band.

Gautama, Flame of Cosmic Peace,
unruly thoughts do hereby cease,
we radiate from you and me
the peace to still Samsara's Sea.

Part 4

1. Gautama Buddha, help women awaken to see that instead of blaming men in general it is constructive to say: "Listen, we are not waiting for the men anymore. We are not waiting for the men to make change happen. We are making change happen ourselves."

Gautama, show my mental state
that does give rise to love and hate,
your exposé I do endure,
so my perception will be pure.

Gautama, Flame of Cosmic Peace,
unruly thoughts do hereby cease,
we radiate from you and me
the peace to still Samsara's Sea.

2. Gautama Buddha, help it is constructive awaken to say: "If the men want to be part of it—fine. But if they do not, we women will come together and make change happen. We will use our attunement to know that things should have been improved and we will improve them, no matter what the men say or do about it."

Gautama, in your Flame of Peace,
the struggling self I now release,
the Buddha Nature I now see,
it is the core of you and me.

Gautama, Flame of Cosmic Peace,
unruly thoughts do hereby cease,
we radiate from you and me
the peace to still Samsara's Sea.

3. Gautama Buddha, help women awaken to say: "We simply will not let men hold us back, let anything on earth hold us back anymore. We will use our inner attunement. We will acknowledge it, acknowledge its validity, and we will make change happen."

Gautama, I am one with thee,
Mara's demons do now flee,
your Presence like a soothing balm,
my mind and senses ever calm.

Gautama, Flame of Cosmic Peace,
unruly thoughts do hereby cease,
we radiate from you and me
the peace to still Samsara's Sea.

4. Gautama Buddha, help women awaken to see that it is not a matter of demanding that the men should make change happen. It is a matter of women deciding to make change happen according to our vision and our attunement.

Gautama, I now take the vow,
to live in the eternal now,
with you I do transcend all time,
to live in present so sublime.

Gautama, Flame of Cosmic Peace,
unruly thoughts do hereby cease,
we radiate from you and me
the peace to still Samsara's Sea.

5. Gautama Buddha, help people awaken to see that men and women who have attunement can work together on making change happen. If they can do this, they can achieve more than any of them could achieve alone.

Gautama, I have no desire,
to nothing earthly I aspire,
in non-attachment I now rest,
passing Mara's subtle test.

Gautama, Flame of Cosmic Peace,
unruly thoughts do hereby cease,
we radiate from you and me
the peace to still Samsara's Sea.

6. Gautama Buddha, help people awaken to see that from the cosmic perspective, the non-dualistic perspective, the outgoing and the contracting forces are the two aspects of creation.

Gautama, I melt into you,
my mind is one, no longer two,
immersed in your resplendent glow,
Nirvana is all that I know.

Gautama, Flame of Cosmic Peace,
unruly thoughts do hereby cease,
we radiate from you and me
the peace to still Samsara's Sea.

7. Gautama Buddha, help people awaken to see that men and women have the potential to lock in to these basic creative forces and therefore balance, supplement and magnify each other so that we can achieve more together than we could alone.

Gautama, in your timeless space,
I am immersed in Cosmic Grace,
I know the God beyond all form,
to world I will no more conform.

Gautama, Flame of Cosmic Peace,
unruly thoughts do hereby cease,
we radiate from you and me
the peace to still Samsara's Sea.

8. Gautama Buddha, help people awaken to see that we can come to the point where we no longer identify ourselves as men or women, we know we are spiritual beings, we just happen to be in a male or female body but we are working together as spiritual beings.

Gautama, I am now awake,
I clearly see what is at stake,
and thus I claim my sacred right
to be on earth the Buddhic Light.

Gautama, Flame of Cosmic Peace,
unruly thoughts do hereby cease,
we radiate from you and me
the peace to still Samsara's Sea.

9. Gautama Buddha, help people awaken to see that from this perspective it is not women who are the key to growth, it is awakened beings who have moved beyond the identification with the body.

Gautama, with your thunderbolt,
we give the earth a mighty jolt,
I know that some will understand,
and join the Buddha's timeless band.

Gautama, Flame of Cosmic Peace,
unruly thoughts do hereby cease,
we radiate from you and me
the peace to still Samsara's Sea.

Part 5

1. Gautama Buddha, help people awaken to see the need to liberate this planet from the influence of the power elite, the fallen beings or the men who are trapped in the mindset of the fallen beings, and cannot or will not see how this mindset is abusing and trapping not only women, but men as well.

Gautama, show my mental state
that does give rise to love and hate,
your exposé I do endure,
so my perception will be pure.

**Gautama, Flame of Cosmic Peace,
unruly thoughts do hereby cease,
we radiate from you and me
the peace to still Samsara's Sea.**

2. Gautama Buddha, help people awaken to see that in order to do something to others, we must already have done it to ourselves. In order to abuse someone else, we must have created a self in our own beings based on that consciousness, that abusive matrix.

Gautama, in your Flame of Peace,
the struggling self I now release,
the Buddha Nature I now see,
it is the core of you and me.

**Gautama, Flame of Cosmic Peace,
unruly thoughts do hereby cease,
we radiate from you and me
the peace to still Samsara's Sea.**

3. Gautama Buddha, help people awaken to see that even if we are not conscious of something, we can still be affected by it. What men do to women is also affecting themselves even if they are not willing to acknowledge it. That means men are actually even more trapped than women on this planet.

Gautama, I am one with thee,
Mara's demons do now flee,
your Presence like a soothing balm,
my mind and senses ever calm.

**Gautama, Flame of Cosmic Peace,
unruly thoughts do hereby cease,**

**we radiate from you and me
the peace to still Samsara's Sea.**

4. Gautama Buddha, help people awaken to see that even though women are trapped, are imprisoned, are being abused, men are even more trapped than women, they are more trapped in these roles and this mindset.

Gautama, I now take the vow,
to live in the eternal now,
with you I do transcend all time,
to live in present so sublime.

**Gautama, Flame of Cosmic Peace,
unruly thoughts do hereby cease,
we radiate from you and me
the peace to still Samsara's Sea.**

5. Gautama Buddha, help people awaken to see that men also feel a certain tension, but most men are not consciously aware of it and they project out that the tension is caused by external circumstances. In reality, the tension is *internal,* is inside the psyche. It is caused by our reaction to external circumstances.

Gautama, I have no desire,
to nothing earthly I aspire,
in non-attachment I now rest,
passing Mara's subtle test.

**Gautama, Flame of Cosmic Peace,
unruly thoughts do hereby cease,
we radiate from you and me
the peace to still Samsara's Sea.**

6. Gautama Buddha, help people awaken to see that if a particular external circumstance that we feel is oppressing us was removed, it does not mean the psychological reactionary pattern was removed, and we would just find another external circumstance to react to.

Gautama, I melt into you,
my mind is one, no longer two,
immersed in your resplendent glow,
Nirvana is all that I know.

Gautama, Flame of Cosmic Peace,
unruly thoughts do hereby cease,
we radiate from you and me
the peace to still Samsara's Sea.

7. Gautama Buddha, help women awaken to see that the key to liberation is to overcome attachments, psychological attachments. When we walk this path, we come to a point where we have overcome our attachments to being in a female body. It no longer matters, it no longer limits, it no longer defines us that we are in a female body.

Gautama, in your timeless space,
I am immersed in Cosmic Grace,
I know the God beyond all form,
to world I will no more conform.

Gautama, Flame of Cosmic Peace,
unruly thoughts do hereby cease,
we radiate from you and me
the peace to still Samsara's Sea.

8. Gautama Buddha, help people awaken to see that this is the ultimate liberation of a woman. When the woman is no longer a woman, *then* we are liberated. When the man is no longer a man, *then* we are liberated. When the human being is no longer a human being but a spiritual being, *then* we are liberated.

Gautama, I am now awake,
I clearly see what is at stake,
and thus I claim my sacred right
to be on earth the Buddhic Light.

Gautama, Flame of Cosmic Peace,
unruly thoughts do hereby cease,

**we radiate from you and me
the peace to still Samsara's Sea.**

9. Gautama Buddha, awaken those who have the potential to apply your teaching and take those last steps and attain the state of liberation that you experienced.

Gautama, with your thunderbolt,
we give the earth a mighty jolt,
I know that some will understand,
and join the Buddha's timeless band.

**Gautama, Flame of Cosmic Peace,
unruly thoughts do hereby cease,
we radiate from you and me
the peace to still Samsara's Sea.**

Sealing

In the name of the I AM THAT I AM, I accept that Archangel Michael, Astrea and Shiva form an impenetrable shield around myself and all constructive people, sealing us from all fear-based energies in all four octaves. I accept that the Light of God is consuming and transforming all fear-based energies that make up the dark forces working against the liberation of women on earth!